The
Transformation
of Judaism

The
Transformation
of Judaism

From Philosophy to Religion

Jacob Neusner

UNIVERSITY OF ILLINOIS PRESS

Urbana and Chicago

© 1992 by the Board of Trustees of the University of Illinois
Manufactured in the United States of America
C 5 4 3 2 1

This book is printed on acid-free paper.

Library of Congress Cataloging-in-Publication Data
Neusner, Jacob, 1932-
   The transformation of Judaism : from philosophy to religion /
Jacob Neusner.
      p.   cm.
   Includes bibliographical references and index.
   ISBN 0-252-01805-2 (alk. paper)
   1. Judaism—History—Talmudic period, 10-425.   2. Judaism and
philosophy.   3. Judaism—Essence, genus, nature.   4. Rabbinical
literature—History and criticism.   I. Title.
BM177.N4833   1992
296'.09'015—dc20   90-27177
                                                               CIP

For colleagues and friends
among the members for 1989-1990
of the Institute for Advanced Study
in appreciation for providing good company
during a happy year,
a time that marked the decisive turning
—in a profound sense, the crisis—
in both my professional career
and my intellectual pilgrimage.

Contents

Preface

Between 200 and 400 C.E. Judaism changed from a philosophy to a religion. In the rest of this book I explain the meaning of that simple sentence, bringing to a culmination twenty years of work of mine, from 1970 to 1990. Defining the word *Judaism* in this context, which is not theological but descriptive, analytical, and comparative, entails understanding a religion as a system of social order formed (whether in fact or in imagination) by the believers. That system is always portrayed in writing, and the problem of description and analysis concerns reading written evidence as testimonies to authors' imagination of the social world. The problem I address here concerns the transformation of a Judaic system of the social order that was fully set forth in its initial document and both carried forward and vastly recast by continuator documents. That problem therefore directs attention to systemic description, analysis, and interpretation of documentary evidence, for by comparing one set of writings with another I compare two different systems of a single religion.

By a religious system (in this case, "a Judaism") I mean a theory of the social order that appeals for validation to supernatural authority and that comprises a worldview (philosophy), a way of life (economics), and a theory of the social entity (politics). These components may be represented as ethos, ethics, and ethnos. So much for the definition of religion that pertains here: a religious theory of the social order that accounts for the way in which (in theory, at least) a social entity sees the world and conducts its affairs.

By (a) Judaism I mean a Judaic system that, in a cogent account of the social order, comprises a worldview, a way of life, and a theory of the social entity called Israel, the sum of which responds to a question deemed urgent and encompassing with an answer found self-evidently valid. The Jews' long history has witnessed the formation of a variety of such Judaic systems. In the first seven centuries of the common era the canonical writings of one such system, the one that has predominated since that time, took shape (the definition of the system and the documentary evidence for it are described presently). That is the Judaic system whose tranformation I discuss in this book. I describe that system as it is attested or adumbrated by the canonical writings produced by sages bearing the title *rabbi*. I read those writings as accounts of the principal parts of the structure and system of society, giving special attention to what seems to me essential: the way of life, or ethics (and in secular social science, economics); the worldview, or ethos (in secular language, philosophy—including science); and the theory of the social entity that realizes the one and lives by the other, or ethnos.

By philosophy I mean very simply a system of thought that, in the context of its time and place, people generally deemed philosophers would have recognized as philosophical, with the proviso that there be no error as to the facts of the matter. In my book *Judaism as Philosophy*[1] I demonstrate that in important ways, the Mishnah, the first canonical writing of Judaism after the Hebrew Scriptures of ancient Israel ("the Old Testament"), is to be read as philosophy in accord with the generally accepted understanding of philosophy of the time (ca. 200 C.E.) and place (the Greek-speaking Near East). By philosophy, both in that study and here, I therefore mean specifically the philosophical tradition of the Greco-Roman world. In particular, as I shall explain at length, I speak of the method of Aristotle united with a proposition important to Middle Platonism, but philosophy in a generic sense demands its place, and by philosophy in general I mean disciplined, rigorous thought that uses valid rules of thought universally applicable as to topic to intelligibly produce generalizations concerning mundane facts to govern or explain a variety of circumstances. A philosophy forms a cogent system of rational thought that treats diverse cases by appeal to a limited set of internally coherent generalizations. Such a system—abstract, intelligible, subject to reasoned explanation in its method, and covering a variety of concrete cases of problems—defines what I mean by philosophy (or a philosophy) and, consequently, philosophical.[2]

The methods I work out here can serve in the study of the history of religions other than Judaism. I mean to speak to a broad reading public interested in how religions form their conceptions of humanity in society. After a long period in which people took for granted that religion does not constitute an independent variable in the definition of politics, economics, and learning or philosophy of science, we now recognize the thesis of inevitable secularization as false. Religion is today the definitive power in the social order in large parts of the globe, and any inquiry into the way in which a religion proposes to set forth a social system and structure will help us make sense of the protean phenomenon that succeeds today where its opponents and enemies fade. Anyone who wishes to grasp what is happening not only in the State of Israel and in Jewry throughout the world but also in much of Europe, Africa, Asia, and the Americas will pay close attention to how the authorships of the documents treated here (called by the reverent "our sages of blessed memory") imagined society. The Judaism that they helped work out, the system and theory of the social order of the "Israel" to whom our sages attended—that Judaism turned out to define all Judaisms from then to now.[3]

For they and their heirs went out and built that imagined community, no less than the heirs and continuators of their contemporary, Augustine of Hippo, went out and framed the whole of the Christian West. In the same age and circumstance—a time of radical turning—but living far apart in worlds that cannot have communicated, local administrators of petty politics thought about the world in cosmic terms, in each case extending the limits of society to encompass Heaven, and throughout the rest of Western history, people devoted their lives and even went to war to define the role and will of Heaven on earth. They still do, which explains why we can understand the world of not the fifth century but the twenty-first century only when we take account of the world-defining and protean force, religion, in not the soul alone but society at large, not the lives of private persons alone but the affairs of state and the disposition of valued resources. The enduring and paramount position of religion in the contemporary political, economic, and intellectual life of peoples and nations explains why I hope that this book will serve more than historians of religion or of Judaism in particular. In these pages I describe how philosophy, which is abstract, elegant, orderly, and intellectual, turned into religion, which is tangible, down-to-earth, chaotic, and concrete—religion as the West has made it.

Like pretty much all of my theoretical books (and most of the others as well), this one was written in my mind long before it was written on paper to allow for experimentation, testing, and final publication. My challenge has been to find means of saying clearly for others what for a long time has been self-evident to me. Like the problem solved by the playwright and director, this challenge always lies in transcending the limitations of the medium, whether turning the theater into the globe or transforming ongoing and inward-turning reflection into intelligible and even useful learning. The topics I cover here are things about which I have thought for a very long time, my whole life, really: what difference religion makes in the world around us, and how it defines what we are and guides what we do.

With the work in its proper intellectual context, it remains to place this book into the context of my unfolding oeuvre. Clearly, I assign to it central importance at a turning in my long-term program. Corresponding to my *Judaism: The Evidence of the Mishnah* (Chicago: The University of Chicago Press, 1982; 2d ed., aug., Atlanta: Scholars Press for Brown Judaic Studies, 1989), this book sets forth, whole and complete, the results of nearly a decade of research on the Judaic system (the "Judaism") portrayed by the documents that reached closure from the conclusion of the Mishnah at the end of the second century of the common era to the completion of the Talmud of the Land of Israel, Genesis Rabbah, Leviticus Rabbah, and Pesiqta deRab Kahana, around the fourth and fifth centuries. The completed research has systematically described the documents of that span of approximately two hundred years, equally systematically analyzing them through comparison and contrast to expose important traits of the system and history of the Judaism they portray.

So I take each of the two sets of documents — the Mishnah and related Midrash compilations and the Talmud of the Land of Israel and associated Midrash collections — as evidence of the system to which it refers or attests, and I claim that those systems exhibit traits I can describe and connections — comparisons and contrasts — I can analyze and interpret. So this book forms an exercise in the study of category formation wherein I show two things. The first is how a continuous literary tradition (the Yerushalmi is construed as a [mere] continuation of, and commentary to, the Mishnah, and the several distinct groups of Midrash compilations are presented as [mere] commentary to Scripture) in fact attests to distinct religious systems. The second is how the categories that frame the initial system are received and dealt with in the successor system. I then analyze literary sources so as to allow the description of religious systems by reference to their characteristic category formations and interpret those sources so as to compare the category formations of one with those of the other.

In the next decade or so I hope to accomplish the same work for the third and final stage in the formation of Judaism, from ca. 450 to ca. 600 C.E.[4] Some of the descriptive and analytical work is now complete, but a fair amount of descriptive study of texts and a still larger amount of analytical study of contexts stands between this work and the third and final interpretive enterprise I have in mind, namely, describing and explaining the passage from religion to theology (terms defined in the introduction). Nevertheless, the theoretical labor for the final stage is now well underway.

Catching up means another go-around in the literary evidence. To undertake systemic analysis on the strength of written evidence, I have systemically reread the classic documents of the Judaism that took shape in the first to the seventh centuries of the common era and that has predominated since then, the Judaism of the dual Torah. These documents—the Mishnah, Midrash compilations, and the two Talmuds—present the collective statement and consensus of authors (none is credibly assigned to a single author and all are preserved because they are deemed canonical and authoritative) and show us how those authors proposed to make a statement to their situation—and, I argue, on the human condition. As I said previously, I generally "write" my major theoretical work mentally and only afterward put the whole down on paper, catching up in research with the results of my abstraction, imagination, and sheer daydreaming. The work of literary analysis is now complete for the Midrash compilations of the third and final state in the formation of Judaism, the late Midrash-Rabbah collections: Ruth Rabbah, Lamentations Rabbati, Song of Songs Rabbah, and Esther Rabbah I.[5] To prepare for literary-analytical studies of the Talmud of Babylonia I have (re)translated the following tractates of the Bavli: Berakhot, Sukkah, Sotah, Bava Mesia, Sanhedrin, Zebahim, Arakhin, Temurah, Bekhorot, Keritot, and Niddah.[6] The planned studies will eventually lead to an account of how the religious system attested by the Talmud of the Land of Israel and related Midrash compilations yielded the theological system adumbrated in the final documents of the formative age of Judaism.[7]

The bibliography lists the books of mine on which I constructed this composition.

I owe to Professor William Scott Green the suggestion that, once the successor system had been described, I compare and contrast the religious system of social order in Augustine's contemporary *City of God*. He was the one to identify Augustine as another theorist of the same sort as the Judaic sages. That seems to me an unusually valuable idea—among many he has given me—even though I cannot claim wholly to have realized its promise.

The contribution of Professor Calvin Goldscheider, Brown University, whose thinking about the sound analysis of theories of the social order has made so deep an impact on my own, is especially appreciated.

I wrote this book while holding a Senior Fellowship of the National Endowment for the Humanities, and I take much pride in offering to that agency of support for humanistic learning my very hearty thanks for the recognition and material assistance the fellowship afforded to me.

Brown University complemented that fellowship with substantial funds enabling me to spend the entire academic year, 1989 to 1990, in full-time research. In my twenty-two years at Brown University, from 1968 to 1990, I have always enjoyed the University's support for every research initiative that I undertook. For that I am grateful.

The Institute for Advanced Study brought me into relationships with colleagues in a variety of fields who stimulated my thinking about my own work, often indirectly. Because I have learned not to take for granted acts of uncommon grace, the dedication of this book bears witness to my genuine appreciation for some of the institute's members for 1989 through 1990. My friends among them in reality formed the community of learning, in that brief time and enchanted place, of which all of us dream.

Because in the middle of writing this book I closed the chapter of my life spent at Brown University and undertook a new chapter in my career, I am minded to cite these words of Jeremiah in connection with my eternally youthful wife, Suzanne, who began as my student four decades ago by studying them, for they aptly capture our circumstance: "*I remember the devotion of your youth, your love as a bride, how you followed me in the wilderness, in a land not sown*" (Jer. 2:2). We perpetually knew whence we came but never could guess where we were heading. We just went. And that tells the tale, not only of our marriage, but, too, of this life of learning of mine: this progress through the wilderness, this pilgrimage to we-never-know-where—until we get there. That is the life I have made for myself, and, the path that, in her patient way, Suzanne has walked with me and for me, and now, as they reach maturity, we surely can claim, our children too have traveled with us together. For all this I give her my thanks.

To my new colleagues and friends at the University of South Florida I give thanks for bringing the journey to a happy conclusion.

Notes

1. Jacob Neusner, *Judaism as Philosophy: The Method and Message of the Mishnah* (Columbia: University of South Carolina Press, 1991).

2. I have further worked out in great detail an account of those passages in the entire Mishnah that are to be classified as philosophical, within the stated criterion, in *The Philosophical Mishnah*, 4 vols. (Atlanta, Ga.: Scholars Press for Brown Judaic Studies, 1989).

3. My field theory of the history of Judaism, to which I allude here, is in these books: *Judaism in the Matrix of Christianity* (Philadelphia: Fortress Press, 1986; British ed., Edinburgh: T. & T. Collins, 1988); *Judaism and Christianity in the Age of Constantine: Issues of the Initial Confrontation* (Chicago: University of Chicago Press, 1987); *Death and Birth of Judaism: The Impact of Christianity, Secularism, and the Holocaust on Jewish Faith* (New York: Basic Books, 1987); *Self-Fulfilling Prophecy: Exile and Return in the History of Judaism* (Boston: Beacon Press, 1987).

4. Michael G. Morony, "Teleology and the Significance of Change," in *Tradition and Innovation in Late Antiquity*, ed., F. M. Clover and R. S. Humphreys (Madison: University of Wisconsin Press, 1989), 21-27, seems to me right on target in his arguments on the character of the final centuries of late antiquity. I am inclined to accept his periodization, but I have not yet done my work on the sixth and seventh centuries.

5. These are as follows: *Esther Rabbah I: An Analytical Translation* (Atlanta, Ga.: Scholars Press for Brown Judaic Studies, 1989); *Ruth Rabbah: An Analytical Translation* (Atlanta, Ga.: Scholars Press for Brown Judaic Studies, 1989); *Song of Songs Rabbah: An Analytical Translation*, vol. 1, *Song of Songs Rabbah to Song Chapters One through Three*, vol. 2, *Song of Songs Rabbah to Song Chapters Four through Eight* (Atlanta, Ga.: Scholars Press for Brown Judaic Studies, 1990); *The Midrash Compilations of the Sixth and Seventh Centuries: An Introduction to the Rhetorical, Logical, and Topical Program*, 4 vols. (Atlanta, Ga.: Scholars Press for Brown Judaic Studies, 1990). See also *Translating the Classics of Judaism: In Theory and in Practice* (Atlanta, Ga.: Scholars Press for Brown Judaic Studies, 1990).

6. These are in *The Talmud of Babylonia: An American Translation,* trans. Neusner (Atlanta, Ga.: Scholars Press for Brown Judaic Studies, 1987-1991).

7. These studies may be described in the following way. 1. *The Bavli's One Voice: The Rules of Composition of the Talmud of Babylonia* (Atlanta, Ga.: Scholars Press for South Florida Studies in the History of Judaism, 1991). The principal issue here and in the next items is how to identify the statements of norms and demonstrate that these norms are cogent with one another. Precisely what do these norms set forth as a system, and why do I maintain that it is a theological system, within my definition of theology? This book asks who it is who speaks through the Bavli. Is it the voice of the penultimate and ultimate authorship, or the voices of a variety of authors and authorships? If the former, then we can proceed to the next problem. 2. *The Bavli's One Statement: The Message of the Method of the Talmud of Babylonia.* What message can we derive from the methods of logical and cogent discourse that are paramount in the Bavli? 3. *The Transformation of Judaism: From Religion to Theology in the Talmud of Babylonia and the Late Midrash Compilations.* Once I have established the method and message of the Bavli, I return to the already completed work on the roughly contemporary Midrash compilations. I compare the category formations of the Yerushalmi and related writings with those of the Bavli and related writings and specify the category structure of the final system of late antiquity. Do I find paramount the same categories or other categories? The principal question finally answered here is, since I have identified statements of norms and demonstrated their mutual consistency, what do these norms set forth as a system, and why do I maintain that it is a theological system, within my definition of theology? 4. *The Bavli and the Denkart: The Judaic and Zoroastrian Response to the Challenge of Nascent Islam.* Are the Zoroastrian sages writing on the same range of issues, or is this simply the collection and arrangement of inherited information, as the prior accounts of the ninth-century Pahlavi books have maintained and the early Islamic era counterpart accounts of Judaism allege?

Introduction

The transformation of Judaism in late antiquity took place in three stages: philosophical, religious, and theological. Three sets of writings attest to each of the stages, respectively. The specific correlations are as follows: the Mishnah, Tosefta, and associated Midrash compilations (Sifra, Sifré to Numbers, and Sifré to Deuteronomy) attest to a philosophical Judaic system; the Talmud of the Land of Israel (the Palestinian Talmud) and its companion Midrash compilations (Genesis Rabbah and Leviticus Rabbah) attest to a religious Judaic system that is in writing continuous with the foregoing but in morphology quite different; and the Talmud of Babylonia and its related Midrash compilations (Lamentations Rabbah, Ruth Rabbah, Esther Rabbah I, and Song of Songs Rabbah) attest to a theological Judaic system. What do the terms *philosophical, religious,* and *theological* denote?

A philosophical system forms its content inductively and syllogistically by appeal to the neutral evidence of rules shown by observing the order of universally accessible nature and society.

A religious system frames its propositions deductively and exegetically by appeal to the privileged evidence of a corpus of writing deemed revealed by God.

A theological system imposes philosophy's systematic modes of thought on the materials of a religious system, regularizing and ordering them in a cogent and intellectually rigorous way.

The movement from the religious to the theological involves the systematization and harmonization of the religious categories, their reformation into a single, tight, and cogent statement that leaves no doubt on what is right and what is wrong, what we are supposed to think and to do, and how all that we are to think and to do coheres.

It is an initiative as radical, in its way, as the passage from the philo-sophical to the religious formation is in its way, for the modes of thought, media of expression, and categorical structure and system are reworked in the enterprise of rendering an order merely imputed within the single heart of the faith as wholly public and subject to sustained, cogent representation and expression, with each component in its proper place in the sequence, beginning, middle, and end. Religious conviction differs from theological proposition as do bricks and mortar from a building.

Religious and theological systems work over the same issues in ways that are common to both and that distinguish them jointly from phil-osophical systems. Nevertheless, the rigorous task of forming from religious attitudes and convictions a cogent composition, a system and not merely a structure of beliefs, imposes on theological systems dis-ciplines of mind and perception, or modes of thought and media of expression, quite different from those that characterize the work of making a religious system. The connection is intimate, for a theological system succeeding and reshaping a religious one appeals to the same sources of truth in setting forth (often identical) answers to (ordinarily) the same urgent questions, but the theological type of system also differs from the religious type in fundamental ways, for although there can be a religious system without theological order, there can be no theological system without a religious core.

To show that categorical transformations and reconsiderations have taken place in the systems in transition, I read literary evidence as testament to systemic formation. The evidence for systems of world construction, such as those found in the history of Judaism, derives from the correct description and analysis of the surviving writings of the formative age. These provide us evidence of how system builders chose to express their ideas (rhetoric), conceived their ideas to express cogent thought and form intelligible statements to be shared by others (logic of cogent discourse), and formed the categories through which the facts acquired sense and constituted orderly and systematic accounts of the world (topical, propositional program). All three together—the mode of discourse, the media of thought and expression, and the message brought to representation through the particular rhetoric and logic at hand—prove accessible when we ask the documentary heritage of the system builders to point us toward the system expressed in detail therein.

In this book, I argue that the movement from the Mishnah and its companions to the Talmud of the Land of Israel and its companions exhibits the transformation of Judaism from a basically philosophical system to a religious one. As we shall see, the raw materials of system building, which are themselves the formations of categories, undergo transformation. As I demonstrate in part 1, when a philosophical system becomes a religious system, the categorical change is more than a reframing or re-formation or re-presentation. What happens is rather the fundamental revaluation of categories, which I call "counterpart categories," a process I detail in part 2. Transvaluation and transformation—these compose the history of religion, so far as history records connections, comparisons, and contrasts between one thing and another. Part 1 sets forth the transformation of the received structure; part 2, the formation of a further set of corresponding categories; and part 3, the consequent recasting of the Judaic system as a whole. The sequence, therefore, is from diachronic comparison (part 1) to synchronic re-presentation (parts 2 and 3). As we shall see, however, the Judaism that emerges is not merely a re-formation of the received system but a fundamentally new system that treats systemically generative categories of the philosophical system as inert and that frames its own systemically definitive categories in their place.

Let me amplify these preliminary remarks. Religions present theories of the social order framed through the power of their rational thought (by "the power of their rational thought" I mean their capacity to explain all data in a single, cogent, and—to an authorship—self-evidently valid way). The framers of the religious documents outlining such theories answer urgent questions posed in language that speaks in that context of public policy in society and politics, economics, and philosophy or science. They thus produce answers deemed self-evidently valid by those whom they mean to address in the formation of their system. When documents such as the Mishnah, Scripture, and the successor writings, the Talmud of the Land of Israel and Midrash compilations, turn out to set forth, in an odd idiom to be sure, the principal parts of a social structure and system, they permit us to describe, analyze, and interpret not merely the documentary statements but also the social implications of those statements. In these pages we will see how the system attested in earlier writings, the Mishnah and its related Midrash compilations, is received and revised by the authorships of later writings that point toward a successor system.

The word *system* recurs throughout this book. Let me define it before proceeding. Writings that are meant (even after the fact) to be read together, such as those of the unfolding canon of Judaism in late antiquity, are held to make a cogent and important statement. I call that encompassing, canonical picture a "system," or a theory of the social order, when it comprises three necessary components: an account of a worldview, a prescription of a corresponding way of life, and a definition of the social entity that finds definition in the one and description in the other. When those three fundamental components fit together, they sustain one another in explaining the whole of a social order and hence constitute the theoretical account of a system.

Defined in this way, systems constitute for their framers a cogent picture of *how* things are to be sorted out and fitted together, *why* things are done in one way rather than another, and *who* acts and thinks in this particular way. When, as is commonly the case, people invoke God as the foundation for their worldview, maintaining that their way of life corresponds to what God wants of them and projecting their social entity in a particular relationship to God, then we have a religious system; when a religious system appeals to the Hebrew Scriptures of ancient Israel (the "Old Testament") as an important part of its authoritative literature or canon, we have a Judaism. In these pages I deal with two such Judaic systems or Judaisms, the first one philosophical and its successor, religious.

The three chapters that form the shank of part 1 and their counterparts in part 2 describe the philosophy, economics, and politics of the two successive systems—the two Judaisms—that are revealed by the successive documents of an ongoing textual community. The successor system conducts its own exercise of category formation, however, not revising what was inherited but essentially preserving the prior system while framing a quite new composition and construction. That is the picture of part 3. This book thus follows the re-presentation of a religious theory of a social world as its constituent categories are transformed from philosophical to religious. Simply put, I set forth the categorical transformation of Judaism from philosophy to religion, terms amply defined in context. This re-presentation took place within a textual community that aimed at defining the social world beyond its circle. The goal, therefore, of examining the sequence of writings produced over these four centuries is to characterize (1) two distinct systems of the social order, the first found in the Mishnah and the second in the Talmud of the Land of Israel, and (2) the striking revision of category formations through which the former became the latter. This is, then, a study of category formation as a tool for the reconstruction of the history and comparison of religion.[1]

My intent is to set forth a theory of the comparison of religions, specifically, an account of category formation and re-formation such as parts 1 and 2 provide. In part 3 I explain why I think the successor system is fundamentally new in categorical definition and structure, and I place the new Judaism into the context of religion by showing the character of its category formation to be religious: not analytical and differentiating but integrative. I further identify what I conceive to be the urgent question and compelling answer that makes the system single and whole, and in a few brief and necessarily superficial observations, I place the Judaic system side by side in its salient systemic traits (but not in its doctrinal ones!) with a contemporary system that seems to me to have asked the same question—the one of world-historical calamity, the utter ruin of the old order—and to have gone about answering it in a manner that was remarkably congruent, namely, system building.

By this example I offer a theory of systemic comparison, with special attention to two religious systems formed within a single religion or religious tradition and therefore connected in important ways with each other. True, my theory of how this is to be done is worked out wholly in terms of a single example, the comparison of two Judaisms (that is, two Judaic systems), with only the most casual allusion to an external system of a similar sort, but other religious systems can be compared by appeal to the same considerations of category formation and redefinition of categories that I spell out in the example.

The basis of comparison and contrast between (and among) systems depends on their imputed relationships, for these classifications of relationships signal the contrast between the first system and its successor. Such religious systems, addressing what is conceived to be a single, continuous social entity,[2] may relate to others in context in one of three ways: they may be (1) autonomous of one another, (2) connected with one another, or (3) continuous with one another. The classification of relationship depends on our observation of the character of the literary evidence: freestanding, contingent, or utterly undifferentiated, respectively. In the case at hand I invoke two of those three possible relationships, the first and the second.[3] The first of the two systems is autonomous, the second, connected to the first but freestanding, and the comparison of the second to the first yields the method of systemic comparison that I mean to set forth here.[4]

My specific contribution to the problem of theory and method, expressed in a concrete case bearing ample generalization as to method, is in three parts. The first step (which so far as I know is a novelty in the study of the history of religion) is to compare religious systems that are both connected to but also distinct from each other.[5] In this way I take account of the important variations that distinguish formations within a single religious tradition, no longer harmonizing or merely ignoring important differences but utilizing them in the description, analysis, and interpretation of the diverse systems that over time a given tradition engenders. To do so I describe the generative categories of the initial system and then ask how the successor system has dealt with these categories. This I do in part 1.

That comparison leads to my second methodological innovation, identifying categorical revision so far-reaching as to require the invention of a new classification of systemic category, which I call the counterpart category, a term I define in context. In part 2 I show how the formation of a counterpart category emerges from the comparison of the way distinct systemic structures frame the same category. I have invented the phrase *counterpart category* to serve my method of systemic comparison; I explain that phrase, and the data that necessitated it, in prologue 2.

The third step, accomplished in part 3, is to explain how a fresh system addresses fundamental problems its framers discerned in a received system, which is done in the two principal parts that together define the new system as coherent: a new theory of the systemic power of the system's worldview and a new coherence imputed to the systemic components of way of life and social entity. I characterize the initial system as philosophical, the successor as religious, and I further show how the religious system has (re)integrated the received categories within the counterpart categories in what is essentially and fundamentally its own fresh statement: a system of Judaism connected with the former but quite clearly intended to deliver its own answers to its own questions.

Let me specify what I conceive to be at stake here. This work derives wholly from the analysis of texts, and what I am attempting to do is find out how to describe a "Judaism" beyond the specific texts, moving beyond the text and the context and toward the matrix of all the canonical texts. What is it that each document takes for granted but no document spells out? To answer that question I have to describe the processes of category formation, to specify the categorical imperative in the description of a Judaism. That accounts for the book's focus on the re-formation of received categories and the formation of new ones, wholly congruent to the received ones but also entirely fresh.

As I previously said, the categories that I bring to the study are those of the social order: philosophy or science, politics, and economics. What makes me so certain that the documents I begin with form a statement of not merely theology and doctrine but also the requirements of the social order? The reason it is legitimate to describe the categorical unfolding of Judaism within the categories of political economy is simple. The Mishnah, which after Scripture is the foundation document of the canonical corpus examined here, sets out a full account of the life of the nation in its social order, to which philosophy, politics, and economics are just as integral as they are to the social order conceived by Greco-Roman philosophy in the tradition of Aristotle. These three constituents of the social order deal with the worldview (in philosophy), the way of life (in economics), and the definition of the social entity (in politics) of the (imagined or real) social order portrayed in documents identified as canonical. The unshakable premise of the Mishnah and all successor documents is that Israel forms a holy society, a community and a nation that lives on its own territory and governs itself. To the various authors and authorships[6] of those writings, that means a political entity that governs itself, constitutes a coherent economy, and furthermore appeals to a cogent and shared worldview.

Thus, at stake in systemic description is the reading of written evidence as it has been combined to form an authoritative statement. In the analysis at hand, I ask what happened in the unfolding of the canon to these categories of description of the social order, to the issues of the way of life, worldview, and definition of the social entity that altogether form the social system imagined by the authors or authorships of authoritative writings. This book provides a detailed answer to that question.

Of the Judaism that reached fruition in the Talmud of Babylonia, the category formation of Greco-Roman political economy (philosophy, politics, and economics) served what would be only the initial system, that is, the Judaic system to which the Mishnah attests. But in many important ways, that Judaism turned out to be far less than wholly symmetrical with the final system of Judaism that emerged from the formative age and has defined matters to the present day. The economics, politics, and philosophy of the initial formation of Judaism set the agenda and formed the court of appeal, but successors and continuators picked and chose, thus framing a fresh definition for the social foundations of the world they proposed to invent. The philosophy, politics, and economics of the next phase in the formation of Judaism, seen on their own but also in relationship with the initial theories, will therefore demand the sustained description, analysis, and interpretation that show the initial system to have been revised and adapted by later system makers. What is ultimately at stake is how intellectuals defined the rationalities of Judaism as a social composition: a theory of the society of Israel, the holy people of God. This work focuses on the successive rationalities of an unfolding Judaism.

I can compare systems because the Judaism that emerged from late antiquity unfolded in three distinct stages, each marked by the distinctive traits of the literature that reached closure at its end. Each stage produced a Judaic system discernable through the examination of the literature that emerged in the three periods. Comparison of the several systems begins, therefore, with attention to the literary evidence. Because this book focuses so uniformly and with such concentration on documentary evidence,[7] a brief word about the particular writings treated here is in order. The initial system is presented in the Mishnah (ca. 200 C.E.), a philosophical system in the form of a law code, and the Tosefta (ca. 300), a systemic amplification and supplement for the Mishnah. Alongside these documents stand the Sifra (a commentary to the book of Leviticus) Sifré to Numbers, and Sifré to Deuteronomy, which are closely related to the Mishnah and the Tosefta. These writings provide access to the initial Judaic system. The successor system is described by reference to the Talmud of the Land of Israel (ca. 400, also known as the Yerushalmi), which is a commentary to the Mishnah, as well as Genesis Rabbah, Leviticus Rabbah, and Pesiqta deRab Kahana (all ca. 400-450), which are commentaries to Scripture.[8] In these pages, I refer to the last-named documents of the late fourth and fifth centuries as the successor documents because one of them, the Talmud of the Land of Israel, presents its materials in the form of a commentary to the Mishnah, which furthermore justifies my insistence that it and its closely allied Midrash compilations of scriptural exegesis present a system connected to the prior one laid out in the pages of the Mishnah.

The transformation to which the title of this book refers therefore speaks of the movement from book to book, from an earlier writing to later compilations represented as continuous with the former document. The "transformation" is a vast re-formation of the Judaic system portrayed in the Mishnah and Tosefta, and the movement is from that Judaism, presented as a philosophical system, to the successor Judaism, which both receives and preserves the initial categories but also defines its own categorical structure through what I call counterpart categories. This Judaism is the one adumbrated in the Talmud of the Land of Israel, Genesis Rabbah, Leviticus Rabbah, and Pesiqta deRab Kahana, the whole now re-presented as a religious system.[9] In these pages, however, I do not mean merely to describe, analyze, and interpret the movement in one set of books to another, of ideas concerning the social order.

The first system, formed in the first 200 years of the common era and represented by the Mishnah and its associated writings, is utterly freestanding. The second, taking shape in the next 200 years and represented by the Talmud of the Land of Israel and its companions, is connected to the first but essentially distinct from it. The third, expressed in documents that reached closure between 400 and 600 C.E. within and around the Talmud of Babylonia, is connected to the second but in important traits distinct from it as well. Ultimately, these three systems, autonomous when viewed synchronically but connected when seen diachronically, constituted at the end of their formative age the single, wholly and utterly continuous structure we call Judaism. In their successive stages of autonomy, however, and then autonomy and connection, the three distinct systems may be classified, respectively, as philosophical, religious, and theological, each one taking over and revising the definitive categories of the former and framing its own fresh generative categories as well. The formative history of Judaism, then, is the story of the presentations and re-presentations of categorical structures. In method it is the exegesis of taxonomy and taxic systems.

Notes

1. The importance of recognizing the autonomy of a given religion's diverse and freestanding systems for the comparative study of religion is self-evident.

No one maintains that there is now, or ever has been, one single "Christianity"; "Buddhism" is an invention of the West; and "Judaism" is a term of convenience standing for whatever people want it to mean. When we see that a given "religion" in fact encompasses a considerable variety of religious systems that neither stand in linear relationship with one another nor harmonize with one another, then we recognize what the comparison of religions requires. It is the comparison, to begin with, between one religious system and other religious systems within the same context, that is, within the same religion: Judaisms compared to one another, so, too, Christianities, Buddhisms, Islams, and the like. That is hardly to argue that there was and is no such thing as "Judaism," only "Judaisms," but merely to point to the necessity of clearly defining what we mean when we refer not to "Judaisms" but to "Judaism," and so throughout. The comparison of religion that consists of observations about "Christianity" in comparison and contrast to "Buddhism" or "Judaism" is simply not plausible in the face of actual data. Nevertheless, I do not think we must leave to theologians the entire task of defining how diverse religious systems may form a single religion. I have shown in *Self-Fulfilling Prophecy: Exile and Return in the History of Judaism,* 2d ed. (Atlanta, Ga.: Scholars Press for South Florida Studies in the History of Judaism, 1990) that even within the framework of the history of religion we can make some progress toward plausible definitions.

2. I say "conceived to be" for I deal with evidence deriving not from observation or field study but from literary, and only literary, statements. In *Judaism and Its Social Metaphors* (Cambridge: Cambridge University Press, 1989), I show the uses of the word "Israel" that diverse Judaisms have made. There is no possibility of simply using a word such as "Israel" or "people," "nation," family," or "community." At hand are what in anthropology are called "imagined communities," and the nature of our evidence—every line of it a much reflected on cultural artifact—attests to only the shared imagination of the persons who wrote the documents, preserved them, and imputed to them definitive authority. In the case at hand, however, I deal with later documents that appeal to earlier ones, hence my claim to speak of what is conceived to be a single, continuous social entity.

3. The relationship of continuity among systems occupies my thought, for I do not understand how a continuous system is composed out of autonomous or connected systems. It seems quite obvious to me, however, that the framers of the Talmud of Babylonia accomplished precisely that when they set forth a single and coherent Judaism comprising all that had come down to them and defining all that would succeed them. Obviously, the work must begin with the literary problems and proceed outward from there, that is, from text, to matrix, to context. I anticipate that just as the last decade has required me to focus on the issue of connectedness, so the next will demand attention to the problem of continuity. The planned works of literary analysis noted in the preface stand between this book and the studies I now contemplate.

4. The companion study to this one, tentatively titled *From Religion to Theology,* will describe a Judaism that has inherited prior systems and recast

them all to form a continuous and seamless statement of its own; only when that system has been shown to emerge from its documentary evidence shall we be able to compare and contrast the three types of systems: autonomous, connected to a prior system, and continuous with all prior systems—a judgment that depends initially on literary evidence, but later also on intellectual and even propositional evidence. All this will be worked out in due course; the first comparison is the one now possible.

5. In general, by comparative religion, people mean the comparison of two or more utterly unrelated religions, e.g., Buddhism and Christianity. Categories such as Christianity and Buddhism are hopeless constructs, however, because they homogenize vast and complex sets of religious systems and treat as one what are many things. "Judaism" through time and change and "Christianity" in all "its" formulations cannot be compared because neither the -*ism* nor the -*ity* ever existed in social reality; there have been only Judaisms and Christianities, and the work of comparison and contrast must entail the study of the differences between two things that are alike, not the contrast of two things that are not alike to begin with—only in likeness do we find the possibility of establishing the context for difference. That is the burden of the exchange between Jonathan Z. Smith and myself in Jacob Neusner, ed., *Take Judaism, for Example: Studies toward the Comparison of Religions* (Chicago: University of Chicago Press, 1983). It has taken me eight years from the time of the conversations that yielded that book to find for myself a contribution to that dialogue, and this book constitutes my reply to Smith's wonderful challenge. Whether it is a suitable and even an adequate reply I cannot claim to know.

6. This term is meant to take account of the collective and social character of much of the literary enterprise. Not a single authoritative book of Judaism in late antiquity bears the name of an identified author, and the literary traits of not a single piece of writing may securely be imputed to a single person. The means for gaining acceptance was anonymity, and the medium of authority lay in recapitulating collective conventions of rhetoric and logic, not to mention proposition. To speak of "authors" in this context is confusing, hence the resort to the word *authorships*.

7. But in my *Symbol and Theology in Judaism* (Minneapolis, Minn.: Fortress Press, 1990) I do try to correlate literary and archaeological evidence.

8. Further definition of the documents that serve this study and how I propose to interpret them is in prologue 1.

9. That simple statement makes it scarcely necessary to add that my synthesis is not a mere reprise of results reached earlier but a large-scale interpretation of those results within the framework of the history of religion—here, the history of the formation of Judaism.

Part One

The Reception
of the
Philosophical System

■

Prologue I
Philosophical Categories

My task in part 1, to characterize and classify the categorical structure of the Mishnah and closely allied writings, requires that I show three things: (1) that the Mishnah's system indeed comprised a philosophy, an economics, and a politics; (2) that the philosophy, economics, and politics of the Mishnah are to be classified as philosophical; and (3) that the successor documents preserve but do not vastly re-form these received categories. This last fact will then open the way to the analysis of the category re-formation I claim is attested in the second phase of the canon of Judaism.

By now, defining the terms of the first proposition hardly requires an elaborate exercise. By *philosophy* I mean discourse that is philosophical in method and in message. An economics in this context must likewise present a theory of the rational disposition of scarce resources that (other) philosophers of the same age would have recognized as familiar and therefore philosophical. Along these same lines, a politics must exhibit the traits of a philosophical politics. Because the Mishnah reached closure in ca. 200 C.E. my definition of philosophy and what may be characterized as philosophical derives from that same age, the Greco-Roman. Within the vast and varied Greco-Roman philosophical tradition, a specific figure emerges as paradigmatic.

In this context, Aristotle defines the model of philosophical method.[1] As to message, I appeal to an important proposition of Middle Platonism that came to full expression only in the writings of Plotinus's Neoplatonism, two generations after the closure of the Mishnah. If I can show that the method of the Mishnah corresponds to that of Aristotle and that a fundamental message of the Mishnah restates within the appropriate idiom a proposition of Middle Platonism, I may fairly characterize the Mishnah's system as philosophical in context, that is, as a system that other philosophers could (with proper education) have recognized as philosophical. As to economics and politics, Aristotle likewise serves to set forth the standard for defining a philosophical system of both.

To briefly restate the results of prior research, in chapter 1 I set forth as philosophical both the method and the principal message of the Mishnah, the one Aristotelian, the other Middle Platonic and fully realized in Plotinus. I then turn to the modes of thought of the successor writings, principally asking how the later documents compare methodologically with the rhetorical and logical modes of thought that are to be classified as philosophical in the Mishnah. I will show that the literary evidence for both the Yerushalmi and the pertinent Midrash compilations consistently points toward rhetoric and logic of an other than philosophical character. That demonstration establishes the point of part 1, which is that in terms of modes of thought and argument expressed in rhetoric and logic (and, as a matter of fact, proposition), a philosophical system is set forth by the Mishnah and faithfully preserved but not replicated in the philsophical manner by the successor documents. These later writers make connections and draw conclusions, portraying the result in a way vastly different from the way of the Mishnah. That sets the stage for the movement from worldview, expressed through philosophy, to way of life and definition of the social entity, which for the Mishnah are economics and politics, respectively.

Does the Mishnah attest to a philosophical economics and politics? Chapter 2 shows in great detail that the Mishnah does set forth an economics — a theory of the rational disposition of scarce resources. That economics, moreover, corresponds point by point with the economics of Aristotle, and its rationality conforms with his. In chapter 3, which builds on the results of chapter 2, I show that the Mishnah also provides a politics — a theory of the legitimate exercise of violence and of the institutions that permanently impose sanctions in the preservation of the social order. Moreover, drawn once more to Aristotle, I compare and contrast the politics of the Mishnah with the philosophical politics of Aristotle, showing the place and message of the political component of the system presented by both. Here the task is both to distinguish the Mishnah's politics from that of the Pentateuch and also to establish points of commonality and contrast between the Mishnah's politics and that of Aristotle.

In both cases a further task remains. Critical to the argument of the book is the demonstration, in chapters 2 and 3, of how the received categories were treated later on. I have to trace the way in which the successor documents received the economics and politics of the Mishnah. That inquiry draws me into the later history of the categories of economics and politics, particularly in the Talmud of the Land of Israel, because that document portrays itself as a systematic commentary to the Mishnah. But attention is required also to the representation of economics in the associated Midrash compilations, themselves represented as commentaries to Scripture.

Now to spell out in some detail the program of part 1: why this, not that? Systemic description begins with the written evidence that points us toward the outlines of the intellectual structure on which the theory of the social order is constructed. That evidence, when deemed authoritative, forms the canon of the system. The canon recapitulates the system that animates the mentality of both the framers of canonical writings and the authorities who adopted those writings for a single canonical composition. To study (a) Judaism, accordingly, we turn to the canon of the Judaism under study and seek its evidence concerning the categories that constitute any account of society: the philosophy, politics, and economics of (a) Judaism.

From beginning to end, the Judaic systems attested by the successive parts of the canon defined as their problem the construction of a social world. The categorical structure of each, in succession, framed intelligible thought by appeal to the issues of the world framed first of all by a particular ethnos, the social entity (the most neutral language I can find) called (an) "Israel." Every Judaic system, moreover, would take as its task the definition of the shared life of (an) Israel: its way of life, or (broadly speaking) ethics, and its worldview, or ethos. So each, presented an account of the social entity or the "Israel" that realized in its shared and corporate being the relevant ethics (again, broadly construed) and explained that ethics by appeal to the ethos. As a matter of definition, a Judaic system is one that derives its generative categories from the (theoretical) requirements of framing a social order: who "we" are, what we do together, and why we are the corporate body that we are — ethnos, ethics, and ethos. And that brings me back to the first of the great Judaic systems that in the end formed Judaism, the system to which the authorship of the Mishnah refers in framing its writing.

The Mishnah set forth in the form of a law code a highly philosophical account of the world ("worldview"), a pattern for everyday and material activities and relationships ("way of life"), and a definition of the social entity ("nation," "people," "us" as against "outsiders," "Israel") that realized that way of life and explained it by appeal to that worldview. There is no difficulty in calling this account of a way of life an economics because the account of material reality provided by the Mishnah corresponds point for point with that given in Aristotle's counterpart. The Mishnah also sets forth a politics by dealing with the same questions about the permanent and legitimate institutions that inflict sanctions that occupied Greek and Roman political thinkers. There is no economics of other-worldly character, no politics of an inner "kingdom of God." All is straightforward, worldly, material, and consequential for the everyday world. The successor documents, closed roughly two centuries later, address the Mishnah's system and recast its categories into a new system, both connected to but different from the first. The character of their reception of the received categories and of their own category formation, emerging in the contrast between one set of documents and another, justifies invoking the term *transformation,* that is, of one thing into something else.

I call the writings that followed the Mishnah, Tosefta, and associated Midrash compilations successors because writings of the late fourth and fifth centuries were formally organized and presented as commentaries on a received text, the Talmud providing exegesis for the Mishnah and the Midrash compilations doing the same for Scripture. So the later authorships insisted, in their own behalf, that they (merely) explained and amplified the received Torah, imparting to their writings the form of a commentary. When these documents attached themselves to the Mishnah, on the one side, and the Hebrew Scriptures, on the other, they gave literary form to the theory of the dual Torah that God gave to Moses at Mount Sinai, the Mishnah standing for the oral revelation and the Scriptures for the written.

Specifically, the Talmud of the Land of Israel formed around thirty-nine of the Mishnah's sixty-two tractates, the Genesis Rabbah and Leviticus Rabbah (joined by Pesiqta deRab Kahana) addressed the first and third books of Moses, respectively, along with some other documents. The very act of choosing only some of the Mishnah's tractates and ignoring others constitutes an act of taste and judgment — system building not only by acts of commission but also by silence. But, much of the Talmud and the principal Midrash compilations does amplify and augment the base documents to which they are attached.[2] In choosing some passages and neglecting others and, more to the point, in working out their own questions and their own answers beyond those of the Mishnah, the authorships attest to a system that did more than merely extend and recast the categorical structure of the system for which the Mishnah stands. They not only took over the way of life, worldview, and social entity defined in the Mishnah's system but also, in systematically amplifying details and framing a program of exegesis around the requirements of clerks engaged in enforcing the rules of the Mishnah, they built their own system.

These authorships formed categories of politics, philosophy, and economics that corresponded to those of the Mishnah, but these categories proved so utterly contrary in structure and definition to those of the Mishnah that, as I shall show, they presented mirror images of the received categories. In due course we shall see how the politics, philosophy, and economics of the Mishnah were joined by what may be called an antipolitics, an antieconomics, and an utterly tranformed mode of learning. In the hands of the later sages, the new mode of Torah study—the definition of what was at stake in studying the Torah—altogether redefined the issues of the intellect. As a matter of fact, the successor system recast not the issues so much as the very stakes of philosophy or science. The reception of the Mishnah's category formations and their transformation therefore stand for the movement from a philosophical to a religious mode of thinking, for the system to which the Mishnah attests is essentially philosophical in its rhetorical, logical, and topical program, whereas the successor system is fundamentally religious in these same principal and indicative traits of intellectual media.

The Mishnah's philosophy, economics, and politics correspond to the categories of worldview, way of life, and social entity previously discussed in the introduction. Its philosophy explains how to think, identifies the agenda for sustained thought and learning, and proves a proposition of fundamental importance. Indeed, even in the context of Greco-Roman philosophy would its method and at least one of its significant propositions be classified as philosophical, the first identical to Aristotle's method of natural history, the second, to Middle Platonism's doctrine of the hierarchical unity of being. The Mishnah's economics sets forth a theory of rational action in the face of scarcity and for the increase and disposition of wealth that, as I previously said, corresponds point by point to the economics of Aristotle: the categories of thought on the rational disposition of scarce resources are the same as Aristotle's, the generative principles the same, and the conclusions the same. Wealth consists of land in both, the notion of true value operates, and distributive, not market economics prevail. Aristotle and the Mishnah's sages concur on the detailed consequences of these economic principles. Finally, the Mishnah's politics lay out a precise account of how power, encompassing legitimate violence and embodied in institutions and their staff, is to realize in everyday social transactions the social entity "Israel." This politics in most of its definitive traits corresponds to that of Aristotle as well.[3]

The Talmud of the Land of Israel and the Midrash compilations Genesis Rabbah and Leviticus Rabbah together with Pesiqta deRab Kahana not only expanded and revised the form of these categories in the Mishnah and Scripture, respectively. These same documents formed their own categories for those served initially by philosophy, politics, and economics. And that explains the entire program of this book: part 1 deals with the transformation of the received categories in the initial structure, that is, the Judaic structure of the social order, laid out philosophically; part 2 identifies the categorical re-formation of the same structure, that is, the Judaic structure of the social order, but now categorized religiously; and part 3 portrays, whole and complete, the systemic consequence of this transformation—Judaism as a religious system.

These general observations explain the task at hand, which is to characterize the basic intellectual traits of the system represented by the Mishnah and to follow the treatment of the same categories in the pages of the Talmud of the Land of Israel, Genesis Rabbah, and Leviticus Rabbah, along with Pesiqta deRab Kahana. Our question is simple: how shall we classify the category formation of the Mishnah in its context? Even on its own terms, part 1 will be more readily grasped when its direction and purpose are clearly stated. Part 2, chapters 4, 5, and 6, asks a more difficult question: in terms of rhetorical and logical classification, are the successor documents' category formations like those of the Mishnah or unlike them? If like, then we classify those documents as we have classified the Mishnah, but if unlike, then how—as a matter of hypothesis—may we classify the system represented by the successor writings?

The title of the opening chapter leaves no doubt as to the thesis that motivates my agenda: the Mishnah is to be classified as philosophical, whereas the successor writings are so fundamentally different as to their rhetorical and logical characteristics as to require an altogether different taxon. The justification for characterizing that taxon as not only *not* philosophical but in fact religious will emerge fully only in later chapters. It suffices at the outset to show a difference and to point to the principal elements of that difference. So we begin with the matter of philosophical method.

But even now, I must show how I identify a system as philosophical or religious. The identification is not subjective nor the criteria private or idiosyncratic; to the contrary, I point only to facts, accurately portrayed and informedly interpreted. To begin with, the indicative traits in both instances derive from and are displayed by documents, for I take as axiomatic that the rhetorical and logical forms of any written system attest to both the method and the message that sustain that system. From how people express themselves, I work my way backward to their modes of thought: how they classify perceived data, how they make connections between fact and fact, how they draw conclusions from those connections, and finally, how they represent conclusions in cogent compositions. All these traits of mind are to be discerned in the characteristics common to all such written compositions — in the rhetoric that conveys messages in proportion and appropriate esthetics, in the logic that imparts self-evidence to the making of connections and the drawing of conclusions, and in the representation of sets of conclusions as cogent and intelligible.

That is why I turn to analyze the evidence of documents when I ask how people think, which in this context means the logic of their intelligible thought and discourse. I further identify the medium by which they frame their message, which in this context means the rules of their formal rhetoric. On the basis of these indicators I can account for that union of disciplined rhetoric and logic that comprises the media of expression and modes of thought of a well-crafted system. Thus, the process of comparing and contrasting the traits discerned in documentary inquiry provides the description of the logical, rhetorical, and topical constraints that allows analysis of the system, for the logic, rhetoric, and topical program of one set of writings can be described and compared with the same traits of another. So evidence for classifying systems that posit a theory of the social order (for instance, as philosophy or religion) derives to begin with from the use of language, in particular, from the rules for correct representation of thought that, in general, we know as rhetoric.

From the surface—the rhetoric—we move inward to the logic of the thought processes encapsulated in the language. This evidence derives from the argumentation in behalf of a proposition, that is, from the kind of evidence adduced and the manner of marshaling that evidence. Active thought takes place when people see a connection between one thing and something else that attempt to explain that connection in one way rather than in some other. The issue is thus what makes a connection self-evident, so that one thing fits with some other, whereas a third thing does not fit in or make sense at all in connection with the first two. We have in hand ample written evidence, of not only the conclusions these authorships reached and the ways in which they framed their propositions but also the expectation that others within the group educated in their writings and manners of thought would find the result compelling.

Two simple questions clarify the issue of continuity in category formation. (1) Have the successor authorships revised or redefined the received categories? (2) Do we find in the Yerushalmi and its companions a considerable extension and re-formation of the philosophical economics and politics set forth by the Mishnah?

If I can show that the philosophers whose ideas are presented by the Mishnah would have been surprised and also informed by what they found in the Yerushalmi's re-presentation of the Mishnah, then it follows that a continuing philosophical reading of an essentially philosophical economics and politics was underway. On the other hand, if it turns out that the Yerushalmi's reading of the Mishnah essentially served the purposes of clarification, extension, and above all, practical application, then it follows that the Yerushalmi and related writings did not undertake a considerable labor of category re-formation at all: not philosophers but something else, its authorships will have given to the Mishnah a decent burial and gone on to other matters.

The criteria for knowing how the Mishnah's system was received are clear. On what problems do the successor authorships concentrate, theoretical or exegetical? What constitutes their continuing intellectual program, the tasks of reconsideration and criticism or the work of practical application? The answers will emerge in a brief survey of exemplary discourses, which repeatedly show a range of questions deriving not from philosophers and theorists but from clerks and judges—people whose concerns in argumentation always end in material reality.

In the case of economics we shall ask about rules governing cases, not definitions of abstractions. In the case of politics we shall find not the extension and elaboration of the received structure but the portrayal of a quite different one. When speaking of the Mishnah the successor writers paraphrase and clarify its sentences. When moving beyond the limits of the Mishnah they make matters their own and set out, side by side with the Mishnah and its message, a quite different account of economics and politics.

The following briefly summarizes what will later be shown in detail. In other than exegetical passages of the Yerushalmi, scarce resources, so far as these are of a material order of being (e.g., wealth as defined by the Mishnah and Aristotle), are systemically neutral. A definition of scarce resources emerges that explicitly involves a symbolic transformation, with the material definition of scarce resources set into contradiction with an other than material one. Thus the successor writings contain both clarification of the details of the received category and adumbration of a symbolic revision: in other words, categorical transformation.

Similarly, the Mishnah's representation of the political structure undergoes clarification as well, but alongside, a quite separate and very different structure also is portrayed. The received structure presents three political classes ordered in a hierarchy; the successor structure presents a single political class that corresponds to a counterpart in Heaven. Here, too, a symbolic transaction has taken place, one set of symbols being replicated but also reversed and a second set of symbols given instead. I express this transformation in a simple way: a structure comprising hierarchically ordered foci of power gives way to a structure made of a single focus of power. That single focus, moreover, now draws boundaries between legitimate and illegitimate violence, boundaries not conceived in the initial system.

So in all three components of the account of the social order the philosophical system gives way to another. The worldview comes to expression in modes of thought and expression—the logic of making connections and drawn conclusions—that differ from the philosophical ones of the Mishnah. The way of life appeals to value expressed in symbols other than those of economics in the philosophical mode. The theory of the social entity comes to concrete expression in sanctions legitimately administered by a single class of persons (an institution) rather than by a proportionate and balanced set of classes of persons in hierarchical order; moreover, that same theory recognizes and defines both legitimate and illegitimate violence, something beyond the ken of the initial system. Clearly, another system is adumbrated and attested in the successor writings. What that other system was, the definition of its categories and how these relate to the categorical requirements of a theory of the social order—these considerations define the questions of part 2.

Notes

1. Do I mean to suggest that our sages of blessed memory hiked down from their Galilean hill towns to Ceasarea on the coast and listened to the public speeches of the masters of the Second Sophistic, who reached a considerable public throughout the Near East? Obviously not. It has not been shown that the Mishnah's sages ever heard a single word of a philosophical address or read a line of a single treatise, and I think it highly unlikely that they did or could have done so. How then does it happen that the Mishnah emerges in its method and message as congruent to philosophical writings long available in the Middle East, such as Aristotle's? How can I explain the obvious parallels in modes of thought, logic, and proof between the Mishnah and the natural philosophy associated with Aristotle in particular? I have no explanation, nor can I think of any. I have to work from the evidence in hand, and what appears time and again are fundamental points of congruence. When items share important traits I classify them within a single taxon. Parallel lines do not meet, and diffusion seems to me an uninteresting mode of explaining anything, but to argue that merely because not a single philosophical term of any consequence occurs in the Mishnah and related writings the authorship of the Mishnah therefore cannot be classified as philosophical is to confuse philology with the history of ideas. The real issues, as I stress a bit later, are traits of writing, of rhetoric, and of argument—the indicative modes of thought. And these are philosophical, not in any merely general sense but in very specific and particular texts. I hasten to emphasize that much more work on the philosophicality of these writings needs to be done. When it is done it will address not only Aristotle and the Mishnah but also Augustine and the fourth- and early fifth-century sages who produced the Talmud of the Land of Israel, Genesis Rabbah, and Leviticus Rabbah, such as I do in part 3, as well as the sages of Zorastrian Iran and the Talmud of Babylonia (e.g., the comparison of the Denkart and the Bavli), which I plan to do when preliminary studies have been completed. So in this and associated works on the Mishnah as philosophy in method and message, economics, and politics,

I mean only to open questions. In my view it is no longer possible either to read these documents in complete isolation from other writings of their class that were produced in antiquity, to regard the sages of the oral Torah as *sui generis* in their context in late antiquity, or to deem their Judaism to be utterly beyond comparison and contrast with any other religious system of their time and place. The comparison of Augustine's and our sages' theories of history obviously opens a road but completes no journey. Once such a comparison is drawn, however, it can no longer be pretended that all we can learn from the Fathers of Christianity is material of philological or exegetical interest and that we can simply ignore, for the study of the formative history of Judaism, the entire intellectual heritage of Christianity. It also cannot be pretended that, beyond the first century, scholars of Christianity have nothing to learn from Judaism.

2. In the tractates I probed, my estimate is that as much as ninety percent of the Talmud of the Land of Israel serves to amplify passages of the Mishnah, and not much more than ten percent contains intellectual initiatives that are fundamentally fresh and unrelated to anything in the Mishnah passage under discussion; see Neusner *Talmud of the Land of Israel*, vol. 35 (Chicago: University of Chicago Press, 1983). Cf. my *Judaism in Society: The Evidence of the Yerushalmi: Toward the Natural History of a Religion* (Chicago: University of Chicago Press, 1983), which aims to show that even the passages that (merely) clarify words or phrases of the Mishnah in fact set forth a considerable autonomous program. See especially pp. 73-112, but what is clearly distinct from the Mishnah is detailed on pp. 113-254.

3. These statements summarize the results of the following books of mine: *Judaism as Philosophy: The Method and Message of the Mishnah* (Columbia: University of South Carolina Press, 1991); *The Economics of the Mishnah* (Chicago: University of Chicago Press, 1990); *The Politics of Judaism: The Initial Structure and System* (Chicago: University of Chicago Press, 1982). *Judaism as Philosophy* is supplemented by *The Philosophical Mishnah*, 4 vols. (Atlanta, Ga.: Scholars Press for Brown Judaic Studies, 1989).

I
Modes of Thought:
From Philosophy to Religion

The philosophers of the Greco-Roman philosophical tradition could have perceived the Mishnah's Judaic system as philosophical not merely in method but also in message. The Mishnah's method of hierarchical classification in important ways is like that of Aristotle's natural history,[1] and the central component of its message is congruent to that of Neoplatonism. Specifically, the Mishnah's Judaic system sets forth in stupefying detail a version of one critical proposition of Neoplatonism, demonstrated through a standard Aristotelian method.[2] The repeated proof through the Aristotelian method of hierarchical classification demonstrates in detail that many things—done enough times, *all* things—really form a single thing: many species, a single genus; many genera, an encompassing, well-crafted, and cogent whole. Every time we speciate—and the Mishnah is a mass of speciated lists—we affirm that position; each successful labor of forming relationships among species, for example, making them into a genus or identifying the hierarchy of the species, proves it again. Further, when we show that many things are really one, or that one thing yields many (the reverse and confirmation of the former), we say in a fresh way this philosophy's immutable truth concerning the unity of all being(s) in an orderly composition within a single taxon. Thus, this Judaism's initial system, the Mishnah's, finds its natural place within philosophy because it appeals to the Aristotelian methods and medium of natural philosophy—classification expressed in the forms of *Listenwissenschaft,* that is, rigorous and disciplined learning through the comparison and contrast of data—to register its position, which is an important one in Middle Platonism and later (close to a century after the closure of the Mishnah) would come to profound expression in Plotinus.[3]

Because I characterize the method as *Listenwissenschaft* and maintain that the Mishnah's use of this mode of thought, which was conventional in the Near East from Sumerian times, corresponds to Aristotle's method of natural philosophy, let me quickly define what I mean by that word. It is the presentation of a proposition (e.g., a rule) through a catalog of facts formed by appeal to common indicative traits. The list of facts is composed so that, through the regularly recurring traits of the entries, it will yield a proposition common to them all. Further still, the list will allow generalization to items not on the list, hence serving a syllogistic purpose. Such a list will therefore be made up of parallel items that together point to a simple conclusion; in the Mishnah the proposed general conclusion may or may not be given at the end of the catalog, but the catalog—by definition—points to it. All the cataloged facts, moreover, are taken to bear self-evident connections to one another, established by those pertinent shared traits implicit in the composition of the list. They therefore also bear meaning and point through the weight of evidence to an inescapable conclusion.

Let us dwell on the philosophical classification of the Mishnah's mode of thought. The Mishnah's method of inquiry is that of natural history, corresponding point by point with that method of natural history characteristic of Aristotle. I do not claim that our sages of blessed memory read, or could have read, Aristotle or any other Greek philosopher. Aristotle's work on natural history and his reflections on scientific method, namely, the *Posterior Analytics*[4]—these works speak in their own language to their own problems, and the Mishnah's authorship has written in a different language about incomparable problems. Nevertheless, when we compare the Mishnaic philosophers' method with that of Aristotle, who also set forth a system that, in part, appealed to the right ordering of things through classification by correct rules,[5] the simple fact becomes inescapable: before us are different people talking about different things but in the same way.

A brief look at the standard textbook picture of Aristotle's taxonomic method will permit a comparison between the philosophical method of the philosophy of Judaism and that of the methodologically paramount natural philosophy of the Greco-Roman world.[6] First of all is the simple observation that the distinction between genus and species lies at the foundation of all knowledge. Adkins states the matter in the most accessible way: "Aristotle, a systematic biologist, uses his method of classification by genera and species, itself developed from the classificatory interests of the later Plato, to place man among other animals. . . . The classification must be based on the final development of the creature."[7] But to classify we must suppose things to be subject to classification, which means they must possess traits that are both essential and indicative, on the one side, but also shared with other things, on the other. The point of direct contact and intersection between the Judaism's philosophy of hierarchical classification and the natural philosophy of Aristotle lies in the shared and critical conviction concerning the true nature or character of things. Both parties concur that there *is* such a true definition—a philosophical commonplace that generates interesting problems, for example, about Platonic Ideas, form and substance, the actual and the potential, and the like.[8]

But how are we to know what are the essential traits by which to classify things, the traits that allow us to define the things' true characters? This is the point at which the comparison between the two systems becomes particular. Aristotle's and Judaism's philosophies share not only conviction about genus and species but also quite concrete conceptions as to how these are to be identified and organized.[9] The basic conviction on both sides is this: objects are not random but fall into classes and so may be described, analyzed, and explained by appeal to the general traits or rules that permit their regularization and ordering in classes. The generative point of comparison is the taxonomic interest in defining through classification.

This definitive trait of natural philosophy is what we find in common between Aristotle's and the Mishnah's philosophical method. The points in common prove far more compelling than those yielded by the general observation that both systems appeal to the identification of genera out of species. In fact, what philosophers call the dialectical approach in Aristotle turns out to be the same approach to the discovery or demonstration of truth that we find in the Mishnah. Like Aristotle, the Mishnah's philosophers compose their taxonomy by appeal to the indicative traits of things rather than to extrinsic considerations of imposed classification, for example, by reference to Scripture.[10] The philosophers whose system appears in the Mishnah appeal to the traits of things, deriving their genera from the comparison and contrast of those inherent or intrinsic traits.

These rather general observations require illustration, for my entire thesis rests on the characterization of the initial system as philosophical and the successor system as nonphilosophical. To show why I maintain that the modes of thought and argument of the Mishnah fall into the same class as Aristotle's method, let me now give one example that shows the framers of the Mishnah presenting the propositions within a labor of classification through comparison and contrast of persons, actions, conditions, matters of status, and the like, and appealing solely to the traits of things in doing so. The logical basis of coherent speech and discourse in the Mishnah derives from *Listenwissenschaft,* which accords with the method of natural history presented by Aristotle. That mode of thought defines a way of proving propositions through classification, thus establishing a set of shared traits that forms a rule that compels us to reach a given conclusion.

Probative facts derive from the classification of data that point in one direction and not in another. A catalog of facts, for example, may be composed so that, through the regularities and indicative traits of the entries, it yields a proposition. A list of parallel items together points to a simple conclusion; the conclusion may or may not be given at the end of the catalog, but the catalog—by definition—points to it. All the cataloged facts are taken to bear self-evident connections to one another, established by those pertinent shared traits implicit in the composition of the list, therefore bearing meaning and pointing through the weight of evidence to an inescapable conclusion. The discrete facts then join together because of some trait common to them all. This mode of classification of facts leads to to both an identification of what the facts have in common and a hierarchical explanation of their meaning.

When, therefore, an author of a passage in the Mishnah wished to make a point, he would appeal to the hierarchical ordering of things. By first classifying discrete data and then ordering the classes of the data he would simultaneously discover and demonstrate a proposition. A very simple case in point derives from Mishnah tractate Sanhedrin, which provides a brief, concrete case of precisely how facts are classified and hierarchized to yield important general propositions—in this instance, of a political character. In the following passage, drawn from Mishnah tractate Sanhedrin, chapter 2, the authorship wishes to say that Israel has two heads, one of state, the other of cult (the king and the high priest, respectively) and that these two offices are nearly wholly congruent with one another, with a few differences based on the particular traits of each. Broadly speaking, therefore, the exercise is one of identifying the genus and the species: the genus is head of holy

Israel; the species are king and high priest. Here are the traits in common and those not shared, and the exercise is fully exposed for what it is, namely, an inquiry into the rules that govern (i.e., the points of regularity and order) in this minor matter of political structure.

My outline, set in boldface type, makes the point important in this setting. The excerpt is from the Mishnah tractate Sanhedrin, chapter 2, paragraphs one and two, hence 2:1, 2:2. The letters, supplied by me, distinguish one whole thought from others fore and aft. The boldface generalizations are my insertions, meant to guide the reader through the exposition.

1. The rules of the high priest: subject to the law, marital rites, conduct in bereavement

2:1A. A high priest judges, and [others] judge him;

B. gives testimony, and [others] do not give testimony about him;

C. performs the rite of removing the shoe [Deut. 25:7-9], and [others] perform the rite of removing the shoe with his wife.

D. [Others] enter levirate marriage with his wife, but he does not enter into levirate marriage,

E. because he is prohibited to marry a widow.

F. [If] he suffers a death [in his family], he does not follow the bier.

G. "But when [the bearers of the bier] are not visible, he is visible; when they are visible, he is not.

H. "And he goes with them to the city gate," the words of R. Meir.

I. R. Judah says, "He never leaves the sanctuary,

J. "since it says, 'Nor shall he go out of the sanctuary' (Lev. 21:12)."

K. And when he gives comfort to others

L. the accepted practice is for all the people to pass one after another, and the appointed [perfect of the priests] stands between him and the people.

M. And when he receives consolation from others,

N. all the people say to him, "Let us be your atonement."

O. And he says to them, "May you be blessed by Heaven."

P. And when they provide him with the funeral meal,

Q. all the people sit on the ground, while he sits on a stool.

2. The rules of the king: not subject to the law, marital rites, conduct in bereavement

2:2A. The king does not judge, and [others] do not judge him;

B. does not give testimony, and [others] do not give testimony about him;

C. does not perform the rite of removing the shoe, and others do not perform the rite of removing the shoe with his wife;

D. does not enter into levirate marriage, nor [do his brothers] enter levirate marriage with his wife.

E. R. Judah says, "If he wanted to perform the rite of removing the shoe or to enter into levirate marriage, his memory is a blessing."

F. They said to him, "They pay no attention to him [if he expressed the wish to do so]."

G. [Others] do not marry his widow.

H. R. Judah says, "A king may marry the widow of a king.

I. "For so we find in the case of David, that he married the widow of Saul,

J. "for it is said '*And I gave you your master's house and your master's wives into your embrace*' (2 Sam. 12:8)."

2:3A. [If the king] suffers a death in his family, he does not leave the gate of his palace.

B. R. Judah say, "If he wants to go out after the bier, he goes out,

C. "for thus we find in the case of David, that he went out after the bier of Abner,

D. "since it is said, '*And King David followed the bier*' (2 Sam. 3:31)."

E. They said to him, "This action was only to appease the people."

F. And when they provide him with the funeral meal, all the people sit on the ground, while he sits on a couch.

3. Special rules pertinent to the king because of his calling

2:4A. [The king] calls out [the army to wage] a war fought by choice on the instructions of a court of seventy-one.

B. He [may exercise the right to] open a road for himself, and [others] may not stop him.

C. The royal road has no required measure.

D. All the people plunder and lay before him [what they have grabbed], and he takes the first portion.

E. *"He should not multiply wives to himself"* (Deut. 17:17)—only eighteen.

F. R. Judah says, "He may have as many as he wants, so long as they *do not entice him* [to abandon the Lord (Deut. 7:4)]."

G. R. Simeon says, "Even if there is only one who entices him [to abandon the Lord]—lo, this one should not marry her."

H. If so, why is it said, "He should not multiply wives to himself"?

I. Even though they should be like Abigail [1 Sam. 25:3].

J. *"He should not multiply horses to himself"* (Deut. 17:16)—only enought for his chariot.

K. *"Neither shall he greatly multiply to himself silver and gold"* (Deut. 17:16)—only enough to pay his army.

L. *"And he writes out a scroll of the Torah for himself"* (Deut. 17:17).

M. When he goes to war, he takes it out with him; when he comes back, he brings it back with him; when he is in session in court, it is with him; when he is reclining, it is before him,

N. as it is said, *"And it shall be with him, and he shall read in it all the days of his life"* (Deut. 17:19).

2:5A. [Others may] not ride on his hourse, sit on his throne, handle his scepter.

B. And [others may] not watch him while he is getting a haircut, or while he is nude, or in the bathhouse,

C. since it is said, *"You shall surely set him as king over you"* (Deut. 17:15)—that reverence for him will be upon you.

The proposition that forms the conclusion concerns the essential likeness of the two offices, except where they are different. The subterranean premise is that we can explain both likeness and difference by appeal to a principle of fundamental order and unity—that is, hierarchical classification. The important contrast comes at the outset. The high priest and king fall into a single genus, but speciation based on traits particular to the king then distinguishes the one from the other. This exercise is conducted essentially independently of Scripture: the classifications derive from the system and are viewed as autonomous constructs; the traits of the things themselves define classifications and dictate what is like and what is unlike. The Mishnah's rhetoric enables freestanding compositions of propositions and their proofs that are entirely syllogistic in inner structure. Its logic of cogent discourse establishes propositions that rest on philosophical bases, for example, by proposing a thesis and composing a list of facts that (e.g., through shared traits of a taxonomic order) prove the thesis. The Mishnah presents rules and treats stories (inclusive of history) as incidental and of merely taxonomic interest. Its logic is propositional, and its intellect does its work through a vast labor of classificatory comparison and contrast that generates governing rules and generalizations.

The philosophical cast of mind is amply revealed in this excerpt, which in concrete terms effects a taxonomy—a study of the genus *national leader* and its two species, *king* and *high priest,* that asks how they are alike, how they are not alike, and what accounts for the differences. The premise is that the two sorts of national leaders are alike and follow the same rule except where they differ and follow the rule opposite from each other. That premise is then proved by the survey of the data consisting of concrete rules, those systemically inert facts that here come to life for the purposes of establishing a proposition. By itself, the fact that, for example, others may not ride on the king's horse bears the burden of no systemic proposition. In the context of an argument constructed for nomothetic, taxonomic purposes, however, the same fact is active and weighty. The whole depends on four premises:

1. The method of comparison and contrast demonstrates essential identity.
2. Like follows the rule of the like.
3. The unlike follows the opposite rule.
4. When we classify, we also hierarchize, which yields the argument from hierarchical classification: if this, which is the lesser, follows rule X, then that, which is the greater, surely should follow rule X.

And that is the sum and substance of the logic of *Listenwissenschaft* as the Mishnah applies it in a practical way.[11]

Let me now generalize on what I conceive to be the philosophical character of the whole. If I had to specify a single mode of thought through which the Aristotelian method establishes connections between one fact and another it would be that of natural history, that is, classification by means of comparison and contrast. Similarly, the Mishnah's sages seek connections between fact and fact or sentence and sentence in the subtle and balanced rhetoric of that document by comparing and contrasting two things that are like and not alike. At the logical level, too, the Mishnah falls into the category of familiar philosophical thought: discovered regularities generate proposed rules. What is like another thing falls under the same rule, and what is not like the other falls under the opposite rule. Accordingly, so far as the species of the genus are alike, they share the same rule; so far as they are not alike, each follows a rule contrary to that governing the other(s). That accounts for the rhetoric of list making and the logic of *Listenwissenschaft* that predominate in the Mishnah. List making places on display the data of the like and the unlike and (ordinarily only implicitly) conveys the rule. It is this resort to list making that accounts for the rhetorical stress on groups of examples of a common principle, three or five, for instance. The authorship assumes that once a series is established the governing rule will be perceived. That explains why, in exposing the interior logic of its authorship's intellect, the Mishnah had to be a book of lists, with the implicit order—the nomothetic traits of a monothetic order—dictating the ordinarily unstated general and encompassing rule. In method, therefore, the Mishnah presents a profoundly philosophical system in that to make a single, general point it employs numerous cases that are analyzed through modes of hierarchical classification commonplace in the philosophy, and particularly the natural history, of Aristotle.

But what about the message? In the context of the Greco-Roman philosophy of Middle Platonism, the Mishnah's message is also philosophical,[12] because the single, characteristically philosophical proposition that the Mishnah repeats in innumerable cases concerns the unity of all being. Specifically, the Mishnah demonstrates over and over again that all things are one, that complex things yield uniform and similar components, and that, rightly understood, there is a hierarchy of being to be discovered through the proper classification of all things. In the Mishnah, many things are teleologically hierarchized in the following two propositions: (1) many things by their nature join into one thing, and (2) one thing yields many things. These propositions complement each other, forming matched opposites that together make an ontological judgment. This judgment is that all things are not only orderly but, in their deepest traits of being, so ordered that many things fall into one classification and that one thing may hold together many things of a single classification. For this philosophy, then, rationality consists in the hierarchy of the order of things, a rationality repeatedly

tested and proved by the ever-present possibility of hierarchically classifying all things. The Mishnah's ontological proposition is thus a theory
of the right ordering of each thing in its taxon, all taxa in correct
sequence, from least to greatest. To show that all things can be ordered
and that all orders can be set into relationship with one another is to
transform the ontological message into its components of proposition,
argument, and demonstration.

The sustained effort of the Mishnah's authorship, therefore, is to
demonstrate the way many classes of things—for example, actions,
relationships, circumstances, persons, places—really form one class.
This work of classification then explores the potentialities of chaos en
route to explicit order. It is classification transformed from the *how*
of intellection to the *why*, the *what for*, and above all, the *what does
it all mean* of philosophical conviction. For the authorship of the
Mishnah, recognition that one thing may fall into several categories
and many things into a single category comes to expression in a simple
way. The authorship shows over and over that diversity in species or
diversification in actions follows orderly lines, thus confirming the claim
that there is that single point from which many lines issue. Carried out
in proper order, the demonstration then leaves no doubt as to the
truth of the matter.

The upshot may be stated very simply. The species point to the
genus, the classes to one class, and all taxa, properly hierarchized, rise
to the top of the structure and the system to form one taxon. So all
things ascend to and reach one thing. All that remains is for the
philosopher to define that one thing as God, but that is a step the
philosophers of the Mishnah did not take. Perhaps—and I assume it
as fact—they did not think they had to make such an obvious point,
but I think there is a further and altogether different reason. Because
they were philosophers, not theologians at all, the document they
produced pursues issues of natural history, never working out a proposition of a theological character—not in a single line! And although
philosophers cite God[13] as both premise and principle, the system does
not derive its generative problematic from that fact. It is not that on
which the system builders proposed to work. For philosophy in this
context served not to demonstrate principles or to explore premises,
but to analyze the unknown, to answer important questions about
what the philosophers did not know but wished to find out. To extend
my argument I appeal once more to the exemplary case of Aristotle,

who asked his analytical questions about natural history, the nature of things, extending his interest from nature to society. What important answers to these questions come from the premise or fact of God (or the gods)? For the natural historian, none.

This observation on the system builders of the Mishnah as philosophers rather than religious thinkers, let alone theologians, returns us to the question of the philosophical classification of the Mishnah's single and paramount proposition: the hierarchical unity of being wherein all things rise to form one thing and all things descend from one thing. The Mishnah's Judaic system—its logic and topic alike—corresponds in its search for the one in the many and the many in the one to the Christian and pagan systems of the same type. This is shown in the comparison of the Judaic, Christian, and pagan philosophical systems within Middle Platonism, as A. H. Armstrong indicates:

> The difference here between pagans and Christians . . . is a difference about the degree of religious relevance of the material cosmos, and, closely connected with this, about the relative importance of general, natural, and special, supernatural, divine self-manifestation and self-communication. On the one side, the pagan, there is the conviction that a multiple self-communication and self-revelation of divinity takes place always and everywhere in the world, and that good and wise men everywhere . . . have been able to find the way to God and the truth about God in and through rational reflection on themselves and on the world, not only the heavens but the earth, and the living unity of the whole. On the other side, the Christian, there is indeed a readiness to see the goodness and beauty of the visible cosmos as a testimony to God's creation . . . but the religious emphasis lies elsewhere. Saving truth and the self-communication of the life of God come through the Incarnation of God as a man and through the human . . . society of which the God-Man is the head, the Church. . . . It is only in the Church that material things become means of revelation and salvation through being understood in the light of Scripture and Church tradition and used by God's human ministers in the celebration of the Church's sacraments. It is the ecclesiastical cosmos, not the natural cosmos, which appears to be of primary religious importance for the Christian.[14]

If God is revealed in the artifacts of the world, then, so pagans in general considered, God must be multiple. No, the philosophy of Judaism is here seen to respond. Here we find a Judaic argument, within the premises of paganism, against paganism. To state with emphasis what I conceive to be that argument, *the very artifacts that appear multiple in fact form classes of things; moreover, these classes themselves are subject to a reasoned ordering, by appeal to this-worldly characteristics signified by properties and indicative traits.* Monotheism is to be demonstrated by appeal to the very data that for paganism prove the opposite.

It follows that Aristotle's medium of hierarchical classification conveys the Middle Platonic message of the unity of being,[15] all expressed in the mundane mode of discourse formed by the framers of the Mishnah. The way to the one God, ground of being and ontological unity of the world, lies through "rational reflection on themselves and on the world" — this world, which yields a living unity encompassing the whole. That claim, which the Mishnah asserts in an argument covering overwhelming detail, directly faces the issue as framed by paganism. Immanent in its medium, it is transcendent in its message. And I hardly need spell out the simple reasons, self-evident in Armstrong's words, for dismissing the Christian reading of the cosmos as irrelevant to their interests. To the Mishnah's sages, it is not (merely) wrong, it is insufficient.

And yet, that is not the whole story, for the Mishnah's sages reach into Scripture for their generative categories, and, in doing so, they address head-on a Christianity that Armstrong centers, with entire soundness, on the life of the Church of Jesus Christ, God-man:[16] "It is only in the Church that material things become means of revelation and salvation through being understood in the light of Scripture and Church tradition and used by God's human ministers in the celebration of the Church's sacraments."

The framers of the Mishnah would have responded, "It is in the Torah that material things are identified and set forth as a means of revelation."

Again, Armstrong: "It is the ecclesiastical cosmos, not the natural cosmos, which appears to be of primary religious importance for the Christian."

To this the philosophers of Judaism would reply, "It is the scriptural account of the cosmos that forms our generative categories, which, by the power of intellect, we show to constitute an ordered, hierarchical unity of being."

So this identification of "the ecclesiastical cosmos" reveals its power when the cosmos of the Mishnah is framed by appeal to its persistent response to the classifications and categories of Scripture. If, as Armstrong portrays matters, the Church first worked out an ecclesiastical cosmos and only later on produced the Bible, the philosophy of Judaism framed a scriptural cosmos and then read it philosophically in the sense I have explained. We may therefore identify three distinct readings of the natural world: the pagan, the Christian, and the Judaic. The one reads nature as a source of revelation. The other two insist on a medium of mediation between nature and intellect. For Christianity, Armstrong says, it is the body of the Church; for Judaism, I claim, it is revelation or the Torah.

There is a philosophical reason for this difference. This reason, which I deem paramount, explains my insistence that this Judaism is, by the criterion of its Greco-Roman context, a philosophy and not a theology in its message and its mode of thought. The Mishnah philosophers accomplished their purposes not merely by appealing to the authority of Scripture but by analyzing the traits of the created world, read in the context of the revealed truths of Scripture. By showing the order and unity inherent within Scripture's list of topics, the philosophers meant to penetrate on their own power into the ground of being as God had revealed matters. They did this by working back from the epiphenomena of creation to the phenomenon of creation and then to the numinous, that is, the Creator. This self-assigned challenge forms an intellectual vocation worthy of a particular kind of philosopher, an Israelite one, and, in my view, it also explains the choice of the form in which the Mishnah philosophers produced their philosophy.

The form, so superficially unphilosophical in its crabbed and obsessive mode of discourse, proves in the end to constitute a philosophy. Judaism in the system of the Mishnah is philosophical in medium, method, and message, but philosophy also is represented as, and within, the Torah in topic and authority. The union of the Torah's classifications and topics with philosophy's modes of thought and propositions marks the system as not only philosophical but also distinctively Judaic. That marriage produced as its first fruits a philosophical Judaism, a Judaic philosophy: the Torah as Moses would have written it had Moses been a philosopher. The offspring of this happy marriage was not to live long, however, and the philosophy of Judaism soon gave way to the theology of Judaism: theology, not philosophy, held sway for a thousand years. Thus, I now turn to the successor system.

I have dwelt at some length on this matter of the philosophical character of both the Mishnah's method and its topical program and system because an adequate understanding of what characterizes the logic and rhetoric of the Mishnah as philosophical will indicate clearly wherein the successor documents' traits of logic and rhetoric differ. These matters of logic and rhetoric lie right on the surface of a piece of writing, and no subjective judgment on their character is required. Anyone who understands how the authorships of the successor documents formulated and expressed their ideas will be able to discern the remarkable shift in the character of the system to which those authorships attest. To characterize the modes of thought that generated the successor system in comparison to those of the initial one, I first of all must compare them with philosophical systems in general.[17]

The single most striking difference, in literary terms, between the Mishnah and both the Talmud of the Land of Israel and the Midrash compilations Genesis Rabbah and Leviticus Rabbah, as well as Pesiqta deRab Kahana, is that the former is freestanding, whereas the latter take the form of commentaries: the Talmud comments on successive paragraphs of the Mishnah and the Midrash compilations comment on verses of Scripture. In the most fundamental aspect, therefore, although the Mishnah's categories derive from its framers' perceptions of the principal classes of actions, objects, and relationships, the successor writings take over the categories of prior documents, either Mishnah or Scripture. Thus, whereas the subcategories of each of the Mishnah's categories are formed by appealing to taxic indicators inherent in those principal classes in a way quite consistent with the initial taxonomy, the subcategories of the successor documents are not formed in that way. So the Mishnah's system sets forth an account of the nature of things based on the things themselves, but the successor writings' categories are contingent and dependent on those of received, authoritative documents.

This means that the Mishnah's organization, and therefore selection, of data for analysis derives from nature, that is, from the traits of things, and the indicative traits are revealed by the things in themselves, as they are. By contrast, the Talmud's and Midrash compilations' organization and selection of data for analysis come from the structure of the Mishnah and Scripture. Because they are not freestanding but contingent in form, their logic of cogent discourse will not be defined by the nature of things. In the case of the Mishnah, as I already have noted at some length, connections are made between and among things by appealing to principles of taxonomy derived from natural history, and fully spelled out propositions (which we should call "paragraphs") are formed into large-scale compositions (which we should call "chapters") by a process of propositional and syllogistic reasoning. But its logic of cogent discourse—the joining of compositions into composites—differs greatly from that of both the Talmud of the Land of Israel and the two Midrash compilations under detailed study here. This difference marks the successor writings as simply not philosophical.

According to the prevailing logic in the successor writings, one thing may join to something else only if both things refer in common to a third thing, not if each thing relates to the other of the pair. A successor writing's fixed association to a received text means that the received text, and not the traits of order and connection intrinsic to the propositions themselves, supplies the rules both of the order in which topics are addressed and of the connection between topics. Thus, for example, sentence A has nothing to do with sentences B, C, D, and E, except that all the five sentences refer to a common verse of Scripture, on the one side, or sentence of the Mishnah, on the other. In a moment I will present an example that shows precisely how this logic of fixed association joins A to B, B to C, and so on, even though A and B together are not otherwise connected in content and do not otherwise form an argument in propositional logic—for example, if A, then B; if not A, then not B; therefore, B if and only if A. However this logic of fixed association is classified, it is not philosophical.

To summarize: in the making of connections, the drawing of conclusions, and the intelligible representation of those conclusions in cogent discourse, the Mishnah is philosophical and the successor writings are not philosophical but something else. That fact, standing by itself, does not show that a fundamental shift in modes of thought has taken place. Two very brief examples of the shift, however, will show what is at stake, the first from the Talmud of the Land of Israel, the second from a Midrash compilation. In addition, this analysis of particular texts will not only make concrete these rather abstract characterizations but also make possible the next step in this chapter's argument.

Given the claims I have made concerning the profound shift in the character of the rhetoric and logic of the Yerushalmi and its companions, the reader will wish to see, first of all, how an already familiar passage is treated in the successor document. Here is how the Yerushalmi's authorship treats the passage about the comparison of the king and the high priest. I give the Mishnah paragraph — now familiar to use — in boldface type.

Mishnah Tractate Sanhedrin 2:3

A. **The king does not judge, and [others] do not judge him;**

B. **does not give testimony, and [others] do not give testimony about him;**

C. **does not perform the rite of removing the shoe, and others do not perform the rite of removing the shoe with his wife;**

D. **does not enter into levirate marriage, nor [do his brothers] enter levirate marriage with his wife.**

E. **R. Judah says, "If he wanted to perform the rite of removing the shoe or to enter into levirate marriage, his memory is a blessing."**

F. **They said to him, "They pay no attention to him if he expressed the wish to do so."**

G. **[Others] do not marry his widow.**

H. **R. Judah says, "A king may marry the widow of a king.**

I. **"For so we find in the case of David, that he married the widow of Saul,**

J. **"For it is said, 'And I gave you your master's house and your master's wives into your embrace' (2 Sam. 12:8)."**

Here is how the Talmud of the Land of Israel reads the foregoing paragraph of the Mishnah. The Yerushalmi gives us a composite of four distinct compositions, signified by Roman numerals, which address the Mishnah passage and clarify it.

I

A. **[The king] does not judge [M. San. 2:3A].** And has it not been written: "*[So David reigned over all Israel] and David administered justice and equity to all his people*" (2 Sam. 8:15).

B. And yet do you say [that the king does not judge]?

C. [From this verse of Scripture, we draw the following picture:]

He would indeed judge a case, declaring the innocent party to be innocent, the guilty party to be guilty. But if the guilty party was poor, he would give him [the funds needed for his penalty] out of his own property. Thus he turned out doing justice for this one [who won the case] and doing charity for that one [who had lost it].

D. Rabbi says, "[If] a judge judged a case, declaring the innocent party to be innocent, and the guilty party to be guilty, [the cited verse of Scripture indicates that] the Omnipresent credits it to him as if he had done an act of charity with the guilty party, for he has taken out of the possession of the guilty party that which he has stolen."

II

A. **And [others] do not judge him (M. San. 2:3A].** This is in line with the verse [in the Psalm of David], *"From thee [alone] let my vindication come!"* (Ps. 17:2).

B. R. Isaac in the name of rabbi: "King and people are judged before Him every day, as it is said '. . . *and may he do justice for his servant and justice for his people Israel, as each day requires'* (1 Kings 8:59)."

III

A. **R. Judah says, "If he wanted to perform the rite of removing the shoe or to enter into levirate marriage, his memory is a blessing"** [M. San. 2:3E].

B. They said to him, "If you rule in this way, you turn out to diminish the honor owing to the king."

IV

A. **Others do not marry the widow of [M. San. 2:3G]** or the woman divorced by a king.

B. This is by reason of that which is said: *"So [David's concubines] were shut up until the day of their death, living as if in widowhood"* (2 Sam. 20:3).

C. R. Yudah bar Pazzi in the name of R. Pazzi in the name of R. Yohanan: "This teaches that David [treating them as forbidden though in law they were not] would have them dressed and adorned and brought before him every day, and he would say to his libido,

'Do you lust after something forbidden to you?' By your life! I
shall now make you lust for something which is permitted to you."

D. Rabbis of Caesarea say, "They were in fact forbidden [20b]
to hand [and it was not merely that he treated the women whom
Absalom had raped as forbidden to him, but the law deemed them
prohibited].

E. "For if a utensil belonging to an ordinary man used by an
ordinary man is prohibited for use of a king, a utensil belonging
to a king which was used by an ordinary man — is not an argument
a fortiori that the king should be forbidden to make use of it?"

What the framers do not do is as indicative as what they do. They
do not address the main point that emerges from the entirety of the
Mishnah composition, the priority of monarch over priesthood. They
do not take up generalizations; these they affirm by dealing only with
details, as if to underline the authority of the main point. Then what
do the framers propose to contribute? First, their task is to compare
what we find in the Mishnah, the oral Torah, with what they find in
Scripture, the written Torah, and that yields a contradiction to be
harmonized at I. Second, they wish not only to harmonize but also to
adduce proof texts from Scripture in support of the Mishnah, and that
is done at II. They proceed to amplify the language of the Mishnah
passage, supplying Judah's opposition with a response in III. And IV
presents no surprises. So if I had to specify the problem pressing on
their minds, indicated by the arguments but never explicitly stated, it
is the relationship between a rule of the Mishnah and the law of the
Scripture. The framers clearly bring their own program of inquiry to
the Mishnah rather than simply continuing its program in some manner.

The fact explains the obvious rhetorical and logical differences that
separate the Mishnah from the Yerushalmi. The rhetoric of the Yerushalmi has nothing in common with that of the Mishnah. The former
is balanced and highly formalized; the latter, loose and not formalized
at all. The former is coherent in addressing a single encompassing
proposition; the latter is made up of compositions that are related not
to one another but only to the passage on which they comment. That
is to say, the four units of the Yerushalmi are discrete compositions,
formed into a composite only through their interest in consecutive
sentences of the same paragraph of the Mishnah. The composite is a
commentary to the Mishnah, not a freestanding proposal of a fresh

proposition or viewpoint; the whole is secondary, derivative, and episodic, unlike the Mishnah's autonomous, well-composed, and carefully crafted discourse.

The same rhetorical and logical modes of expression serve a variety of types of passages of the Mishnah, not only the narrowly topical legal ones. A theological discussion that invites generalization, expansion, elaboration, proof, and the like exhibits precisely the same traits. There are, therefore, no distinctions as to genre of material: the Yerushalmi's voice is single and uniform throughout, as is the Mishnah's,[18] but it is a very different voice, indeed. The following example shows that different voice just as clearly as the previous one does. Here, too, the Mishnah paragraph forms the Talmud's occasion for discourse, and the initial task is to amplify and clarify that paragraph. The passage at hand is Mishnah tractate Sanhedrin 10:1, again set in boldface type.

Mishnah Tractate Sanhedrin 10:1

All Israelites have a share in the world to come, as it is said, "Your people also shall be all righteous; they shall inherit the land forever, the branch of my planting, the work of my hands, that I may be glorified" (Isa. 60:21).

And these are the ones who have no portion in the world to come:

(1) He who says the resurrection of the dead is a teaching which does not derive from the Torah, (2) and the Torah does not come from Heaven; and (3) an Epicurean.

R. Aqiba says, "Also: He who reads in heretical books, and he who whispers over a wound and says 'I will put none of the diseases upon you which I have put on the Egyptians; for I am the Lord who heals you' (Exod. 15:26)."

Abba Saul says, "Also: He who pronounces the divine Name as it is spelled out."

On this passage, the Talmud of the Land of Israel tractate Sanhedrin, 10:1.X and XI,[19] gives the following, first citing a clause of the Mishnah:

X

A. **He who whispers over a wound and says, "I will put none of the diseases upon you which [28b] I have put on the Egyptians; for I am the Lord who heals you"** (Exod. 15:26).

B. Rab said, "But this [statement is prohibited] only if the one who says it then spits."

C. R. Joshua b. Levi said, "Even if one has said, '*When a man has on the skin of his body a swelling or an eruption or a spot, and it turns into a leprous disease on the skin of his body*' (Lev. 13:2), and then has spat—he has no portion in the world to come."

XI

A. **Abba Saul says, "Also: he who pronounces the divine Name as it is spelled out" [M. San. 10:1G].**

B. R. Mana said, "For example, the Cutheans, who take an oath thereby."

C. R. Jacob bar Aha said, "It is written YH[WH] and pronounced AD[onai]."

There are no changes in the prevailing rhetoric or logic of the second example. My previous remarks on the modes of coherence and cogency show how these two paragraphs are made up. What joins the proposition of XI to X? The whole is not an argument advanced by the movement from one proposition to the next. There is no order that is required and that therefore explains why XI must follow X and X must precede XI, except for one: both X and XI refer to a text in common, and their order is dictated by that fixed text with which both compositions are associated. Hence, the logic of intelligible discourse that collects two compositions (here, paragraphs) into a single composite is that of fixed association.

Again, whatever the logic, it is simply not philosophical by the criteria now established concerning the manner in which philosophical discourse was carried on in this time and place. Nevertheless, the logic is propositional within each composition, for the several authorities address the same topic and make points pertinent to the same proposition. A given paragraph will contain contrary viewpoints on a single matter of common concern, one party taking this position, the other, that position—a dialogue, and one of a philosophical order. So the compositions appeal to a propositional, and indeed, syllogistic logic, whereas the composite (and most of the composites of the Yerushalmi, as a matter of fact) appeals to a quite different logic, that of fixed association.[20] The rhetorical forms of a commentary to a text therefore adumbrate an other than philosophical mode of thought.

Now if we ask ourselves what we have and what we do not have the answer is simple: we have a contingent and dependent discourse, one in which the Talmud of the Land of Israel clarifies and amplifies a prior document but in no way asserts its own propositions, in its own terms, and for its own purposes. That pattern occurs twice, at X and at XI. An inspection of how the Talmud in general carries on its program of thought would show by far the greater part to be made up of precisely the kind of discourse exemplified here. The Midrash compilations follow suit,[21] its framers reading Scripture as the Talmud's framers read the Mishnah.[22]

The next step is to generalize on the exemplary materials in hand. Precisely how was the Mishnah studied in the Talmud?[23] It was studied line by line, word by word. The modes of study were mainly three. First, sages asked about the meanings of words and phrases. Second, they compared one set of laws or propositions with another, finding the underlying principles of each and comparing and harmonizing those principles. The example from Genesis Rabbah in appendix 1, which concerns the task of harmonizing the goodness of creation with the evil in creation, is a case in point. Thus, the sages formed of the rather episodic rules a tight and large fabric. Third, they moved beyond the narrow limits of the Mishnah or of Scripture into still broader and more speculative areas of thought. The whole, it is clear, is now traditional and not freestanding; the source texts dictate the program and its problematic, the Mishnah on the one side, Scripture on the other.

This is not to suggest that philosophy cannot conduct its discussions through receiving and reworking a tradition of thought. To the contrary, like religious and theological systems, philosophical systems may, and very often do, take over a tradition and rework it, expressing the essentially new within the framework and discipline of the received. A philosophical system may easily be set forth as a commentary on a received text, for example, the traditional form of scholastic response to Aristotle. Part of the esthetic challenge to the framer of a new system requires the re-formation of the new within the rhetorical givens of the old. Thus, the formal change from a freestanding to an exegetical representation of thought, broadly characterized as rhetorical, does not by itself demonstrate a shift in mode of thought from philosophical to some other.

What does show that shift is something much more profoundly

embedded in a system, namely, the mode of thought. This has two aspects: first, how people made connections between one thing and something else, which is to say, the media of cogent thought that produced conclusions of one sort rather than another; second, how people expressed their ideas in a manner calculated to be understood by others, which is to say, the method of intelligible discourse. These two aspects instantiate and exemplify at the deepest layers of intellect the sort of shift from system to system that I posit in this book. Accordingly, when we grasp how the Mishnah's thinkers conducted their mental experiments in addition to how they expressed the result as part of the spinning out of a received tradition, we see that the rules governing thought have changed. This realization lets us draw accurate and well-founded conclusions on the nature of the shift, which I wish to characterize as one that leaves philosophy behind.

A final point requires clarification. In describing the movement from the Mishnah to the successor documents, I do not mean to suggest that a system formerly philosophical and not ("really") religious became religious. The Mishnah's philosophical system is a philosophy of religion, of what we now know as Judaism. The successor system inherits the literature and the system of the Mishnah, as the previous examples amply demonstrate, but the successor system makes its statement not in a philosophical idiom and for philosophical purposes but rather in a different medium and to deliver a message of a different character. That shift takes place in three ways. First, the inherited categories are expanded and reshaped. Second, the received structure of categories is recast, introducing fresh, characteristically religious categories alongside the received ones. Third, the consequence structure of the system is itself vastly transformed from what it had been in the representation of the initial document.

The character of the shift I claim to discern becomes pellucid when we realize that the philosophical proposition also yields in philosophical form a religious one. As the previously made observations about the Middle Platonic philosophical world show, this proposition concerns the belief in one and singular God from whom all being comes. In the Mishnah's massive and detailed account of the realm of nature, the rules that govern the ordering of all things in a cogent, ascending structure rise to the affirmation of one God. But philosophy can attend to religious questions without turning itself into an essentially religious statement and expression.

The difference between the Mishnah's system and its successor becomes clear at this point. In the case of the Mishnah, the focus of the document is on a philosophical proof of a philosophical proposition. That judgment is easily validated: the place of God in the system is classified as philosophical deism[24] even if at no point in the entire writing does someone announce the conclusion: all existence points to a single source, the one God. This conclusion is implicit in proposition and infuses the method of hierarchical classification, even though it is nowhere explicitly stated. Accordingly, the Mishnah is to be characterized in proposition and in method as a philosophical Judaism. The contrary indicative traits of a religious Judaism will show us the contrast.[25]

So although profoundly Israelite in its implicit proposition concerning the unity of being in creation by one, unique God, the Mishnah is yet everywhere systematic and philosophical and only rarely, and then episodically, religious (let alone theological). Two-thirds of all tractates focus on issues critical to philosophy, problems of hierarchical classification in particular; except for liturgical settings, however, scarcely a line of the Mishnah invokes the word "God" or—more to the point—calls on the active presence of God. The data derive not only from philological evidence, for example, whether the name of God is invoked or whether the immediate activity of God is invited (though it is in every prayer). More germane is the shape of the topical program, which attests to the categorical transformation, not merely the modification, effected by the successor documents. The Mishnah's agenda never encompass—even in philosophical terms—such characteristically theological questions as the meaning and end of history, the nature of prophecy, nature and supernature, the being of God, miracles, and the like.[26] Issues justified by revelation rather than observation of this world do not arise.

True, answers to these questions as much as to those of natural history assuredly lie, or even lay, at the foundations for the philosophical structure, but the system and structure represented by the Mishnah ask the questions philosophers ask concerning the nature of things and answer them in the way the philosophers answer them, that is, orderly sifting data in the taxonomic process of natural philosophy. The only point of difference is subject matter, but philosophers in the great tradition took up multiple questions; some worked on this, some on that, and no single question predominated.

That which in its authorship's fundamental traits of intellect marks the Mishnah's system as essentially philosophical is therefore not merely its focus on the propositions about how things are but the explanation—implicit in their modes of thought—of why they are the way they are. The authorship of the Mishnah appeals to *this-worldly* data and rules susceptible to *this-worldly* demonstration to explain what it means that things are this way rather than some other. I emphasize the this-worldly character of not only the data but also the identification of indicative traits because in the successor systems, which I classify as religious, the data derive not only from the observed experience of humanity and the perceived characteristics of the natural world but also from revelation, the Torah in particular.

The identification both of a source of classification and of fact that is not limited to the world of sense observation and experience but extends to the supernatural world, on the one side, and the experience of transcendence, on the other, differentiates the successor writings from the Mishnah. As the examination of their logic of cogent discourse and rhetoric has shown, the former appeal to revelation in the form of the Torah (written in Scripture, hence serving the Midrash compilations, and oral in the Mishnah,[27] hence serving the Talmud of the Land of Israel) as the source of taxa and therefore of structure and order. Once more, the Mishnah falls comfortably within the classification of philosophy.

To conclude: the Mishnah's systemic statement, its representation of a Judaic system (a Judaism) as philosophy, demonstrates that all things in place, in proper rank and position in the hierarchy of being, point to or stand for one thing. The Mishnah's philosophical method accords with Aristotle's method of natural history, and its propositional program aims at the hierarchical classification of all things leading to the one that was found critical by Middle Platonism—thus, the Mishnah's system is a philosophical Judaism.[28] By contrast, the successor documents' traits of rhetoric and logic, although in theory serviceable for philosophical thinking, bear no meaningful relationship with the modes of discourse characteristic of the counterpart philosophies; certainly the fixed associative logic of coherent thought and cogent presentation characteristic to the successor documents would have found no comprehension whatever in so orderly an intellect as Aristotle's.

If the Mishnah in its fundamental traits of program and argument is philosophical, which it is, the successor documents, however they are to be categorized, are assuredly something other than philosophical. That point established, I can in due course turn to define and classify the result of the movement from philosophical to other than philosophical movements of thought, with special attention to the topical initiatives surfacing only later on—for instance, to topics that require classification as religious and not as philosophical.

But first I proceed to economics to underline the fundamentally philosophical character of the Mishnah's system and to show that the system was undergoing revision through categorical reformation and not merely modification in the successor documents. The Mishnah represents economics in a manner entirely congruent with philosophical economics, but recapitulates it,[29] for the framers of the new system worked out not expansions and revisions of the received categories but entirely fresh and unprecedented counterpart categories in which data hitherto neglected were collected and evaluated so as to yield propositions previously not considered in a sustained way, if at all.[30] To signal the direction this argument will take, what happens in the successor system is not so much the effort to treat new subjects in the old way but rather to encompass altogether other things than those to which economics attends.[31] The new system comes to expression not in how it receives the old but rather in how it invents the new; it is not continuous with what has gone before.

Notes

1. But a great deal of further study must show in all specificity how the Mishnah's method of hierarchical classification compares in detail with that of Aristotle. My observations are only the beginning of the matter.

2. And I hardly need add that the very eclecticism of the philosophy of Judaism places it squarely within the philosophical mode of its time. See J. M. Dillon and A. A. Long, eds., *The Question of "Eclecticism": Studies in Later Greek Philosophy* (Berkeley: University of California Press, 1988). But these are only general observations, not meant to suggest direct connection or even to imply that an explanation drawn from "what was floating in the air" seems to me to pertain; I have no explanation.

3. That proposition on the essential unity of the hierarchical nature of all being forms one important, generative premise of Neoplatonism, which I discuss in a moment. Thus, a philosophical method is used to establish a philosophical proposition. That, sum and substance, is what I claim to demonstrate.

4. I consulted Jonathan Barnes, *Aristotle's Posterior Analytics* (Oxford: Clarendon Press, 1975).

5. As to the proposition about the hierarchical ordering of all things in a single way, or the unity of all being in right order, although we cannot show and surely do not know that the Mishnah's philosophers knew anything about Plato, let alone Plotinus's Neoplatonism (which came to expression only in the century after the closure of the Mishnah!), we can compare our philosophers' proposition with that of Neoplatonism. For that philosophy, as we shall see, did seek to give full and rich expression to the proposition that all things emerge from one thing and that one thing encompasses all things, and that constitutes the single proposition animating the system as a whole.

6. That is not to suggest Aristotle was an influential figure in the philosophy done in the same time and place as sages; nothing in these observations about a shared method requires us to postulate contact, intersection, or even diffusion of ideas. For this matter of Aristotle's philosophical method, I relied only on standard textbook descriptions, including the following:

Adkins, A. W. H., *From the Many to the One: A Study of Personality and Views of Human Nature in the Context of Ancient Greek Society, Values, and Beliefs* (Ithaca, N.Y.: Cornell University Press, 1970).

Allan, D. J., *The Philosophy of Aristotle* (London: Oxford University Press/ Geoffrey Cumberlege, 1952).

Armstrong, A. H., s.v.v. "Platonism and Neoplatonism," *Encyclopaedia Britannica* (Chicago, 1975) 14:539-45.

Armstrong, A. H., s.v. "Plotinus," *Encyclopaedia Britannica* (Chicago, 1975) 14:573-74.

Bréhier, Émile, *The History of Philosophy: The Hellenistic and Roman Age,* trans. Wade Baskin (Chicago: University of Chicago Press, 1965).

Cherniss, Harold, *Selected Papers,* ed. Leonardo Tarán (Leiden: E. J. Brill, 1977).

Feldman, Louis H., s.v. "Philo" *Enclyclopaedia Britannica* (Chicago, 1975) 14:245-47.

Goodenough, Erwin R., *An Introduction to Philo Judaeus,* 2d ed. (Lanham: University Press of America Brown Classics in Judaica, 1986).

Merlan, P., "Greek Philosophy from Plato to Plotinus," in A. H. Armstrong, ed., *The Cambridge History of Later Greek and Early Medieval Philosophy* (Cambridge: Cambridge University Press, 1967), 14-136.

Minio-Paluello, Lorenzo, s.v. "Aristotelianism," *Encyclopaedia Britannica* 1:1155-61.

Owens, Joseph, *A History of Ancient Western Philosophy* (New York: Appleton-Century-Crofts, 1959).

Parker, G. F., *A Short History of Greek Philosophy from Thales to Epicurus* (London: Edward Arnold, 1967).

Reale, Giovanni, *A History of Ancient Philosophy*: vol. 3, *The Systems of the Hellenistic Age* ed. and trans. from the third Italian edition by John R. Catan (Albany: State University of New York Press, 1985).

7. A. W. H. Adkins, *From the Many to the One,* 170-71.

8. But only Aristotle and the Mishnah carry into the material details of economics that conviction about the true character or essence of definition

of things. The economics of the Mishnah and the economics of Aristotle begin in the conception of "true value," and the distributive economics proposed by each philosophy then develops that fundamental notion. The principle is so fundamental to each system that comparison of one system to the other in those terms alone is justified. This is a matter to which I return in chapter 2.

9. If the parallels in method are clear, where do we find the difference between Aristotle's system and the Mishnah's? It is that the goals of Aristotle's system (the teleological argument in favor of the unmoved mover) and the goal of Judaism's system (the demonstration of the unity of being) are essentially contradictory, marking utterly opposed positions on the fundamental character of God and the traits of the created world that carries us upward to God. So we establish the philosophical character of the method of the Mishnah's system only at the cost of uncovering a major contradiction: the proposition that animates the one system stands in direct opposition as to its premises, implications, and explicit results with the results of the other. Aristotle's God, attained through teleological demonstration accomplished through the right classification of all things, and the Mishnah's God, whose workings in the world derive from the demonstration of the ontological unity of all things, cannot recognize each other. And that is the case even though they are assuredly one. Accordingly, we must ask ourselves, *cui bono?* Or more precisely, not to whose advantage, but rather, *against* whose position did the Judaic philosophical system propose to argue? When we realize that at stake is a particular means for demonstrating the unity of God, we readily identify as the principal focus the pagan reading of the revealed world of the here and the now, and, it must follow, Judaism as a philosophy stood against the pagan philosophy of the world of its time and place. The fundamental argument in favor of the unity of God in the philosophy of Judaism is to show the hierarchical order and therefore the unity of the world. The world therefore is made to testify to the unity of being, and—to say the obvious with very heavy emphasis—*the power of the philosophy derives from its capacity for hierarchical classification.* When we compare the pagan and the Christian philosophical ontology of God, we see that it is the pagan position, and not the Christian one, that forms the target of this system. The Christian position is simply not perceived and not considered.

10. And for that decision they are criticized by all their successors, chief among them, the authorship of Sifra. See my *Uniting the Dual Torah: Sifra and the Problem of the Mishnah* (Cambridge: Cambridge University Press, 1990).

11. Any claim that the document at hand merely reorganizes information available from Scripture and simply depends for all important traits (and propositions!) on Scripture, by the way, is shown here to be null. The subordination of Scripture to the classification scheme is self-evident. Scripture supplies facts. The traits of things—kings, high priests—dictate classification categories on their own, without Scripture's dictate.

12. I cannot take seriously the preoccupation with whether the authorship

of the Mishnah not only was philosophical but knew ("self-consciously") that it was philosophical. There is no evidence on the basis of which to address that peculiarly modern question of pseudopsychology, and anyhow, I do not see much at stake in the answer. I suppose one might argue from the case of the duck: the creators of the Mishnah quack like philosophers and waddle like philosophers, so whether they knew it, they were philosophers. That does not seem to me to yield an important analytical datum, however, nor do I find myself responsible to explain how the medieval Judaic Aristotelians missed the Aristotelian character of Mishnaic thought completely, as they did. It is the simple fact that they did; specialists in the study of, for example, Gersonides can worry about why. My guess is that, to begin with, they studied the Mishnah in bits and pieces, as episodic problems of exegesis rather than as a set of well-crafted demonstrations of propositions. The reason, then, would lie in the character of the Talmud of Babylonia and its reading of the Mishnah, which left no possibility of grasping the Mishnah as a statement on its own, appealing to its own method to set forth its own statement. Among the medieval Mishnah commentators, only Maimonides read the document as a freestanding and autonomous statement, but his interests in addressing the Mishnah were in law, not in philosophy, and I suppose that he did not imagine the law to contain philosophy because his intent was to set the law into perspective, not highlight it, so as to make a place for philosophy in its own abstract terms. If that accounts for his error, then it was indeed a formidable one.

13. And whether it is one God or many gods, a unique being or a being that finds a place in a class of similar beings, hardly is germane!

14. A. Hilary Armstrong, "Man in the Cosmos," *Plotinian and Christian Studies* (London: Variorum Reprints, 1979), no. 27, p. 11.

15. Both Plato and Plotinus assert this proposition.

16. That judgment does not contradict the argument of my *Uniting the Dual Torah: Sifra and the Problem of the Mishnah* (Cambridge: Cambridge University Press, 1990) concerning the critique the Sifra's authorship made of the Mishnaic philosophers' stress on classification through intrinsic traits of things rather than through classes set forth solely by the Torah. I mean only to stress the contrast between appeal to Scripture and to nature, which I find in the philosophy of Judaism, and appeal to the ecclesial cosmos. This point registers immediately.

17. Modes of thought that are not to be classified as philosophical do not on that account fall into the category of religious, so the second task—in many ways the easier of the two—will be to demonstrate that they were fundamentally religious. In the literary evidence for the successor system, the two propositions—not philosophical but *religious*—flow together in a way in which they do not in abstract proposition. For, as the rest of this part of the book will show, in framing their systemic writings, the authorships representative of the successor system rejected philosophical viewpoints in favor of religious modes of perceiving and organizing matters.

18. There are a few exceptions of consequence, specifically, Eduyyot and Abot.

19. This is by my numbering system for the Talmud of the Land of Israel. I preserve the received numbering system of the Mishnah with which each Talmud passage commences; thus, the chapter is the chapter of the Mishnah, the paragraph likewise, and the subsequence discussion is the Talmud's amplification thereof. The Mishnah reference then is 10:1, meaning, Mishnah tractate Sanhedrin, chapter 10, paragraph 1. I have then subdivided the Talmud between 10:1 and 10:2 into complete units of thought, marking these with Roman numerals, and further subdivided the components of these compositions or complete units of thought, marking each component by a letter. The letter then indicates the smallest whole unit of thought; subdividing a lettered passage (in general, a sentence) would yield no intelligible group of words at all. There is no other system of marking that permits us to distinguish one thing from anything else except by page reference, as in p. 93b, which means the obverse side of a Talmud folio; in the Yerushalmi editions we have Mishnah numbers, as indicated, and also page references, which may then be four: a, b, c, and d. All this is very helpful except if we are asking analytical questions and must signify and refer to what we think are the individual sentences and paragraphs. All description yielding analysis must start with the smallest whole units of material that are subject to analysis, however. Understanding the analytical system I have devised is fundamental to grasping the analysis that follows from it.

20. I hasten to qualify that judgment. There is an argument to be made that the logic of *Listenwissenschaft* takes over in the Midrash compilations, so that in the *davar-aher* constructions ("another matter . . . another matter") we have multiple restatements of what is in fact the same matter. That rhetoric then proves expressive of the logic of list making in the service of propositional presentation and demonstration. The logic of framing composites out of diverse compositions is not in play in the Yerushalmi, however, as even the tiny snippet before us shows. It does serve in important ways in the two Midrash compilations we are considering, being fundamental to Leviticus Rabbah. Whereas the Yerushalmi therefore works with two logics, one for composites, the other for compositions, the Midrash compilations tend to appeal to syllogistic demonstration of propositions for large-scale composites. Differentiating them from the Mishnah and showing they are religious rather than philosophical will take a different tack from the present one. I expand, in a preliminary way, on these points in *From Literature to Theology: Three Preliminary Experiments* (Atlanta, Ga.: Scholars Press for Brown Judaic Studies, 1989). For reasons obvious to the readers of this book, however, the theological inquiry must await the results of the next phase of the work, which will in due course attend to the third and final phase in the formation of Judaism, that attested by the Talmud of Babylonia and related documents.

21. To ease the burden on the reader, I give my example as appendix 1.

22. But that statement requires the caveat just now introduced in note 20.

23. And how was Scripture studied in the Midrash compilations represented by Genesis Rabbah?

24. I have expanded on this point in *The Incarnation of God: The Character of Divinity in Formative Judaism* (Philadelphia: Fortress Press, 1988). See also my *Foundations of the Theology of Judaism* (Northvale, N.J.: Jason Aronson, 1991), vol. 1, *God*.

25. Presentation of these traits will require protracted discussion, and in this chapter my interest is only in the rhetorical and logical differences between system and system, not in the topical differences, let alone the propositional ones. These will come in due course.

26. The suspicious attitude toward miracles expressed at M. Ta. 3:8 in the famous story about Honi the Circle-drawer forms a very minor footnote. Silences testify far more eloquently than occasional observations or pointed stories.

27. The representation of the Mishnah as (part of) the oral Torah appears for the first time in the canonical sequence in the Talmud of the Land of Israel. This is spelled out at some length in my *Foundations of Judaism* (Atlanta, Ga.: Scholars Press for Brown Judaic Studies, 1988), vol. 2, *Torah: From Scroll to Symbol in Formative Judaism*.

28. What makes the philosophy a philosophical system of (a) Judaism in particular is defined by the context of Scripture, with its insistence that Israel's God is one and unique. We may identify as distinctively Judaic the premise defined by that fundamental and ancient affirmation of Israel.

29. As we see in chapter 2.

30. As we see in chapter 5.

31. I shall show how a philosophical system is turned into a religious one in the revision of what is meant by scarce resources. The justification for calling the successor system not philosophical but *religious* emerges in the result of the transformation of categories, not merely in their extension and expansion: that is my argument in part 2.

2

Scarce Resources:
Philosophical Economics
Reproduced

The heirs of the initial, philosophical Judaism received a system
that used the subject of economics—the rational disposition of
scarce resources—to make a systemic statement of fundamental importance. Although they made every effort to affirm and apply the
details of that statement, they in no way contributed to the theoretical
work that the economics of the Mishnah could and should have precipitated. Consequently, their system repeated the given but made no
significant use of it. Instead, as I shall show, the heirs of the Mishnah
invented what I call a counterpart category, that is, a category that still
dealt with problems of the rational utilization of scarce resources, but
not with the same scarce resources defined by the Mishnah's philosophical system. The systemic category for the aborning religious system
was not an economics, but its position and role in the new system
corresponded to the position and role of economics in the old.

A theory of a social entity has an economics if, in designing the
social order, it explains how and why scarce resources are distributed,
rationally or otherwise, to any particular persons, institutions, classes,
and so on, rather than to others.[1] Among all the Judaic (and Christian)
systems of late antiquity,[2] the Mishnah's system alone set forth as part
of its systemic composition a fully articulated economics, entirely congruent with the philosophical economics of Aristotle and answering
questions concerning the definition of wealth, property, production
and the means of production, ownership and control of the means of
production, the determination of price and value, and the like.

This distinction signifies that the Judaic system to which the Mishnah
attests is philosophical not only in method and message but in its very
systemic composition. In their basic definitions and indicative traits,

the principal components of its theory of the social order—its account of the way of life of its Israel and its picture of the conduct of the public policy of its social entity—correspond in detail with the economics and the politics of Greco-Roman philosophy in the Aristotelian tradition. To be more precise, the Mishnah's economics, in general its theory of the rational disposition of scarce resources and the management and increase thereof and specifically its definitions of wealth, ownership, production, and consumption, closely corresponds to that of Aristotle.[3]

To be sure, sayings relevant to an economics may take shape within a religion or a philosophy without that religion or philosophy providing an economics, for unsystematic opinions on this and that (for instance, episodic sayings about mercy to the poor or recommendations of right action, fairness, honesty, and the like) do not by themselves add up to an economics. Indeed, one mark that a system lacks an economics is the presence of merely occasional and ad hoc remarks about matters of wealth or poverty that, all together, attest to complete indifference to the systemic importance of a theory of the rational disposition of scarce resources, their preservation and increase. By contrast, when issues of the rational disposition of scarce resources are treated in a sustained, systematic, internally coherent theory that programmatically explains specific details and defines the market in relation to ownership of the means of production, then we have a systematic account of an economics. In addition, the economics will serve the interests of the system of which it is part if it makes a statement in behalf of that larger system, as is the case in Aristotle's economics. The Mishnah's system makes a critical part of its systemic statement through economics, and its authorship found economics, and only economics, the appropriate medium for making that part of its statement.

But of all the systems of antiquity, only two—Aristotle's and the Mishnah's—delivered principal parts of systemic statements on economics. There are no other candidates for inclusion on the list of significant thinkers and system builders to whom an account of an economics mattered in a systematic way in a systemic composition.[4] Whereas other system builders made episodic reference to topics of economic interest (for example, Plato) and any number of other figures alluded to issues of wealth (Jesus being the most important example, but his model influenced a great many important figures in early Christianity), none produced a well-crafted account of the wealth, the market, exchange, money, value, the definition of the unit and means of production, and other basic components of an economics, let alone a composition of all those things into a coherent statement. More to the point, none but the Aristotelian and the Mishnaic systems undertook to make a fundamental point in its discussion of topics of economic interest. Aristotle's and the Mishnah's systems not only did so, they did so in this-worldly terms by appealing to well-crafted philosophical principles about the character of society and politics. That is why I characterize the Mishnah's economics as philosophical and why the fact that the Mishnah sets forth an economics in the way it does shows economics to form an indicator of the philosophical character of the Mishnah as a system.[5]

The general point common to Aristotle's and the Mishnah's economics comes first: for both systems, economics forms a chapter in a larger theory of the social order. The power of economics as framed by Aristotle, the only economic theorist of antiquity worthy of the name, was to develop the relationship between the economy to society as a whole.[6] The framers of the Mishnah did precisely that when they incorporated issues of economics at a profound theoretical level into the system of society they proposed to construct. That is why the authorship of the Mishnah seems to attack the problem of man's livelihood within a system of sanctification of a holy people with a radicalism far beyond that of later religious thinkers about utopias. None has ever penetrated deeper into the material organization of man's life under the aspect of God's rule. In effect, they posed, in all its breadth, the question of the critical, indeed definitive, place occupied by the economy in a society under God's rule.

The more specific similarities in Aristotle's and the Mishnah's economics prove no less indicative. Both Aristotle and the Mishnah presented an anachronistic system of economics. The theory of both falls into the same classification of economic theory, that of distributive economics, a sort familiar in the Near and Middle East from Sumerian times down to, but not including, the age of Aristotle (let alone that of the Mishnah, five centuries later). On the other hand, market economics had been well established prior to Aristotle's time. Let me briefly explain the difference between the two, which is a fundamental indicator in classifying economics.

In market economics merchants transfer goods from place to place in response to the working of the market mechanism, which is expressed in price; in distributive economics traders move goods from point to point in response to political commands. In market economics merchants make the market work by calculations of profit and loss; in distributive economics there is no risk of loss on a transaction.[7] In market economics money forms an arbitrary measure of value, a unit of account; in distributive economics money gives way to barter and bears only intrinsic value, as do the goods for which it is exchanged. Money is understood as "something that people accept not for its inherent value in use but because of what it will buy."[8] The idea of money requires the transaction to be completed in the exchange not of goods but of coins. The alternative is the barter transaction, in which, in theory at least, the exchange takes place when goods change hands. In distributive economics money is an instrument of direct exchange between buyers and sellers, not the basic resource in the process of production and distribution that it is in market economics. Aristotle's economics is distributive for systemic reasons, whereas the Mishnah's replicates the received principles of the economics planned by the Temple priests and set forth in the priestly code of the Pentateuch, Leviticus in particular. The result—fabricated or replicated principles—was the same.

Both systems—the Mishnah's and Aristotle's—expressed in vast detail the ancient distributive economics, their theories of fixed value and their conception of the distribution of scarce resources appealing to forces other than the rationality of the market. The theory of money characteristic of Aristotle (but not of Plato) and of the Mishnah, for instance, conforms to that required by distributive economics; exchange takes place through barter, not through the abstract price-setting mechanism represented by money. Consequently, the representation of the Mishnah as a philosophical Judaism derives from not only general characteristics but very specific and indicative traits held in common with the principal figure of the Greco-Roman philosophical tradition in economics.[9]

There was a common social foundation for the economic theory of both systems.[10] Both Aristotle and the Mishnah's framers deemed the fundamental unit of production to be the household; the larger social unit, the village that the households composed, marked the limits of the social entity. The Mishnah's economic tractates, such as the Babas, which treats civil law, invariably refer to the householder, making him the subject of most predicates; where issues other than economics are in play, for example, in the political tractates such as Sanhedrin, the householder scarcely appears as a social actor. In addition, both Aristotle and the authorship of the Mishnah formed the conception of "true value," the notion that something—an object or a piece of land—possesses a value extrinsic to the market and intrinsic to itself, so that if a transaction varied from that imputed true value by (in the case of the Mishnah) eighteen percent, the exchange was null. Further, the sole definition of wealth for Aristotle's and the Mishnah's economics is real estate, however small. Because land does not contract or expand, the conception of an increase in value through other than a steady-state exchange of real value, "true value,"[11] between parties to a transaction lies outside this theory of economics. Therefore, all profit is classified as usury, is illegitimate, and must be prevented.

Episodic details of these and similar positions could have been, and surely were, entertained by a variety of system builders in the same age: Plato, for instance, had a theory of money; Jesus, a theory of the negative value of wealth and ownership; and so on. Only for Aristotle and the Mishnah's framers, however, do these conceptions coalesce to form an economics worthy of the name, one that moreover bears an important part of the systemic message, for in both cases the entire purpose of the system comes to expression in (among other aspects) the matter of a fully articulated economics. Aristotle's interest in economics derived from his larger program of framing a political economics for the community at large. As Polanyi states,

> whenever Aristotle touched on a question of the economy he aimed at developing its relationship to society as a whole. The frame of reference was the community as such, which exists at different levels within all functioning human groups. In terms, then, of our modern speech Aristotle's approach to human affairs was sociological. In mapping out a field of study he would relate all questions of institutional origin and function to the totality of society. Community, self-sufficiency, and justice were the focal concepts. The group as a going concern forms a community (*koinonia*) the members of which are linked by the bond of good will (*philia*). Whether *oikas* or *polis* [household or village], or else, there is a kind of *philia* specific to that *koinonia,* apart from which the group could not remain. *Philia* expresses itself in a behavior of reciprocity . . . , that is, readiness to take on burdens in turn

and share mutually. Anything that is needed to continue and maintain the community, including its self-sufficiency . . . is "natural" and intrinsically right. Autarchy may be said to be the capacity to subsist without dependence on resources from outside.[12]

Economics therefore forms an important building block in Aristotle's system, and distributive economics in detail bears meanings for the larger political economy he was developing.

For Aristotle, the postulate of self-sufficiency governs all else; such trade as is required to restore self-sufficiency is natural and right, but that is all.[13] The fundamental principle, with ample instantiation in the Mishnah's economics as well, is therefore natural self-sufficiency attained by the *oikos* and the *polis* made up thereof: political economy. "The institution of equivalency exchange was designed to ensure that all householders had a claim to share in the necessary staples at given rates, in exchange for such staples as they themselves happened to possess. . . . Barter derived from the institution of sharing of the necessities of life; the purpose of barter was to supply all householders with those necessities up to the level of sufficiency. . . . "[14] Accordingly, Aristotle's economic theory rests on the sociology of the self-sufficient community, made up of self-sufficient, if mutually dependent, households.

Aristotle's is not the only economics to provide a parallel and counterpart to that of the Mishnah. The economics of the Mishnah's Judaism replays, with important variations, the old and well-established distributive theory of economics in the priestly code, which was spelled out in the rules of Leviticus and Numbers and on whose details the Mishnah's authorship drew very heavily. In doing so, the economics of the Mishnah took its leave in important details from that of Aristotle, for in its most basic and distinctive conviction, the economics of the Mishnah's Judaism rests on the theory of God's and the Israelite householder's joint ownership of a designated piece of real estate. In that system, *all* that matters as wealth is ownership shared between God and partners of a certain genus of humanity whose occupancy of a designated piece of real estate—but no other—affects the character of the dirt in question. Aristotle could never have accepted so particular and so enchanted a conception of wealth!

The theology of wealth found in both the priestly code and the Mishnah consists of an account of what happens when ground of a certain locale is subject to the residency and ownership of persons of a certain genus of humanity. The generative conception of the theology involves a theory of the effect — the enchantment and transformation — that results from the intersection of "being Israel": land, people, and individual person alike. Any evidence that *wealth* has meanings in successor documents other than Israelite (normally, male) ownership of a piece of real estate, in the Land of Israel in particular, is evidence of the expansion and revision of the economics defined in the Mishnah.

The economic program of the Mishnah derived in detail from the priestly code and other priestly writings within the pentateuchal mosiac. Indeed, at point after point, that authorship clearly intended merely to spin out details of the rules set forth in Scripture in general and, in economic issues such as the rational use of scarce resources, the priestly code in particular. The priestly code assigned portions of the crop to the priesthood and Levites as well as to the caste comprising the poor; it intervened in the market processes affecting real estate by insisting that land could not be permanently alienated but reverted to its "original" ownership every fifty years; it treated some produce as unmarketable even though it was entirely fit; it exacted for the temple a share of the crop; and it imposed regulations on the labor force that were not shaped by market considerations but by religious taboos, for example, naming days on which work might not be performed or might be performed only in a diminished capacity.

The authorship of the Mishnah made its own points however. The single most striking, already noted, is that the Mishnah's system severely limited its economics — and therefore the social vision and pertinence of the realm of the system — to Israelite householders, meaning landowners, and among these, only those who lived on real estate held to fall within the Land of Israel.[15] The economics of the Mishnah eliminated from its conception of the economy gentiles in the Land of Israel, Israelites outside the Land of Israel, and Israelites in the Land of Israel who did not own land — which is to say, nearly everybody in the world. So the definition of "scarce resources" proved so particular as to call into question the viability of the economics as such and to recast economics into a (merely) systemic component. For when the Mishnah speaks of the economic person, the one who owns "land," it is only land that produces a crop liable to the requirements of the sacerdotal taxes.

It follows, therefore, that ownership of land speaks of a very particular acreage, specifically, the territory known to the framers of the Mishnah as the Land of Israel, and that alone. The Mishnah does not impute the same legal status and traits to land not subject to the sacerdotal taxes. There is a second, equally critical qualification, however. Real property in the Land of Israel that is liable to sacerdotal taxes must be owned by an Israelite—a qualification beyond the imagination of the priestly authorship of Leviticus seven hundred years earlier. Gentiles are not expected to designate portions of their crop as holy, and if they do so, the portions they designate as holy nonetheless are deemed secular. Thus, this system presents an exceedingly specific set of conditions in hand, and further, to miss what is excluded is to fail to grasp the odd and distinctive character of the Mishnah's economics. For the system of the Mishnah, wealth is not ownership of land in general, for example, land held by Jews in Babylonia, Egypt, Italy, or Spain. It is ownership of land in a very particular place. And wealth for that same system is not wealth in the hands of an undifferentiated owner but of an Israelite owner in particular.

Wealth is ownership of *land of Israel* in two senses, both of them contained within the italicized words. It is ownership of land located in the *Land of Israel,* and it is ownership of land located in the *Land of Israel* that is *of Israel,* that is, belonging to an Israelite. *Israel* then forms the key to the meaning of wealth, because it modifies persons and land alike: only an Israel(ite) can possess the domain that signifies wealth; only a domain within the land called *Israel* can constitute wealth. It is in the enchanted intersection of the two Israels (ownership of the land and by the people) that the Mishnah's notion of wealth finds realization. Like Aristotle's selective delimitation of the economy, the Mishnah's economics describes a tiny part of the actual economic life of the time, place, and community.

Not only is the Mishnah's economics rather truncated in its definition of wealth, but the range of economic theory in its distributive mode (as distinct from the market mode) deals with only one kind of scarce resource: food. Although goods and services, primarily food and housing, are valued and understood to have value, these are dealt with generally as components of the market, not of the distributive economics that is assumed to predominate. Within the mixed economics at hand, food is the component of the market's goods and services subject to distributive and not market economics. Food alone is subject to the distributive system at hand, and nothing else, certainly not capital or even money. Manufactured goods and services, such as shoes on the last or boards in the vise, not to mention intangibles such as medical and educational services, the services of clerks and scribes, goods in trade, commercial ventures of all kinds—none of these is subject to the tithes and other sacerdotal offerings. The possibility of a mixed situation, in which a distributive economics leaves space for a market economics, rests on the upshot of the claim that God owns the holy land. It is the land that God owns, not the factory or shop, stall or store, ship or wagon, or other instruments and means of production. Indeed, the sole unit of production for which the Mishnah legislates in rich and profound exegetical detail is the agricultural one. The distributive component of the economy, therefore, is the one responsible for the production of food, including sheep, goat, and cattle production.

The key, then, is what and where wealth is. The curious, narrow, geographical-genealogical framework of the system provides the answer: wealth is land held by Israelites in the Land of Israel. That framework must be broadened considerably, however, for the definition of wealth leads to an issue of considerable systemic consequence: ownership of the means of production, which amplifies the received theory of wealth. Wealth is the formation of (1) the unit and (2) means of production, the household, defined in terms of (3) an ownership's command of a landed domain, however small. Thus, wealth is located in the household, which along with other households constitutes the village; the village defines the market in which all things hold together in an equal exchange of a stable population in a steady-state economy.

In this context, wealth is conceived as material, not figurative, metaphorical, or spiritual,[16] but like real property, it also is held to be perfect and therefore unchanging, not subject to increase or decrease— hence, the notion of true value imputed to commodities. If we imagine an ideal world in which no one rises and no one falls and in which wealth is essentially stable, then we want to know what people understand by money, on the one hand, and how they identify riches, on the other. The answer is simple: for the system of the Mishnah, wealth is that which is of lasting value, and what lasts is real property (in the Land of Israel), and that alone. Real estate (in the Land of Israel) does not increase in volume; it is not subject to the fluctuation of the market (so it was imagined); it is permanent, reliable, and, however small, always useful for something. It was perceived to form the medium of enduring value for a society made up of households engaged in agriculture. Accordingly, the definition of wealth as real and not movable, as real estate (in the Land of Israel) and nowhere else, and as real estate and not other kinds of goods conforms to the larger systemic givens. A social system composed of units of production (households) engaged in particular in agricultural production made a decision entirely coherent with its larger conception and character in identifying real estate as the sole measure of wealth. Nor would Aristotle have been surprised, except perhaps by the rather peculiar definition of the sole real estate deemed of worth.

How was the philosophical economics of the Mishnah received? To begin with, the heirs of the Mishnaic system read that document not whole and complete but phrase by phrase and sentence by sentence, breaking up its large units of discourse into discrete parts. Consequently, as a matter of hermeneutics, they received not the system but only its constitutent pieces; to those they devoted sustained efforts at clarification. Their exegetical method precluded a perceptive assessment of the document as a whole, however, focusing as it did on details. That explains why, as I shall show, the economics of the Mishnah defined not a category for exploration, expansion, revision, renovation, and reformation but only a topic for discussion.

To fully grasp the fate of philosophical economics in the successor documents is to understand the full dimensions of the fourth- and fifth-century authorships' achievement in building an essentially new and fresh system while at the same time receiving and preserving the words of the ancients. A consideration of how the philosophical economics was received will illuminate the traits of intellect of the system builders whose work is realized by the successor documents. Rather than begin with generalizations on the method of the new authorships, let me turn directly to the concrete case at hand. The details will provide a basis on which to interpret the entire work of the fourth- and fifth-century authorships in its own terms.

Nearly every discourse—perhaps ninety percent of the whole—of the Yerushalmi addresses one main point: the meaning of the Mishnah, read sentence by sentence. That fact gives the false impression that for the Yerushalmi the life of Israel reaches the level of analysis within the integument of the Mishnah. One might say that the Mishnah is about life whereas the Yerushalmi is about the Mishnah. So a literary analysis will suggest. However, the full subtlety and polemical power of the Yerushalmi, which seems to be a mere commentary, appears only in the realization that, right alongside its reading of the Mishnah, the authorship of the Yerushalmi and companion documents is bringing to expression a system of its own, one not at all continuous in its categories with the system of the Mishnah. That commentary form implies that the traits of the Mishnah have defined the intellectual and political problematic confronting the heirs of the Mishnah, the faithful disciples of the final generation of the Mishnah's redaction and formulation onward. On the contrary, in the invention of a categorical system entirely their own, these people make a statement of their own, even while purporting to focus on statements of others prior to themselves.[17]

The Yerushalmi's authorship invariably subjects the Mishnah to one of the following four processes: (1) textual criticism; (2) exegesis of the meaning of the Mishnah sentence or paragraph under discussion, including glosses and amplifications; (3) addition of scriptural proof texts of the Mishnah's central propositions; and (4) harmonization of one Mishnah passage with another such passage or with a statement of Tosefta.[18] The first two of these four procedures remain wholly within the narrow frame of the Mishnah passage subject to discussion. The second two take an essentially independent stance vis-à-vis the Mishnah pericope at hand.

Briefly surveying the Yerushalmi's reading of passages of economic importance indicates that it reads the Mishnah as a composite of discrete and essentially autonomous rules, a set of atoms rather than an integrated molecule, so to speak.[19] This process obliterates the most striking formal traits of the Mishnah. More important, the Mishnah as a whole and complete statement of a viewpoint no longer exists. Its propositions are reduced to details. On occasion, the details may be restated in generalizations encompassing a wide variety of other details across the gaps between one tractate and another. This immensely creative and imaginative approach to the Mishnah vastly expands the range of discourse, but the first and deepest consequence is to deny to the Mishnah both its own mode of speech and its distinctive and coherent message.

How, then, does the Yerushalmi deal with the principal components of the Mishnah's economics, such as the definitions of money, true value, wealth, and like indicators of a sophisticated system of economics? It amplifies, refines, and complements them, but it does not revise, innovate, or even renovate them. For example, in the discussion, critical to an understanding of the philosophical economics of the Mishnah, of the rule "silver acquires gold, but gold does not acquire silver; copper acquires silver, but silver does not acquire copper," the Yerushalmi's anonymous voice states as its opener: "This is the summary principle of the matter: Whatever is of lesser value than its fellow effects acquisition of its fellow [when it is drawn or lifted up]" (Y. Baba Mesia 4:1:I.A). The supplied language (mine) is justified by the fact that, to the authorship of the Mishnah—and also therefore to the voice of the Yerushalmi—silver and gold are commodities, pure and simple, and all trade is *au fond* solely barter.

There is, furthermore, an interest in authorities, for example, "Said R. Hiyya bar Ashi, 'Who taught this Mishnah paragraph, that silver acquires gold?'" Implications are made explicit: "The implication of what the rabbi has said is that gold is in the status of a commodity." We are given cases, for example, "The daughter of R. Hiyya the Elder lent Rab golden denars. She came and asked her father [how to collect the debt, since in the meantime, gold had risen in value vis-à-vis silver]. He said to her 'Take from him good and substantial denars [of the same weight as those you lent]'" (Y. Baba Mesia 4:1.I.H). That is the case even though she would profit handsomely in trading the gold for silver. There is, furthermore, interest in comparing one rule of the Mishnah to another rule of the same origin, and this governs much of the subsequent discussion.

The principal point of expansion, however, concerns not the conception of gold and silver as commodities for barter but rather a quite different issue, hardly prominent in this Mishnah paragraph though admittedly entirely present there. It has to do with the rules of acquisition, the point in a transaction at which one party has fully acquired ownership of the object from the other. Not surprisingly, a variety of cases and expansions of the received rule treat this issue, for administrators of the law are far less occupied with the issues of legal theory concerning abstract problems of economics than with concrete cases of who owns property or a person at a given instant. All these cases derive from the basic principle that transfer of funds does not complete a transaction: money is a commodity, and only when the object itself has been handed over by the seller and received by the buyer is the transaction done. Up to that point, either party may still retract, even though money has changed hands.

So the facts of the law of the Mishnah govern, but the category of economics is essentially untouched. When the authorship of the Yerushalmi learns "silver acquires gold, but gold does not acquire silver," it wishes to spell out rules of acquisition, but not principles of commodity barter as against the abstract conception of money, such as Aristotle had set forth and the Mishnah's sages instantiated in the case of gold and silver. The rest of Mishnah tractate Baba Qamma chapter 4 is also treated within that same concrete and immediate focus of interest. So what is made concrete is the Mishnah's conception of money, not the principle of money, let alone the category of economics as it relates to principles of the steady-state, self-sufficient economic entities, the household and the village of which it is part.

What about the fundamental (if to us mysterious) conception of true, as distinct from market, value? Here, too, there is neither revision nor renovation, but only restatement; the conception is made no clearer by what the Yerushalmi's authorship has to say than it was in the Mishnah. There is no effort to explain, only to apply to concrete cases or to harmonize with other principles of law the conception that objects have an intrinsic worth that is not dictated by the market but to which the market must conform. For example, Mishnah tractate Baba Mesia 4:3A gives a definition of fraud: "Fraud is an overcharge of four pieces of silver out of twenty-four pieces of silver to the sela, one-sixth of the purchase price." The given conception of a true value or inherent worth independent of the market that is to be given by the purchaser and received by the seller of the object ("fraud applied to the buyer and the seller alike") is restated, but the focus is on the application.

A brief account of the Talmud's treatment of the subject shows the character of its reception of the Mishnah's category. It begins with the position that the assessment of fraud at a sixth overcharge is fact: fraud is defined as an overcharge of a sixth of the true value of an object, so R. Yohanan maintains that it would apply to the price paid for the object, not only to the true value of the object. The issue then addressed is whether the transaction is null or whether the purchaser may return the amount by which he had defrauded the merchant and keep the object, thus complicating the issue of retraction. Finally, there is a discussion of a change in the market value of the object prior to the completion of the transaction: "If one sold an object worth five for six, but did not complete the transaction before the market price of the object went up to seven, so that the purchaser, who had been subject to fraud, now wishes to complete the purchase, what is the rule?" Here again, the Talmud clarifies the received rule but in no way expands, contracts, or revises the category that the rule realizes in detail.

So far as the Mishnah sets forth the conception of wealth, the Yerushalmi retains it: the Yerushalmi respectfully receives and precisely and accurately restates exactly what the Mishnah's authorship has said, without expanding or redesigning it, let alone redefining that conception in any material way. The conception of wealth as fixed and unchanging is associated with the scripturally based prohibition against what is narrowly translated as interest or increase (Mishnah tractate Baba Mesia 5:1A) but what is in fact nothing other than either profit or more than eighteen percent of the true value of the object, on the one side, or interest on a loan of any kind, on the other. Trading in naked futures, for example, is forbidden, for it involves transactions concerning things that are not now in being. The prohibition against profit or interest on loans is extended to gifts in kind or even generous gestures or attitudes. The Yerushalmi then works out this rule. For example, may the judges exact usurious interest from one who has received it? "If from this man you exact what he has unlawfully gained, then we shall leave not a thing in the estates of the great nobles of the Land of Israel" (Y. Baba Mesia 5:1.IC). But bonds containing interest clauses are unenforceable in court.

The Yerushalmi clarifies the language of the Mishnah and fills in details left open by the earlier document. A case involving interest in kind—free rent—is worked out: "A man lent money to his fellow. The latter let him space in his building. Later on the borrower said to the lender, 'Pay me rent for my building.' The lender said to him, 'Give me back my money. [I had assumed you would not charge me rent so long as my money was in your hands.]' The case came before R. Ba bar Mina, who ruled, 'Now does the lender get what he had imagined was free [merely because he has assumed it was free? Obviously not. He was wrong and has no claim on free rent at all.]'"

The case is further expanded, but the character of the discussion is entirely clear and the upshot is obvious. The Yerushalmi faithfully reads the Mishnah's important discussions of economics, reproducing, clarifying, and complementing the received rules, but the powerful abstraction of the Mishnah's intellectual method, stating in detail general principles of an encompassing character, finds no counterpart. In general, the Mishnah's statements are treated not as concrete expressions of abstract principles but rather as mere cases and rules. Thus, the document's basic philosophicality is subverted, its economics, which had been an exercise in theory capable of holding its own with Aristotle's, turned into mere rules. What that means is simple: the Yerushalmi and its companion documents express their points in ways that do not involve the sustained reconsideration of problems of economic theory. What is obvious, therefore, is that the Mishnah's heirs faithfully preserved their inheritance without taking over its categorical structure and system. They paid all due respect to the inherited system while— as chapter 5 will show—at the same time constructing their own counterpart system with its counterpart categories.

These counterparts emerge in freestanding, non-exegetical passages, compositions framed outside the orbit of the Mishnah. The received economics is simply bypassed in these passages. Extensive passages of this sort, in which the Mishnah is left far behind, normally are of two kinds: (1) exegesis of narrative or theological passages of Scripture and (2) fables about heroes. These latter are divided into tales about rabbis and historical accounts, but no important distinction exists between the two except that the former speaks of what rabbis said and did whereas the latter tell about events on a more generous scale. Thus, when the Yerushalmi presents ideas or expressions of a world related to, but fundamentally separate from, that of the Mishnah—that is, when it expresses something other than what the Mishnah says and means—it takes up one of these two modes of discourse. Either it provides exegesis of biblical passages, with the value system of the rabbis read into the scriptural tales, or it tells stories about holy men and paradigmatic events, once again in such a way that a didactic purpose is served.[20] And in such passages, there is no economics in the received and conventional sense.

So far as the issues of economics arise in the Yerushalmi, they invariably are introduced by the requirement of dealing with sentences of the Mishnah, and they are fully spelled out. But is there independent thinking about the same issues? A survey of the tractates of the Yerushalmi fails to yield a *single* important case in which the kinds of writing particular to the Yerushalmi vis-à-vis the Mishnah produce any thought at all on economic topics. Quite to the contrary, those non-exegetical passages of the Yerushalmi portray a world in which no one is thinking about the kinds of scarce resources and their rational utilization, protection, and increase that economics considers. To state the fact simply: so far as scarce resources are of a material order of being—for example, wealth defined as the Mishnah and Aristotle defined it, true value understood as philosophy understood it, and matters of profit, increase, market economics, and the rest—they are systemically neutral in the successor documents. Where wealth, money, trading, and profit enter discourse at all, they are not part of a system that expresses its basic structure through the category of economics. They are trivialized and made to exemplify categories of a different system altogether.

To demonstrate that fact, let me turn to some examples of how the companion writings treat issues of market and wealth. What repeatedly emerges is the simple fact that these matters, which are systemically necessary, independent variables in the Mishnah's structure, are treated explicitly as contingent and dependent. In explaining the fight between Cain and Abel, one version has the argument concern the relative merit of real estate as against movables, but another restates the matter entirely, thus, R. Joshua of Sikhnin in the name of R. Levi: "Both of them took the real estate of the world, and both of them took the movables. Then what was the quarrel about? This one said 'in my domain will the house of the sanctuary be built' and that one said 'in my domain.' 'And when they were in the field' (Gen. 4:8) [indicates it, for] the word field can refer only to the house of the sanctuary, as it is said, 'Zion shall be ploughed as a field' (Micah 3:12). And, as matters played themselves out: 'Cain rose up against his brother Abel and killed him' (Gen. 4:8)."[21] The basic conviction of the biblical story that at issue is Cain's jealousy because God had favored Abel is curiously absent in all three explanations. The first theory of the dispute is that it concerned material things; the second, that it concerned the sacred service; the third, that it concerned who would possess woman. Substituting for the possession of the house of the sanctuary the prestige accruing to the one who possesses that domain, at issue in the mind of the compositor of the whole are wealth, prestige, and sex. The notion that God favors one brother because of his superior offering and turns against the other because of his niggardly one falls away from the story, which becomes an account of human greed, arrogance, and lust. In terms of economic concepts, what is interesting is simple. Real estate and movables are not to be prized; these do not constitute wealth. They are contingent and dependent. Not only does wealth not take the form of land or movables, but prosperity is a source of sin.[22]

Pisqa Ten of Pesiqta deRab Kahana, which deals with tithing, makes an explicit polemic against wealth. Its base verse is Deuteronomy 14:22. At X:I.4 it gives a very precise treatment to a principal concern of economics, proper estate management. Xenophon would not have made much sense of the following:

4A. R. Levi interpreted the cited verse [*The miser is in a hurry to grow rich, never dreaming that want will overtake him* (Prov. 28:22)] to speak of those who do not set aside the required tithes as is proper.

B. For R. Levi said, "There is the case of one who would set aside his required tithes as was proper.

C. "Now the man had one field, which produced a thousand measures of grain. He would separate from it a hundred measures for tithe. From the field he would derive his livelihood all his days, and from it he would nourish himself all his life. When he was dying, he called his son and said to him, 'My son, pay attention to this field. Such and so has it produced, such and so I would separate from the crop for tithe, and from that field I derived my livelihood all my days, and from it I nourished myself all my days.'

D. "In the first year [following the father's death], the son sowed the field and it produced a thousand measures of grain, from which the son set aside a hundred measures for tithe. In the second year the son became niggardly and deducted ten measures, and the field produced a hundred measures less, and so he deducted ten and it produced a hundred measures less, and so he deducted ten and it produced a hundred less, until the field yielded only the amount that had originally been set aside as tithe.

E. "When the man's relatives realized it, [a sign of rejoicing] they put on white garments and cloaked themselves in white and assembled at his house. He said to them, 'Why have you come to rejoice over that man who has been afflicted?'

F. "They said to him, 'God forbid! We have come only to rejoice with you. In the past you were the householder, and the Holy One, blessed be he, was the priest [collecting the tithes as his share of the crop]. Now you have been turned into the priest, and the Holy One, blessed be he, has become the householder [keeping back the larger share of the crop, nine-tenths of the former yield, for himself]. [So we are rejoicing at your rise in caste status!]'"

G. Said R. Levi, "After he had deducted [the priests' share] year by year, yearly the field reduced its yield."

H. Therefore Moses admonished Israel, saying to them, [*Year by year] you shall set aside a tithe [of all the produce of your seed, of everything that grows on the land. You shall eat it in the presence of the Lord your God in the place which he will choose as a dwelling for his name — the tithe of your corn and new wine and oil, and the first-born of your cattle and sheep, so that for all time you may learn to fear the Lord your God]* (Deut. 14:22-23).

The message cannot be missed: obedience to the law of the Torah yields prosperity; its violation yields want. The sarcasm of the relatives underlines the main point. What the householder prized, he lost. His father had left the right message: obedience to God, giving God the proper share of the jointly owned property, ensures prosperity. That point is made explicitly at Pesiqta deRab Kahana XI:X.1.B-C: ". . . *tithing, you shall tithe* — so that you will get rich. Said the Holy One, blessed be he, 'Give a tithe of what is mine, and I shall enrich what is yours.' "

These and other stories, which occur in numbers, show that in place of one rationality, that of careful management and increase of scarce resources, another rationality, that of a transcendent sort, has come into place. That other rationality places a high value on matters of an other than material character; Leviticus Rabbah III:V, for example, presents stories on the high worth of the poor man, the poor man's offering, the widow's meal offering, and like. These tales present no important economic insight but instead contrast worldly value with real value. Indeed, examining sustained discussions of sin and venality, such as that at Leviticus Rabbah XVI:I, shows sins of a material order to be rarely at issue. The entire matter of scarce resources is omitted in numerous moral passages.

Sayings and stories of this type are commonplace in systems that lack all interest in economics. No early Christian writer would have found alien the denigration of wealth and the identification of value in something of an other than material classification that are expressed in the documents of the fourth and fifth centuries. Instead of carrying forward systematic thought on a system of economics, let alone a system that makes a statement through economics, they present episodic and trivial observation on economic topics, making points hardly pertinent at all to economics as a sustained and systematic field of thought.

What takes the place of those scarce resources that form the critical interest of philosophical economics? The following passage clearly states the answer, which shows explicitly the utterly new rationality as to the definition of value and wealth that would emerge in the successor system:

Leviticus Rabbah XXXIV:XVI

1B. R. Tarfon gave to R. Aqiba six silver centenarii, saying to him, "Go, buy us a piece of land, so we can get a living from it and labor in the study of Torah together."

C. He took the money and handed it over to scribes, Mishnah teachers, and those who study Torah.

D. After some time R. Tarfon met him and said to him, "Did you buy the land that I mentioned to you?"

E. He said to him, "Yes."

F. He said to him, "Is it any good?"

G. He said to him, "Yes."

H. He said to him, "And do you not want to show it to me?"

I. He took him and showed him the scribes, Mishnah teachers, and people who were studying Torah, and the Torah that they had acquired.

J. He said to him, "Is there anyone who works for nothing? Where is the deed covering the field?"

K. He said to him, "It is with King David, concerning whom it is written, 'He has scattered, he has given to the poor, his righteousness endures forever' (Ps. 112:9)."

It would be difficult to invent more explicit proof that a drastic shift has taken place. Instead of defining wealth as land, land is defined as not-wealth, and something else is now defined as wealth in its place.

That is evidence of not the re-formation of received categories but the formation of new ones, not continuous with the old. The representation of matters is clearly articulated in the contrast between wealth as real estate and wealth as Torah. How does real estate become Torah? That transvaluation of values is worked out, once more quite explicitly, in the following statement (Y. Megillah 4:1.IV. P-Q): " 'I can write the whole Torah for two hundred copper coins.' What did he do, he went and bought flax seed worth two hundred copper coins, sowed it, reaped it, made it into ropes, caught a deer, and wrote the entire Torah on the deer hide." The three operative components here are money, land, and Torah. The Mishnah defined real wealth as real estate. So first money is transformed into land. Then the definition of wealth shifts, and the symbolic shift is blatant: turn money into real wealth, then real wealth produces the wherewithal of making a Torah. That rather stunning symbolic transformation projects a world wholly different from the one in which scarce resources are identified with matters of material, palpable value and in which economics is the theory of the rational disposition of scarce resources of capital, labor, movables, real estate, and the like.

What appears, therefore, is not the revision, let alone the expansion, of a received category, but adumbrations of the transformation of the category into a counterpart category, one that systemically addresses the same issue but presents a mirror image of the received category's meanings and doctrines. How does the received economics change as a continuing category? In my view, the received economics does not undergo categorical revision at all. Have we found, beyond the valuation of land, the conception of true value, and other traits of Aristotelian economics, appreciation of other media of material wealth and value, for example, the marketplace, capital, and the like? I think not. I can identify in the documents under examination no new thinking on economic questions. For instance, I can locate no interest in the market, in the production of goods and services distinct from produce of land, that would signify reflection on the limitations of philosophical economics and the expansion of the range of concern beyond the theoretically constricted limits of the Mishnah's economics. There simply is no new thinking on economics. Instead, as I shall show in due course, a new "scarce resource" essentially beyond the limits of the old—that is, a supernatural resource—defined a new category, and a new rationality superseded the received one. Before following the new, however, I want to examine the third component of the initial system, its politics. Here, too, we shall see that dual process of amplification of the literary expression of the given system and also the utter reformulation of its category formation.

Notes

1. But not all systems work out an economics or require one. A system will address the rationality required for the disposition of scarce resources

when, and only when, a systemic message may be set forth through the exemplification (or even specification) of that rationality. No Christianity developed an economics of systemic consequence prior to the medieval Christian encounter with Aristotle. And one of the marks of the Aristotelian character of the Mishnah's economics, as I show in this chapter, is its forthright utilization of economics in the formation and expression of its systemic message and in the point-by-point replication of Aristotle's particular doctrines in the composition of that economics. I think the basic reason, as with politics, is that the Mishnah's framers took for granted that their "Israel" formed not merely an ethnic group or a religious community (our terms, not theirs) but a nation living on its land; the enlandisement of their system necessitated address to the rational disposition of scarce resources, defined as real estate, and the givenness of the nationhood of their system's social entity led them to reflect on the legitimate uses of violence. They took for granted that theirs was an empowered social entity. Only in the diaspora do Judaic systems bypass economics and politics as media for the making of the system's larger statement, even though episodic sayings on economic action (e.g., in ethics) or on politics (ordinarily, in a supernatural context) do make their appearance here and there. The fundamental criterion for sorting out Judaisms must be, then, whether they are enlandised and empowered—all systems must fall on one side of another of that line. If the hypothesis just now suggested is sound, then no diaspora Judaism should resort to economics or politics as principal systemic components. The shift I trace in part 2 is not so odd, then, because although located in the Land of Israel, the framers had entered a period in which their Israel no longer governed within the land, let alone overseas, and furthermore progressively was losing command of the real estate of what they called the Land of Israel to Christians, who called the same territory Palestine. The successor system's utter reversal of the conventional meanings of politics and economics forms a response, of a kind, to that worldly transformation of the Jews' economic and political circumstances. The really interesting question lies elsewhere: whether and how the system to which the Talmud of Babylonia and related writings attest yields the stigmata of disenlandisement and disempowerment. If it does not, then the criterion of provenance in the Land of Israel does not serve so decisively as, at the present, it seem to me to do.

2. For instance, history defined an important, systemically critical category for Augustine, whereas economics did not.

3. And, as I shall show in chapter 3, the Mishnah's politics is worked out along lines entirely congruent to those dictated by Aristotle's mode of political theory.

4. For Plato the issue was episodic and bore no important systemic message; for Christian thinkers, economics makes its first consequential appearance in medieval times, with the renewal of Aristotelianism.

5. My argument should be clarified here. I do not mean to suggest that all systems to be systemic require an economics, nor do I propose that any philosophical system lacking an economics is not philosophical. My task in

this part of the book is to demonstrate that the Mishnah's is a distinctively philosophical system, and I have taken as my evidence the demonstration that its system is congruent in method and composition (and, as a matter of fact, here and in the next chapter, in doctrine as well) to a system everyone concedes to be philosophical, which is Aristotle's. So not all systems require an economics, and not all philosophies require an economics, but when the Mishnah's system presents its economics, it shows itself to be structurally congruent with Aristotle's, and, as it happens, the Mishnah's economics says the same things, and for the same purpose, that Aristotle's economics says. In this context that proves the philosophical character of the Mishnah's system.

6. Polanyi, "Aristotle Discovers the Economy," in Karl Polanyi, Conrad M. Arensberg, and Harry W. Pearson, *Trade and Market in the Early Empires: Economies in History and Theory* (Glencoe, Ill.: Free Press, 1957), 79.

7. William I. Davisson and Hames E. Harper, *European Economic History* (New York: Appleton-Century-Croft), vol. 1, *The Ancient World*, 130.

8. Ibid., 131.

9. A basic point in common should be noted. Both Aristotle and the Mishnah composed economic theories that defied the economics of their own day. In each case a version of the then-anachronistic theory of distributive economics was made to bear the burden of the systemic message, while market economics was accorded only a subordinate place within the larger theoretical structure (market economics coming into being in Greece in the very period— the sixth century B.C.E.—in which the priestly code was composed). Aristotle theorized about an economics entirely beyond anyone's ken and stated as principle the values of an economics (and a social system, too) long since transcended. Market economics, moreover, had been conveyed in practice to the Middle East a century and a half or so later by Alexander. By the time of the Mishnah, seven centuries after the Pentateuch was closed, market economics was well established as the economics of the world economy in which, as a matter of fact, the Land of Israel and Israel, that is, the Jews of Palestine, had been fully incorporated.

10. Though, as I shall show in chapter 3, the politics of the Mishnah was disembedded from its economics, whereas the politics of Aristotle was embedded, so that the latter presents a political economy, the former does not.

11. I do not claim to grasp the meaning of "true value."

12. Polanyi, "Aristotle Discovers the Economy," 79.

13. Ibid., 88.

14. Ibid., 90. Also Karl Polanyi, *The Livelihood of Man*, ed. Harry W. Pearson (New York: Academic Press, 1977), see in particular pp. 145-276.

15. The borders of the Land of Israel were notoriously difficult to specify; they did not coincide with any political boundaries to which we can now point. In general, what was meant by the *Land of Israel* seems to me to have been both land settled and held by the immigrants in the time of Joshua, on the one side, and that settled and held in the time of the return to Zion, on the other, with the former real estate more deeply sanctified and more fully constituting land of the Land of Israel than the latter. The holiness of the

holy land depended on the joint ownership of that particular property between God and (an) Israel(ite), and the longer the Israelite held the land, the holier the land became. So the holy land is not an absolute, geographical fact, but a relative, (in our terms) social one. Israelites outside the Land of Israel did not impart holiness to the land on which they lived, and gentiles within the Land of Israel also did not impart holiness to the land on which they lived. Further, all real estate outside the Land of Israel was held to be cultically unclean in the level of corpse-uncleanness, which is the most virulent source of uncleanness. So the entire matter of "land as wealth," or "land is the only form of wealth," which was an absolute commonplace in ancient economics, has to be recast in the context of (a) Judaism. There are numerous details of the law that rest on precisely that supposition. Then Israelites living on land nearby, for example, in Syria, imparted to that land holiness as well, though less holiness inhered in that land than in land in the Land of Israel occupied by Israelites. So the system admits gradations, that is to say, land is both classified and also hierarchized. That hierarchical classification seems to me yet another striking piece of evidence for the philosophical character that permeates the Mishnah's system; it is surely a conception of which the priestly authors of Leviticus and Numbers, after 500 B.C.E., were entirely oblivious. But it is critical to the problematic of a variety of legal discussions in the Mishnah.

16. And that must govern the definition of wealth in the expansion of the category at hand, that is, rational disposition of scarce resources. When I speak presently of scarce resources of another type, I will not identify virtue as a scarce resource in the way in which land is a scarce resource but will identify, in chapter 5, scarce resources that produce worldly comfort and ease and other benefit, as valuable as land, as desired as gold, as productive as a vineyard or a field. That may prove "spiritual" or "immaterial" or "metaphorical," but systemically, wealth throughout is understood as palpable and real and consequential for the material well-being of the owner of such wealth. I cannot overemphasize the danger of assuming that wealth is either material or spiritual; in this system's secondary phase, there is wealth that is entirely palpable and produces precisely the same good life that owning fields and villages does, but it is not wealth in real estate at all, and, all the more so, assuredly not wealth in the form of liquid capital. I think no form of wealth identified by us proved so incomprehensible to the system builders before us as capital.

17. It remains to stress that the Yerushalmi's exegetes of the Mishnah brought to the document no distinctive program of their own. I perceive no hidden agenda. To state matters negatively, before they began to work on a law of the Mishnah, the exegetes did not know facts about the passage not contained (at least implicitly) within the boundaries of the language of the Mishnah passage itself (except only for facts contained within other units of the same document). Rejecting propositions that were essentially a priori, they proposed to explain and expand precisely the wording and the conceptions supplied by the document under study. I cannot point to a single instance in

which the Yerushalmi's exegetes appear to twist and turn the language and message of a passage, attempting to make the words mean something other than what they appear to say. Whether the exegetical results remain close to the wording of a passage of the Mishnah or whether they leap beyond the bounds of the passage, the upshot is the same. There is no exegetical program revealed in the Yerushalmi's reading of the Mishnah other than that defined, to begin with, by the language and conceptions of one Mishnah passage or another.

18. These four taxa encompass all the Yerushalmi's units of discourse that relate to the Mishnah at all, ninety percent of the whole of Yerushalmi tractates surveyed in *Talmud of the Land of Israel: A Preliminary Translation and Explanation* (Chicago: University of Chicago Press, 1983), vol. 35, *Introduction: Taxonomy.*

19. Let me briefly amplify the matter of how the Yerushalmi proposes to provide a systematic exegesis of selected passages of the Mishnah. I review a taxonomy of these exegeses. What are the sorts of approaches we are apt to find? These are four, of which two are nearly indistinguishable, the third highly distinctive, and the fourth barely consequential.

a. *Citation and gloss of the language of the Mishnah* (meaning of a phrase or concrete illustration of a rule). A unit of discourse of this type will contain a direct citation of a sentence of the Mishnah. The word choices or phrasing of the Mishnah will be paraphrased or otherwise explained through what is essentially a gloss, or the rule of the Mishnah will be explained through an example or a restatement of some kind.

b. *Specification of the meaning of the law of the Mishnah or the reason for it.* Items of this type stand very close to those of the former. What differentiates the one from the other is the absence, in the present set of units of discourse, of direct citation of the Mishnah or close and explicit reading of its language. The discussion tends to allude to the Mishnah or to generalize while remaining wholly within its framework. In some units of discourse scriptural proof texts are adduced in evidence of a Mishnah passage. These frequently spill over into discussion of the reason for a rule.

c. *Secondary implication or application of the law of the Mishnah.* Units of discourse of this catalog generalize beyond the specific rule of the Mishnah. The discussion will commonly restate the principle of the rule at hand or raise a question invited by it. Hence, if the Mishnah's law settles one question, participants in this type of discourse will use that as the foundation for raising a second and consequent question. Two or more rules of the Mishnah (or of the Mishnah and Tosefta) will be contrasted with one another and then harmonized, or two or more rulings of a specific authority will be alleged to conflict and then shown not to stand at variance with one another.

d. *The matter of authorities and their views: case law.* In a handful of items, concrete decisions are attached to specific laws of the Mishnah, or the harmonization or identification of the opinions of Mishnah's authorities forms the center of interest.

From this taxonomy it follows that there was a severely circumscribed repertoire of intellectual initiatives available to the authorities of the Yerushalmi. Approaching a given rule of the Mishnah, a sage would do one of two things: (1) explain the meaning of the passage or (2) extend and expand the meaning of the passage. In the former category fall all the items in the first and second approaches, as well as those units of discourse in which either a scriptural proof text is adduced in support of a law or an alleged variant reading of a text is supplied. In the latter category fit all items in the third and fourth approaches, as well as those in which the work is to harmonize laws or principles, on the one side, or to cite and amplify Tosefta's complement to the Mishnah passage, on the other. Within these two categories, which produce, in all, four subdivisions, we may find a place for all units of discourse in which the focus of discussion is a passage of the Mishnah. Of the two sorts, the straightforward explanation of the plain meaning of a Mishnaic law by far predominates. If I may state the outcome very simply: what the framers of the Yerushalmi want to say—whatever else their purpose or aspiration— is what they think the Mishnah means in any given passage.

20. Then when does the Yerushalmi speak for itself, not for the Mishnah? If we collect all units of discourse, or larger parts of such units, in which exegesis of the Mishnah or expansion on the law of the Mishnah is absent— about ten percent of all the Yerushalmi's units of discourse in my proble— we find at most four types, which in fact are only two.

a. *Theoretical questions of law not associated with a particular passage of the Mishnah.* Some tendency exists to move beyond the legal boundaries set by the Mishnah's rules themselves. More general inquiries are taken up. These remain within the framework of the topic of one tractate or another, athough some larger modes of thought are characteristic of more than a single tractate. To explain, I point to the mode of thought in which the scriptural basis of the law of the Mishnah will be investigated, without regard to a given tractate. Along these same lines, I may point to a general inquiry into the count under which one may be liable for a given act, to comments on the law governing teaching and judging cases, and the like. But these items tend not to leave the Mishnah far behind.

b. *Exegesis of Scripture separate from the Mishnah.* It is under this rubric that we find the most important instances in which the Yerushalmi presents materials essentially independent of the Mishnah. They pursue problems or themes through what is said about a biblical figure, expressing ideas and values simply unknown to the Mishnah.

c. *Historical statements.* The Yerushalmi contains a fair number of statements that something happened or narratives about how something happened. Although many of these are replete with biblical quotations, in general they do not provide exegesis of Scripture, which serves merely as illustration or reference point.

d. *Stories about, and rules for, sages and disciples separate from discussion of a passage of the Mishnah.* The Mishnah contains a tiny number of tales about rabbis. These serve principally as precedents for, or illustrations of, rules. The Yerushalmi, by contrast, contains a sizable number of stories about sages and their relationships to other people. Like the items in the second and third lists, these too may be adduced as evidence of the values of the people who stand behind the Yerushalmi and the things they thought important. These tales rarely serve to illustrate a rule or concept of the Mishnah. The main, though not the only, characteristic theme is the power of the rabbi, the honor due to the rabbi, and the tension between the rabbi and others, whether the patriarch, on the one side, the heretic on the second, or the gentile on the third. Units of discourse (or large segments of such units) independent of the interests of the Mishnah are not numerous. Varying in bulk from one tractate to the next, as I said, in my proble of five tractates of the Yerushalmi they added up to not much more than ten percent of the whole. Furthermore, among the four types of units of discourse before us, the items on the first do not move far from the principles and concerns of the Mishnah.

21. Gen. Rabbah XII:VII.2.

22. See the appendix to chapter 2 for further illustrations of that position.

3
Legitimate Violence:
From Hierarchized Foci to
Unitary Focus of Power

When setting forth its view of power—specifically, the legitimate use of violence—and the disposition of power in society, the Mishnah's authorship describes matters in a fundamentally political manner, inventing a political structure and system integral to its plan for the social order. In the Mishnah's system Israel forms a political entity, fully empowered in an entirely secular sense, just as Scripture describes matters. Political institutions of the social order—king, priest, and court or civil administration—are assigned the right, each in its jurisdiction, to exercise violence here on earth, corresponding to, and shared with, the same empowerment accorded to institutions of Heaven. Moreover, these institutions are conceived to ration and rationalize the uses of that power permanently. The picture is this-worldly, but because it does not distinguish crime from sin, it is not secular, for the same system that legitimates king, high priest, and court posits in Heaven a corresponding politics, with God and the court on high exercising jurisdiction for some crimes or sins, the king, priesthood, or court below for others.

Among prior Judaisms only the scriptural system defined with the closure of the Pentateuch sets forth a politics at all. The appeal to politics in presenting a theory of the social order of this particular "Israel" would have provoked some curiosity among, for one example, the framers of the Judaism portrayed by the Essene library uncovered at Qumran and, for another, the framers of the Christianity of the Land of Israel in the first century. Both groups, heirs to the ancient Scriptures as much as were the framers of the Mishnah, found in politics no important component of the systemic structure they constructed.

By contrast, the integration of a politics within a systematic account of the social order would not have surprised the great figures of Greco-Roman philosophy, Plato and Aristotle, for example. That fact is of consequence because the Pentateuch simply does not provide an adequate basis from which to make sense of the institutions that the politics of Judaism designs. The pentateuchal politics invokes priest and prophet, Aaron and Moses, but says nothing of a tripartite government involving king, priest, and sage, nor do the royal narratives concede power to the priest or sage. On the other hand, as I shall show, knowledge of the *Politics* of Aristotle and the *Republic* of Plato gives perspective on the politics of the Mishnah.

Although the Pentateuch defines the principles and details of the Mishnah's distributive economics, it contributes nothing to the Mishnah's scheme of routine government by king, high priest, and sages' court. On the contrary, the Pentateuch's prophetic rule and constant appeal to God's immediate participation in the political process and, in particular, in the administration of sanctions and acts of legitimate violence, fall into the category of the politics of charisma. The difference is not merely in the pentateuchal institutions' appeal to prophet and priest but also in how the structure works as a political system, for the pentateuchal myth that serves to legitimate coercion — rule by God's prophet, in the model of Moses, and governance through explicitly revealed laws that God has dictated for the occasion — plays no active and systemic role whatsoever in the formulation and presentation of the politics of Judaism. By contrast, philosophical systems use politics to set forth the rules and unchanging order of legitimate exercise of power, its teleology and its structure. Plato and Aristotle make no place for godly intervention on any particular occasion.

Of the types of political authority contained within the scriptural repertoire, the Mishnah's philosophers, like the Greco-Roman philosophers, reject the prophetic and charismatic and deem critical the authority governing and governed by rules in an orderly, rational way. The principal political figures — king, high priest, and the disciple of the sage — are carefully nurtured through learning of rules, not through cultivation of gifts of the spirit. The authority of sages in the politics of Judaism in particular does not derive from charisma, for example, from a revelation by God to the sage, who makes a ruling in a given case, or even from the sage's general access to God. So the politics of the Pentateuch — structure and system alike — in no way forms the model for the politics of the Mishnah. Hence, the correct context for the classification of the Mishnah's politics must be located elsewhere than in a Judaism between the Pentateuch's and the Mishnah's, ca. 500 B.C.E. to 200 C.E. But what about the Greco-Roman tradition of philosophical politics?

Given the pentateuchal precedent, the mere presence of a highly orderly and systematic political structure and system is insufficient evidence of the philosophical character of the Mishnah's politics. Three specific traits, however, do indicate a philosophical classification for the Mishnah's politics in framing a systemic composition, even though the parallels prove structural and general rather than detailed and doctrinal, unlike the case with economics.

First, like the politics of Plato and Aristotle, the Mishnah's politics describes only a utopian politics, a structure and system of a fictive and a fabricated kind: an intellectuals' conception of a politics. Serving the larger purpose of system construction, politics of necessity emerges as invention, for example, by Heaven or in the model of Heaven, not as a secular revision and reform of an existing system. Although in the middle of the second century Rome incorporated their country, Israel, into its imperial system, denying Jews access to their capital, Jerusalem, and permanently closing their cult-center, its Temple, the authorship of the Mishnah described a government of a king, a high priest, and an administration fully empowered to carry out the law through legitimate violence. So the two politics—the Mishnah's and the Greco-Roman tradition represented by Plato's and Aristotle's—share common origins in intellectuals' theoretical and imaginative lives and concretely realize within those lives a larger theory of matters. In strange and odd forms, the Mishnah's politics falls into the class of the *Staatsroman,* or political novel, the classification that also encompasses Plato's *Republic* and Aristotle's *Politics,* but the same may be said for the strange politics of the Pentateuch.

Second, and more to the point, the Mishnah's sages stand well within the philosophical mode of political thought that begins with Aristotle, who sees politics as a fundamental component of his system when he says, "political science . . . legislates as to what we are to do and what we are to abstain from," and as to the institutionalization of power, I cannot imagine a more ample definition of the Mishnaic system's utilization of politics than that.[1] Although that statement also applied to pentateuchal politics, the systemic message borne by politics within the pentateuchal system and that carried by politics in the Mishnaic system do not correspond in any important ways. Aristotle and the philosophers of the Mishnah use politics to make systemic statements that correspond to one another, in that both comparison and contrast prove apt and pointed. Both speak of an empowered social entity; both take for granted that ongoing institutions legitimately govern in accord with a rationality discerned by distinguishing among those empowered to inflict sanctions; both see politics as a medium for accomplishing systemic goals that derive from the larger purpose of the social order, to which politics is subordinate and merely instrumental.

Third, the comparison also yields a contrast of importance. Specifically, because political analysis depends on the results of prior inquiry into a social system's disposition of scarce resources and theory of control of means of production, the results of the preceding chapter's comparison of economics leads to a comparison of the politics of Aristotle and the politics of the Mishnah. For when we know who commands the means of production, we turn to ask who tells whom what to do and why: who legitimately coerces others, even through violence. And here the Mishnah's system decisively parts company with that of the Pentateuch and also with that of Aristotle.

The distributive economics of the Pentateuch, as outlined in the priestly code, assigns both economic and political privilege to the same class of persons, the priesthood, which effects distributive economics and distributive politics. That is not the way things are in the Mishnah's politics, which distinguishes the one controlling the means of production from the one possessing the right to commit violence. The former, the householder, is not a political entity at all: dominant as the subject of most sentences in the economic tractates, he never appears in the political ones.

When we come to Aristotle, the point in common underlines the difference. Both Aristotle and the Mishnah's philosphers name the householder as the "person" (in our century we prefer "class," "caste," or other more abstract and impersonal categories) who forms the commanding presence in control of the means of production. For the systems of Aristotle and the Mishnah's sages, the fundamental unit of economic thought and the generative social metaphor is the householder. The givens of the Mishnah's framers' theory of economics, embedded in a larger systemic plan, correpond point by point with the economic program of Aristotle. That correspondence simply does not apply to pentateuchal politics, however. Accordingly, the context in which the political structure and system of the Mishnah find their proper place is the Greco-Roman philosophical one; the differences from the pentateuchal politics, both in detail and in overall structural traits, decisively remove the Mishnah's politics from the scriptural tradition. Nevertheless, these same differences set the Mishnah's politics apart from Aristotle's as well.

So, as I said, that important difference between Aristotle and the Mishnah's authorship is to be seen only within the context of the similarity that permits comparison and contrast. Although the economics of both Aristotle and Judaism commence by considering the place and power of the person ("class," "caste," or economic interest) in control of the means of production, the social metaphors that animate the politics of the two systems part company. In the *Politics,* Aristotle is consistent in starting with that very same person ("class") when he considers issues of power, producing a distributive politics to match his distributive economics. The Mishnah's philosophers, however, build their politics with an altogether different set of building blocks. The simple fact is that the householder, fundamental to their economics, does not form a subject of political discourse and in no way constitutes a political class or caste. When the Mishnah's writers speak of economics, the subject of most active verbs is the householder; when they speak of politics, the householder never takes an active role or even appears as a differentiated political class. In this sense, the economics of the Mishnah is disembedded from its politics, and vice versa, whereas the economics and politics of Aristotle's system are deeply embedded within a larger, nurturing, wholly cogent theory of political economy.

The difference is of sufficient weight to justify amplification. For Aristotle, both economics and politics originate in the agglomeration of households into villages and of villages into the city, or *polis,* which was the social metaphor of his thought on political questions. The politics of the Mishnah's philosophers does not follow suit, however. The politics of Judaism appeals to a fundamental building block selected from the political entities of the social order (persons or classes), which in no way correspond to the householder of the economics of Judaism. These are, as I said, the king and the priest, representing the monarchy and the Temple, and the court or administration, made up of what they called sages and representing what we should call the civil service and bureaucracy. These institutions are represented in their order and hierarchy: king at the top, priest on the one side, sage on the other. In Heaven, God stands at the top, corresponding to the king.[2]

A very simple observation shows that these three classes of persons — king, priest, sage — defined the political structure and controlled the political system. In examining who could legitimately invoke violence and inflict penalties, whether to persons or to property, or against individuals or groups, the point of differentiation among the appropriate mundane institutional powers invariably turns on those three classes and no others. The householder, the building block of economy and society, although in command of the means of production (so far as the economics of the Mishnah was concerned), in no way defines a point of differentiation on the imposition of legitimate violence. The point is simple. The economics of the Mishnah and the economics of Aristotle bore important parts of the systemic message of the respective systems, and it was essentially the same message. Nevertheless, although like Aristotle's politics the politics of the Mishnah falls into the category of a philosophical politics, the systemic message it assigns to the political component is not the same as the systemic message assigned to Aristotle's politics.

More precisely, the systemic message that the system builders of the Mishnah assigned to the political components concerns the hierarchical classification of society, just as my account of the Mishnah's philosophy suggests. In the present context, the sense is a simple one. Given that society is viewed as classified and hierarchized, the task of politics is to designate who is on top, who is in the middle, and who is on the bottom — to explain who does what to whom in that well-ordered social structure that the Mishnah's framers envisaged. The hierarchical ordering of power through a theory of politics comes to expression in a political myth, one that exhibits itself in the identification of what differentiates the sanctions (that is, power in its brute and pure form) among the several jurisdictions. The next task is to differentiate jurisdictions, to discern the hierarchical ordering effected through politics, which is to say, sytemically expressed through the imagined structure and system embodied in legitimate sanctions.

Understanding the differentiating force of myth that imparts to politics its activity and dynamism will help explain the systemic message, conveyed through the political component of the system, that animates the structures of the politics and propels the system. Appealing to a myth of taxonomy, the politics of the system accomplishes its tasks by explaining why this and not that, telling as its foundation story a myth about the classification of power. The myth appeals in the end to the critical bases for classifying institutions in terms of a generalized power to coerce. Moving from sanctions to the myth expressed in the application and legitimation of those sanctions shows a complex but cogent politics sustained by a simple myth; specifically, the encompassing framework of rules, institutions, and sanctions is explained and validated by the myth of God's shared rule, the counterpart to God's shared ownership of land. That dominion, exercised by God and God's surrogates on earth, is focused partly in the royal palace, partly in the Temple, and partly in the court. But which part falls where, and why? The political myth of Judaism answers that question, and consequently, the Judaic political myth comes to expression in its details of differentiation, which permits an answer to the generative question of politics: who imposes which sanction, and why?

Four types of sanctions must be differentiated, each deriving from a distinct institution of political power and each bearing its own mythic explanation. To understand these points of differentiation is to be prepared to recognize how vastly the politics changed in the successor documents, for, as I shall show, the later politics makes no such differentiation but recognizes only one legitimate political institution on earth. For the Mishnah's politics, the first class of sanctions is what God and the heavenly court can do to people. The second is what the earthly court can do to people—the legitimate violence of which political theory ordinarily speaks. The third is the sanction imposed by the cult's requirements, which can deprive people of their property as legitimately as can a court. The fourth is the self-imposed sanction: conformity to consensus; the issue in this case becomes whose consensus it is and who defines it. In play are four types of coercion, including violence of various kinds, psychological and social as much as physical. The types of sanction that the system concedes to other than judicial-political agencies surely prove violent and legitimately coercive, even though the violence and coercion are not the same as those carried out by courts.

Power exercised invariably and undifferentiatedly in the name and by the authority of God in Heaven is kept distinct. Concrete application of legitimate violence by Heaven covers matters different from the parts of the political and social world governed by the policy and coercion of the this-worldly political classes. And both sorts of violence have to be kept distinct from the community-imposed sanction effected not through institutional force and expression but through the weight of attitude and public opinion. The politics works in such a way that all political institutions — God, the court, the Temple, and the monarchy — all agencies with the power to bestow or take away life or property or to inflict physical pain and suffering, cooperate in a single continuum so as to deal with the same crimes or sins.

The orderly character of the Mishnah's hierarchization of power is shown by a simple fact: God's direct intervention is quite absent from the politics, which decisively distinguishes the Mishnah's political theory from the Pentateuch's. In the Mishnah's system God's ad hoc and episodic intervention in the life of the community does not serve to explain obedience to the law in the here and now. What sort of evidence would indicate that God intervenes in ways that could justify obedience to the law on an everyday basis? Invoking God's immediate presence, a word said, a miracle performed — any of these would suffice, but in the more than 550 chapters of the Mishnah and the much larger corpus of the Tosefta no one ever prays to have God supply a decision in a particular case. There is no counterpart to Moses' asking God whether women can inherit, absent a male heir, for instance. The later position that prophecy has ceased can readily account for this fact, however, so it is more to the point to observe that no judge asks God to execute a convicted felon. If the judge wants the felon killed, he kills him. On the other hand, it may be argued that the Mishnah's system does appeal to extirpation, meaning that Heaven, too, participates in the system. This is so, but only because of the hierarchical order set forth, for when God intervenes, it is on the jurisdiction assigned to God, not to the court, and then the penalty is different from execution.

Penalties fall into four classifications: (1) what Heaven does, (2) what cultic institutions do, (3) what the civil administration and court system do, and (4) what is left to the coercion of public opinion, or consensus, with special attention to the definition of the "public" that has effective opinion to begin with. This final realm of power, conferring or withholding approval, proves constricted, but the first three prove critical. (1) God takes care of *deliberate* violation of God's wishes. If a sin or crime is inadvertent, the penalties are of one order; if deliberate, of a different order. The most serious infraction of the law of the Torah is identified not by what is done but by the attitude of the sinner or criminal. If the violation of God's rule is deliberate, then God intervenes; if the violation if inadvertent, then (2) the Temple imposes the sanction. The difference is considerable. In the former case, God, acting through the heavenly court, ends the felon's or sinner's life. A person who defies the relevant laws, which concern sexual conduct, attitude toward God, and relationships within the family, will be penalized either (if necessary) by God or (if possible) by the earthly court. That means that (3) the earthly court exercises God's power, and the myth of the system as a whole, so far as the earthly court constitutes the principal institutional form of the system, emerges not merely in a generality but in all its specificity. These particular judges, here and now, stand for God and exercise the power of God. In the case of social coercion, the Temple takes over jurisdiction; a particular offering is called for, as the book of Leviticus specifies, but there is no need for God or the earthly court in God's name to take a position. The power of social coercion, for example, ostracism, is systemically unimportant.

Power therefore flows through three distinct but intersecting dominions, each with its own concern, all sharing some common interests. The heavenly court attends to *deliberate* defiance of Heaven, the Temple to *inadvertent* contradiction — therefore not defiance — of Heaven. The earthly court attends to matters subject to its jurisdiction, by reason of sufficient evidence, proper witnesses, and the like, and these same matters will come under heavenly jurisdiction when the earthly court finds itself unable to act. Who then tells whom to do what? Power comes from two conflicting forces: the commanding will of God and the free will of the human being. Power expressed in immediate sanctions is mediated through these same forces: Heaven above, human beings below, with the Temple mediating the two. Power works its way in the interplay between what God has set forth in the law of the Torah and what human beings do, whether intentionally or inadvertently, obediently or defiantly.

The myth differentiates and therefore of necessity also hierarchizes, and the point of differentiation within the political structures, supernatural and natural alike, lies in the attitude and intention of a human being. A person who comes into conflict with the system, rejecting the authority claimed by the powers that be, does so deliberately or inadvertently. The myth accounts for the following hierarchization of action and penalty, infraction and sanction: (1) If the deed is deliberate, then one set of institutions exercises jurisdiction and utilizes supernatural power. (2) If the deed is inadvertent, another institution exercises jurisdiction and utilizes the power made available by that same super-natural being. The ordering of power relationships and the hierarchization of the political institutions therefore present a single, well-composed political structure and system. And that brings us to the politics portrayed in the successor writing, with the difference simply characterized in this way: from a realm of order and hierarchy (in this context, a redundant combination) in which power is diffused but well focused, we turn to a disorderly politics indeed.

The successor system, speaking on its own and not in response to the Mishnah, exhibits none of the traits of the Mishnah's politics; instead, it sets forth those of its own. Where the Mishnah's politics is orderly and hierarchical, the Yerushalmi's scarcely distinguishes within the Israelite sphere at all; it has one political entity and class, not three on earth corresponding to one in Heaven. It contains not the marvelously differentiated and classified penalties and sanctions on which the Mishnah's authorship lovingly dwells in such tractates as Keritot and Sanhedrin but rather a quite undifferentiated system of sanctions, each serving for the correct context. And context is always the point of differentiation: doing what one can, when one can, where one can, and appealing to Heaven to do the rest. In due course these points of difference will serve to highlight the more profound differences between the philosophical politics of the Mishnah and what I shall show is the religious politics of the Yerushalmi, differences to be observed only in the constructive account of part 2. It suffices here to draw the contrast and establish the simple fact that the Mishnah's and the Yerushalmi's politics bear little in common, except where the latter simply paraphrased and clarified details of the former.

The Talmud of the Land of Israel and related writings portray not the (imagined) orderly and inner-facing politics of Israelites living by themselves under God, king, priest, and sage but the palpable chaos of Jews living among gentiles, governed by a diversity of authorities, and lacking all order and arrangement. The politics of the Mishnah is classified with that of philosophers because it deals with logic and order in abstract terms. The politics of the successor documents reveals politicians deeply involved in the administration of the concrete social group, describing its "Israel" as a real-life community. The later authorships, in the fourth and fifth centuries, prove analogous not to philosophers but to men of affairs—judges, lawyers, bureaucrats, heads of local governments. That general thesis corresponds to the results of my overview of how the Yerushalmi and its friends treat philosophical economics. The successor documents exhibit an interest in not theory but practice, and the important distinctions and points of clarification all have to do with the workaday application of the law. That observation justifies the view that the Yerushalmi and related writings reveal how men of affairs faithfully read but realistically translated philosophy into public policy.

It is true that both the Mishnah's and the successor documents' politics in the end put sages in charge of everything, but in the first system sages form only one component of a well-ordered structure in which monarchy, priesthood, and clerkdom also contribute to a cogent structure; together, each doing its assigned task, all these components administered an orderly world in an orderly way. In the second system, sages are represented as the sole legitimate authority, competing with such illegitimate authorities as the patriarch within and the gentile government of Rome beyond. The practical politics then dealt with Jews who lived under both the local rabbis, who settled everyday disputes of streets and households, and also distant archons of a nameless state, to be manipulated and placated on earth as in Heaven. The Yerushalmi's portrait of legitimate power, as distinct from illegitimate violence, appeals to the legitimation of the Torah serving solely for the sages, whereas the Mishnah's account differs in ways now entirely obvious. Indeed, what I find most striking as I look back on the Mishnah's politics is that although legitimate power is carefully parceled out, illegitimate power is ignored. In the Yerushalmi's politics, by contrast, the issue is the distinction between illegitimate power, worked by patriarch within and Rome beyond, and legitimate power, focused solely on sages. The issues thus shift, even while the category remains the same. That shift seems to indicate a decay in categorical cogency; the Mishnah's category of politics is preserved but then bypassed, as issues not formerly considered intervene and drastically revise the character of the whole—even in its initial context and definition. A look at the counterpart category to philosophical politics will clearly show how a new, less-cogent category simply supplants the received and preserved one.

The Mishnah's politics breathes the pure air of public piazza and stoa; the politics of the Talmud of the Land of Israel and its associated Midrash compilations, the ripe stench of private alleyway and courtyard. That is why the comparison of the Mishnah's politics with philosphical politics and of the Yerushalmi's with an other than philosophical politics is amply justified.[3] The image of the Mishnah's politics evokes the majestic Parthenon, perfect in all its proportions, conceived in a single moment of pure rationality. The successor system is a scarcely choate cathedral in process, the labor of many generations, each part the conception of diverse moments of devotion, all of them the culmination of an ongoing and evolving process of revelation in the here and now. The Mishnah's system presents a counterpart to Plato's *Republic* and Aristotle's *Politics,* a noble theory of it all. In literary terms, the transition from the Mishnah to the successor writings leaves behind the strict and formal classicism of the Mishnah, which like Plato's *Republic* describes for no one in particular an ideal society never to be seen in its day. The focus instead comes to be on the disorderly detail of the workaday world, the successor writings taking the utopian Mishnah along in its descent into the streets, where people really do commit acts of violence against one another and where authority really does have to sort out legitimate acts of force and ongoing institutions able to perform such acts from illegitimate acts and nonpriviledged institutions.

Given the fate of the Mishnah's economics, the dual reception accorded to the Mishnah's politics is hardly surprising, it being amplified, on the one side, and supplanted, on the other. As to the first of these two now-familiar modes of dealing with the received system's categories, the evidence of the Yerushalmi, Genesis Rabbah, Leviticus Rabbah, and Pesiqta deRab Kahana shows the continuing authority of the inherited politics. But how has the category of politics been revised or broadened, essentially within the limits defined by the received definition? The question of the rest of this chapter is whether the successor documents recognize authorites other than king, temple, and court as able to coerce and otherwise utilize legitimate violence. The decay—within the theoretical structure—of the received political institutions is reflected in the fact that, as the sage becomes the recognized government, the king and high priest (in the persons of their avatars, the patriarch and the priesthood) are no longer accorded legitimate rights of violence of any kind. The former is represented as illegitimate, a part of an illegitimate alien government; the latter is treated as no longer a political entity at all, for the most violent act a priest can commit is to seize the priestly rations owing to the priesthood in general by a particular farmer. What sorts of power does the sage alone now exercise, and how is the inherited politics revised?[4]

The basic shift in political thinking is marked by two complementary traits. In the representation of the Yerushalmi and its associated compilations, the high priest is now absent; more to the point, the king is less differentiated and, like the priesthood, more remote, whereas the sage is ever more differentiated, always concretely present in the here and now. Let me make this point clear. When the Yerushalmi's framers speak independently and not as Mishnah exegetes, the role of the king is no longer differentiated within an overarching system of sanctions: the king is treated in general terms and not in a specific way. There is no recognition whatsoever that the king or patriarch legitimately inflicts some sanctions, the sage, others. Use of force by the patriarch is illegitimate, but its use by the sage is always and everywhere legitimate. The differentiation of sanctions focuses on what the sage does in distinct kinds of cases, not on what the king does in one kind of case and what the sage does in some other. It follows quite naturally that the role of the sage is much more richly differentiated, amplified by cases, for instance, so that the focus of political discourse, defined as it is by the legitimate exercise of power, comes to bear solely on the sage and his court. The king occupies center stage, but only in parables, in which the king or prince stands for everyman, not in concrete accounts of legitimate violence, let alone in autonomous exercises on the differentiation of the authorities that exercise legitimate violence.

It is to be expected that the Yerushalmi will spell out the Mishnah's points entirely within the framework of the Mishnah's structure and system. It is when the authorship of the Yerushalmi speaks not about the Mishnah but about other matters that it makes its own statement; in such cases it attests to a system quite different from the Mishnah's politics. Let us take only one example of how, when the Yerushalmi's exegetes read the Mishnah's rules of politics, they paraphrase and amplify what the Mishnah says, whereas when they take initiatives on their own, they make an altogether different statement. That will suffice to show once again the familiar fact that, when they read the Mishnah, the successor authorships amplify and clarify but do not innovate. It is only when they move on to their own program that they make a statement particular to themselves, and when they do, it is not the statement of the Mishnah, but a different one, signified by categories for which the Mishnah makes no place.

Here is a single instance of the Yerushalmi's reading of the Mishnah on politics. I give the Mishnah passage in boldface type, then the Talmud's treatment of the passage in regular type.

Mishnah Tractate Sanhedrin 2.1

A. **A high priest judges, and [others] judge him;**

B. **gives testimony, and [others] give testimony about him;**

C. **performs the rite of removing the shoe [Deut. 25:7-9], and [others] perform the rite of removing the shoe with his wife.**

D. **[Others] enter levirate marriage with his wife, but he does not enter into levirate marriage,**

E. **because he is prohibited to marry a widow.**

F. **[If] he suffers a death [in his family], he does not follow the bier.**

G. **"But when [the bearers of the bier] are not visible, he is visible; when they are visible, he is not.**

H. **"And he goes with them to the city gate," the words of R. Meir.**

I. **R. Judah says, "He never leaves the sanctuary,**

J. **"since it says, 'Nor shall he go out of the sanctuary' (Lev. 21:12)."**

I

A. It is understandable that he judges others.

B. But as to others judging him, [is it appropriate to his station?]

C. Let him appoint a mandatory.

D. Now take note: What if he has to take an oath?

E. Can the mandatory take an oath for his client?

F. Property cases involving [a high priest] — in how large a court is the trial conducted?

G. With a court of twenty-three judges.

H. Let us demonstrate that fact from the following:

I. **A king does not sit in the sanhedrin, nor do a king and a high priest join in the court session for intercalation [T. San. 2:15].**

J. [In this regard,] R. Haninah and R. Mana — one of them said, "The king does not take a seat on the Sanhedrin, on account of suspicion [of influencing the other judges].

K. "Nor does he take a seat in a session for intercalation,

because of suspicion [that it is in the government's interest to intercalate the year].

L. "And a king and a high priest do not take a seat for intercalation, for it is not appropriate to the station of the king [or the high priest] to take a seat with seven judges."

M. Now look here:

N. If it is not appropriate to his station to take a seat with seven judges, is it not an argument *a fortiori* that he should not [be judged] by three?

O. That is why one must say, property cases involving him are tried in a court of twenty-three.

II

A. [What follows is verbatim at M. Hor. 3:1] **Said R. Eleazar, "A high priest who sinned—they administer lashes to him, but they do not remove him from his high office."**

B. Said R. Mana, "It is written, '*For the consecration of the anointing oil of his God is upon him: I am the Lord*' (Lev. 21:12).

C. [Here omitted:] ("That is as if to say: 'Just as I [stand firm] in my high office, so Aaron [stands firm] in his high office,' ")

D. [Here omitted:] (Said R. Abun, " '*He shall be holy to you [for I the Lord who sanctify you am holy]*' (Lev. 21:8).)

E. "That is as if to say, 'Just as I [stand firm] in my consecration, so Aaron [stands firm] in his consecration.' "

F. R. Haninah Ketobah, R. Aha in the name of R. Simeon b. Laqish: "An anointed priest who sinned—they administer lashes to him [by the judgment of a court of three judges].

G. "If you rule that it is by the decision of a court of twenty-three judges [that the lashes are administered], it turns out that his ascension [to high office] is descent [to public humiliation, for if he sins he is publicly humiliated by a sizable court]."

The preceding discussion remains wholly within the framework of the Mishnah's interest, but the following moves on to other questions, leaving behind the politics of the king and high priest and entering a new realm altogether, one of not the king but the *nasi,* the patriarch. At stake in what follows is the very stark question: whose acts of violence are legitimate, and whose illegitimate? The sages' acts of violence are legitimate, and the patriarch's not, even though sages must concede that greater power inheres in the patriarchal government than in theirs. The claim that "they"—the sages—possess authority to administer sanctions to the patriarch now is at issue. The theoretical clarity of the Mishnah is lost in the practical politics of real power, leaving the Mishnah's politics far behind, but that understates the shift. I cannot point to a single passage in the Mishnah or the Tosefta in which the several components of the political structure are represented as competing, let alone one in which the sages' component, in *political* terms and contexts of legitimation of violence (as distinct from mere status), is set above that of the king or the high priest. The following therefore not only digresses from Mishnah exegesis but also makes a point entirely beyond the framework of the Mishnah's politics.[5]

III

A. R. Simeon b. Laqish said, "A ruler who sinned—they administer lashes to him by the decision of a court of three judges."

B. What is the law as to restoring him to office?

C. Said R. Haggai, "By Moses! If we put him back into office, he will kill us!"

D. R. Judah the Patriarch heard this ruling [R. Simeon b. Laqish's] and was outraged. He sent a troop of Goths to arrest R. Simeon b. Laqish. [R. Simeon b. Laqish] fled to the Tower, and, some say, it was to Kefar Hittayya.

E. The next day R. Yohanan went up to the meetinghouse, and R. Judah the Patriarch went up to the meetinghouse. He said to him, "Why does my master not state a teaching of Torah?"

F. [Yohanan] bagan to clap with one hand [only].

G. [Judah the Patriarch] said to him, "Now do people clap with only one hand?"

H. He said to him, "No, nor is Ben Laqish here [and just as one cannot clap with one hand only, so I cannot teach Torah if my colleague, Simeon b. Laqish, is absent]."

I. [Judah] said to him, "Then where is he hidden?"

J. He said to him, "In a certain tower."

K. He said to him, "You and I shall go out to greet him tomorrow."

L. R. Yohanan sent word to R. Simeon b. Laqish, "Get a teaching of Torah ready, because the patriarch is coming over to see you."

M. [Simeon b. Laqish] came forth to receive them and said, "The example which you [Judah] set is to be compared to the paradigm of your Creator. For when the All Merciful came forth to redeem Israel [from Egypt], he did not send a messenger or an angel, but the Holy One, blessed be He, himself came forth, as it is said, 'For I will pass through the Land of Egypt that night' (Exod. 12:12)—and not only so, but he and his entire retinue.

B. "[Here omitted:] ['What other people on earth is like thy people Israel, whom God went to redeem to be his people' (2 Sam. 7:23).] 'Whom God went' (sing.) is not written here, but 'Whom God went' (plural) [meaning, he and all his retinue].")

O. [Judah the Patriarch] said to him, "Now why in the world did you see fit to teach this particular statement [that a ruler who sinned is subject to lashes]?"

P. He said to him, "Now did you really think that because I was afraid of you, I would hold back the teaching of the All Merciful? [And lo, citing 1 Sam. 2:23f.,] R. Samuel b. R. Isaac said, '[Why do you do such things? For I hear of your evil dealings from all the people.] No, my sons, it is no good report [that I hear the people of the Lord spreading abroad]. [Here omitted:] (If a man sins against a man, God will mediate for him; but if a man sins against the Lord, who can intercede for him? But they would not listen to the voice of their father, for it was the will of the Lord to slay them' [1 Sam. 2:23-25]. [When] the people of the Lord spread about [an evil report about a man], they remove him [even though he is the patriarch].")

This brief abstract suffices to make the simple point that the politics of the Mishnah, treated by the Yerushalmi, is carried forward without noticeable change as to basic structure and system. But when—as at III—the Yerushalmi then portrays power relationships not in the context of Mishnah exegesis, it provides a quite different picture.

Now the issue is not the king but the patriarch, not the sages' court with clearly differentiated power to administer sanction but with a generalized power to do what the sages want—if it can. And whereas the Mishnah's king exercises violence legitimately, the Yerushalmi's patriarch uses foreign troops and enjoys no more legitimacy than does the foreign government that has supplied those troops.

Therefore, although the Yerushalmi and related writings carry forward the politics of the Mishnah, they also express a quite separate conception of political institutions and relationships: a political structure in which sages administer sanctions and make decisions. Where others intervene, their sanctions—whether the patriarch's or the gentile's—are illegitimate. Legitimate violence is executed solely by one political entity, the sages' court. Demonstrating that fact suffices for the present stage in the argument, for all that is necessary now is to demonstrate that the politics of the Yerushalmi and its companions is other than philosophical.[6]

That observation draws attention to the sanctions legitimately in the hands of sages alone. These are differentiated not in principle but only in context: what matters is what works. And the differentiation is circumstantial, expressed through a description of cases that is never theoretical and principled. Nevertheless, there should be no doubt that the issue is violence and not merely voluntary acquiescence. Sages' power is political and not merely moral, routine and not charismatic in any sense. Thus, the Talmud of the Land of Israel portrays sages as exercising authority effected through concrete sanctions not only over their own circles, people who agreed with them, but over the Jewish community at large. This authority was practical and involved very specific powers. The first and most important type of power a rabbi maintained he could exercise, under some circumstances and in some cases, was the power to sort out and adjudicate rights to property and personal status affecting property. The rabbi is described as able to take chattel or real estate from one party and give it into the rightful ownership of some other. The second sort of power rabbis are supposed to have wielded was the right to tell people what to do or not to do in matters not involving property rights; they could, for example, administer floggings, violence in its most personal form. The Talmud claims that rabbis could tell people outside the circles of their own disciples and estate how to conduct themselves. A rabbi is presented as able to coerce an ordinary Jew to do what he might otherwise not wish to do or to prevent him from doing what he wanted. That other authorities existed, and even competed with rabbinical authorities, is taken for granted. What is important to this part of my inquiry into systemic transformation is that the Yerushalmi portrays legitimate violence in a manner quite asymmetrical with the pattern set forth in the Mishnah.[7]

The Talmud of the Land of Israel takes for granted that rabbis could define the status of persons so as to affect property and marital rights and standing. It is difficult to imagine a more effective form of social authority. The Talmud treats as settled fact a range of precedents out of which the character of the law is defined. In those precedents, rabbis declare a woman married or free to marry; permitted as the wife of a priest to eat food in the status of leave-offering or prohibited from doing so; entitled to the support of a husband's estate or left without that support; and entitled to collect a previously contracted marriage settlement or lacking that right. The rabbis held that they governed the Jewish community as effective political authorities in all these ways, as much as in their control of real estate, commercial, and other material and property transactions among Jews. The rabbis did not use moral suasion or pretense of magical power to instill beliefs or values in the people, or to realize them in the collective life of the community. It was not hocus pocus they appealed to but political power resting on the force of government authority. They could tell people what to do and force them to do it.[8]

The Talmud of the Land of Israel is remarkably reticent about the basis for the rabbis' power over the Jews' political institutions: who bestowed the this-worldly legitimacy and supplied the force? The systematic provision of biblical proof texts for Mishnaic laws presents an ample myth for the law and its enforcement, however: sages act by right of their mastery of the Torah and therefore in the status of Heaven. Given by God to Moses at Mount Sinai, the law of the Torah, including the Mishnah's laws, represents the will of Heaven. Nevertheless, given all the faith in the world in such an assertion about God's will, the losing party to litigation over a piece of real estate would surely have surrendered his property only with the gravest reservations—if at all. He more likely would have complained to some other authority, if he could. Short of direct divine coercion, on which a legal system cannot be expected to rely, there had to be more reliable means of making the system work.

What these were, however, the Talmud of the Land of Israel hardly tells us. That silence underlines the political theory of the document: the sage acts for Heaven just as, in the Mishnah's politics, the king, high priest, and sage represent an earthly counterpart to the power and activity of Heaven. Each party, on earth as in Heaven, carries out its assigned and proper task. It seems clear that the sage is the sole focus of legitimate authority on earth and that Heaven's rule is no more explicit than the role of the king (or high priest) is legitimate. The differentiated foci of the Mishnah's philosphical politics now give way to the unitary focus of the Yerushalmi's theory of the same matter. The Mishnah's politics, at least in theory, calls for a diffusion of power within an articulated order and hierarchy; by contrast, the focus of power in the Yerushalmi is no longer cogent, but multiple and incoherent; legitimacy is now single and singular, and therein lies the shift.

The Talmud of the Land of Israel, therefore, clearly recognizes that rabbis competed with other authorities for rule over the Jewish community, but it claims that sages alone exercise power legitimately; all other political institutions by definition are illegitimate. True, the relationship of the rabbis as judges and administrators to other Jewish community judges and administrators who may have carried out the same tasks and exercised the same responsibilities in regard to the Jewish nation of the Land of Israel is not clarified, either in cases or as to theory. But here, too, the silence is indicative: it is a tacit judgment, and a devastatingly eloquent one. The Talmud's picture of legitimate violence comes to concrete expression in its account of what rabbis could force people to do because of their political power and position. The sovereignty of rabbinical courts in property disputes derived from the courts' power not only to persuade or elicit general support but also to call the power of the state to transfer ownership of real and movable property from one party to another.

Another sanction derived from the public fear of ostracism and from the active support of the people at large. Determinations of personal status by rabbinical courts depended on the power of public opinion that the sages manipulated. Although the courts might call on the state to back up their rulings about property, they are not likely to have enjoyed equivalent support in matters to which the government was probably indifferent, such as whether a given woman was betrothed and so not free to marry anyone but her fiancé. Persistent meddling in such affairs could have generated only widespread protest, unless the community at large acquiesced and indeed actively supported the right of the courts to make such decisions. Nonetheless, even behind these evidences of rabbinical authority, based as they are on sanctions of moral authority quite distinct from the imperial government's ultimate threat of force, there still were elements of property or commodity exchange.

As a matter of fact, the authorities who stood behind the Talmud of the Land of Israel preserved a vast number and wide variety of cases in which rabbinical courts exercised a kind of authority that was solely political and bureaucratic. Persons and property of Israel came under their authority, so the Talmud of the Land of Israel represents its authorities as judges of litigation and administrators of questions of personal status. Decisions are represented, moreover, as precedents, accepted in theorizing about law and uniformly authoritative for courts spread over a considerable territory. Accordingly, rabbinical judges saw themselves as part of a system and a structure, not merely local strong men or popular sages. The Yerushalmi describes a fully articulated system of politics and government, staffed by people who knew the Mishnah and how to apply its law to concrete cases and who had the full power to do so. Rabbinical judges knew what to do and had full confidence in their authority to do it. The Talmud of the Land of Israel portrays rabbis' power over the estates and possessions of the Jews, including communal property and behavior.

Rabbis furthermore made decisions or gave opinions in a domain quite distinct from that of property or of property joined to determination of personal status. These decisions, which influenced personal behavior in private rather than coercing it in public, were meant to establish rules for good public order and decent behavior. Whether rabbis enjoyed the power to force people to behave in the way they wanted is not at issue. So far as these issues related not to property and public policy but to individual conduct, the authority that the rabbis claimed to exercise was generally moral rather than civil and political. But the sanctions were every bit as rich in the potential for violence as those of a more narrowly political order.

The rabbi stood on the intersecting borders of several domains: political and private, communal and individual. He served as both legal and moral authority: decisor and exemplar, judge and clerk, administrator and governor, but also holy man and supernatural figure. What is important here is the representation of the rabbi—and the rabbi or sage alone, not the high priest (or priesthood) and the monarch (or patriarch), too—as the sole public authority deemed to exercise supernatural power. His task was to use his supernatural power in pretty much the same context and for the same purpose as he used his political-judicial and legal power and learning, on the one side, and his local influence and moral authority, on the other. In the following story the sage as public official protects the town from a siege and the illegitimate violence of the gentile.

Y. Taanit 3:8.II

A. As to Levi ben Sisi: troops came to his town. He took a scroll of the Torah and went up to the roof and said, "Lord of the ages! If a single word of this scroll of the Light has been nullified [in our town], let them come up against us, and if not, let them go their way."

B. Forthwith people went looking for the troops but did not find them [because they had gone their way].

C. A disciple of his did the same thing, and his hand withered, but the troops went their way.

D. A disciple of his disciple did the same thing. His hand did not wither, but they also did not go their way.

E. This illustrates the following apothegm: "You can't insult an idiot, and dead skin doesn't feel the scalpel."

The power of the sage to ward off the siege was based upon his saintliness, which consisted in his obedience to the Torah and the people's obedience to him. So whatever public authority the rabbi exercised is credited, in the end, to his accurate knowledge and sincerity in living up to his own teachings, on the one side, and the people's willingness to accept his instructions, on the other. Nothing in the Mishnah prepares us for such an account of the supernatural politics focused on the sage.[9] Concommitantly, the contrast between the sages' legitimate power and the gentiles' illegitimate violence underlines the contrast between the power of the Torah and the violence of the troops.

The illegitimacy of violence then forms a complementary component of the Yerushalmi's theory of politics, a matter simply bypassed as irrelevant in the Mishnah and the Tosefta. The Yerushalmi's tales about illegitimate Jewish authority portray the patriarch as exercising authority over rabbis. Some of the patriarchal tales place the patriarch into close relationship with Romans of the highest rank, including the emperor. On the basis of these tales, the Talmud of the Land of Israel posits the existence, in addition to the rabbinical bureaucrats, of a patriarch who hired them, used their services for the administration of the local affairs of the Jewish nation in the Land of Israel, and validated their decisions, even while maintaining his autonomy from, and superiority over, the clerks who made those decisions. So in the Talmud's view the context of rabbinical authority found definition in a figure—the patriarch—at the margins of both the rabbinical estate and the Roman administration of the Land of Israel. The rabbinical judges and clerks depended for political legitimation of their decisions and orders upon that government beyond themselves, both close at hand, in the patriarchate, and far away, in the Roman government itself. They clearly did not confuse the mere practicalities of politics with legitimacy, however, and they assuredly saw themselves as the sole legitimate political figures within Israel.

A theory of politics is different from a portrait of the political actualities of the time. The Talmud of the Land of Israel concedes that the rabbi was part of the administraiton of a man who stood at the margins of the rabbinical estate, one foot in, the other out. The sage was further limited in his power by popular will and consensus, by established custom, and by other sorts of Jewish local authorities. Furthermore, as the Talmud represents matters, the rabbi as clerk and bureaucrat dealt with matters of surpassing triviality, a fair portion of them of no interest to anyone but a rabbi, I should imagine. He might decide which dog a flea might bite, but would the fleas listen to him? Accordingly, the Talmud presents a politics that sorts out inconsequentialities. On the one side, the rabbi could make some practical decisions; on the other, he competed for authority over Israel with the patriarch and with local village heads, and, in general, no Jew decided much. From the viewpoint of the Roman empire, moreover, the rabbi was apt to have been one among many sorts of invisible men, self-important nonentities, treating as consequential things that concerned no one but themselves, doing little, changing nothing.

These realities bear no more consequence for the political theory at hand than the everyday facts of life shaped the politics of the initial system, the one represented by the Mishnah and its related writings. Just as the Mishnah's systemic statement effected through a theory of politics contains not a single line that concedes legitimacy to things that have actually happened, so the Yerushalmi's contains not a word that takes account of the givens of the day, and that is not at all surprising. What is not to be gainsaid is the systemic transformation of the relevant concepts, represented by the reconsideration not of the details of politics but of the very category. Thus far all I have shown is that the received category is recapitulated when the Mishnah is under discussion but re-presented when not. I have not yet shown where and how the Judaic system attested by the Yerushalmi and Midrash compilations associated with it have set forth not the Mishnah's categories revised and re-formed, but altogether new categories of their own: counterpart categories. To these I now turn.

Notes

1. Cited by R. G. Mulgan, *Aristotle's Political Theory* (Oxford: Clarendon Press, 1977), 3.

2. The heavenly court of angels is undifferentiated and in the Mishnah plays no role.

3. And what that other comparison yields will be clear presently.

4. This formulation of matters deliberately ignores the wholly new definition of the political entity, Israel, as family and of power as merit. These are treated in a different systemic context, specifically, in part 2, chapter 5, and part 3, chapter 8. What we see in chapter 2 and this chapter is the revision and expansion of the range of the received categories.

5. Mishnah tractate Horayyot proves this point. Developing the pentateuchal rules of Leviticus, chapter 4, that tractates refers to the requirement of an authority who has sinned to bring an offering to the Temple. It says nothing of removing such a person from office; that is not the issue. So the sinning ruler does not fall under the authority of the court of the sages. That is not the issue of the tractate as the Mishnah treats the subject of the sinning politician. Contrast Simeon b. Laqish's statement!

6. Classification of that politics within an other than philosophical systemic framework will receive ample attention in part 2, chapter 6.

7. I omit reference to the companion writings because they are not pertinent to the present issue, which pertains solely to the reception of the Mishnah's politics and the disposition of that politics. I observe nothing pertinent to the Mishnah's political theory in the Midrash compilations, and the sole issue of this chapter, the reception of the Mishnah's political structure and system and the diffusion of the power to inflict legitimate violence, is sufficiently worked out through a brief survey of the Yerushalmi's consideration of the matter. In its treatment of the counterpart category, chapter 6 reviews the political system and structure adumbrated in the Midrash compilations that form companions to the Yerushalmi.

8. The details are spelled out in my *Judaism and Society: The Evidence of the Yerushalmi* (Chicago: University of Chicago Press, 1984), chap. 3. Note also my *Foundations of the Theology of Judaism* (Northvale, N.J.: Jason Aronson, 1991), vol. 2, *Israel*.

9. The supernatural power vested in Honi the Circle-drawer (M. Ta. 3:8) is not of a political order and does not involve the exercise of legitimate violence in the conduct of public policy.

Part Two

The Formation
of Counterpart Categories
and the New Structure

Prologue II
Counterpart Categories

By definition, a theoretical system formed to describe the social order must attend to the way of life, worldview, and definition of the social entity that it puts forth. By "way of life" or "worldview," however, no two systems need mean—or even refer to—exactly the same category of data. Moreover, the constituent categories need not be functionally equivalent, which for obvious reasons would be as irrelevant as the judgment of relativism. This last claim forms an excuse for differences among systems, not a reason. It does not explain why one system sets forth its way of life by selecting data of one kind, whereas another chooses data of a completely different order for the same purpose, which is the kind of systemic comparison at stake here. Also at stake are the description, analysis, and interpretation of systems on their own and (in the case of systems that prove continuous in their canonical expression) in relationship with one another. For that purpose, the claim that "this functioned in system A as that functioned in system B" proves simply irrelevant.

Let me restate matters as I think a rigorous definition requires. A system selects its data to expose its systemic categories; it defines its categories in accord with the systemic statement that it wishes to set forth; and it identifies the urgent question(s) to which the systemic message compellingly responds. To understand a system, we begin with the whole and work our way inward toward the parts; the formation of categories then is governed by the system's requirements: the rationality of the whole dictates the structure of the categorical parts, and the structure of the parts then governs the selection of what fits into those categories.[1]

Now that I have shown the philosophical character of the initial system's worldview, way of life, and theory of the social entity (that is, its philosophy, economics, and politics), I ask how these same categories fared in the successor system's documentary evidence. As a matter of simple fact, although sharing the goal of presenting a theory of the social order, the initial, philosophical Judaic system and the successor system differ in a fundamental way as to their categorical formations and structures. Stated very simply, the successor system held up a mirror to the received categories and so redefined matters that everything was reversed. Left became right, down became up, and as I shall show, in a very explicit transvaluation of values, power was turned into weakness and things of real value were transformed into intangibles. This transvaluation, which altogether transforms the prior system, is articulated and not left implicit; it is a specific judgment made concrete through mythic and symbolic revision by the later authorships.[2] A freestanding document, received with reverence, precipitated the transvaluation of all its own values.

The categorical transformation that was underway, which signaled the movement from philosophy to religion, surfaces in answering the following simple questions: Precisely what do the authorships of the successor documents, speaking not about the Mishnah but on their own account, mean by economics, politics, and philosophy? To what kinds of data do they refer when they speak of scarce resources and legitimate violence, and exactly how do they define correct modes of thought and expression, logic and rhetoric, and even the topical program worthy of sustained inquiry? These questions arise because the results of part 1 show that the received categories were in no way subjected to redefinition. The next three chapters answer these questions.

The components of the initial category formations were examined thoughtfully and carefully, paraphrased and augmented and clarified, but the received categories were not continued, not expanded, and not renewed. Merely preserved intact, as they had been handed on, the received categories hardly encompass all the points of emphasis and sustained development that characterize the successor documents—or, as a matter of fact, any of them. On the contrary, when the framers of the Yerushalmi, for one example, moved out from the exegesis of the Mishnah passages, they left behind the topics of paramount interest in the Mishnah and developed altogether other categories.[3] The framers of the successor system defined their own counterparts in these other categories. These counterpart categories redefined matters while following the main outlines of the structure of the social order manifest in the initial system. The counterpart categories set forth an account of the social order just as the ones of the Mishnah's framers did, but they defined the social order in very different terms. That redefinition exposes the transformation of the received system, and the traits of the new system fall into the classification of not philosophy but religion.

The successor thinkers did not continue and expand the categorical repertoire but instead set forth a categorically fresh vision of the social order—a way of life, worldview, and definition of the social entity—with appropriate counterpart categories. What is decisive is that these served, as did the initial categories, within the generative categorical structure definitive for all Judaic systems. So there was a category corresponding to the generative component of worldview, but it was not philosophical; another corresponding to the required component setting forth a way of life, but in the conventional and accepted definition of economics it was not an economics; and finally, a category to define the social entity "Israel," which any Judaic system must explain, but in the accepted sense of a politics it was not politics.

Addressing the issues ordinarily treated by the method and message of philosophy, economics, or politics, the counterpart categories nonetheless supplied for the social order a worldview, way of life, and definition of the social entity. Indeed, the Judaism that emerged from late antiquity adopted as its categorical structure the counterpart categories I will define and explore, recasting the Mishnah within them. The transformation of Judaism, therefore, from an essentially philosophical account of the social order to a fundamentally religious one was accomplished by the system builders whose conceptions came to literary expression in the Talmud of the Land of Israel, Genesis Rabbah, Leviticus Rabbah, and Pesiqta deRab Kahana. In so stating, alas, I have moved beyond my story.

Let me return to this process of category formation that yielded not a revision of the Mishnah's modes of philosophical thought and proposition—its philosophy, philosophical economics, and philosophical politics—but an entirely new categorical structure: mode of thought, definition of scarce resources, and conception of the social entity. Exactly how was this categorical re-formation accomplished? To state matters first in the most abstract way, it was done by reversing the direction of the attribution, specifically, by taking the predicate of a proposition and moving it to the position of the subject, that is, commencing not from subject but from predicate. From "economics is the rational disposition of scarce resources," the category of way of life was rephrased as "the rational disposition of scarce resources is (a given system's) economics."

The reverse reading therefore yields the counterpart category, defined by this sentence: a (any) theory of rational action with regard to scarcity is (for the system at hand) its economics. The same procedure serves, *mutatis mutandis,* for discerning the later systems' politics and science, learning, or philosophy. Precisely what the framers worked out as their economics, politics, and philosophy is laid out in this part of the book, and the result, as the third part of this book will show, was a quite new system. This transvaluation of values, not merely the re-formation but the utter transformation of categories, set forth an essentially fresh answer to a fundamentally new urgent question. But here, the answer is the main point of interest.

Let me make more concrete this matter of the reverse definition of economics, placing the predicate as the subject. Previously, I claimed that the Judaism of the Mishnah presents a theory of economics because it addresses the definition of rational action with regard both to the allocation of scarce resources and to the increase and disposition of wealth. It was a specifically philosophical economics because, in structure and in doctrine, it conformed with that of Aristotle. Now the question is what the successor system means by "scarce resources" and how to define the rationality it requires for the disposition of such resources. When I say "a (or any) theory of rational action with regard to scarcity *is* (an) economics," I mean any account of what is deemed to be scarce and therefore to require rational action as to allocation, increase, and disposition—functions defining the successor system's category that is the counterpart to economics in the philosophical system of the Mishnah. It answers the same question, but it utterly recasts the terms of the question.

Why have I found it necessary to invent the conception of a counterpart category? The results of part 1 compel a consideration of what, in the successor documents, constitutes an economics, politics, mode of thought, and worldview. My premise is that a religious theory of the social order will comprise an account of a way of life, a worldview, and the social entity that realizes the one and explains itself by appeal to the other. In the Mishnah, as in other philosophical systems, the way of life finds definition in economics, the worldview in philosophy (both as to method and as to proposition), and the account of the social entity in a politics. That is simply not the case in the successor documents, however, and what serve as way of life, worldview, and definition of the social entity in no way conform to what had defined these same categories.

That fact is hardly surprising, for as I have already noted, there are quite elaborate and well-composed systems of the social order that, though they fully spell out a way of life, a worldview, and a definition of the social entity, simply have no economics at all in the received and accepted sense of economics as a theory of the rational disposition of scarce resources. Augustine's design and account in *The City of God*, for example, which I shall briefly discuss in chapter 9, introduces its own categories in response to the same requirements of definition and articulation of the social order. The history of salvation deriving from the Christian Bible, for instance, forms the critical center, and philosophy, while profoundly influencing Augustine's thought, hardly generates the primary categorical structures. Indeed, in their first twelve hundred years, Christian system builders found it entirely possible to set forth the Christian social order's way of life without defining an economics for themselves.[4]

It does not follow that for failing to present an economics, accounts of the social order do not define a way of life. To the contrary, when they do define a way of life in terms of scarce resources, what they mean is not what we ordinarily mean by economics. True, such systems omit all reference to such topics as wealth and money, production and distribution, work and wage, ownership and conduct of economics entities, or else they treat them as systemically inert and inconsequential. The entire repertoire of subjects constituting economic action in all its forms simply is lacking. But the issues of tangible wealth and material goods do emerge — must emerge — and it follows that the systems must identify for themselves something other than real wealth (real estate or capital, for instance) when they design those societies that express the respective systems' messages: urgent question, self-evidently valid answer, integrating the whole and rendering the system cogent and coherent.

The question remains of how to deal with accounts of the social order that lack an economics, politics, or a philosophy in the familiar senses of these categories. To answer that methodological question in the analysis of category formation, I have to discover and define what in the nonphilosophical system plays the role that economics plays in a philosophical system. To do so—as stated in abstract form just now— I propose the notion that "a (any) theory of rational action with regard to scarcity *is* economics." Matters that hardly fall into the category of economic theory may yet yield points of congruency; as a matter of fact, they may also validate those systemic comparisons and contrasts that indicate the history of an ongoing system from its philosophical to its religious formulation. I will justify all these claims by showing that the authorships of the successor systems recognized and selected the principal symbolic expression of a received category and turned it on its head: land becomes Torah learning, and that is made explicit in one stunning instance. It is not merely my post facto reading of one system as a reversal of a prior one that has yielded the counterpart category, but the documents themselves.

Let me now spell out why I find this two-directional reading critical— first, "*economics is* (or encompasses) the theory of rational action with regard to scarcity"; second, "a theory of rational action with regard to scarcity *is encompassed by economics*," To state matters negatively, if one system presents a conventional economics and another does not, then I cannot compare the one to the other (beyond the observation that one has an economics and the other does not). On the positive side, if I can show how one body of coherent thought in one system addresses the same question that another body of equally coherent thought takes up in the other, then I can compare the two systems at the point not of detail but of the main beams of structure. The sole undemonstrated premise is that any system must explain in its account of the social order what people are to think and do and how they are to define themselves as a social entity, but the very phrase *social order* comprises these three components: society and order in both intellect and practice. So at stake is the comparison of systems.

In this context, by the comparison of system I mean the contrast of one rationality to another.[5] The comparison of rationalities then is made possible by the dual and reciprocal definition of economics as the theory of rational action with regard to scarcity and of the theory of rational action with regard to scarcity as economics. The same is so, of course, for philosophy and politics.[6] Understanding the particular rationality of the economics of—to take the case at hand—the Judaism of the Mishnah provides a way to translate into intelligible categories of rationality that Judaism's (to us) familiar category with the (to us) alien and odd rationality of the Yerushalmi's counterpart, which, as I shall show, covers matters we do not conceive to fall under the rubric of economics at all but that answered the same questions to which, for us and the philosophical economics of the Mishnah, economics attends.

Thus, to see that a category in an alien system and its rationality constitutes *its* economics and therefore forms a counterpart to economics within a different rationality is to learn how to translate from system to system for a critical component. This justifies statements like "In that system, within its rationality, that category of activity forms a component of economic theory, whereas in this system, within its rationality, that category of activity is not considered a component of economic theory at all." And this does not require a posture of relativism, for example, claiming that one economics and its associated rationality is pretty much the same, or as at least as valid, as another. Framing the relativist judgment in that way, it is simply not relevant to what is at stake. That kind of interpretation of matters is not pertinent to my exercise in translation and comparison carried out through the definition and examination of counterpart categories.

Part 2 begins with the systemic counterpart to philosophy, then proceeds to economics, and concludes with politics, following the order of part 1. My first task is to follow the categorical formation of a new worldview generated by the received mode of thought, a worldview that fundamentally differed from the philosophical one at every point.

Notes

1. None of these points intersects with either relativism or functionalism; the issues are wholly other. After all, at stake in systemic description, analysis, and interpretation is ultimately the comparative study of rationalities, but this conclusion carries us far beyond the argument of this part of the book — and, indeed, of the book as a whole.

2. I underline that fact, for all that follows on the transvaluation of values through the formation of what I have invented as "counterpart categories" appeals to explicit statements, not a very general, post facto observation on my part.

3. That fact is demonstrated in my *Talmud of the Land of Israel: A Preliminary Translation and Explanation* (Chicago: University of Chicago

Press, 1983), vol. 35, *Introduction: Taxonomy.* There I show that when Mishnah exegesis is concluded, a quite separate agendum takes center stage, the emphases of which find no counterpart in the Mishnah. That seems to me to justify the consideration of counterpart categories such as I introduce here.

4. As with the sages of Judaism, so with the first important Christian economics. It was the encounter with Aristotle (and not with Scripture) that made urgent the formation of a Christianity encompassing, for the way of life of its social order, elaborate attention to the expression of theological truth in economics and rules for the Christian management and preservation of scarce resources, defined in the conventional sense of philosophical economics.

5. I allude to the great conception of Max Weber in his studies of China, India, and ancient Israel. In asking why capitalism here and not there he founded the comparative study of rationalities. Many present themselves as his successors, some with more reason than others, but in the aggregate, I have not found a rich theoretical literature that vastly revises Weber's definition of issues. In this regard philosophy has gone far beyond the limits of theory in social science.

6. Would I extend the matter to, let us say, medicine, technology, city planning, mathematics, the provision of a water supply, a department of defense, or any of the other diverse components of the social order and its culture, whether intellectual or institutional? At this moment, I should have to decline an invitation to descend into such unbounded relativism, for then everything is the equivalent of something, and nothing is to be defined in itself. For the moment I leave matters at the basic components of any and all social orders, as I have identified them.

4
Learning and the Category Torah

In the Mishnah's system Torah serves as a taxic indicator, that is, the status of Torah is distinct from other (lower) status, for example, Torah teaching in contradistinction to scribal teaching.[1] By contrast, the category formation attested in the successor documents confers the status of the Torah on what the sage says. It is Torah *because the sage is Torah incarnate.* Knowledge of the Torah yields power over this world and the next, the capacity to coerce to the sage's will the natural and supernatural worlds alike. The Torah is thus transformed from a philosophical enterprise of sifting and classifying mundane facts into a gnostic process of changing persons through knowledge. It is on that basis that I claim the Torah to be, in the Yerushalmi and related writings, the counterpart category to philosophy in the Mishnah.

This is a new intellectual category: Torah, meaning religious learning *in place of* philosophical learning. What is the difference between the two? First, the former appeals to revealed truth, the latter to perceived facts of nature and their regularities; second, unlike the latter, the former conceives of an other-worldly source of explanation and develops a propositional program focused not on nature but on Scripture and not on nations in general but on Israel in particular; and third, the former gnosticizes knowledge in the conception that knowing works salvation, whereas the latter rationalizes knowledge.

The Mishnah's characteristic philosophical modes of thought, which use list making to discover rules of data classification yielding the hierarchical classification of all things, also characterize the logical and even rhetorical program of the documents that set forth the successor system. What was to change, therefore, was not the mode of thought. After all, *Listenwissenschaft* had characterized intellectual life in the

Near and Middle East for three thousand years, reaching its apex with Aristotle's natural philosophy.[2] What was new, rather, were the propositions to be demonstrated philosophically, and what made these propositions new were the focus of interest and data assembled by way of demonstrating them. The focus moved from a philosophical proposition within the framework of freestanding philosophy of religion and metaphysics that the Mishnah's system aimed to establish to religious and even theological propositions within the setting of contingent exegesis of Scripture.

What shows that what was changing was not merely topical and propositional but *categorical* in character? The answer lies in the symbolic vocabulary that was commonly used in the late fourth- and fifth-century writings but not used at all, or not in the same way, in the late second-century ones. When people select data not formerly taken into account and represent the data by appeal to symbols not formerly found evocative or expressive, or not utilized in the way in which they later on were used, then—so I claim—we are justified in raising questions about category formation and the development of new categories alongside, or instead of, the received ones. In the case at hand, the character of the transformation is shown by the formation of a symbol to represent a category, and that is not a matter of subjective judgment, for the explicit substitution of one category for another category, one symbol for another symbol, is right on the surface.

To signal what is to come, the successor system contains the quite bald statement that, in comparing the value of capital (which in this time and place meant land or real property) and Torah, Torah is worthwhile and land is not—a symbolic syllogism that is explicit, concrete, repeated, and utterly fresh. On the basis of that quite explicit symbolic comparison I speak of transformation—symbolic and therefore *categorical* transformation, not merely thematic shifts in emphasis or even propositional change. That is why I hold that the successor writings exhibit the formation of a system connected with, but asymmetrical to, the initial, philosophical one. For the worldview of the transformed Judaism, the counterpart category to philosophy is formulated by appeal to the symbolic medium for the theological message, and it is the category of the Torah expressed by the symbol of *Torah*.[3]

Let me deal first with what continued, for the continuities justify my interpretation of these phenomena as the transformation of a received system and structure, not the invention of an altogether new one. That the Yerushalmi, Genesis Rabbah, Leviticus Rabbah, and Pesiqta deRab Kahana carried forward and maintained connections with the initial writings, the Mishnah and the Tosefta, is shown not merely by the literary character of the later writings, framed as they were as commentaries on the earlier ones. A much more important connection is established by the paramount role that philosophical modes of thought play in all of them. The successor documents continued the work of comparing and contrasting species in quest of the genus and the rule governing that genus, but their inquiry led them in directions not contemplated by the framers of the system portrayed in part by the Mishnah—at least, so far as the Mishnah, their end product, tells us. It moreover produced results concerning a set of issues not considered in the Mishnah and its related writings. The persistence of list making shows how the intellects whose system is adumbrated in the Yerushalmi, Genesis Rabbah, Leviticus Rabbah, and Pesiqta de Rab Kahana remained well within the received modes of thought,[4] but what they learned about how to think did not dictate to them the program for reflection. The propositions of their documents, shown in particular in the Midrash compilations, indicate that the formation of a category counterpart to the philosophical one had gotten underway.

Proceeding from modes of thought to message and only then to the categorical formation at hand, I start with the matter of list making. List making places on display the data of the like and the unlike and (ordinarily) implicitly conveys the rule. The authorship assumes that once a series is established the governing rule will be perceived, which explains why, in exposing the interior logic of its authorship's intellect, the Mishnah had to be a book of lists, with the implicit order, the nomothetic traits of a monothetic order, dictating the ordinarily unstated general and encompassing rule. The purpose of list making in the Mishnah is to make a single statement, endless times over, and to repeat in a mass of tangled detail precisely the same fundamental judgment. To form their lists, the framers of the Mishnah appealed solely to the traits of things. Establishing a set of shared traits that form a rule compelling a given conclusion, Mishnaic list makers assembled probative facts to derive from the classification of data whatever conclusions they reached.

As an example of the mode of thought characteristic to the writings of the successor system, Leviticus Rabbah argues in behalf of a given proposition through an argument based on accumulation of facts, all classified in the same way to make the same point. These examples, drawn from Scripture, form the counterpart to the facts concerning the natural world that yield, in the Mishnah, propositions of hierarchical classification ascending toward the One (God) that dominate in the Mishnah. Lists of examples deriving from Scripture provide an entirely logical—because factual—demonstration. The proposition is a simple one: if X, then Y; if not X, then not Y. If Israel carries out its obligations, then God will redeem Israel; if not, then God will not redeem but will punish Israel. That simple commonplace is given numerous illustrations.

An example of the proposition demonstrated by facts is that Israel in times past repented, so God saved them. Israel in times past sinned, so God punished them. Another proposition is that God loves the humble and despises the haughty; therefore, God saves the humble and punishes the haughty. Let me give one example of how, in the Midrash compilations of the late fourth and fifth centuries, the mode of compiling lists of data that bear shared taxonomic traits serves to demonstrate propositions. The proposition to be proved in the following composition is that the third day marks the salvific occasion, with the further implication that salvation comes at the end of a series of three. The mode of argument, which is what is pertinent here, is the familiar one of presenting a variety of facts that point to the same conclusion, and, in context, only to that conclusion.

Genesis Rabbah LVI:I

1A. "*On the third day Abraham lifted up his eyes and saw the place afar off*" (Gen. 22:4):

B. "*After two days he will revive us, on the third day he will raise us up, that we may live in his presence*" (Hos. 16:2).

C. On the third day of the tribes: "*And Joseph said to them on the third day, 'This do and live'*" (Gen. 42:18).

D. On the third day of the giving of the Torah: "*And it came to pass on the third day when it was morning*" (Exod. 19:16).

E. On the third day of the spies: "*And hide yourselves there for three days*" (Josh. 2:16).

F. On the third day of Jonah: "*And Jonah was in the belly of the fish three days and three nights*" (Jonah 2:1).

G. On the third day of the return from the Exile: "*And we abode there three days*" (Ezra 8:32).

H. On the third day of the resurrection of the dead: "*After two days he will revive us, on the third day he will raise us up, that we may live in his presence*" (Hos. 16:2).

I. On the third day of Esther: "*Now it came to pass on the third day that Esther put on her royal apparel*" (Esther 5:1).

J. She put on the monarchy of the house of her fathers.

K. On account of what sort of merit?

L. Rabbis say, "On account of the third day of the giving of the Torah."

M. R. Levi said, "It is on account of the merit of the third day of Abraham: '*On the third day Abraham lifted up his eyes and saw the place afar off*'" (Gen. 22:4).

2A. "*. . . lifted up his eyes and saw the place afar off*" (Gen. 22:4):

B. What did he see? He saw a cloud attached to the mountain. He said, "It would appear that that is the place concerning which the Holy One, blessed be He, told me to offer up my son."

The third day marks the fulfillment of the promise of the resurrection of the dead at the end of time and of Israel's redemption at appropriate moments. The reference to the third day at Genesis 22:2 then invokes the entire panoply of Israel's history.

Another commonplace mode of argument may be noted. If one condition is met, the other will come about. This too is set forth with its corpus of examples, which in context form demonstrations, and the whole is given the form of the list, that is, example after example of a single proposition. The thirty-seven *parashiyyot* of Leviticus Rabbah thus form the counterpart to the lists that defined the labor of the Mishnah's philosophers; a nomothetic definitive trait serves to demonstrate the rules that apply throughout. Although the rules in this case concern the social life, rather than the natural world on which so much of the Mishnah (for example, the Division of Purities) concentrates, the mode of thought is consistent. For the Midrash compilations that shared method appeals to the rhetoric of joining distinct examples by the use of "another matter" (in Hebrew, *davar-aher;* hence, the *davar-aher* construction). Sequences of comments on the same verse joined by "another matter" mean to establish compositions of taxically joined facts, that is, lists. To recognize that obvious fact is to be drawn back to the Mishnah's method, which is also that of list making.

Thus, the mode of thought common to both the Mishnah and the later Midrash compilations hardly suggests the formation of a counterpart category whose message, medium, and especially symbolic formulation differ markedly from the philosophical category that the Mishnah sets forth. As a matter of fact, evidence for the formation of that counterpart category comes, to begin with, from vast differences in propositional program; only at the end of this investigation can the differences in the symbolic formulation of the counterpart category be seen. The results of learning accomplished through list making in the philosophical setting of the Mishnah vastly differ from those of the same method of learning worked out in the theological setting of the Midrash compilations of the fourth and fifth centuries. So let me now ask how the successor documents used familiar methods to yield a new message. And, not forgetting my thesis, I also must indicate the basis on which I characterize that new message as not philosophical but religious.

In the Mishnah, philosophy yields a system concerning the orderly classification of things, whereas in the Midrash compilations, the same modes of thought yield propositions of fixed truth about God and God's relationship with Israel. However diverse the language and however original the arrangement of the relevant data, now drawn from Scripture rather than from nature, the message is uniform throughout, articulated essentially through the repetition in marginally different theological "things" of the same thing: *davar-aher* stands for "another matter" that is in fact the same matter. So the same method of learning is used for different purposes, the one philosophical, systematizing the evidence of nature, the other religious in substance, if not theological in structure,[5] recapitulating the evidence of supernature revealed by God in the Torah.[6]

The propositional programs of Leviticus Rabbah, Genesis Rabbah, and Pesiqta deRab Kahana set forth on the basis of facts of not nature but Scripture propositions of a religious, rather than a philosophical, character. Why the difference? Philosophy generalizes and aims at classification of all data in a single way, accounting for exceptions, but only by appeal to appropriate rules to explain exceptions. Religion, however—at least in the present case—concerns itself with integrating the traits of a single category, for example, a unique social entity, a holy and therefore separate and different way of life, a revealed worldview not to be discovered within the facts of nature but only through the data of supernature, supernaturally revealed (in the case of a Judaism). Accordingly, instead of dealing with the nature of things, these not philosophical and general but religious and particular propositions deal with the special traits of Israel, setting forth not how humanity in general conducts itself or how nature in general is structured but the rules particular to the holy people in its holy way of life. The emerging worldview pertains to only the theologically identified social entity, Israel, and it follows that Israel is no longer a taxic indicator that distinguishes diverse species of a common genus but is a social entity *sui generis*.[7] Let me now rapidly survey the propositions that a synthetic reading of the several documents may yield.

In the writings under examination, philosophy sought the generalizations that cases might yield, as did religion (and, later, theology), but the range of generalization vastly differed. Philosophy spoke of the nature of things, whereas theology represented the special nature of Israel in particular. Philosophy appealed to the traits of things; theology, to the special indicative qualities of Israel. In Leviticus Rabbah, for example, the framers systematically adopted for themselves and adapted to their own circumstance the reality of the Scripture, its history and doctrines. They transformed that history from a sequence of one-time events, leading from one place to some other, into the fixtures of the enduring tableau of an ever-present mythic world. That is what I mean by generalizing on the basis of particular cases: persons who lived once now operate forever; events take on that trait of recurrence, circularity, or replicability that allows them to happen again and again, every day, all because events are seen to yield rules, and the rules apply throughout: philosophical mode of thought, but religious proposition.

No longer was there one Moses, one David, one set of happenings of a distinctive and never-to-be-repeated character. Whatever events the framers of the successor system proposed to discuss must be entered and absorbed into that established and ubiquitous pattern and structure founded in Scripture. One-time history is therefore transformed into all-time social structure. It is not that biblical history repeats itself or is turned from a one-way path into a cyclical system; rather, biblical history no longer constitutes history as a story of things that happened once, long ago, and pointed to some one moment in the future but becomes an account of things that happen every day—hence, an ever-present mythic world, or, in anachronistic terms, history turned into social science.

The organizing rhetoric carries the same message. The verses that are quoted ordinarily shift from the meanings they convey to the implications they contain, speaking about something, anything, other than what they seem to be saying. What the sages of the system adumbrated by Leviticus Rabbah proposed was a reconstruction of existence along the lines of the ancient design—the social rules—of Scripture as they read it. What that meant was that everything that happened was turned from a sequence of one-time and linear events into a repetition of known and already experienced paradigms, hence, a mythic being. The source and core of the myth derive from Scripture—Scripture reread, renewed, and reconstructed along with the society that revered Scripture. In an exact sense, these sages were engaged in a labor of natural history: classifying data, forming species, and re-forming species into genera. By treating history as social science, the successor system produced a kind of natural history that was counterpart to the Mishnah's natural philosophy. That explains the movement to Scripture as the organizing structure, for Scripture was history and dictated the contents of history, laying forth the structures of time, the rules that prevailed and were made known in events.

A category requires structure and order, so I must identify the lines of structure of the counterpart category in process. The principal lines of structure flow along the borders with the world beyond: Israel's relationships with others. These are horizontal (with other nations) and vertical (with God), but from the viewpoint of the framers of the document the relationships form a single, seamless web, for Israel's vertical relationships dictate the horizontals as well: when God wishes to punish Israel, the other nations do the work. In contrasting philosophy, with its concern for generalization and classification and its reading of "Israel" as a taxic indicator, to religion, with its interest in the distinctive, the specific, and the special, this is precisely the result to be expected: the turning from a horizontal perspective on everybody in the same way to a vertical vision of Israel seen from above, all by itself.

Moreover, the relationships that define Israel prove dynamic in that they respond to the movement of the Torah through Israel's history. When the Torah governs, then the vertical relationship is stable and felicitous and the horizontal one secure; when not, God obeys the rules and the nations obey God.

So the first and paramount category takes shape within the themes associated with the national life of Israel. The principal lines of structure flow along the fringe, namely, Israel's relationships with others, but the relationships form a single, seamless web, for Israel's vertical relationships dictate the horizontals as well. Finally, the relationships that define Israel prove dynamic in their response to the movement of the Torah through Israel's history.

What of the propositional program that the document sets forth? The Mishnah's philosophical program used the facts and traits of things to demonstrate the hierarchical order of all being, with the obvious if merely implicit proposition that God stands at the head of the social order. The religious propositions of the successor documents speak in other words of other things, having simply nothing in common with the propositional program of the Mishnah's philosophy. For Leviticus Rabbah, for example, the principal propositions are these: God loves Israel, so he gave its people the Torah, which defines their life and governs their welfare. Israel is alone in its category (*sui generis*), so what is a virtue to Israel is a vice to the other nations and what is life giving to Israel is poison to the gentiles. True, Israel sins, but God forgives that sin, having punished the nation on account of it. Such a process has yet to end, but it will culminate in Israel's complete regeneration. Meanwhile, Israel's assurance of God's love lies in the many expressions of God's special concern for even the humblest and most ordinary aspects of the national life: the food the nation eats and the sexual practices by which it procreates. These life-sustaining, life-transmitting activities draw God's special interest as a mark of his general love for Israel. Israel, then, is supposed to achieve its life in conformity with the marks of God's love. These indications also signify the character of Israel's difficulty, namely, subordination to the nations in general, but to the fourth kingdom, Rome, in particular. Both food laws and skin diseases stand for the nations. There is yet another, social category of sin that is collective and generates collective punishment. The moral character of Israel's life, the people's treatment of one another, the practice of gossip and small-scale thuggery—these too draw down divine penalty. The nation's fate therfore corresponds to its moral condition. The moral condition, however, emerges not only from the current generation. Israel's richest hope lies in the merit of the ancestors and thus in the scriptural record of the merits attained by the founders of the nation, those who originally brought it into being and gave it life.

The world to come is portrayed so as to restate these same propositions. Merit overcomes sin, and doing religious duties or super-erogatory acts of kindness will win merit for the nation that does them. Israel will be saved at the end of time, and the age or world to follow will be exactly opposite to this one. Much that exists in the account of Israel's national life, which is worked out through the definition of the liminal relationships, recurs in slightly altered form in the picture of the world to come. The world to come will right all presently unbalanced relationships; what is good will go forward, and what is bad will come to an end. The simple message is that the things people revere, the cult and its majestic course through the year, will go on: Jerusalem will come back, so will the Temple, both in all their glory. Israel will be saved through the merit of the ancestors, atonement, study of Torah, and practice of religious duties. The prevalence of the eschatological dimension at the formal structures, with its messianic and other expressions, here finds its counterpart in the repetition of the same few symbols in the expression of doctrine. The theme of the moral life of Israel produces propositions concerning not only the individual but, more important, the social virtues that the community as a whole must exhibit.

This brings me to the laws of society for Israel's holy community as the authorship of Leviticus Rabbah set forth those laws. In this context, the message to the individual constitutes a revision of the address to the nation: humility as against arrogance, obedience as against sin, constant concern not to follow the natural inclination to do evil or to overcome the natural limitations of the human condition. Israel must accept its fate, obeying its laws and relying on both the merits accrued through the ages and God's special love. Both the individual in his ordinary affairs and great men and women, that is, individual heroes, must conform to this paradigm of patience and submission, exemplifying the national virtues. Among the latter, Moses stands out; he has no equal. The special position of the humble Moses is complemented by the patriarchs and by David, all of whom knew how to please God and left as an inheritance to Israel the merit they had thereby attained.

As for further recurring themes or topics, there is one so common-place that a complete list of its occurrences would include the majority of paragraphs of discourse. It is an exercise in *Listenwissenschaft,* such as occurs in the Mishnah, but what is listed is not a taxonomy of traits of the natural world but rather the catalog of events in Israel's history, meaning in this context Israel's history in scriptural times down through the return to Zion. The one-time events of the generation of the Flood; Sodom and Gomorrah; the patriarchs and the sojourn in Egypt; the Exodus; the revelation of the Torah at Sinai; the golden calf; the Davidic monarchy and the building of the Temple; Sennacherib, Hezekiah, and the destruction of northern Israel; Nebuchadnezzar and the destruction of the Temple in 586 B.C.E.; the life of Israel in Babylonian captivity; Daniel and his associates; Mordecai and Haman—these individuals and events occur over and over again, serving as paradigms of sin and atonement, steadfastness and divine intervention, and equivalent lessons. In fact, there is a fairly standard repertoire of scriptural heroes or villains, on the one side, and conventional lists of Israel's enemies and their actions and downfall, on the other. The boastful, for instance, include the generation of the flood, Sodom and Gomorrah, Pharoah, Sisera, Sennacherib, Nebuchadnezzar, and the wicked empire (Rome), which is contrasted to Israel, "despised and humble in this world." The four kingdoms recur again and again, always ending with Rome and the repeated message that after Rome will come Israel. But Israel has to make this happen through its faith and submission to God's will. Lists of enemies repeatedly refer to Cain, the Sodomites, Pharoah, Sennacherib, Nebuchadnezzar, and Haman.

Accordingly, the mode of thought brought to bear on the theme of history remains exactly the same as before: list making, with data exhibiting similar taxonomic traits drawn together into lists based on common monothetic traits or definitions. In the Mishnah, *Listenwissenschaft* yields a composition of natural philosophy; in the successor documents, one of natural history. The lists in Leviticus Rabbah make a single enormous point through the power of repetition: they prove a social law of history. The catalogs of exemplary heroes and historical events serve a further purpose, however, providing a model of how contemporary events are to be absorbed into the biblical paradigm. Because biblical events exemplify recurrent happenings—sin and redemption, forgiveness and atonement—they lose their one-time character. At the same time and in the same way, current events find a place within the ancient but eternally present paradigmatic scheme. Thus, other than exemplary episodes in the lives of heroes, no new historical events demand narration because the framers of Leviticus Rabbah could discuss what was happening in their times through what was said about the past. This mode of dealing with biblical history and contemporary events produces two reciprocal effects. The first is the mythicization of biblical stories, their removal from the framework of ongoing, unique patterns of history and sequences of events and their transformation into accounts of things that happen all the time. The second is the generalization of contemporary events and their placement within the paradigmatic framework of established mythic existence. So (1) the Scripture's myth happens every day, and (2) every day produces reenactment of the Scripture's myth.

Israel is God's special love, and that love is shown in a simple way. Israel's present condition of subordination derives from its own deeds. It follows that God cares, so Israel may look forward to redemption on God's part in response to Israel's own regeneration through repentance. When the exegetes proceeded to open the scroll of Leviticus, they found numerous occasions to state that proposition in concrete terms and specific contexts. The sinner brings on his own sickness, but God heals through that very ailment. The nations of the world govern in heavy succession, but Israel's lack of faith guaranteed their rule and its moment of renewal will end it. Israel's leaders—priests, prophets, and kings—fall into an entirely different category from those of the nations, as much as does Israel. In these and other concrete allegations, the same classical message comes forth. Accordingly, at the foundations of the pretense lies the long-standing biblical-Jewish insistence that Israel's sorry condition in no way testifies to Israel's true worth—the grandest pretense of all. All the little evasions of the primary sense in favor of some other testify to this, the great denial that what counts is what is. Leviticus Rabbah makes that statement with art and imagination, but it is never subtle about saying so.

Salvation and sanctification join together in Leviticus Rabbah, which takes the laws of the book of Leviticus, focused as they are on the sanctification of the nation through its cult, to indicate the rules of salvation as well. The message of Leviticus Rabbah treats the book of Leviticus as if it had come from prophecy and addressed the issue of the meaning of history and Israel's salvation, but the book of Leviticus came from the priesthood and speaks of sanctification. The paradoxical syllogism—the as-if reading, the opposite of how things seem—of the composers of Leviticus Rabbah therefore reaches simple formulation. The very setting of sanctification ensures the promise of salvation. The topics of the cult and the priesthood expose the national and social issues of the moral life and redemptive hope of Israel. The

repeated comparison and contrast of priesthood and prophecy, sanctification and salvation, produce a complement that comes to most
perfect union in the text at hand.

The focus of Leviticus Rabbah and its laws of history is on the
society of Israel, its national fate and moral condition. Indeed, nearly
all of the *parashiyyot* of Leviticus Rabbah deal with the national, social
condition of Israel in three contexts: (1) Israel's setting in the history
of the nations; (2) the sanctified character of the inner life of Israel
itself; and (3) the future, salvific history of Israel. Thus, the biblical
book that deals with the holy Temple is shown to address the holy
people. Leviticus really discusses not the consecration of the cult but
the sanctification of the nation—its conformity to God's will laid forth
in the Torah and to God's rules. Reviewing the document as a whole,
therefore, in pursuit of the something else that the base text is supposed
to address, it turns out that the sanctification of the cult stands for
the salvation of the nation. The nation is like the cult, the ordinary
Israelite like the priest. The holy way of life lived through acts to
which merit accrues corresponds to the holy rites. The process of
metamorphosis is full, rich, and complete. When everything stands for
something else, the something else repeatedly turns out to be the nation.
This is what Leviticus Rabbah spells out in exquisite detail, yet never
missing the main point. It is in the context of that highly cogent message
that I shall ask whether Sifra sets forth any propositions, let alone a
cogent and stunning judgment as powerfully laid out as that in Leviticus
Rabbah. First, however, I must demonstrate that the treatment of the
book of Leviticus by the authorship of Leviticus Rabbah is particular
and significant, not simply a repetition of generally prevailing propositions in a singular context.

Lest readers suppose I present them with a series of one, I must also
ask whether Genesis Rabbah and Pesiqta deRab Kahana also point
toward the shape and structure of the successor system. In fact, the
mode of thought paramount in Leviticus Rabbah proves entirely congruent with the manner of reflection characteristic of Genesis Rabbah,
and the propositions concerning history and the social laws of Israel
are the same. If I had to point to the single most important proposition
of Genesis Rabbah, it would be the message of the meaning and end
of the life of the Jewish people that it expresses in the story of the
beginnings of creation, humanity, and Israel. This appeal to not history
but rule-making precedent runs parallel to the equivalent interest in

regularities in Leviticus Rabbah. Where the authorship of Genesis Rabbah differs is in the choice of the paradigm, which is now the age of beginnings; that choice leads to distinctive propositions that nevertheless prove quite congruent to those important in Leviticus Rabbah.

As the rules of Leviticus become the social laws of Israel's history in Leviticus Rabbah, so the particular tales of Genesis are turned into paradigms of social laws in Genesis Rabbah.[8] The deeds of the founders supply signals for the children about what will come in the future. Thus, the biographies of Abraham, Isaac, and Jacob constitute the paradigm by which to interpret the history of Israel later on. If the sages could announce a single syllogism and argue it systematically, that is the proposition on which they would insist. The sages understood that Genesis presents stories about the progenitors that define the human condition and proper conduct for their children, Israel, in time to come. Accordingly, they systematically asked Scripture to tell them how they were supposed to conduct themselves at the critical turnings of life. Let me briefly restate what I conceive to be the conviction of the framers of Genesis Rabbah about the message and meaning of the book of Genesis, as I might word matters:

> We now know what will be in the future. How do we know it? Just as Jacob had told his sons what would happen in time to come, just as Moses told the tribes their future, so we may understand the laws of history if we study the Torah. And in the Torah, we turn to beginnings: the rules as they were laid out at the very start of human history. These we find in the book of Genesis, the story of the origins of the world and of Israel. The Torah tells not only what happened but why. The Torah permits us to discover the laws of history. Once we know those laws, we may also peer into the future and come to an assessment of what is going to happen to us—and, especially, of how we shall be saved from our present existence. Because everything exists under the aspect of a timeless will, God's will, and all things express one thing, God's program and plan, in the Torah we uncover the workings of God's will. Our task as Israel is to accept, endure, submit, and celebrate.

In Genesis Rabbah the entire narrative of Genesis is construed so as to point toward the sacred history of Israel, the Jewish people: its slavery and redemption, its coming Temple in Jerusalem, and its exile and salvation at the end of time. The powerful message of Genesis in Genesis Rabbah proclaims that the world's creation commenced a single, straight line of events, leading in the end to the salvation of Israel and, through Israel, of all humanity. Israel's history constitutes the counterpart of creation, and the laws of Israel's salvation form the foundation of creation. Therefore, a given story out of Genesis (for example, about creation, or events from Adam to Noah and Noah to Abraham, or the domestic affairs of the patriarchs, or Joseph) bears a deeper message about what it means to be Israel, on the one side, and what will happen to Israel in the end of days, on the other.

The persistent program of religious inquiry into God's place in Israel's history thus requires sages to search in Scripture for the meaning for their own circumstance and for the condition of their people. The message of the meaning and end of the life of the Jewish people is supplied in the story of the beginnings of creation, humanity, and Israel. The deeds of the founders supply signals for the children about what will come in the future; the biographies of Abraham, Isaac, and Jacob constitute a protracted account of the history of Israel later on. If the sages could announce a single syllogism and argue it systematically, that is the proposition on which they would insist. The sages read the book of Genesis as if it portrayed the history of Israel and Rome. Why Rome in the form it takes in Genesis Rabbah? And why the obsessive character of the sages' disposition of the theme of Rome?

Were their picture merely of Rome as tyrant and destroyer of the Temple, there would be no reason to link the text to the problems of the age of redaction and closure. But Genesis Rabbah portrays Rome as Israel's brother, counterpart, and nemesis, Rome as the one thing standing in the way of Israel's, and the world's, ultimate salvation. So the stakes are different and much higher. It is not a political Rome but a Christian and messianic Rome that is at issue: Rome as surrogate for and obstacle to Israel. Why? It is because Rome at this time confronted Israel with a crisis, and, I argue, the program of Genesis Rabbah constitutes a response to that crisis. Rome in the fourth century became Christian. Sages responded by facing that fact quite squarely and saying, "Indeed, it is as you say, a kind of Israel, an heir of Abraham as your texts explicitly claim. But we remain the sole legitimate Israel, the bearer of the birthright—we and not you. So you are our brother: Esau, Ishmael, Edom." And the rest follows.

The authorship of Genesis Rabbah focuses its discourse on the proposition that the book of Genesis speaks to the life and historical condition of Israel, the Jewish people. Therefore, a given story will bear a deeper message about what it means to be Israel, on the one side, and what in the end of days will happen to Israel, on the other. And that is precisely the proposition endlessly represented by the authorship of Leviticus Rabbah. The subjects change, the point remains the same. This leaves the third compilation of Midrash exegeses adduced as evidence of the successor system, Pesiqta deRab Kahana, to be included in this account of the successor system's propositional program.

Pesiqta deRab Kahana is closely related to Leviticus Rabbah in that its authorship borrowed five *parashiyyot* from the earlier writing, but its framers moved beyond the appeal to scriptural history (as in Genesis Rabbah) or to scriptural case law (as in Leviticus Rabbah). Instead of inheriting propositions they set forth propositions entirely independent of the received Scripture and so produced their era's most uniformly theological compilation of Midrash exegeses, worked out in the modes of argument of philosophy and in the idiom of scriptural exegesis. In Pesiqta deRab Kahana I see three propositions, all religious and none philosophical within my previously stated definitions. The following discussion provides abstracts of the passages containing these propositions.

The first is that God loves Israel, that his love is unconditional, and that Israel's response to God must be obedience to the religious duties God has assigned, which will produce merit. Much of the argument for this proposition draws on the proof of history as laid out in Scripture and appeals to history transformed into paradigm. Israel's obedience to God is what will save Israel. Thus, Israel must observe the religious duties as required by the Torah, which is the mark of God's love for — and regeneration of — Israel. The tabernacle symbolizes the union of Israel and God. When Israel does what God asks above, Israel will prosper down below. If Israel remembers Amalek down below, God will remember Amalek up above and will wipe him out; a mark of Israel's loyalty to God is remembering Amalek. God does not require the animals that are sacrificed, for man could never match God's appetite, if that were the issue, but the savor pleases God (as a mark of Israel's loyalty and obedience). The first sheaf returns God's fair share of the gifts that God bestows on Israel, and those who give it to God benefit, whereas those who hold it back suffer. Observing religious duties, typified by the rites of the Festival, brings a great reward of the merit that ultimately leads to redemption. God's ways are just, righteous and merciful, as shown by God's concern that the offspring remain with the mother for seven days. God's love for Israel is so intense that he wants to hold its people back for an extra day after the Festival to spend more time with them, because, unlike the nations of the world, Israel knows how to please God. This is a mark of God's love for Israel.

The second proposition concerns not the ontology but the history of that *sui generis* social entity that is Israel: God is reasonable, and when Israel has been punished, it is in accord with God's rules. God forgives penitent Israel and is abundant in mercy. The good and the wicked die in exactly the same circumstance or condition. Laughter is vain because it is mixed with grief. A wise person will not expect too much joy, but when people suffer there ordinarily is a good reason for it. That is only one sign that God is reasonable and never did anything lawless and wrong to Israel or made unreasonable demands, and there was, therefore, no reason for Israel to lose confidence in God or to abandon him. God punished Israel, but this was done with reason. Nothing happened to Israel of which God did not give fair warning, and Israel's failure to heed the prophets brought about its fall. But God will forgive a faithful Israel: even though the Israelites sinned by making the golden calf, God forgave them and raised them up. On the New Year, God executes justice, but the justice is tempered with mercy. The rites of the New Year bring about divine judgment and also forgiveness because of the merit of the fathers. Israel must repent and return to the Lord, who is merciful and will forgive them for their sins. The penitential season of the New Year and Day of Atonement is the right time for confession and penitence, and God is sure to accept penitence. By exercising his power of mercy, the already merciful God grows still stronger in mercy.

The third proposition is that God will save Israel personally at a time and circumstance of his own choosing. While I take for granted that the hope for future redemption animates the other compilations, some of them, Sifra, for a prime example, show no evidence of an equivalent obsession with messianic questions. Israel may know what the future redemption will be like because of the redemption from Egypt. The paradox of the red cow—that what imparts uncleanness, namely, touching the ashes of the red cow, produces cleanness—is part of God's ineffable wisdom, which humanity cannot fathom. Only God can know the precise moment of Israel's redemption. That is something humanity cannot find out on its own, but God will certainly fulfill the predictions of the prophets about Israel's coming redemption. The Exodus from Egypt is the paradigm of the coming redemption. Israel has lost Eden but can yet come home and, with God's help, will. God's unique power is shown through Israel's unique suffering. God will redeem Israel in his own time. The lunar calendar, particular to Israel, marks Israel as favored by God, for the new moon signals the coming of Israel's redemption, and the particular new moon that will mark the actual event is that of Nisan. When God chooses to redeem Israel, Israel's enemies will have no power to stop him, for God will force Israel's enemies to serve Israel because of Israel's purity and loyalty to God. Israel's enemies are punished, and what they propose to do to Israel, God does to them. Both directly and through the prophets, God is the source of true comfort, which he will bring to Israel. Israel thinks that God has forsaken it, but it is Israel that forsook God; God's love has never failed and will never fail. Even though he has been angry, his mercy still is near, and God has the power and will to save Israel. God has designated the godly for himself and has already promised to redeem Israel. He will assuredly do so. God personally is the one who will comfort Israel. While Israel says there is no comfort, God will comfort Israel. Zion/Israel is like a barren woman, but Zion will bring forth children, and Israel will be comforted. Both God and Israel will bring light to Zion, which will give light to the world. The rebuilding of Zion will be a source of joy for the entire world, not for Israel alone. God will rejoice in Israel and Israel in God, like bride and groom.

There is a profoundly cogent statement made through the composition of this document, and this is the message of Pesiqta deRab Kahana: God loves Israel, his love is unconditional, and Israel's response to God must be obedience to the religious duties that God has assigned, which will produce merit. God is reasonable, and when Israel has been punished, it is in accord with God's rules. God forgives penitent Israel and is abundant in mercy. God will save Israel personally at a time and circumstance of his own choosing. Israel may know what the future redemption will be like because of the redemption from Egypt. Pesiqta deRab Kahana, therefore, has been so assembled as to exhibit a viewpoint or purpose of its particular authorship, one quite distinctive in its own context (if not in a single one of its propositions!) to its framers or collectors and arrangers. Why the authorship of Leviticus Rabbah did not concur in a general way I cannot say, but I cannot find these propositions in Leviticus Rabbah, which as I have shown presents its own points.[9] Both Pesiqta deRab Kahana and Leviticus Rabbah address issues of salvation, but I find the former's message of salvation couched in explicitly messianic terms, which is not the case in the latter. Indeed, the altogether different emphases in Sifré to Deuteronomy, Sifré to Numbers, and Sifra underscore the centrality in the Rabbah compilations of historical-salvific issues.

Enough has been said to show how the three Midrash compilations under scrutiny present propositions that, although consistent with the range of positions and attitudes of the Mishnah and the Tosefta, simply play no role whatsoever in those expressions of the initial system. By appealing to my initial definition of the difference between a philosophical and religious system,[10] I may bypass extensive reiteration of an obvious point, namely, that the successor writings concern themselves not with natural philosophy, yielding philosopy of religion, but with revealed truths—Scripture, in particular—yielding a religious account of the social order. It suffices to say simply that the single definitive difference between the philosophical system adumbrated by the Mishnah and the religious system to which these Midrash compilations attest lies in the rhetorical form, constant appeal to Scripture, and the propositional result, namely, rules that derive not from the nature of things, applying without differentiation to all of nature, but from the history of Israel, pertaining solely to Israel. I now must give sustained attention to my claim concerning the formation of a counterpart category, one that serves to portray a worldview just as philosophy does but that forms a category essentially different from the philosophical one.

If I ask the Mishnah for a verbal symbol for philosophy, the document remains dumb. Philosophy for the Mishnah serves as source of method and taxon of proposition, but the Mishnah's framers have no word for philosophy, natural science, learning, system, or any of my other analytical categories.[11] Nor, despite their formidable powers of abstraction in thought and expression, do they even set forth the abstract proposition concerning the hierarchical unity of being that in point of fact is their principal result. The Mishnah uses the symbol *Torah,* like *Israel,* only as a taxic indicator and not to convey more than it expresses; "Torah," with or without the definite article, with or without an initial capital, serves no symbolic functions and bears no symbolic valence. And there is, in the Mishnah, no other. Whatever single symbol captures the entirety of the Mishnah's message in the Mishnah's own language, it is not the symbol of Torah.[12]

By contrast, if I ask the Midrash compilations associated with the Yerushalmi to express, in a single word, the medium and the message that constitute their worldview, they have that word and use it constantly: it is the word *Torah*. It is the Torah that conveys the generative facts of learning; it is Torah, losing its definite article, that defines the range of truth. To grasp the re-presentation of Torah and *the* Torah in the successor writings is to be able to follow the outlines of the counterpart category that the new system uses to express its worldview in the way that the old one used philosophy. The very symbolization of learning, or of philosophy, in the word *Torah* (and in such visual symbols as the Torah may have generated in context) signals the formation of the new category, or, in slightly different language, the categorical formation and re-formation that is taking place.

Let me give a single example of the generative symbol *Torah* and its concretization in *the* Torah that characterizes the successor system. In what follows, the Torah forms not the *post facto* description of the facts of the world but the design of the world that God followed in creation. The Torah comes prior to reality, that of nature as much as that of history, and its rules prove descriptive of how things were made later on—a stunning reversal of the order of nature and a clear and decisive proof that a categorical re-formation is afoot. The Mishnah's source of truth was nature; the successor documents' source of truth, the Torah: clear evidence for the formation of a counterpart category indeed! The following expresses the priority of the Torah:

Genesis Rabbah I:I.1

1A. "*In the beginning God created*" (Gen. 1:1):

B. R. Oshaia commenced [discourse by citing the following verse:] " '*Then I was beside him like a little child, and I was daily his delight [rejoicing before him always, rejoicing in his inhabited world, and delighting in the sons of men]*' (Prov. 8:30-31).

C. "The word for 'child' uses consonants that may also stand for 'teacher,' 'covered over,' and 'hidden away.'

D. "Some hold that the word also means 'great.'

E. "The word means 'teacher,' in line with the following: '*As a teacher carries the suckling child*' (Num. 11:12).

F. "The word means 'covered over,' as in the following: '*Those who were covered over in scarlet*' (Lam. 4:5).

G. "The word means 'hidden,' as in the verse, '*And he hid Hadassah*' (Esther 2:7).

H. "The word means 'great,' in line with the verse, '*Are you better than No-Ammon?*' (Nah. 3:8). This we translate, 'Are you better than Alexandria the Great, which is located between rivers.' "

2A. Another matter:

B. The word means "workplan."

C. [In the cited verse] the Torah speaks, "I was the workplan of the Holy One, blessed be He."

D. In the accepted practice of the world, when a mortal king builds a palace, he does not build it out of his own head, but he follows a workplan.

E. And [the one who supplies] the workplan does not build out of his own head, but he has designs and diagrams, so as to know how to situate the rooms and the doorways.

F. Thus the Holy One, blessed be He, consulted the Torah when he created the world.

G. So the Torah stated "*By means of 'the beginning'* [that is to say, the Torah] *did God create . . .*" (Gen. 1:1).

H. And the word for "beginning" refers only to the Torah, as Scripture says, "*The Lord made me as the beginning of his way*" (Prov. 8:22).

The list before us—the initial proposition, then "another matter"—makes the simple point that the Torah comes prior to creation and reveals the plan of creation. If people appeal to the facts of nature, therefore, they err, because it is in the Torah, not in natural philosophy, that they will discover how things are meant to be and actually are. This shows the link between the Torah and Israel, which explains why the special rules governing Israel derive from the Torah in particular.

There are then two sets of facts, those of nature, pertaining to the world in general, and those of Scripture, dealing with Israel in particular.

Genesis Rabbah I:IV.1

A. ["*In the beginning God created*" (Gen. 1:1):] Six things came before the creation of the world, some created, some at least considered as candidates for creation.

B. The Torah and the throne of glory were created [before the creation of the world].

C. The Torah, as it is written, *"The Lord made me as the beginning of his way, prior to his works of old"* (Prov. 8:22).

D. The throne of glory, as it is written, *"Your throne is established of old"* (Ps. 93:2).

E. The patriarchs were considered as candidates for creation, as it is written, *"I saw your fathers as the first ripe in the fig tree at her first season"* (Hos. 9:10).

F. Israel was considered [as a candidate for creation], as it is written, *"Remember your congregation, which you got aforetime"* (Ps. 74:2).

G. The Temple was considered [as a candidate for creation], as it is written, *"You, throne of glory, on high from the beginning, the place of our sanctuary"* (Jer. 17:12).

H. The name of the Messiah was kept in mind, as it is written, *"His name exists before the sun"* (Ps. 72:17).

I. R. Ahbah bar Zeira said, "Also [the power of] repentance.

J. "That is in line with the following verse of Scripture: *'Before the mountains were brought forth'* (Ps. 90:2). From that hour: *'You turn man to contrition and say, Repent, you children of men'* (Ps. 90:3)."

K. Nonetheless, I do not know which of these came first, that is, whether the Torah was prior to the throne of glory, or the throne of glory to the Torah.

L. Said R. Abba bar Kahana, "The Torah came first, prior to the throne of glory.

M. "For it is said, *'The Lord made me as the beginning of his way, before his works of old'* (Prov. 8:22).

N. "It came prior to that concerning which it is written, *'For your throne is established of old'* (Ps. 93:2)."

2A. R. Huna, R. Jeremiah in the name of R. Samuel b. R. Isaac: "Intention concerning the creation of Israel came before all else.

B. "The matter may be compared to the case of a king who married a noble lady but had no son with her. One time the king turned up in the marketplace, saying 'Buy this ink, inkwell, and pen on account of my son.'

C. "People said, 'He has no son. Why does he need ink, inkwell, and pen?'

D. "But then people went and said, 'The king is an astrologer, so he sees into the future and he therefore is expecting to produce a son!'

E. "Along these same lines, if the Holy One, blessed be He, had not foreseen that, after twenty-six generations, the Israelites would be destined to accept the Torah, he would never have written in it, 'Command the children of Israel.' [This proves that God foresaw Israel and created the world on that account.]"

3A. Said R. Benaiah, "The world and everything in it were created only on account of the merit of the Torah.

B. " '*The Lord for the sake of wisdom* [Torah] *founded the earth*' (Prov. 3:19)."

C. R. Berekhiah said, "It was for the merit of Moses.

D. " '*And he saw the beginning for himself, for there a portion of a ruler* [Moses] *was reserved*' (Deut. 33:21)."

The power of the exposition is the link it forges between the natural world of creation and the historical world of Israel, its life and salvation. The world was created because of Israel. That simple proposition lays down a judgment that leads the exegete to join details of creation and of the stories of the patriarchs to details of the history of Israel, with the gross effect of showing the correspondence between Israel's salvific existence and the natural order of the world. The preceding example provides a set piece exposition of the opening proposition, that is, the six things preceding the creation of the world. That topic, and not the exposition of Genesis 1:1, explains the composition at hand. Following the necessary catalog of the six things the dicussion proceeds at no. 2 to a secondary exposition of the same matter. The passage then introduces creation for the sake of the Torah, followed by a complementary proposition on other things for the sake of which the world was created—this is the point at which Genesis 1:1 serves as a proof text.

This protracted representation of matters through abstracts should not obscure the simple point the citations are meant to make. Let me state the point with emphasis: *the Torah now defines the category of worldview.* As a symbol, the Torah no longer denotes a particular book, let alone the contents of such a book. In fact, in the Talmud of the

Land of Israel and its associated writings, the Torah, with or without its definite article and an initial capital, connotes a broad range of clearly distinct categories of noun and verb, concrete fact and abstract relationship alike.[13] *Torah* stands for a kind of human being. It connotes a social status and a sort of social group and refers to a type of social relationship. It further denotes a legal status and differentiates among legal norms. As symbolic abstraction, the word encompasses things and persons, actions and status, points of social differentiation and legal and normative standing, as well as "revealed truth."

The main points of insistence of the whole of Israel's life and history come to full symbolic expression in that single word. When people wanted to explain how they would be saved, the used the word *Torah*. When they wished to sort out their parlous relationships with gentiles, they also used the world *Torah*. Torah stood for salvation and accounted for Israel's this-worldly condition and the hope, for both individual and nation, of life in the world to come. For the successor system, therefore, the word *Torah* stood for everything. The Torah symbolized the whole, at once and entire. There is no counterpart in the Mishnah, no symbol that captures in itself the entire sense of "worldview," the weight of what is now categorized as "knowledge," "learning," and "science" in the broadest sense. As the successor system's generative symbol, however, the total, exhaustive expression of the system as a whole, the Torah stood for exactly these things: knowledge, learning, and science.

A brief catalog of the senses of the word *Torah* suffices for the present purpose. When the Torah refers to a particular thing, it is to a scroll containing divinely revealed words. The Torah may further refer to revelation, not as an object but as a corpus of doctrine. When one "does Torah" the disciple "studies" or "learns" Torah and the master "teaches" it. Hence, although the word *Torah* never appears as a verb, it does refer to an act. The word also bears a quite separate sense, torah as category, classification, or corpus of rules; for example, "the torah of driving a car" is a usage entirely acceptable to some documents. This generic usage of the word does occur. The word *Torah* very commonly refers to a status, distinct from and above another status, for example, the "teachings of Torah" as against the "teachings of scribes." For the two Talmuds that distinction is absolutely critical to the entire hermeneutic enterprise, but it is important even in the Mishnah. Finally, the word *Torah* refers to a source of salvation, often fully worked out in stories about how the individual and the nation will be saved through Torah. In general, the sense of the word "salvation" is not complicated. It is simply salvation in the way in which Deuteronomy and the Deuteronomic historians understand it: kings who do what God wants win battles; those who do not, lose. Similarly, people who study and do Torah are saved from sickness and death, and Israel can save itself from its degradation through Torah.

This range of meanings that the successor system imputes to Torah, the word now made into a symbol, vastly exceeds the limits of the Mishnah's nonsymbolic use of the word. Critical to this symbolic use is the literary definition of Torah as encompassing an oral component beginning with the Mishnah. To show the categorical novelty of Torah, it suffices to note that the framers of the Mishnah nowhere claim, implicitly or explicitly, that what they have written forms part of the Torah, enjoys the status of God's revelation to Moses at Sinai, or even systematically carries forward secondary exposition and application of what Moses wrote down in the wilderness. By contrast, the symbol of Torah takes on mythic expression with the Yerushalmi's position that God's revelation of the Torah at Sinai encompassed the Mishnah as much as it did Scripture. Following its revelation, so the story goes, the Mishnah was handed on through oral formulation and oral transmission from Sinai to the framers of the document as it now exists. These two convictions, fully exposed in the ninth-century letter of Sherira, in fact emerge from the references of both Talmuds to the dual Torah: one part was written, the other was oral and now is in the Mishnah.

It is easy to show that the authorship of the Mishnah and its associated writings knew nothing of the symbol—and therefore the category—of Torah as it would take shape in the successor system. The Mishnah contains not a hint that anyone has heard any such myth. The earliest apologists for the Mishnah, represented in Abot and the Tosefta alike, say nothing of the fully realized myth of the dual Torah of Sinai, of which the Mishnah as a document forms a principal component. The Yerushalmi marks the change.

True, the Mishnah places a high value on studying the Torah and on the status of the sage. A "*mamzer* disciple of a sage takes priority over a high priest *am-haares,*" as is claimed at M. Hor. 3:8 (a *mamzer* is a person whose parents never could have married legally, for example, because they were consanguineous; *am-haares* in this context refers to a person who has not studied the Torah with a qualified sage and is therefore ignorant). So the rights of caste position are set aside — though the caste status is unchanged — but that judgment, distinctive though it is, cannot settle the question. All it shows is that the Mishnah pays due honor to the sage, but if the Mishnah does not claim to constitute part of the Torah, then what makes a sage a sage is not mastery of the Mishnah in particular. Thus the Mishnah merely continues the established and familiar position of the wisdom writers of old. Wisdom is important; knowledge of the Torah is definitive. To maintain that position, however, it is hardly necessary to profess the fully articulated Torah myth of rabbinic Judaism. Proof of that fact, after all, is the character of the entire wisdom literature prior to the Mishnah itself.

Abot draws into the orbit of Torah talk the names of authorities of the Mishnah, but Abot does not claim the Mishnah to form part of the Torah. Nor does the tractate mention the doctrine of two Torahs. Only beginning with the Talmuds is there clear and ample evidence of that doctrine. Moreover, Abot does not mean by the word *Torah* much more than the framers of the Mishnah do. Not only does the established classification scheme remain intact, but the sense essentially replicates already familiar usages, producing no innovation; on the contrary, I find a diminution in the range of meanings.[14] In Abot, Torah is instrumental. The figure of the sage, his ideals and conduct, forms the goal, focus, and center. To state matters simply: Abot regards study of Torah as what a sage does. The substance of Torah is what a sage says, whether or not the saying relates to scriptural revelation. The content of the sayings attributed to sages endows those sayings with self-validating status. The sages usually do not quote verses of Scripture and explain them, nor do they speak in God's name, yet it is clear that sages talk Torah. If a sage says something, what he says is Torah. More accurately, what he says falls into the classification of Torah. *Torah* thus forms a taxic indicator in Abot as much as it does in the Mishnah.

The Yerushalmi is the first document to represent the Mishnah as equivalent to Scripture (Y. Hor. 3:5). Once the Mishnah entered the status of Scripture, it would take but a short step to a theory of the Mishnah as part of the revelation at Sinai — hence, oral Torah. Here are the first glimmerings of an effort to theorize, in general and not merely in detail, about how specific teachings of Mishnah relate to specific teachings of Scripture. The citing of scriptural proof texts for the Mishnah's propositions would not have caused much surprise to the framers of the Mishnah; they themselves included such passages, though not often. But what conception of the Torah underlies such initiatives, and how did the Yerushalmi's sages propose to explain the phenomenon of the Mishnah as a whole? The following passage (Y. Hagigah 1:7.V) gives one statement; it refers to the assertion at M. Hag. 1:8D that the laws on cultic cleanness presented in the Mishnah rest on deep and solid foundations in the Scripture.

> B. R. Zeira in the name of R. Yohanan: "If a law comes to hand and you do not know its nature, do not discard it for another one, for lo, many laws were stated to Moses at Sinai, and all of them have been embedded in the Mishnah."

The Mishnah is claimed here to contain statements made by God to Moses. Neither how these statements found their way into the Mishnah nor which passages contain them is stated. That is hardly important, however, given the fundamental assertion at hand. The passage proceeds to a further and far more consequential proposition. It asserts that part of the Torah was written down and part was preserved in memory and transmitted orally. In context, moreover, that distinction must encompass the Mishnah, thus explaining its origin as part of the Torah. Here is a clear and unmistakable expression of the distinction between two forms in which a single Torah was revealed and handed on at Mount Sinai, part in writing, part orally.

Short of explicit allusion to Torah-in-writing and Torah-by-memory, which (so far as I am able to discern) appears mainly in the Talmud of Babylonia, the ultimate theory of Torah in formative Judaism is at hand in what follows:

Yerushalmi Hagigah 1:7.V

> D. R. Zeirah in the name of R. Eleazar: " *'Were I to write for him my laws by ten thousands, they would be regarded as a strange thing'* (Hos. 8:12). Now is the greater part of the Torah written down? [Surely not. The oral part is much greater.] But more abundant are the matters which are derived by exegesis from the written [Torah] than those derived by exegesis from the oral [Torah]."
>
> E. And is that so?
>
> F. But more cherished are those matters which rest upon the written [Torah] than those which rest upon the oral [Torah]. . . .
>
> J. R. Haggai in the name of R. Samuel bar Nahman, "Some

teachings were handed on orally, and some things were handed on in writing, and we do not know which of them is the more precious. But on the basis of that which is written, '*And the Lord said to Moses, Write these words; in accordance with these words I have made a covenant with you and with Israel*' (Exod. 34:27), [we conclude] that the ones which are handed on orally are the more precious."

K. R. Yohanan and R. Yudan b. R. Simeon—one said, "If you have kept what is preserved orally and also kept what is in writing, I shall make a covenant with you, and if not, I shall not make a covenant with you."

L. The other said, "If you have kept what is preserved orally and you have kept what is preserved in writing, you shall receive a reward, and if not, you shall not receive a reward."

M. [With reference to Deut. 9:10: "*And on them was written according to all the words which the Lord spoke with you in the mount,*"] said R. Joshua b. Levi, "He could have written 'On them,' but wrote 'and on them.' He could have written 'all,' but wrote 'according to all.' He could have written 'words,' but wrote 'the words.' [These then serve as three encompassing clauses, serving to include] Scripture, Mishnah, Talmud, laws, and lore. Even what an experienced student in the future is going to teach before his master already has been stated to Moses at Sinai."

N. What is the Scriptural basis for this view?

O. "*There is no remembrance of former things, nor will there be any remembrance of later things yet to happen among those who come after*" (Qoh. 1:11).

P. If someone says, "See, this is a new thing," his fellow will answer him, saying to him, "This has been around before us for a long time."

Here is absolutely explicit evidence that people believed part of the Torah had been preserved not in writing but orally. Linking that part to the Mishnah remains a matter of implication, but it surely comes fairly close to the surface when it is said that the Mishnah contains Torah traditions revealed at Sinai. From that view it requires only a small step to the allegation that the Mishnah is the oral part of the Torah.

I adduce as evidence of a categorical transformation—that is, in this context, the formation of a counterpart category—the representation of the worldview as Torah, through the symbol of Torah, because the Torah is now re-presented as a source of salvation.[15] That is a profoundly fresh conception, without consequential antecedent[16] in the Mishnah and related writings. There (the) Torah forms a taxic indicator, and although merely knowing the Torah—without commensurate caste status or wealth—imparts status to the one who knows it, knowledge—*mere* knowledge—in no way constitutes the source of salvation. By contrast, that profoundly gnostic conception of knowledge in which (merely) knowing something ("the truth") changes the one who knows comes to the surface time and again in the successor documents. This power of personal transformation through knowledge of the Torah is a matter to which I shall return in chapter 7.

In the canonical documents up to the Yerushalmi and its companions, there simply are no sayings or stories that fall into such a category. It was no doubt believed that, in general, Israel would be saved by obedience to the Torah, a claim that surely would not have surprised any Israelite writer from the Deuteronomists of the seventh century B.C.E. down through the final redactors of the Pentateuch in the time of Ezra and onward through the next seven hundred years, but in the rabbinical corpus from the Mishnah forward, the specific and concrete assertion that by taking up the scroll of the Torah, standing on the roof of his house,[17] and confronting God, a sage could take action against an expected invasion—that kind of claim is not located, so far as I know, in any prior composition.[18]

This shift points not merely toward a revision of a received category, philosophy, but toward the formation of a new category altogether: the definition of the counterpart category to philosophy formed by (the) Torah. The new category, conveyed by the symbol *Torah*, treats the knowledge represented by the Torah (whether scroll, contents, or act of study) as source and guarantor of salvation. Accordingly, the category denoted by the word *Torah* encompasses the centerpiece of a theory of Israel's history, on the one side, and an account of the teleology of the entire system, on the other. Indeed, Torah has ceased to constitute a specific thing or even a category or classification in stories about studying the Torah that yield not a judgment as to status (i.e., praise for the learned man) but promise for supernatural blessing now and salvation in time to come. The new category, which corresponds to philosophy in its mode of thought and is counterpart to philosophy in its message, must be classed as a fundamentally religious category, in that in this system knowledge forms the medium of salvation: knowing the Torah changes the one who knows it, whereas, in the Mishnah and related writings, knowing the hierarchical structure and order of things, pointing toward the unity of the natural order, does not lead to the transformation of the one who knows the facts that yield the knowledge. It is thus no wonder that, in the Yerushalmi, mastery of Torah transforms the man engaged in Torah learning into a supernatural figure who can do things ordinary folk cannot do.

The transformation of the Judaic worldview encompassed new subjects, a new source of truth, and a new program of learning. How that new program of learning redefined scarce resources and re-formed the institutions that carried out the legitimate exercise of violence remains to be seen. Therefore, I turn next to reconsider a simple but fundamental representation of the successor system, one in which the symbolic transaction is quite concrete: scarce resources, valued things, are redefined other than they were.

Notes

1. In the present matter I see Abot as an intermediate document, but not as a mediating or transitional one. In Abot the Torah indicated who was a sage and who was not. Accordingly, the apology of Abot for the Mishnah was that the Mishnah contained things sages had said. What sages said formed a chain of tradition extending back to Sinai. Hence it was equivalent to the Torah. The upshot is that words of sages enjoyed the status of the Torah. The small step beyond, I think, was to claim that what sages said was Torah, as much as what Scripture said was Torah. And, a further small step (and the steps need not have been taken separately or in the order here suggested) moved matters to the position that there were two forms in which the Torah reached Israel: one in writing, the other handed on orally, that is, in memory.

2. I repeat what I have already emphasized, lest my proposition be misinterpreted. The intellectuals whose system(s) I here analyze did not live in the great metropolitan centers of intellectual life and cannot be expected, in the back country, fundamentally to have rethought the very processes of thought that were the givens of intellect from Sumerian times onward. Among them was no one who, like Kant, could address in the abstract the most general questions of intellect. Such utter independence of mind, moreover, lay beyond the social circumstances of clerks and petty administrators. Quite to the contrary, I find genuinely awesome the capacity of these rather minor figures to undertake the world construction that I am going to examine. The category formation they inherited, with all its prestige and force of mind, did

not inhibit their own enterprise of category re-formation—or even very much influence it. That power of independent thought seems to me to form a counterpart to Kant's.

3. Much that is said here alludes to the results of my *Torah: From Scroll to Symbol in Formative Judaism* (Philadelphia: Fortress, 1985).

4. But list making would change in form and, I think, in character; I do not mean to take for granted that *Listenwissenschaft* beginning to end was everywhere and always pretty much the same thing. In my treatment of "another matter," I show both that *Listenwissenschaft* defined the method of the late Midrash compilations and also that this method underwent considerable revision for the purposes of the compilers of those documents. I refer specifically to *From Literature to Theology in Formative Judaism: Three Preliminary Studies* (Atlanta, Ga.: Scholars Press for Brown Judaic Studies, 1989).

5. The distinction made here will form the problematic of the study of the transformation of a religious into a theological system.

6. I have vastly elaborated on this conception of the Torah in *Uniting the Dual Torah: Sifra and the Problem of the Mishnah* (Cambridge: Cambridge University Press, 1989). There is no need to recapitulate that argument here.

7. In *Judaism and Its Social Metaphors* (Cambridge: Cambridge University Press, 1989) I have set forth the standing of "Israel" in the Mishnah as a taxic indicator by contrast to the uses of "Israel" in the successor documents as referring to a genus with no counterpart, Israel as *sui generis* in one of two ways: a family different from all other families and unrelated to them; or a holy society bearing no points in common with any other society, being in fact of a different genus from societies in general. That is the basis for the statement made here.

8. The parallel mode of thought in Sifré to Deuteronomy and in Sifra is the exercise of inclusion and exclusion, which turns a case or an example into a law with clear-cut application or exclusion. That mode of generalizing law forms the counterpart to the interest in generalizing laws from incidents or anecdotes that is characteristic of Genesis Rabbah. In both cases we observe the move from an ad hoc and episodic mode of thinking to a philosophical and scientific one. The profound interest in generalization, rather than merely precedent or ad hoc observation, characteristic of the authorships of Sifra and Sifré to Deuteronomy for law and of Leviticus Rabbah and Genesis Rabbah for history, seems to be one of the deepest and most indicative traits of mind of the Judaism of the dual Torah in its intellectual origin, and one that marks that Judaism as deeply philosophical. No student of the writings of the Church fathers can find that fact surprising, even though the idiom of the formative intellects of the Judaism of the dual Torah is less accessible, within the philosophical mode, than that of the formative intellects of Christianity, particularly Catholic (not Gnostic) Christianity. But the gnostic side to the successor system will presently emerge as a principal characteristic.

9. I immediately qualify that there are chapters of Pesiqta deRab Kahana that orgininate in Leviticus Rabbah. In form and in polemic, in plan and in

program, the materials assembled in Pesiqta deRab Kahana cohere to such a degree that, on the basis of traits of cogency, I can differentiate the materials in Pesiqta deRab Kahana original to Leviticus Rabbah from those distinctive to Pesiqta deRab Kahana.

10. Pp. ix-x.

11. And that fact has rightly impressed those who have not recognized the philosophical character of the document; there is no philological evidence that suggests knowledge of any concrete philosophical modes of thought, let alone propositions.

12. The truth is, I can think of no single symbol that serves the entirety of the Mishnah as a medium of expressing the whole or evoking it. Surely, in tractate Abot, fifty years or so later, we may readily point to "Torah" as that symbol, referring to not a document but a status, but vividly so and not merely (as with the Mishnah) as a medium of taxonomic thought. That is to say, in tractate Abot we can point to the object, the Torah, speak of words of Torah, identify the status of a person or a gesture or action within the classification of Torah, and so in a single symbol speak of the whole and state the message of the whole. In the Mishnah, by contrast, I find no such symbolic centerpiece. I could make the case that the symbolic system of the Mishnah comes to expression not pictorially or visually or verbally (as with the object "Torah") but rather in what is as recurrent in the Mishnah as Torah is in tractate Abot, and that is the deepest structures of syntax, the orderly formation of thought in well-patterned language. But if I can find in any few sentences of the Mishnah the whole of the Mishnah in its syntactic structure (and, I have claimed, also its message as well, as in my *History of the Mishnaic Law of Purities* [Leiden: Brill, 1977], vol. 21, *The Redaction and Formulation of the Order of Purities in the Mishnah and Tosefta*), that does not seem to me to be the same thing as a symbol of the order of Torah or the Torah. But then, it seems fair to claim, philosophers in that context conveyed their messages through not symbolic but rather verbal discourse and argument, and the Mishnah's very philosophicality explains its failure to give us in a single way a medium for saying many things. To take a step further, the formation of the religious counterpart category for worldview, Torah, for philosophy, in medium and message alike, is signaled by the symbolic transaction represented by the word *Torah*.

13. Again, the basis of these statements is in my *Torah: From Scroll to Symbol in Formative Judaism*.

14. Yet Abot in the aggregate does differ from the Mishnah. The difference has to do with the topic at hand. The other sixty-two tractates of the Mishnah contain Torah sayings here and there, but they do not fall within the framework of Torah discourse. They speak about other matters entirely, and the consideration of the status of Torah rarely pertains to that speech. Abot, by contrast, says a great deal about Torah study; the claim that Torah study produces direct encounter with God forms part of Abot's thesis about the Torah.

15. The counterpart category in part 3 will be shown to constitute on its own an utterly fresh statement. The conception of knowledge as not merely

illuminating but salvific transforms what is at stake in the category of world-view from philosophical into religious truth.

16. Given the state of manuscript evidence for all ancient Judaic documents, we cannot claim as decisive the fact that a word or a phrase appears or does not appear in some one piece of writing. The manuscript evidence is too sparse to appeal to the occurrence or absence of a word or a pharse, or to count up the number of occurrences and draw consequences from the result. We can work with large-scale and well-attested aggregates, for example, the simple fact that all manuscripts of a given document concur on the basic topical program and organization, rhetorical preferences, logical principles of coherent discourse; these do vary from one document to another, and they do represent the choices of the initial authorship of a given document. That is why, as a matter of fact, the state of the evidence does allow us to characterize the fundamental literary structure and intellectual system of documents, for that characterization rests not on details but on the entire evidence in hand. One would have to claim that the Mishnah, for example, yields such diverse manuscript evidence that we can say nothing about its generative conceptions and fixed and formal traits, but the simple fact, proven decades ago by Y. N. Epstein in his *Introduction to the Text of the Mishnah* (Jerusalem: Magnes, 1957), is that manuscript variations affect words and phrases. That means the basic structures as to form and topical program are secure. My characterization rests not on details of the the nonappearance of a word here or there but rather on the large-scale and secure characteristics of the several documents as a whole. Hence, I stress the systemic infrastructure and the place of a given word or phrase in that infrastructure. If the word *Torah* occurs in a salvific sense, for example, in the Mishnah, that singleton bears no systemic weight whatsoever in the Mishnah overall. This distinction between the mere appearance or absence of a given word in a document and the systemic importance accorded to the concept represented by that same word in a document is worked out for *zekhut* in chapter 8. There we see that *zekhut* in the sense important later on does occur in documents generally held to have reached closure prior to the Yerushalmi and related Midrash compilations, but when used earlier, the concept is systemically inert, not active and indicative, and this we know because we can identify, in these prior appearances, no systemic burden carried by the word or concept of *zekhut*. In the appearances in the later documents, by contrast, *zekhut* proves to stand at the very center of discourse, a judgment concerning not the number of times the word occurs but the place of the concept in the systemic structure. Justification for characterizing the usage in a systemically active and not inert way will be set forth in context, but even here I must underline that, though the salvific value accorded to Torah (e.g., Torah study) may appear episodically in some document prior to the ones deemed critical in this book, the place of that concept in the earlier system is not established by an ad hoc usage. That can have been an addition of a later scribe; it also can have been present in the original version of the document (as it can have been in the mind of this one or that one in the circles of sages, and probably was) without making

an impact on the shape and structure of the system attested by the document containing that episodic usage.

17. This story is cited verbatim at the outset of chapter 7.

18. Precisely what I claim in this "canonical history" of ideas must be made explicit. It is that we deal with a symbolic transaction portrayed in the succession of usages of a given word or symbol as we move from one document to the next. Our survey concerns the description, analysis, and interpretation of successive systems, which I claim were not successor systems. My argument is that knowledge—the intellectual integument of the worldview—in the Mishnah is not Torah and is not salvific, whereas knowledge in the Yerushalmi and associated writings is Torah and is salvific. I do not know what others, not represented by these writings, were thinking; I cannot even say that systems other than those represented by the successive groups of writings existed. I surely do not claim that the belief that the Torah in the hands of the sage constituted a source of magical, supernatural, and hence salvific power did not flourish prior, let us say, to ca. 400 C.E. We cannot show it, hence we do not know it (and anyhow, I very much doubt it). All we can say with assurance is that no stories containing such a viewpoint appear in any rabbinical document associated with the Mishnah. So what is critical here is not the generalized category—the genus—of conviction that the Torah serves as the source of Israel's salvation. It is the concrete assertion—the speciation of the genus—that in the hands of the sage and under conditions specified, the Torah may be utilized in pressing circumstances as Levi, his disciple, and the disciple of his disciple used it. That is what is new and in my judgment forms decisive evidence for a categorical re-formation—in my language, the formation of a counterpart category—effected by the system builders whose views are attested in the documents under study.

5

The Transvaluation of Value

Consideration of the transvaluation of value leads to the category in the successor systems that is the counterpart to the concrete, this-worldly, and material definition of value that the Mishnah makes in conformity with philosophical economics.[1] I must now ask what the new system set forth in place of the received definition of value and the economics thereof.

The transformation of economics involved redefining scarce and valued resources in so radical a manner that the concept of value, while remaining material in consequence and character, nonetheless took on an altogether different sense.[2] As formulated by the authorships responsible for the final composition of the Yerushalmi, Genesis Rabbah, Leviticus Rabbah, and Pesiqta deRab Kahana, the counterpart categories of the successor system concerned themselves with the same questions as did the conventional economics, presenting an economics in function and structure, but one that concerned things of value other than those identified by the initial system. They constitute an economics, but an economics of something other than real estate.

Nonetheless, it was an economics as profoundly embedded in the social order, as deeply a political economics, and as pervasively a systemic economics as the economics of the Mishnah and of Aristotle. Why so? Because issues such as the definition of wealth, the means of production and the control thereof, the disposition of wealth through distributive or other media, the theory of money, reward for labor, and the like, all found their resolutions in the counterpart category of economics as much as in the received and conventional philosophical economics. The new "scarce resource" accomplished what the old did, but it was a different resource, a new currency. Thus, at stake in the category, which was meant to address the issues of the way of life of the social entity, were precisely the same considerations as confront economics in its (to us) conventional, commonplace, and philosophical sense. Because the definition of wealth changes from land to Torah, however, as I have already shown, much else also was transformed.

This explains why the formation of the counterpart category of value other than real value but nonetheless value in function and in social meaning reveals the transformation of a system from philosophy to religion. It would be a profound error to suppose that, in contrasting land to Torah and affirming that true value lies in Torah, the framers of the successor system formulated an essentially spiritual or otherwise immaterial conception, that is, a surrogate for economics in the conventional sense. That is not what happened. What they created was an economics that answers the questions economics answers but that uses a value different from real value—real estate, in the initiator system—as its definition of the scarce resource that requires a rational policy for its preservation and enhancement. Land produced a living; so did Torah. Land formed the foundation of the social entity; so did Torah.

The transvaluation of value was such that an economics concerning the rational management and increase of scarce resources worked itself out so as to answer, for things of value quite different from real property or capital, precisely the same questions that the received economics addressed in connection with wealth of a real character: land and its produce. Systemic transformation comes to the surface in articulated symbolic change. The utter transvaluation of value finds expression in a jarring juxtaposition, an utter shift of rationality—specifically, the substitution of Torah for real estate. Recall how in a successor document (but in none prior to the fifth-century compilations) Tarfon thought wealth took the form of land, whereas Aqiba explained to him that wealth takes the form of Torah learning. That the sense is material and concrete is explicit: land for Torah, Torah for land. Thus, to repeat the matter of how Torah serves as an explicit symbol to convey the systemic worldview, let me note the main point of the now familiar passage:

Leviticus Rabbah XXXIV:XVI

1B. R. Tarfon gave to R. Aqiba six silver centenarii, saying to him, "Go, buy us a piece of land, so we can get a living from it and labor in the study of Torah together."

C. He took the money and handed it over to scribes, Mishnah teachers, and those who study Torah.

D. After some time R. Tarfon met him and said to him, "Did you buy the land that I mentioned to you?"

E. He said to him, "Yes."

F. He said to him, "Is it any good?"

G. He said to him, "Yes."

H. He said to him, "And do you not want to show it to me?"

I. He took him and showed him the scribes, Mishnah teachers, and people who were studying Torah, and the Torah that they had acquired.

J. He said to him, "Is there anyone who works for nothing? Where is the deed covering the field?"

K. He said to him, "It is with King David, concerning whom it is written, 'He *has scattered, he has given to the poor, his righteousness endures forever*' (Ps. 112:9)."

The successor system has its own definitions not only for learning, symbolized by the word *Torah,* but also for wealth, expressed in the same symbol. Accordingly, the category re-formation for worldview, Torah in place of philosophy, dictates a still more striking category re-formation in which the entire matter of scarce resources is reconsidered and a counterpart category set forth. When "Torah" substitutes for real estate, then, exactly what does the successor system take to be scarce resources, and how is the counterpart category constructed?

Let me begin with a simple definition of "value." Although it bears a variety of inchoate meanings associated with belief, conviction, ideal, moral preference, and the like, the word initially bears an entirely concrete sense. Value means that which people value under ordinary circumstances, what they hold to be of concrete, tangible, material worth. What is "of value" conventionally is what provides a life of comfort, sustenance, and material position.[3] In commonplace language, "value" (as distinct, therefore, from the vague term, "values") refers to those scarce resources that economics aims at rationally managing and increasing: real wealth,[4] which in our contemporary context means capital and in the context of Aristotle's and the Mishnah's economics means real estate.[5] When I speak of the transvaluation of value, I mean that the material and concrete things of worth were redefined, even while being subjected to an economics functioning in the system as the counterpart to the initial economics of the Mishnah and of Aristotle. The successor writings thus contrast ownership of land, even in the Land of Israel, with wealth in another form altogether, and the contrast was material and concrete, not merely symbolic and spiritual. It was material, tangible, and palpable because it produced this-worldly gains, for example, a life of security, comfort, and ease, as these too found definition in the systemic context of the here and the now.

It follows that, although the successor system's theory of the social order encompasses an economics in its way-of-life component, it is an economics of scarce resources defined as something other than particular real estate. I insist that these questions are economic in character because they deal with the rules or theory of the rational management of scarce resources, their preservation and increase, and do so in commonplace terms of philosophical economics, for example, the control of the means of production, the definitions of money and value, the distribution of valued goods and services (whether by appeal to the market or to a theory of distributive economics), the theory of the value of labor, and the like. Although the structure remained the same, however, the contents differ radically—hence, the transvaluation of value. It is as if a new currency were issued to replace the old, then declared of no value, capable of purchasing nothing worth having. Such an economics suggests far more than a currency reform; this is a complete economic revolution, a new beginning, as much as a shift from socialism to capitalism. The transvaluation in the case at hand was more thoroughgoing still, however, for it involved the very reconsideration of the scarcity of scarce resources. Both elements, then, underwent transvaluation: the definition of resources of value and the rationality involved in the management of scarcity. Stated baldly, although real estate cannot increase and by definition must always prove scarce, the value represented by Torah can expand without limit. Value thus can increase indefinitely and desired and scarce resources can be made ever more abundant in the transformed economics of the successor system.

When responding to the same questions of that same part of the social order with which the received category concerned itself, the economics that emerged in no way proves discontinuous with the received economics. Why do I not simply call it another economics, different from the philosophical one already considered? The reason is that so abrupt and fundamental a reworking has taken place that the category—way of life—*while yet an economics* nonetheless has become a wholly other economics, one completely without relationship to the inherited definition of way of life (manner of earning a living) as to both structure and system.

For at stake is not merely the spiritualization of wealth, that is to say, the re-presentation of what "wealth" *really* consists of in other-than-material terms.[6] That would represent not an economics but a theology. For example, the familiar saying in tractate Abot, "Who is rich? One who is happy in his lot," simply does not constitute a statement of economics at all. Like sayings in the Gospels that denigrate wealth, this one tells nothing about the rational management (e.g., increase) of scarce resources; it merely tells about appropriate moral attitudes of a virtuous order: how life is worth living, which does not answer an economic question at all. On the other hand, the tale that contrasts wealth in the form of land and its produce with wealth in the form of Torah (whatever is meant by "Torah") does constitute a statement of economics. The reason is that the storyteller invokes precisely the category of wealth—real property—that conventional economics defines as wealth. If I have land, I have wealth, and I can support myself; if I have Torah, I have wealth, and I can support myself. Those form the two components of the contrastive equation before us, but then wealth is disenlandised, and the Torah substituted for real property of all kinds. That forms not a theology, not an economics in any conventional sense, but rather an anti-economics. The same will be seen to be so in politics.

Take, for example, the following explicit statement that a sentence of the Torah is more valuable than a pearl:

Y. Peah 1:1 XVII (trans. by Roger Brooks)

E. Ardavan sent our holy Rabbi a priceless pearl and said to him, "Send me something as valuable as this."

F. He sent him a doorpost scroll [*mezuzah* containing words of Torah].

G. Ardavan said to him, "I sent you an item beyond price, but you send me something worth but a few cents."

H. Rabbi said to him, "Your precious things and my precious things are not equivalent. You sent me something I have to guard, but I sent something that guards you while you sleep: '*When you walk along, [the words of Torah] will lead you, when you lie down, they will watch over you*' (Prov. 6:22)."

If I have words of the Torah in hand, there are scarce resources in my possession that I otherwise do not have: security, for example, against whatever demons may want to harm me in my sleep.[7]

I insist that these kinds of stories deal with scarce resources in a concrete sense because in both cases cited to this point the upshot of possessing Torah is this-worldly, concrete, tangible, and palpable. The rewards are not described as "filling treasuries in the heart," nor do they "enrich the soul," nor are they postponed to the world to come (as would be the case in a kind of capitalistic theology of investment on earth for return in heaven). The tale concerning Aqiba and Tarfon, like the one involving Rabbi and Ardavan, insists on precisely the same *results* from possessing wealth or value in the form of "Torah" as from wealth or value in the form of real estate. The key language is this: "Go, buy us a piece of land, *so we can get a living from it* and labor in the study of Torah together." Tarfon assumes owning land buys leisure for Torah study; Aqiba does not contradict that assumption, he steps beyond it.

Thus, one thing forms the counterpart and opposite of the other — anti-economics and economics, in this case — but both yield a single result: wealth sustains leisure, which any reader of Xenophon's handbook on economics (estate management, in his context) would have found an entirely commonplace and obviously true judgment. That explains why the form that wealth takes in the successor system — Torah rather than real estate — presents a jarring contrast, one that is, of course, the point of the story. As a matter of fact, as I shall show in just a moment, that jarring contrast would have proved unintelligible to any authorship prior to the second stage in the formation of the canonical writings and explicitly contradicts the sense of matters that predominates in the first stage: the Torah is not to be made "a spade to dig with" (whatever that can have meant). In Tarfon's mind, therefore, real (in the theological sense) value is real (in the economic sense) wealth, that is, real estate, because if you own land, you can enjoy the leisure to do what you really want to do, which (as every philosopher understood) is to study (in the sages' case) the Torah together. To Aqiba, however, that is beside the point, for the real (in the theological sense) value (in the economic sense, that is, what provides a living—food, for instance) is Torah (study), and that in itself suffices. The sense is, if I have land, I have a living, and if I have Torah, I also have a living that is no different from the living that I have from land but that, as a matter of fact, is more secure.

Owning land involved control of the means of production, and so did knowing the Torah. But more to the point, land provided people with a living, and Torah provided people a living in *precisely* the same sense—that is to say, in the material and concrete sense—as land did. That is alleged time and again, so at stake is not the mere denigration of wealth but the transvaluation of value. The transvaluation consisted in (1) the disenlandisement of value, and (2) the transvaluation of (knowing or studying) the Torah, the imputation to Torah of the value formerly associated with land. This validates the claim for Torah's status as a counterpart category: it is the system's economics, its theory of the way of life of the community and account of the rational disposition of those scarce resources that made everyday material existence possible and even pleasant. It is economics of wealth, but of wealth differently defined while similarly valued and utilized.[8]

Like Aristotle, when the authorship of the Mishnah conducted discourse on economic questions, it understood wealth entirely in this-worldly terms. The Torah formed a component in the system of hierarchical classification, not a unit of value or a measure of worth. By contrast, as I shall show, the successor system portrayed by the Talmud of the Land of Israel, Genesis Rabbah, Leviticus Rabbah, and their companions linked the concept of scarce resources to the conception of Torah and so gave it altogether fresh meanings, but in exactly the same context and producing exactly the same material consequence (e.g., having food and shelter) as its counterpart in the initiator system. This in turn requires a redefinition of that which serves the category of "economics." This is necessary because of those stunning transvaluations, already cited, of value stated explicitly and baldly in the contrast between land and Torah. When the successor documents contrast the received value with the value they recognize, issues arise about the formation of the counterpart category and how to make sense of that category.

Accordingly, I now have to show that when a successor system authorship speaks of Torah, it addresses the issues of scarce resources in the same way in which the authorship of the Mishnah or Aristotle speaks of real wealth in addressing those same issues. Then I must provide an account of the goods and services assigned the status of "scarce resources" and define the theory of rational disposition that constitutes the economics in the successor system. The questions are the same, but they are addressed to different things of value, different scarce resources altogether, and the systemic goal is to make abundant what has been scarce.

Because Torah—left undefined for the moment—forms the definition of wealth in the successor system,[9] the following question immediately arises: has the sense of the word really changed so considerably from its representation in the first stratum of the literature that it must be imputed meanings that are represented as both fresh and simply not considered in the initial economics of the first Judaism? That is to say, was Torah in the Mishnah not that same ultimate value that it became in the successor system? If it was, then any claim that Torah has replaced real estate as the definition of value and worth— the transvaluation of value in a very concrete sense—is simply beside the point. In the initial system, it may be claimed, Torah stood for something of ultimate worth, right alongside real property and its equivalents, each in its own context, each for its own purpose. Thus, I now must return to the issue of the standing and meaning of Torah in the Mishnah and demonstrate that in the Mishnah, Torah, now to be defined as Torah learning, in no way functions as a scarce resource; it in no way occupies the position as a statement of real worth and value that it gained in the successor system and in the writings that adumbrate it. According to the Mishnah, if I know Torah, I enter a certain status, for knowledge of Torah forms part of the taxic structure of the Mishnah's social system. Even if I know the Torah, however, I have still to earn a living, and scarce resources are defined by real estate and equivalents.

To make that point stick, I must now show that, in the Mishnah, Torah stands for status but produces no consequences of a material order or, as a matter of fact, even for caste status. It is the simple fact that studying the Torah is deemed an action to which accrues unlimited benefit. This is made explicit:

M. Peah. 1:1A-E (trans. Brooks)

A. These are things that have no specified measure: the quantity of produce designated as *peah*; the quantity of produce given as

first fruits, the value of the appearance offering, the performance
of righteous deeds, and time spent in study of Torah.

B. These are things the benefit of which a person enjoys in this
world, while the principal remains for him in the world to come:
deeds in honor of father and mother, performance of righteous
deeds, and acts which bring peace between a man and his fellow.

C. But the study of Torah is as important as all of them all
together.

The study of Torah, or knowledge of the Torah, is equivalent to a
variety of other meritorious actions, for example, designating produce
as "corner of the field" for use by the scheduled castes, bringing an
offering of high cost, or honoring parents. Study of the Torah enjoys
pride of place among these comparable deeds, but the rewards are not
worldly, material, or palpable. If I know the Torah, I enjoy a higher
status than if I do not, but I still must work for a living.[10]

Knowledge of the Torah did not define the qualifications of the
highest offices; for instance, a member of the priestly caste could be
high priest and not have mastered the Torah:

M. Yoma 1:6A-D

A. If the high priest was a sage, he expounds the relevant Scriptures of the Day of Atonement, and if not, disciples of sages
expound for him. If he was used to reading Scriptures, he read,
and if not, they read for him.

In addition, the Mishnah says nothing of using holy funds to support
disciples of sages (see, e.g., M. Meg. 3:1: townsfolk who sold a street
of a town buy with its proceeds a synagogue, and so on). Mishnah
tractate Sheqalim, with its account of the use of public funds for the
Temple, never supposes that disciples of sages associated with the
Temple may be paid from the public funds represented by the *sheqel*
tax.

This underlines the simple fact that in the Mishnah a disciple of a
sage is not assumed to get support on account of his Torah study, nor
the sage assumed to make his living through Torah study or other
Torah activities. Knowledge of the Torah or the act of study enjoys
no material value. For instance, an act of betrothal requires an exchange
of something of value; among the examples of value the act of study
or teaching of the Torah is never offered; for example, "Lo, thou art

betrothed to me in exchange for my teaching you [or your brother or your father] a teaching of the Torah" is never suggested as a possibility. So Torah learning is not material and produces no benefits of a material character. Sages' status may derive from knowledge of Torah, but that status is not conflated with the material consideration involved in who may marry whom. In M. Qid. 4:1 sages do not form a caste. "Ten castes came up from Babylonia," but the "status" of sage has no bearing upon caste status. Then what difference does Torah study or Torah knowledge make? It is, as I have stressed, one of taxic consequence and one of status, but with no bearing whatsoever on livelihood. Here are the important statements of the taxic value of knowing Torah, and in none of them is what is gained of a material or concrete order:

M. Baba Mesia 2:11

A. [If he has to choose between seeking] what he has lost and what his father has lost,

B. his own takes precedence;

C. what he has lost and what his master has lost,

D. his own takes precedence;

E. what his father has lost and what his master has lost,

F. that of his master takes precedence.

G. For his father brought him into this world.

H. But his master, who taught him wisdom, will bring him into the life.

I. But if his father is a sage, that of his father takes precedence.

J. [If] his father and his master were carrying heavy burdens, he removes that of his master, and afterward removes that of his father.

K. [If] his father and his master were taken captive,

L. he ransoms his master, and afterward he ransoms his father.

M. But if his father is a sage, he ransoms his father, and afterward he ransoms his master.

In this passage Torah learning has not attained practical consequence. That is to say, there is no theory that, because the master has studied Torah, therefore the master does not have to earn a living ("carrying heavy burdens"). The same is so in the following:

M. Horayot 3:6-8

3:6A. Whatever is offered more regularly than its fellow takes precedence over its fellow, and whatever is more holy than its fellow takes precedence over its fellow.

B. [If] a bullock of an anointed priest and a bullock of the congregation [M. Hor. 1:5] are standing [awaiting sacrifice]—

C. the bullock of the anointed [high priest] takes precedence over the bullock of the congregation in all rites pertaining to it.

3:7A. The man takes precedence over the woman in the matter of the saving of life and in the matter of returning lost property.

B. But a woman takes precedence over a man in the matter of [providing] clothing and redemption from captivity.

C. When both of them are standing in danger of defilement, the man takes precedence over the woman.

3:8A. A priest takes precedence over a Levite, a Levite over an Israelite, an Israelite over a *mamzer*, a *mamzer* over a *Netin*, a *Netin* over a proselyte, a proselyte over a freed slave.

B. Under what circumstances?

C. When all of them are equivalent.

D. But if the *mamzer* was a disciple of a sage and a high priest was an *am haares*, the *mamzer* who is a disciple of a sage takes precedence over a high priest who is an *am haares*.

What is explicit here is that knowledge of the Torah does not change one's caste status, for example, priest or *mamzer* or *Netin* (Temple servant) and that caste status does govern whom one may marry, a matter of substantial economic consequence. It does change one's status as to precedence of another order altogether, however, one that is curiously unspecific at M. Horayot 3:8. Hierarchical classification for its own sake, lacking all practical consequence, characterizes the Mishnah's system, defining, after all, its purpose and its goal! Along these same lines, the premise of tractate Sanhedrin is that the sage is judge and administrator of the community: knowledge of the Torah qualifies him, but knowledge of the Torah does not provide a living or the equivalent to a living. No provision for supporting the sage as administrator, clerk, or judge is suggested in the tractate.

What about knowledge of Torah as a way of making one's living? In the list of professions by which men make a living we find several positions. First is that of Meir and Simeon:

Mishnah Qiddushin 4:14

E. R. Meir says, "A man should always teach his son a clean and easy trade. And let him pray to him to whom belong riches and possessions.

G. "For there is no trade which does not involve poverty or wealth.

H. "For poverty does not come from one's trade, nor does wealth come from one's trade.

I. "But all is in accord with a man's merit."

J. R. Simeon b. Eleazar says, "Have you ever seen a wild beast or a bird who has a trade? Yet they get along without difficulty. And were they not created only to serve me? And I was created to serve my Master. So is it not logical that I should get along without difficulty? But I have done evil and ruined my living."

One's merit or sinfulness makes the difference between poverty and wealth. A more practical position is that which follows in the continuation of the passage.

K. Abba Gurion of Sidon says in the name of Abba Gurya, "A man should not teach his son to be an ass driver, a camel driver, a barber, a sailor, a herdsman, or a shopkeeper. For their trade is the trade of thieves."

L. R. Judah says in his name, "Most ass drivers are evil, most camel drivers are decent, most sailors are saintly, the best among physicians is going to Gehenna, and the best of butchers is a partner of Amalek."

The third view is that of Nehorai, who holds that Torah suffices as a means for making a living:

M. R. Nehorai says, "I should lay aside every trade in the world and teach my son only Torah.

N. "For a man eats its fruits in this world, and the principal remains for the world to come.

O. "But other trades are not that way.

P. "When a man gets sick or old or has pains and cannot do his job, lo, he dies of starvation.

Q. "But with Torah it is not that way.

R. "But it keeps him from all evil when he is young, and it gives him a future and a hope when he is old.

s. "Concerning his youth, what does it say? *They who wait upon the Lord shall renew their strength*' (Isa. 40:31). And concerning his old age what does it say? *They shall still bring forth fruit in old age*' (Ps. 92:14).

T. "And so it says with regard to the patriarch Abraham, may he rest in peace, *And Abraham was old and well along in years, and the Lord blessed Abraham in all things*' (Gen. 24:1).

U. "We find that the patriarch Abraham kept the entire Torah even before it was revealed, since it says, *Since Abraham obeyed my voice and kept my charge, my commandments, my statutes, and my laws*' (Gen. 26:5)."

Does Nehorai tell us that if we study the Torah, we will have all our worldly needs met, as Aqiba tells Tarfon that Torah is the counterpart of real estate but a more secure investment? I think not. Quite to the contrary, precisely why Torah works as it does is made explicit at R: "It keeps him from evil when he is young." That is to say, the position of Meir and Simeon is repeated, only in a fresh way. If I know the Torah, I will not sin. The conception that if I study Torah I automatically get food and shelter is not at issue here, where the concern is with being kept from evil in youth and enjoying God's blessing in old age on account of keeping the Torah—a very different thing, as I shall show presently.

The first apologia for the Mishnah, tractate Abot, takes the view that one should not make one's living through study of the Torah. That is made explicit in Torah sayings of tractate Abot, which explicitly rejects the theory of Torah study as a means of avoiding one's obligation to earn a living. Torah study without a craft is rejected and Torah study along with labor at a craft is defined as the ideal way of life. The following sayings make that point quite clearly:

M. Abot 2:2 and 3:17

2:2A. Rabban Gamaliel, a son of Rabbi Judah the Patriarch says: Fitting is learning in the Torah along with a craft, for the labor put into the two of them makes one forget sin. And all learning of the Torah which is not joined with labor is destined to be null and causes sin.

3:17A. R. Eleazar b. Azariah says, ". . . If there is no sustenance [lit.: flour], there is no Torah learning. If there is no Torah learning, there is no sustenance."

Here there is no contrast between two forms of wealth, one less secure, the other more. The way of virtue lies rather in economic activity in the conventional sense, joined to intellectual or philosophical activity in the sages' sense. Again, Xenophon would not have been surprised. The labor in Torah is not an economic activity and produces no solutions to this-worldly problems of getting food, shelter, and clothing. To the contrary, labor in Torah defines the purpose of human life; it is the goal, but it is not the medium for maintaining life and avoiding starvation or exposure to the elements. So, too, Tosefta's complement to the Mishnah is explicit in connection with M. Gittin 1:7A, "a commandment pertaining to the father concerning the son":

T. Qiddushin 1:11E-G

It is to circumcise him, redeem him [should he be kidnapped], teach him Torah, teach him a trade, and marry him off to a girl.

There clearly is no conception here that one who studies Torah need not work for a living, nor in the Tosefta's complement to the Mishnah does anyone imagine that merit is gained by supporting those who study the Torah.

Yohanan ben Zakkai speaks of Torah study as the goal of a human life, on the one side, and of a reward paid for Torah study, clearly in a theological sense and context, on the other. That the context of Torah study is religious and not economic in any sense is shown by Hananiah's saying, which is explicit: if people talk about the Torah, the presence of God joins them to participate:

M. Abot 2:8, 2:16, 3:2

2:8A. Rabban Yohanan ben Zakkai received [the Torah] from Hillel and Shammai. He would say: If you have learned much Torah, do not puff yourself up on that account, for it was for that purpose that you were created.

2:16A. He would say: It is not your job to finish the work, but you are not free to walk away from it. If you have learned much Torah, they will give you a good reward. And your employer can be depended upon to pay your wages for what you do. And know what sort of reward is going to be given to the righteous in the coming time.

3:2B. R. Hananiah b. Teradion says, "[If] two sit together and between them do not pass teachings of the Torah, lo, this is a seat of the scornful, as it is said, '*nor sits in the seat of the scornful*' (Ps. 1:1). But two who are sitting, and words of the Torah do pass between them—the Presence is with them, as it is said, '*Then they that feared the Lord spoke with one another, and the Lord hearkened and heard, and a book of remembrance was written before him, for them that feared the Lord and gave thought to his name*' (Mal. 3:16)." I know that this applies to two. How do I know that even if a single person sits and works on the Torah, the Holy One, blessed be He, sets aside a reward for him? As it is said, "*Let him sit alone and keep silent, because he has laid it upon him*" (Lam. 3:28).

Do worldly benefits accrue to those who study the Torah? The rabbi cited in the following statement maintains that it is entirely inappropriate to utilize Torah learning to gain either social standing or economic benefit:

M. Abot 4:5

B. R. Sadoq says, "Do not make [Torah teachings] a crown in which to glorify yourself or a spade with which to dig." So did Hillel say, "He who uses the crown perishes. Thus have you learned: Whoever derives worldly benefit from teachings of the Torah takes his life out of this world."

I cannot think of a statement more likely to startle the author of the story involving Aqiba and Tarfon than this one, for Aqiba's position is precisely the one rejected here. The bulk of opinion in the Mishnah and in tractate Abot identifies Torah learning with status within a system of hierarchical classification, not with a medium for earning a living, although that is not the only position presented. The following seems to me to contrast working for a living with studying Torah and to maintain that the latter will provide a living without recourse to hard labor:

M. Abot 3:15

A. R. Nehunia b. Haqqaneh says, "From whoever accepts upon himself the yoke of the Torah do they remove the yoke of the state and the yoke of hard labor. And upon whoever removes from himself the yoke of the Torah do they lay the yoke of the state and the yoke of hard labor."

The prevailing view, however, represented by the bulk of sayings, treats Torah study as an activity that competes with economic venture and insists that it take precedence, even though it is not of economic value in any commonplace sense of the words. This is explicitly imputed to Meir and to Jonathan in the following:

M. Abot 4:10

4:10A. R. Meir says, "Keep your business to a minimum and make your business the Torah. And be humble before everybody. And if you treat the Torah as nothing, you will have many treating you as nothing. And if you have labored in the Torah, [the Torah] has a great reward to give you."

4:9A. R. Jonathan says, "Whoever keeps the Torah when poor will in the end keep it in wealth. And whoever treats the Torah as nothing when he is wealthy in the end will treat it as nothing in poverty."

Torah study competes with, rather than replaces, economic activity. That is the simple position of tractate Abot, extending the conception of matters explicit in the Mishnah. If I had to make a simple statement of the situation prevailing at ca. 250, it would be that sages contrast their wealth, which is spiritual and intellectual, with material wealth, they do not deem the one to form the counterpart of the other, but only the opposite.

That brings me to consider the re-presentation of wealth in the successor documents and to seek a richer sample of opinion than the story that ended the preceding chapter and that, I maintain, frames the new economics of the successor system. A system that forbids using the Torah as a spade with which to dig (i.e., as a means of making a living) will have found proof for its position in the numerous allegations in Wisdom literature that the value of wisdom, understood as the Torah, is beyond price: "*Happy is the man who finds wisdom . . . for the gain from it is better than gain from silver, and its profit better than gold; she is more precious than jewels, and nothing you desire can compare with her*" (Prov. 3:13-15). Neither this nor its numerous parallels were understood to mean that if people devoted themselves to the study of the Torah and the teaching thereof they would not have to work any more. Nor do the praises of wisdom specifically contrast Torah learning with land ownership. In the successor writings, however, that is precisely what is commomplace, and the conclusion is drawn that one may derive one's living from study of the Torah, which thus becomes a spade with which to dig, as much as a real spade serves to dig in the earth to make the ground yield a living.

The issue of scarce resources in the context of a society that highly valued honor and despised and feared shame was phrased in terms not only of material wealth but also of worldly repute. Knowledge of the Torah served as did coins, that is, to circulate the name of the holy man or woman (Abraham or Sarah, in the following example), all figures to whom heroic deeds of Torah learning and teaching were attributed:

Genesis Rabbah XXXIX:XI.5

A. R. Berekhiah in the name of R. Helbo: "[The promise that God will make Abram great] refers to the fact that his coinage had circulated in the world.

B. "There were four whose coinage circulated in the world.

C. "Abraham: '*And I will make you*' (Gen. 12:2). And what image appeared on his coinage? An old man and an old woman on the obverse side, a boy and a girl on the reverse [Abraham, Sarah, Isaac, and Rebekkah].

D. "Joshua: '*So the Lord was with Joshua and his fame was in all the land*' (Josh. 6:27). That is, his coinage circulated in the world. And what image appeared on his coinage? An ox on the obverse, a wild ox on the reverse: '*His firstling bullock, majesty is his, and his horns are the horns of a wild ox*' (Deut. 33:17). [Joshua descended from Joseph.]

E. "David: '*And the fame of David went out into all lands*' (1 Chron. 14:17). That is, his coinage circulated in the world. And what image appeared on his coinage? A staff and a wallet on the obverse, a tower on the reverse: '*Your neck is like the tower of David, built with turrets*' (Song of Sol. 4:4).

F. "Mordecai: '*For Mordecai was great in the king's house, and his fame went forth throughout all the provinces*' (Esther 9:4). That is, his coinage circulated in the world. And what image appeared on his coinage? Sackcloth and ashes on the obverse, a golden crown on the reverse."

"Coinage" is meant to be jarring, to draw an ironic contrast between true currency, which is the repute that is gained through godly service, and worldly currency; as kings use their coins to make their persons and policies known, so do the saints. By itself, however, this is not a saying that assigns to Torah the value equivalent to coins.

Indeed, it cannot make such an assignment, for the value imputed to Torah study and teaching compares not to (mere) currency, which in the context of Aristotelian and Mishnaic economics bears the merely contingent value of a commodity, but only to land. So the issue is whether successor writings make clear affirmations, beyond the one now cited concerning Tarfon and Aqiba, that compare land with the Torah. For one thing, the Torah serves as Israel's deed to the land; therefore, knowledge of the Torah is what demonstrates the right to possess the one resource worth having:

Genesis Rabbah I:II.1

1A. R. Joshua of Sikhnin in the name of R. Levi commenced [discourse by citing the following verse]: " *'He has declared to his people the power of his works, in giving them the heritage of the nations'* (Ps. 111:6).

B. "What is the reason that the Holy One, blessed be He, revealed to Israel what was created on the first day and what on the second?

C. "It was on account of the nations of the world. It was so that they should not ridicule the Israelites, saying to them 'Are you not a nation of robbers [having stolen the land from the Canaanites]?'

D. "It allows the Israelites to answer them, 'And as to you, is there no spoil in your hands? For surely: *"The Caphtorim, who came forth out of Caphtor, destroyed them and dwelled in their place"* (Deut. 2:23)!

E. " 'The world and everything in it belongs to the Holy One, blessed be He. When he wanted, he gave it to you, and when he wanted, he took it from you and gave it to us.'

F. "That is in line with what is written, '. . . *in giving them the heritage of the nations, he has declared to his people the power of his works'* (Ps. 111:6). [So as to give them the land, he established his right to do so by informing them that he had created it.]

G. "He told them about the beginning: *'In the beginning God created . . .'* (Gen. 1:1)."

While pertinent, the passage is hardly probative; it links Torah to land, but for merely instrumental purposes. Moreover, the conception of riches in the conventional philosophical sense certainly persisted. "Abram was very rich in cattle" is understood quite literally, interpreted in line with Psalms 105:37: "*He brought them forth with silver and gold, and there was none that stumbled among his tribes.*"[11] Along these same lines, "Jacob's riches" of Genesis 30:43 are understood to be material and concrete: sixty-thousand dogs, for example.[12] One may therefore interpret the story of the disinheritance of Eliezer b. Hyrcanus on account of his running off to study the Torah with Yohanan ben Zakkai as a contrasting tale. The father intends to disinherit the son from his property because he has gone to study the Torah but then, impressed by the son's achievements, goes and gives him the whole estate.[13] But that would require reading into the story a symbolic transaction that is not explicit. So too, the allegation that "Torah" is represented by bread does not require, and perhaps does not even sustain, the interpretation that Torah learning forms a scarce resource that provides bread, is worth bread, and serves as bread does:

Genesis Rabbah LXX:V.1

A. ". . . will give me bread to eat and clothing to wear":

B. Aqilas the proselyte came to R. Eliezer and said to him, "Is all the gain that is coming to the proselyte going to be contained in this verse: '. . . *and loves the proselyte, giving him food and clothing*' (Deut. 10:18)?"

C. He said to him, "And is something for which the old man [Jacob] beseeched going to be such a small thing in your view namely, '. . . will give me bread to eat and clothing to wear'? [God] comes and hands it over to [a proselyte] on a reed [and the proselyte does not have to beg for it]."

D. He came to R. Joshua, who commenced by saying words to appease him: " 'Bread' refers to Torah, as it is said, '*Come, eat of my bread*' (Prov. 9:5). 'Clothing' refers to the cloak of a disciple of sages.

E. "When a person has the merit of studying the Torah, he has the merit of carrying out a religious duty. [So the proselyte receives a great deal when he gets bread and clothing, namely, entry into the estate of disciples.]

F. "And not only so, but his daughters may be chosen for marriage into the priesthood, so that their sons' sons will offer

burnt offerings on the altar. [So the proselyte may also look forward
to entry into the priests' caste. That statement will now be spelled
out.]

G. " 'Bread' refers to the show bread.

H. " 'Clothing' refers to the garments of the priesthood.

I. "So lo, we deal with the sanctuary.

J. "How do we know that the same sort of blessing applies in
the provinces? 'Bread' speaks of the dough offering [that is sep-
arated in the provinces], while 'clothing' refers to the first fleece
[handed over to the priest]."

Here too it is reasonable to interpret the passage in a merely symbolic
way: "bread" stands for Torah learning because just as bread sustains
the body, so Torah learning sustains the soul. That and similar inter-
pretations offer plausible alternatives to the conception that for the
successor system Torah learning forms the scarce resource that defines
value in the way in which land does for Aristotle or Israelite-occupied
land in the Land of Israel does for the Mishnah.

There are passages that are quite explicit, however: land is wealth,
or Torah is wealth, but not both; owning land is power and studying
Torah permits (re)gaining power. The following presents the first of the
two propositions in its most explicit formulation:

Leviticus Rabbah XXX:I.4

A. R. Yohanan was going up from Tiberias to Sepphoris. R.
Hiyya bar Abba was supporting him. They came to a field. He
said, "This field once belonged to me, but I sold it in order to
acquire merit in the Torah."

B. They came to a vineyard, and he said, "This vineyard once
belonged to me, but I sold it in order to acquire merit in the
Torah."

C. They came to an olive grove, and he said, "This olive grove
once belonged to me, but I sold it in order to acquire merit in
the Torah."

D. R. Hiyya began to cry.

E. Said R. Yohanan, "Why are you crying?"

F. He said to him, "It is because you left nothing over to support
you in your old age."

G. He said to him, "Hiyya, my disciple, is what I did such a light thing in your view? I sold something that was given in a spell of six days [creation] and in exchange I acquired something that was given in a spell of forty days [of revelation].

H. "The entire world and everything in it was created in only six days, as it is written, '*For in six days the Lord made heaven and earth*' (Exod. 20:11).

I. "But the Torah was given over a period of forty days, as it was said, '*And he was there with the Lord for forty days and forty nights*' (Exod. 34:28).

J. "And it is written, '*And I remained on the mountain for forty days and forty nights*' (Deut. 9:9)."

5A. When R. Yohanan died, his generation recited concerning him [the following verse of Scripture]: "*If a man should give all the wealth of his house for the love*" (Song of Sol. 8:7) with which R. Yohanan loved the Torah, "*he would be utterly destitute*" (Song of Sol. 8:7). . . .

B. When R. Eleazar b. R. Simeon died, his generation recited concerning him [the following verse of Scripture]: "*Who is this who comes up out of the wilderness like pillars of smoke, perfumed with myrrh and frankincense, with all the powders of the merchant ?*" (Son of Sol. 3:6)

D. What is the meaning of the clause, "with all the powders of the merchant"?

E. [Like a merchant who carries all sorts of desired powders,] he was a master of Scripture, a repeater of Mishnah traditions, a writer of liturgical supplications, and a liturgical poet.

The sale of land for the acquisition of "merit in the Torah" introduces two principal systemic components, merit and Torah.[14] For my purpose, the importance of the statement lies in the second of the two, which deems land the counterpart—and clearly the opposite—of the Torah.

Now one can sell a field and acquire Torah, meaning in the context established by the exchange between Tarfon and Aqiba the opportunity to gain leisure to (acquire the merit gained by) the study of the Torah. That the sage has left himself nothing for his support in old age makes explicit the material meaning of the statement, and the comparison of the value of land, created in six days, and the Torah, created in forty days, is equally explicit. The comparison of knowledge of Torah to the merchant's wares simply repeats the same point, but in a lower register. So too does the this-worldly power of Torah study make explicit in another framework the conviction that study of the Torah yields material and concrete benefit, not just spiritual renewal. Thus R. Huna states, "All the exiles will be gathered together only on account of the study of Mishnah teachings."[15]

In addition, the sage devoted to study of the Torah has to be supported because he can no longer perform physical work. Study of the Torah deprives him of physical strength, and that contrast and counterpart represented by land and working of the land as against Torah and the study of the Torah comes to symbolic expression in yet another way:

Leviticus Rabbah XI:XXII.1

A. R. Eleazar bar Simeon was appointed to impress men and beasts into forced labor [in the corvée]. One time Elijah, of blessed memory, appeared to him in the guise of an old man. Elijah said to him, "Get me a beast of burden."

B. Eleazar said to him, "What do you have as a cargo [to load on the beast]?"

C. He said to him, "This old skin-bottle of mine, my cloak, and me as rider."

D. He said, "Take a look at this old man! I [personally] can take him and carry him to the end of the world, and he says to me to get a beast ready!"

E. What did he do? He loaded him on his back and carried him up mountains and down valleys and over fields of thorns and fields of thistles.

F. In the end [Elijah] began to bear down on him. He said to him, "Old man, old man! Make yourself lighter, and if you don't, I'll toss you off."

G. [Elijah] said to him, "Now do you want to take a bit of a rest?"

H. He said to him, "Yes."

I. What did he do? [Elijah] took him to a field and set him down under a tree and gave him food and drink. When he had eaten and drunk, he [Elijah] said to him, "All this running about— what is in it for you? Would it not be better for you to take up the vocation of your fathers?"

J. He said to him, "And can you teach it to me?"

K. He said to him, "Yes."

L. And there are those who say that for thirteen years Elijah of blessed memory taught him until he could recite even Sifra [the exegesis of Leviticus, which is particularly difficult].

M. But once he could recite that document, [he had so lost his strength that] he could not lift up even a cloak.

2A. The household of Rabban Gamaliel had a member who could carry forty *seahs* [of grain] to the baker [on his back].

B. He said to him, "All this vast power do you possess, and you do not devote yourself to the study of Sifra."

C. When he could recite that document, they say that even a single *seah* of grain he was unable to bear.

D. There are those who say that if someone else did not take it off him, he would not have been able to take it off himself.

I include these stories about physical weakness as a mark of the sage only because they form part of the (in this instance, secondary) composition of Eleazar b. Simeon. They nonetheless do form part of a larger program of contrasting Torah study with land ownership and intellectual prowess with physical power and of weighing the superiority of the one over the other. No wonder sages would in time claim that their power protected cities, which then needed neither police nor walls. These were concrete claims, affecting the rational utilization of scarce resources as much as the use and distribution of land constituted an expression of a rationality concerning the preservation and increase of scarce resourses.

In alleging that the pertinent verses of Proverbs were assigned a quite this-worldly and material sense, so that study of the Torah really was worth more than silver, I say no more than the successor compilations allege in so many words. Thus the following, which faces head on the fact that masters of the Torah are paid for studying the Torah, so confirming the claim that the Torah served as a spade with which to dig:

Pesiqta deRab Kahana XXVII:I

1A. R. Abba bar Kahana commenced [discourse by citing the following verse]: "*Take my instruction instead of silver, and knowledge rather than choice gold*" (Prov. 8:10).

B. Said R. Abba bar Kahana, "Take the instruction of the Torah instead of silver.

C. "Take the instruction of the Torah and not silver.

D. " '*Why do you weigh out money? [Because there is no bread]*' (Isa. 55:2).

E. "Why do you weigh out money to the sons of Esau [Rome]? [It is because] there is no bread, because you did not sate yourselves with the bread of the Torah.

F. " '*And [why] do you labor? Because there is no satisfaction*' (Isa. 55:2).

G. "Why do you labor while the nations of the world enjoy plenty? Because there is no satisfaction, that is, because you have not sated yourselves with the bread of the Torah and with the wine of the Torah.

H. "For it is written, '*Come, eat of my bread, and drink of the wine I have mixed*' (Prov. 9:5)."

2A. R. Berekhiah and R. Hiyya, his father, in the name of R. Yosé b. Nehorai: "It is written, '*I shall punish all who oppress him*' (Jer. 30:20), even those who collect funds for charity [and in doing so, treat people badly], except [for those who collect] the wages to be paid to teachers of Scripture and repeaters of Mishnah traditions.

B. "For they receive [as a salary] only compensation for the loss of their time, [which they devote to teaching and learning rather than to earning a living].

C. "But as to the wages [for carrying out] a single matter in the Torah, no creature can pay the [appropriate] fee in reward."

The obvious goal, the homily at 1:E, surely stands against my claim for allegations of concrete and material value, namely, the imputation to the learning of the Torah of the status of "scarce resources." The whole of number 2, however, makes the contrary position explicit: wages are paid to Torah teachers. The following makes the same point:

Y. Nedarim 4:3.II

A. It is written, "*Behold, I have taught you statutes and ordinances*" [Deut. 4:5].

B. Just as I do so without pay, so you must do so without pay.

C. Is it possible that the same rule applied to teaching Scripture and translation [cf. M. Ned. 4:3D]?

D. Scripture says, "Statutes and ordinances."

E. Statutes and ordinances must you teach without pay, but you need not teach Scripture and translation without pay.

F. And yet we see that those who teach Mishnah collect their pay.

G. Said R. Judah b. R. Ishmael, "It is a fee for the use of their time [which they cannot utilize to earn a living for themselves] which they collect."

True, this transformation of Torah study into something of real worth is rationalized as salary in compensation for loss of time, but the same rationalization clearly did not impress the many masters of the initial system who insisted that the sage must practice a craft to make a living and study the Torah only in his leisure time. The contrast between the two positions appears quite explicitly in what follows.

Y. Peah 1:1.VII (trans. Brooks)

D. It is forbidden to a person to teach his son a trade, in as much as it is written, "*And you shall meditate therein day and night*" (Joshua 1:8).

E. But has not R. Ishmael taught, "*You shall choose life*" (Deut. 30:19)—this refers to learning [Torah] and practicing a trade as well. [One both studies the Torah and also a trade.]

There is no harmonizing the two views by appeal to this rationalization. In fact, study of the Torah substituted for practicing a craft, and it was meant to do so, as A alleges explicitly. In all, therefore, there is firm evidence for the proposition that in the successor system Torah becomes a material good and, further, is transformed into the ultimate scarce resource, explicitly substituting for real estate, even in the Land of Israel.

That ultimate value—Torah study—surely bears comparison with other foci of value, such as prayer, using money for building synagogues, and the like. It is explicitly stated that spending money on synagogues is a waste of money, whereas spending money supporting Torah masters is the right use of scarce resources. There is the further claim that synagogues and schoolhouses—communal real estate—form the property of sages and their disciples, who may dispose of them just as they want, as any owner may dispose of his property according to his unfettered will. In Y. Sheqalim we find the former allegation; in Y. Megillah, the latter:

Y. Sheqalim 5:4.II

A. R. Hama bar Haninah and R. Hoshaia the Elder were strolling in the synagogues in Lud. Said R. Hama bar Haninah to R. Hoshaia, "How much money did my forefathers invest here [in building these synagogues]!"

B. He said to him, "How many lives did your forefathers invest here! Were there not people who were laboring in Torah [who needed the money more]?"

C. R. Abun made the gates of the great hall [of study]. R. Mana came to him. He said to him, "See what I have made!"

D. He said to him, " 'For Israel has forgotten his Maker and built palaces' (Hos. 8:14)! Were there no people laboring in Torah [who needed the money more]?"

Y. Sotah 9:13.VI

C. A certain rabbi would teach Scripture to his brother in Tyre, and when they came and called him to do business, he would say, "I am not going to take away from my fixed time to study. If the profit is going to come to me, let it come in due course [after my fixed time for study has ended]."

Y. Megillah 3:3:V

A. R. Joshua b. Levi said, "Synagogues and schoolhouses belong to sages and their disciples."

B. R. Hiyya bar Yosé received [guests] in the synagogue [and lodged them there].

C. R. Immi instructed the scribes, "If someone comes to you with some slight contact with Torah learning, receive him, his asses, and his belongings."

D. R. Berekhiah went to the synagogue in Beisan. He saw someone rinsing his hands and feet in a fountain [in the courtyard of the synagogue]. He said to him, "It is forbidden to you [to do this]."

E. The next day the man saw [Berekhiah] washing his hands and feet in the fountain.

F. He said to him, "Rabbi, is it permitted to you and forbidden to me?"

G. He said to him, "Yes."

H. He said to him, "Why?"

I. He said to him, "Because this is what R. Joshua b. Levi said: 'Synagogues and schoolhouses belong to sages and their disciples.' "

Not all acts of piety are equal, and the one that takes precedence over all others (just as is alleged at Mishnah tractate Peah 1:1) is study of the Torah. The point is a much more concrete one, however, namely, that through study of the Torah, sages and their disciples gain possession over communal real estate, which they may utilize in any way they wish. That is a quite concrete claim indeed, as the preceding story illustrates.

No wonder, then, that people in general were expected to contribute their scarce resources for the support of sages and their disciples. Moreover, society at large was obligated to support sages, and the sages' claim on others was enforceable by Heaven. Those who gave sages' disciples money so that they would not have to work would get it back from Heaven, and those who did not would lose what they had:

Y. Sotah 7:4.IV

F. R. Aha in the name of R. Tanhum b. R. Hiyya: "If one has learned, taught, kept, and carried out [the Torah], and has ample means in his possession to strengthen the Torah and has not done so, lo, such a one still is in the category of those who are cursed." [The meaning of "strengthen" here is to support the masters of the Torah.]

G. R. Jeremiah in the name of R. Hiyya bar Ba, "[If] one did not learn, teach, keep, and carry out [the teachings of the Torah], and did not have ample means to strengthen [the masters of the Torah] [but nonetheless did strengthen them], lo, such a one falls into the category of those who are blessed."

H. And R. Hannah, R. Jeremiah in the name of R. Hiyya: "The Holy One, blessed be He, is going to prepare a protection for those who carry out religious duties [of support for masters of Torah] through the protection afforded to the masters of Torah [themselves].

I. "What is the Scriptural basis for that statement? 'For the protection of wisdom is like the protection of money' (Qoh. 7:12).

J. "And it says, '[*The Torah] is a tree of life to those who grasp it; those who hold it fast are called happy*' (Prov. 3:18)."

Such contributions form the counterpart to taxes, that is, scarce resources taken away from the owner by force for the purposes of the public good, and thus constitute the ultimate meeting point of economics and politics, the explicit formation of distributive, as against, market, economics. What is distributed and to whom and by what force forms the centerpiece of the systemic political economy, and the answer is perfectly simple: all sorts of valued things are taken away from people and handed over for the support of sages:

Pesiqta deRab Kahana V:IV.2

A. "*A man's gift makes room for him and brings him before great men*" (Prov. 18:16).

B. M'SH B: R. Eliezer, R. Joshua, and R. Aqiba went to the harborside of Antioch to collect funds for the support of sages.

C. [In Aramaic:] A certain Abba Yudan lived there.

D. He would carry out his religious duty [of philanthropy] in a liberal spirit, but had lost his money. When he saw our masters, he went home with a sad face. His wife said to him, "What's wrong with you, that you look so sad?"

E. He repeated the tale to her: "Our masters are here, and I don't know what I shall be able to do for them."

F. His wife, who was a truly philanthropic woman—what did she say to him? "You only have one field left. Go, sell half of it and give them the proceeds."

G. He went and did just that. When he was giving them the money, they said to him, "May the Omnipresent make up all your losses."

H. Our masters went their way.

I. He went out to plough. While he was ploughing the half of the field that he had left, the Holy One, blessed be He, opened his eyes. The earth broke open before him, and his cow fell in and broke her leg. He went down to raise her up, and found a treasure beneath her. He said, "It was for my gain that my cow broke her leg."

J. When our masters came back, [in Aramaic:] they asked about a certain Abba Yudan and how he was doing. They said, "Who can gaze on the face of Abba Yudan [which glows with prosperity]—Abba Yudan, the owner of flocks of goats, Abba Yudan, the owner of herds of asses, Abba Yudan, the owner of herds of camels."

K. He came to them and said to them, "Your prayer in my favor has produced returns and returns and returns."

L. They said to him, "Even though someone else gave more than you did, we wrote your name at the head of the list."

M. Then they took him and sat him next to themselves and recited in his regard the following verse in Scripture: "*A man's gift makes room for him and brings him before great men*" (Prov. 18:16).

What is at stake here in the scarce resource represented by Torah study? It cannot be a (merely) spiritual benefit, when I get rich in consequence of giving money to sages so they will not have to work. Moreover, the matter of position is equally in play: I get rich, and I also enjoy the standing of sages, sitting next to them. So far as social position intersects with wealth, the Torah constitutes the wealth that, in this systemic context, defines "scarce resources": a source of this-worldly gain in practical terms, of public prestige in social terms, and of validation of the use of force—in this context, psychological force—for taking away scarce (material) resources in favor of a superior value. The entire system comes to expression in this story: its economics, its politics, and, as a matter of fact, its philosophy. But all three are quite different from what they were in the initial structure and system.

No wonder then that sages protect cities. It is claimed that sages are the guardians of cities, and later on that would yield the further allegation that sages do not have to pay taxes to build walls around cities, because their Torah study protects the cities:

Pesiqta deRab Kahana XV:V.1

A. R. Abba bar Kahana commenced discourse by citing the following verse: "*Who is the man so wise that he may understand this? To whom has the mouth of the Lord spoken, that he may declare it? Why is the land ruined and laid waste like a wilderness, [so that no one passes through? The Lord said, It is because they forsook my Torah which I set before them; they neither obeyed me nor conformed to it. They followed the promptings of their own*

*stubborn hearts, they followed the Baalim as their forefathers had
taught them. Therefore these are the words of the Lord of Hosts
the God of Israel: I will feed this people with wormwood and give
them bitter poison to drink. I will scatter them among nations
whom neither they nor their forefathers have known; I will harry
them with the sword until I have made an end of them]"* (Jer.
9:16).

B. It was taught in the name of R. Simeon b. Yohai, "If you
see towns uprooted from their place in the Land of Israel, know
that [it is because] the people did not pay the salaries of teachers
of children and Mishnah instructors.

C. "What is the verse of Scripture that indicates it? *Why is the
land ruined and laid waste like a wilderness, [so that no one passes
through]?* What is written just following? *It is because they forsook
my Torah [which I set before them; they neither obeyed me nor
conformed to it].*

2A. Rabbi sent R. Yosé and R. Ammi to go and survey the towns
of the Land of Israel. They would go into a town and say to the
people, "Bring me the guardians of the town."

B. The people would bring out the head of the police and the
local guard.

C. [The sages] would say, "These are not the guardians of the
town, they are those who destroy the town. Who are the guardians
of the town? They are the teachers of children and Mishnah
teachers, who keep watch by day and night, in line with the verse,
'*And you shall meditate in it day and night*' (Josh. 1:8)."

D. And so Scripture says, "*If the Lord does not build the house,
in vain the builders labor*" (Ps. 127:1).

7A. Said R. Abba bar Kahana, "No philosophers in the world
ever arose of the quality of Balaam ben Beor and Abdymos of
Gadara. The nations of the world came to Abdymos of Gardara.
They said to him, 'Do you maintain that we can make war against
this nation?'

B. "He said to them, 'Go and make the rounds of their synagogues and their study houses. So long as there are there children
chirping out loud in their voices [and studying the Torah], then
you cannot overcome them. If not, then you can conquer them,
for so did their father promise them: "*The voice is Jacob's voice*"
(Gen. 27:22), meaning that when Jacob's voice chirps in synagogues

and study houses, the hands are *not* the hands of Esau [so Esau has no power].

C. " 'So long as there are no children chirping out loud in their voices [and studying the Torah] in synagogues and study houses, the hands are the hands of Esau [so Esau has power].' "

The reference to Esau (Rome) links the whole to the contemporary context and alleges that if the Israelites will support those who study the Torah and teach it, then their cities will be safe, and, still more, the rule of Esau/Rome will come to an end; then the Messiah will come, so the stakes are not trivial.

The disenlandisement of economics, the transvaluation of value so that Torah replaced land as the supreme measure of value and also of social worth—these form (an) economics that is fully the counterpart to the philosophical economics based on real estate as true value that Aristotle and the framers of the Mishnah constructed, each party for its own systemic purpose. Indeed, there is no need to review the components of this Torah-based economics—the theory of means of production and who controls the operative unit of production of value or the consideration of whether it promotes a market or a distributive economics. It is perfectly obvious that the sage controlled the means of production and fully mastered the power to govern them; the sage distributed valued resources—supernatural or material, as the case required—and the conception of a market was as alien to that economics as it was to the priestly economics revised and replicated by the Mishnah's system. Enough has been said, therefore, to establish beyond reasonable doubt the claim that the idea of Torah provides the successor system's counterpart category of economics.

And yet that very fact calls into question my insistence that this system produced not (merely) another economics, with a different value, but a counterpart economics. For I claim that Torah is a systemic counterpart to economics, not the same thing in another form: an anti-economics and the transvaluation of value, not merely the redefinition of what is to be valued. Obviously, I have reservations that have led me to this claim. A shift from valuing land to valuing liquid capital (or from valuing beads to valuing conchs, for that matter) would require neither the invention of the category of counterpart economics nor the rather protracted argument offered earlier concerning the movement from the subject to the complement of the operative language of definition. Why, then, my rather odd claim that the system transvalues economics instead of merely redefining it?

I make the claim because economics deals with scarce resources, and the disenlandisement of economics in the successor Judaism turned on its head the very focus of economics: scarcity and the rational confrontation with scarcity. Nature sets rigid limits to land, and still more narrow ones apply to the Holy Land, but knowledge of the Torah has no such limits. The resulting economics thus concerns not the rational utilization of scarce resources but the very opposite: the rational utilization of what can and ought to be the opposite of scarce. In identifying knowledge and teaching of the Torah as the ultimate value, the successor system has not simply constructed a new economics in place of an old one, finding of value something other than what had earlier been valued; it has redefined economics altogether, and it has done so in a manner that is entirely familiar, by setting forth in place of an economics of scarcity an economics of abundant productivity.

Disenlandising value thus transvalues value by insisting on its (potential) increase as the definition of what is rational economic action. The task is not preservation of power over land but increase of power over the Torah, because one can only preserve land, but one can increase one's knowledge of the Torah. To revert to the theoretical point that in context seemed so excessive, the economics of the initial system concerns the rational disposition of the scarce resource of particular real property; the rational increase of the potentially abundant resource of Torah learning is—that is, serves and functions as—the economics of the successor system.

Notes

1. An economics that the Mishnah set forth but the successor documents did not develop.

2. Let me recapitulate a point made earlier but important here. Does that fact then suggest the new system's theory of the social order set forth no economics at all? After all, there is no reason that a theory of the social order requires an economics, for a variety of theories of the social order of the same time and place other than Aristotle's and the Mishnah's—Plato's for one, the Gospels' for another, the Essene Community at Qumran's for a third—managed to put forth a compelling theory of society lacking any sustained, systematic, and systemically pertinent attention to economics at all. I insist, however, that the successor system put forth a theory of the way of

life that must be characterized as an economics—not as a theology that made passing reference to topics of economic interest, but as an economics. It was, however, one involving a value different from the ultimate value of real property that characterizes Aristotle's and the Mishnah's economics.

3. I define matters narrowly in economic terms, rather than encompassing such valid considerations of sociology as status, for my claim to demonstrate a counterpart category requires a rigorous and rigid definition of economics. It would be facile and self-serving to introduce into political economy considerations of status; I can readily demonstrate shifts therein, but so what? Later on, however, I shall have to concede the social embeddedness of the new economics of the successor system, in a way in which, in my consideration of the initial system, I never had to do. As I show in *The Politics of the Mishnah*, the economics of the Mishnah is disembedded from the politics, so that we have a politics and an economics but not a political economy in the way in which Aristotle's system sets forth a political economy. But the economics of the successor system is profoundly embedded in its politics (and in its philosophy, as a matter of fact), so the system is a much more tightly integrated one than the initial system. All of this takes on greater detail in due course.

4. I use the word *real* in the technical sense, meaning landed wealth or property: real estate. Any other usage draws me into questions of theology or philosophy, with which economics does not deal. I shall presently argue that there is no spiritualizing or moralizing or philosophizing "value," which bears concrete meanings and material consequences in the documents considered here.

5. For Aristotle, land could be anywhere; for the Mishnah's economics, the ultimate value was a particular piece of land, which was the Land of Israel occupied by holy Israel.

6. Now the word *real* is used in its nontechnical sense, with which sense theologians and philosophers are more at ease.

7. I present in this chapter a richer selection of abstracts than I thought required in the others because my claim here is somewhat out of the ordinary. That makes it necessary to show, through concrete passages, that what I claim is happening in the successor documents is amply instantiated in them.

8. At this point in the argument of the book, readers may conclude that the systemic center lay in the symbol and concept of Torah, because both the worldview and the way of life define themselves within that category and the data pertinent to it. But we shall see in chapters 7 and 8 that Torah is subordinate to another and deeper consideration; it is contingent and a dependent variable, in no way the independent variable and point of final destination that mark a system's center. Torah produces what we really want— that is the upshot of chapters 7 and 8. Consequently, readers are cautioned not to identify the materials under discussion in chapters 4 and 5 as the end of the matter; counterpart categories serve to describe their system, but they do not define the systemic center at all. They simply guide us to that center.

9. Hence the title of this chapter, which alleges that value is transvalued.

At the end of the chapter I explain precisely why I insist that the successor system does not merely identify a new scarce resource in place of the received one, but that the disenlandisement of value constitutes in this context an utter redefinition of what can be meant by economics, hence, the transvaluation of value.

10. To be sure, the distinction between *haber* and *am haares* does not encompass Torah study. Only in later strata of the canon did the value of Torah knowledge contrast with the disvalue (disgrace) of ignorance, distinguishing the *haber* from the *am haares*. And when that distinction was made, the opposite of *am haares* was sage or disciple of a sage.

11. Genesis Rabbah XLI:III.1.A-B.

12. Genesis Rabbah LXXIII:XI.1.D.

13. Genesis Rabbah XLII:I.1.

14. In a well-crafted system, principal parts prove interchangeable or closely aligned, and that is surely the case here, but I have already observed that the successor system is far more tightly constructed than the initial one, in that the politics and the economics flow into one another in a way in which, in the initial, philosophical system, they do not. The disembedded character of the Mishnah's economics has already been discussed.

15. Pesiqta deRab Kahana VI:III.3.B.

6

Empowerment and the Category
The People Israel

Stated roughly, philosophical politics tells who may legitimately do what to whom. When a politics sets forth who ought *not* to be doing what to whom, it formulates the counterpart category to the received politics.[1] The received category set forth politics as the theory of legitimate violence; the conterpart category, politics as the theory of *illegitimate* violence. The received politics had been one of isolation and interiority, portraying Israel as *sui generis* and autocephalic in all ways. The successor documents portray a politics of integration among the nations; a perspective of exteriority replaces the inner-facing one of the Mishnah, which recognized no government of Israel but God's — and then essentially *ab initio*. The issues of power had found definition in questions concerning who legitimately inflicts sanctions on whom within Israel. In the later documents they shift to give an account of who illegitimately inflicts sanctions on ("persecutes") Israel. The points of systemic differentiation are radically revised, and the politics of the successor system becomes not a revision of the received category but a formation that in many ways mirrors the received one: once more, a counterpart category. Just as, in the definition of scarce resources, Torah study replaced land, so now weakness forms the focus in place of strength, illegitimacy in place of legitimacy. Once more the mirror image of the received category presents the perspective of the counterpart category.

The politics of the successor system turns outward, its attention focused on the world in which Israel finds itself. Israel differentiated by its castes, Israel as taxic indicator — these categories no longer form the center of exegetical attention. Instead, with Israel viewed whole, the opposite of "Israel" is not "Levite, then Priest" or (in the opposite direction) "gentile," but "the nations." Israel is one and whole vis-à-vis outsiders, who are seen as many and distinct. Israel as the victim of illegitimate violence and the nations as illegitimately empowered now define the main beams in the categorical structure of the successor system's politics. That fact justifies the classification of the system's politics as not a mere revision but an utter inversion, hence, a counterpart category. The received components of way of life, worldview, and social entity are recast in category, not merely content; this transmutation explains why, in regard to the definition of the social entity and, in particular, the realm of empowerment, to be "Israel" is to be the victim of the illegitimate exercise of power. The new system classifies Israel in context and transitively, as a nation among nations and subject to the will of outsiders, not out of context and intransitively, as an autonomous and freestanding social entity.

When they speak on their own account and not in clarification of the Mishnah and related writings, the successor documents offer data that shift in character. They answer questions about to whom violence is illegitimately done and who may not legitimately inflict violence. With the move from the politics of legitimate to that of illegitimate power, the systemic interest comes to lie in defining not who legitimately does what but rather to whom or against whom power is illegitimately exercised. This movement represents not the revision of the received category but its inversion, for thought on legitimate violence is turned on its head, and a new category of empowerment is worked out alongside the old. The entity that is the victim of power is at the center, rather than the entity that legitimately exercises power. That entity is now Israel *en masse,* rather than the institutions and agencies of Israel on earth and Heaven above—a very considerable shift in thought on the systemic social entity. Rather than king, high priest, and sage as Israel's media of empowerment, Israel as disempowered defines the new system's politics.

In laying claim to the status of empowerment, the successor system's discussions on legitimate violence ask about the illegitimacy of violence inflicted on social entities—which nonetheless also are conceived as political entities—rather than the legitimacy of violence inflicted by them.[2] This is as much a new mode of classification, an utterly fresh category, as the odd and unpredicatable economics reconsidered in the transvaluation of value. But as that remained an economics, so in hand is still a politics. The reason is that the question it seeks to answer remains the same as before: who inflicts sanctions on whom, and why? The answer is found in the entities on which discussions of violence focus.

This is a political question addressed to an empowered entity, but the answer—the focus of attention within political thought—now centers on the violence inflicted on Israel as a nation, and differentiation is among those who illegitimately act violently. True, when they speak of who legitimately exercises violence (in addition to Heaven, of course), sages refer to the sage. This constitutes a mere extension of the received system, which assigned sages mastery of the courts alongside the monarchy and the high priesthood. When the successor writings specify on whom and by whom violence is illegitimately exercised, however, there is a wholly new realm of thinking going on.

Recall that the Mishnah's government for Israel comprises, on earth, a tripartite structure of high priest, king, and administrative courts of sages, ascending upward to the authority of the Temple mount. Above, and corresponding, is the court in Heaven. That court bears its jurisdiction for some actions, the earthly political institutions each exercise jurisdiction for others, and the point of differentiation sets forth the urgent and compelling systemic issue in the political component of the system, just as it did in the other components. The Talmud of the Land of Israel and its companion compilations of scriptural exegeses do not even pretend that such an ordered, self-governing world existed in their time—or ever would, for that matter. They portray an administration by an unstructured set of small-claims courts standing outside an appellate structure of authority, petty bureaus of adminsitration for trivial things presided over by rabbis, who were defined as judges, lawyers, and masters of disciples in the law. At the head of it all is not a king but a patriarch, on the one side, or a priest anointed for the purpose, on the other. And the patriarch is variously represented as honorable and not. A variety of well-composed political institutions gives way to a single kind of institution, and a vertical structure is set aside by a horizontal one. These institutional differences as to fact signal a deeper difference as to system.

The Mishnah's account of practical politics and that of the Yerushalmi prove discontinuous not only in structure but also in system, for the discontinuity reveals itself in the theory of empowerment. The successor system deems gentiles not only empowered but also subject to differentiation. The earlier system concerned itself with the internal politics of (an) Israel, with politics seen as the principal taxic indication of the social order. The later politics, by contrast, turned toward the external relationships of (an) Israel located in the disorderly world of nations. Thus, the new politics not only inverted the issue of violence and turned its illegitimate side upward, it also revised the systemic vision so that attention faced outward, differentiation among the outsider vis-à-vis (an) undifferentiated Israel being the result. Consequently, in defining what is at stake in the theory of legitimate violence that forms the centerpiece of politics, the successor system proves wholly other.

The burden of the systemic message assigned to the component of politics remained as heavy in the successor system as in the prior one, but the contents proved quite dissimilar. The Mishnah's political theory focused on the inner structure and composition of Israel's social order; politics served the systemic purpose of setting forth the hierarchical taxonomy of power, just as each of the other principal parts of the Mishnah's statement of the social order represented the classification and ordering of all classes of things. When the Mishnah's politics spells out who within Israel legitimately inflicts sanctions on whom within Israel, the principle of differentiation yields a clear picture of the organization of Israelite society. The role of politics in the philosophical statement of Judaism is to represent the theoretical standing of the empowered institutions, the ones that bear the political role and responsibility. As I shall show, the task of politics in the successor system accomplished a different sort of differentiation altogether.   .

The systemic message now concerned an Israel lacking all capacity to effect violence and requiring an explanation of its illegitimacy. No longer an empowered nation, Israel — within the systemic writings of the late fourth and the fifth centuries — speculates on who is the worst among the nations, what will come of Israel, and when Israel will once more take charge of its own affairs. That explains why the systemic message was bound up not only with the *illegitimate* exercise of power but with differentiation among the entities, institutions, and persons that illegitimately inflict violence.[3] Where the former system sorted out who properly inflicts which sanction on whom, the new system's political analysis concerns the equally illegitimate actor and victim. That inversion brings me back to my interest in not the re-formation of received categories but the formation of the counterpart ones: to what systemic purpose was this effected? The answer lies right at the surface for the economics of never-scarce Torah of the successor system. What about the politics of weakness?

At stake is always the social entity, for a politics—commonplace and conventional or counterpart and odd—must define the social entity of the encompassing system. Here I locate the systemic message delivered by the antipolitics. The counterpart category rejects as beside the point what makes a politics political, namely, the legitimate use of violence. The data that will be sought attest to the very opposite facts, for now, all violence but God's and the sages' is illegitimate. The political entity that Israel is to form is an antipolitical one in that it defines itself not by appeal to its legitimate exercise of sanctions but rather by its exercising no power at all. The social entity in the politics at hand is made, therefore, to affirm the status of the victim, once again, a social entity for an antipolitics.

This political ideal reaches its simplest formulation in the bald statement that God—after all, the All-Powerful—wants only the victim, done to but never doing:[4]

Leviticus Rabbah XXVII:V.1

A. "*God seeks what has been driven away*" (Qoh. 3:15).

B. R. Huna in the name of R. Joseph said, "It is always the case that 'God seeks what has been driven away' [favoring the victim].

C. "You find when a righteous man pursues a righteous man, 'God seeks what has been driven away.'

D. "When a wicked man pursues a wicked man, 'God seeks what has been driven away.'

E. "All the more so when a wicked man pursues a righteous man, 'God seeks what has been driven away.'

F. "[The same principle applies] even when you come around to a case in which a righteous man pursues a wicked man, 'God seeks what has been driven away.' "

2A. R. Yosé b. R. Yudan in the name of R. Yosé b. R. Nehorai says, "It is always the case that the Holy One, blessed be He, demands an accounting for the blood of those who have been pursued from the hand of the pursuer.

B. "Abel was pursued by Cain, and God sought [an accounting for] the pursued: '*And the Lord looked [favorably] upon Abel and his meal offering*' (Gen. 4:4).

C. "Noah was pursued by his generation, and God sought [an accounting for] the pursued: '*You and all your household shall come into the ark*' (Gen. 7:1). And it says, '*For this is like the days of Noah to me, as I swore [that the waters of Noah should no more go over the earth]*' (Isa. 54:9).

D. "Abraham was pursued by Nimrod, 'and God seeks what has been driven away': '*You are the Lord, the God who chose Abram and brought him out of Ur*' (Neh. 9:7).

E. "Isaac was pursued by Ishmael, 'and God seeks what has been driven away': '*For through Isaac will seed be called for you*' (Gen. 21:12).

F. "Jacob was pursued by Esau, 'and God seeks what has been driven away': '*For the Lord has chosen Jacob, Israel for his prized possession*' (Ps. 135:4).

G. "Moses was pursued by Pharaoh, 'and God seeks what has been driven away': '*Had not Moses His chosen stood in the breach before Him*' (Ps. 106:23).

H. "David was purused by Saul, 'and God seeks what has been driven away': '*And he chose David, his servant*' (Ps. 78:70).

I. "Israel was pursued by the nations, 'and God seeks what has been driven away': '*And you has the Lord chosen to be a people to him*' (Deut. 14:2).

J. "And the rule applies also to the matter of offerings. A bull is pursued by a lion, a sheep is pursued by a wolf, a goat is pursued by a leopard.

K. "Therefore the Holy One, blessed be He, has said, 'Do not make offerings before me from those animals that pursue, but from those that are pursued': '*When a bull, a sheep, or a goat is born*' (Lev. 22:27)."

I can offer no better evidence that a new sense altogether has been imputed to the consideration of the legitimacy of power. No longer does politics explain the uses of power, specifying, for example, what sort of institutions may use it and on the basis of what kind of rationale. The issue is now exactly the opposite: the legitimacy of powerlessness and the illegitimacy of (nearly all) power. That these issues are political, not (merely) theological, is underlined when Israel as such enters: it is Israel contrasted with the nations, and as the latter form political entities, so does the former. This shows what I mean when I speak of an antipolitics, an inversion of the category to focus on not the legitimate but the illegitimate exercise of power, on not the actor but the victim.

This new thinking draws attention to new foci of differentiation as well. Formerly, it was the social entity Israel that was differentiated by its taxic components. Claims about who could legitimately inflict sanctions on whom were found in the diverse components of that social entity, analyzed and differentiated within the interiorities of its order and structure. Now the nondifferentiation of Israel—no longer ordered by its castes, for instance—finds its mirror, opposite, and counterpart in the differentiation of the nations (and Israel among them). These are ordered in the manner in which the Israelite castes had been ordered;[5] so hierarchical taxonomy now indicates how to sort out the affairs of nations in relationship to Israel. But what can this possibly mean? It is that the violence inflicted on Israel by one nation, as I shall show, may be more illegitimate than that inflicted on Israel by another.

The successor writings included Israel's history in their systemic discourse, with the acts of one gentile ruler compared to those of some other now enjoying importance as a medium for differentiation among outsiders. "Israel" thus became a historical entity, subject to historical narratives. The Mishnah and related writings had not presented historical narratives and did not find their provision systemically necessary. By contrast, successor documents portray Israel as the hero of a story with a crisis and denoument. In an infinity of ways, the story bearing the systemic message of the social entity in a political form always told a tale about what it means to be empowered but also subject to the power of others.

The stories about illegitimate violence, then, told what it means to form a social entity with traits that are intrinsic, concrete, and material, not merely indicative aspects of abstract relationships of comparison and contrast.[6] The successors' systemic "Israel" now became transitive and contextual, not merely occupying a given, transitive position within a hierarchical order of being or exhibiting certain taxic indicators of hierarchical meaning. As a corollary, other important systemic categories, such as "gentile," also acquired material definition and concrete nuance, as the systemic exercise in differentiation affected diverse components of the whole. In the successor system, Israel bears three meanings: (1) family, that is, a social entity different from the nations because it is formed by a common genealogy; (2) nation among nations; and

(3) Israel as *sui generis,* different not in indicative traits but categorically, that is to say, different in its very category from all other nations.

To begin with, when sages of the successor documents wished to know what (an) "Israel" was, they reread the scriptural story of Israel's origins for the answer. Scripture told them the story of a man named Jacob. His children, therefore, were "the children of Jacob." That man's name was also "Israel," thus "the children of Israel" comprised the extended family of that man. By extension upward, "Israel" formed the family of Abraham and Sarah, Isaac and Rebecca, and Jacob, Leah, and Rachel. "Israel" therefore invoked the metaphor of genealogy to explain the bonds that linked persons unseen into a single social entity; the shared traits were imputed, not empirically demonstrated. That social metaphor of "Israel"—a simple one, really, and easily grasped—bore consequences in two ways. First, children in general were admonished to follow the good example of their parents. The deeds of the patriarchs and matriarchs therefore taught lessons on how the children were to act. Second, and of greater interest in an account of "Israel" as a social metaphor, is the notion that "Israel" lived twice, once in the patriarchs and matriarchs, a second time in the lives of the heirs, as the descendants relived those earlier lives. The stories of these families were carefully reread as providing meaning to the latter-day events of the descendants. Accordingly, the lives of the patriarchs signaled the history of Israel.[7]

The metaphor of Israel as family supplied an encompassing theory of society, accounting for that sense of constituting a corporate social entity that clearly infused the documents of the Judaism of the dual Torah from the very outset. Such a theory did far more than explain who "Israel" was as a whole: it set forth the responsibilities of Israel's social entity, its society; it defined the character of that entity; it explained who owes what to whom, and why, therefore also explaining the politics of empowerment; and it accounted for the inner structure and interplay of relationship within the community, here and now, constituted by Jews in their villages and neighborhoods. Accordingly, "Israel" as family bridged the gap between an account of the entirety of the social group and a picture of the components of that social group as they lived out their lives in their households and villages. "Israel" viewed as extended family provided an encompassing theory of society, covering all components from least to greatest and holding the whole together in correct order and proportion.

Genesis Rabbah presents an example of the consequence of representing Israel as a family. Here, Israel as family is also understood to form a nation or people. This nation-people held a rather peculiar enchanted or holy land that, in its imputed traits, the metaphorical thought of the system at hand took to be as *sui generis* as Israel was (as I shall show presently). Competing for the same territory, Israel's claim to what it called the Land of Israel—*of Israel* in particular—now rested on right's of inheritance such as a family enjoyed, and this was made explicit. The following passage shows how high the stakes were in the claim to constitute the genealogical descendant of the ancestors.

Genesis Rabbah LXI:VII.1

A. "*But to the sons of his concubines, Abraham gave gifts, and while he was still living, he sent them away from his son Isaac, eastward to the east country*" (Gen. 25:6):

B. In the time of Alexander of Macedonia the sons of Ishmael came to dispute with Israel about the birthright, and with them came two wicked families, the Canaanites and the Egyptians.

C. They said, "Who will go and engage in a disputation with them?"

D. Gebiah b. Qosem [the enchanter] said, "I shall go and engage in a disputation with them."

E. They said to him, "Be careful not to let the Land of Israel fall into their possession."

F. He said to them, "I shall go and engage in a disputation with them. If I win over them, well and good. And if not, you may say, 'Who is this hunchback to represent us?' "

G. He went and engaged in a disputation with them. Said to them Alexander of Macedonia, "Who lays claim against whom?"

H. The Ishmaelites said, "We lay claim, and we bring our evidence from their own Torah: '*But he shall acknowledge the firstborn, the son of the hated*' (Deut. 21:17). Now Ishmael was the firstborn. [We therefore claim the land as heirs of the firstborn of Abraham.]"

I. Said to him Gebiah b. Qosem, "My royal lord, does a man not do whatever he likes with his sons?"

J. He said to him, "Indeed so."

K. "And lo, it is written, '*Abraham gave all that he had to Isaac*' (Gen. 25:2)."

L. [Alexander asked,] "Then where is the deed of gift to the other sons?"

M. He said to him, " '*But to the sons of his concubines, Abraham gave gifts, [and while he was still living, he sent them away from his son Isaac, eastward to the east country]*' (Gen. 25:6)."

N. [The Ishamelites had no claim on the land.] They abandoned the field in shame.

The metaphor now shifts, moving away from the notion of Israel as the family of Abraham, which was distinct from the Ishmaelites, yet also of the same family. But the theme of family records persists. Canaan has no claim, for though Canaan was also a family, comparable to Israel, it descended from a slave. The power of the metaphor of family is that it can explain not only the social entity formed by Jews but also the social entities confronted by them. All fell into the same genus, making up diverse species. The theory of society presented here—that is, the theory of "Israel"—thus also accounts for the existence of all societies and, as I shall show when I deal with Rome, does so with extraordinary force.

O. The Canaanites said, "We lay claim, and we bring our evidence from their own Torah. Throughout their Torah it is written, 'the land of Canaan.' So let them give us back our land."

P. Said to him Gebiah b. Qosem, "My royal lord, does a man not do whatever he likes with his slave?"

Q. He said to him, "Indeed so."

R. He said to him, "And lo, it is written, '*A slave of slaves shall Canaan be to his brothers*' (Gen. 9:25). So they are really our slaves."

S. [The Canaanites had no claim to the land and in fact should be serving Israel.] They abandoned the field in shame.

The same metaphor serves both "Israel" and "Canaan." Each formed the latter-day heir of the earliest family, and both lived out the original paradigm. The mode of thought at hand assigns both social entities to the same genus and then distinguishes between the two species.

The final claim in the passage moves away from the metaphor of family, but the notion of a continuous, physical descent is implicit here as well. "Israel" has inherited the wealth of Egypt. Because the notion of inheritance forms a component of the metaphor of family (a conception critical, as I shall show in the next section, to the supernatural patrimony of the "children of Israel" in the merit of the ancestors), the conclusion of the passage falls within the metaphor's scope.

T. The Egyptians said, "We lay claim, and we bring our evidence from their own Torah. Six hundred thousand of them left us, taking away our silver and gold utensils: '*They despoiled the Egyptians*' (Exod. 12:36). Let them give them back to us."

U. Gebiah b.Qosem said, "My royal lord, six hundred thousand men worked for them for two hundred and ten years, some as silversmiths and some as goldsmiths. Let them pay us our salary at the rate of a *denar* a day."

V. The mathematicians went and added up what was owing, and they had not reached the sum covering a century before the Egyptians had to forfeit what they had claimed. They abandoned the field in shame.

V. [Alexander] wanted to go up to Jerusalem. The Samaritans said to him, "Be careful. They will not permit you to enter their most holy sanctuary."

W. When Gebiah b. Qosem found out about this, he went and made for himself two felt shoes, with two precious stones worth twenty-thousand pieces of silver set in them. When he got to the mountain of the house [of the Temple], he said to him, "My royal lord, take off your shoes and put on these two felt slippers, for the floor is slippery, and you should not slip and fall."

X. When they came to the most holy sanctuary, he said to him, "Up to this point, we have the right to enter. From this point onward, we do not have the right to enter."

Y. He said to him, "When we get out of here, I'm going to even out your hump."

Z. He said to him, "You will be called a great surgeon and get a big fee."

The Ishmaelites, Abraham's children, deprived as they were of their inheritance, fall into the same genus as does Israel; so does Canaan. As to the Egyptians, that is a different matter. This last "Israel" is that same "Israel" of which Scripture spoke. The social metaphor shifts within the story, though the story is not affected.

This genealogical metaphor leads naturally to a picture of Israel as victim of illegitimate power, such as formed the centerpiece of the counterpart category of politics. Illegitimate power was exercised by a member of the same family, and the illegitimacy of his power derived from his genealogical illegitimacy. Indeed, the metaphor of family made possible the differentiation in material and concrete terms between the legitimate and the illegitimate, for, after all, these initially formed genealogical classifications and only by analogy and metaphor formed classifications of other sorts of data. Thus, the consequence of this appeal to the genealogical metaphor for the categorization of Israel emerges when attention shifts from the legitimate to the illegitimate political entity.

The illegitimate entity is, of course, Rome. The comparison of one line of a family to another line of the same family, the legitimate and the illegitimate, prepares the way for the system's project of comprehensively interpreting world politics. The following passage shows how the comparison and contrast of political entities within the genealogical metaphor take place.

Genesis Rabbah LXX:XV.1

A. "*Now Laban had two daughters, the name of the older was Leah, and the name of the younger was Rachel*" (Gen. 29:16):

B. They were like two beams running from one end of the world to the other.

C. This one produced captains and that one produced captains, this one produced kings and that one produced kings, this one produced lion tamers and that one produced lion tamers, this one produced conquerers of nations and that one produced conquerers of nations, this one produced those who divided countries and that one produced dividers of countries.

D. The offering brought by the son of this one overrode the prohibitions of the Sabbath, and the offering brought by the son of that one overrode the prohibitions of the Sabbath.

E. The war fought by this one overrode the prohibitions of the Sabbath, and the war fought by this one overrode the prohibitions of the Sabbath.

F. To this one were given two nights, and to that one were given two nights.

G. The night of Pharaoh and the night of Sennacherib were for Leah, and the night of Gideon was for Rachel, and the night of Mordecai was for Rachel, as it is said, *"On that night the king could not sleep"* (Esther 6:1).

The genealogical metaphor therefore encompasses not only "Israel" but also "Rome." It makes sense of all the important social entities, for in this metaphor, "Israel" is consubstantial with other social entities, which relate to "Israel" just as "Israel" as a society relates to itself, present and past.

What is important in the metaphor of Israel as family is how that metaphor governs the conceptualization of the other political components of the sages' world. The result appears in the treatment of Rome: Rome is Edom, or Ishmael, or Esau—always the rejected line of the authentic ancestor. History works out the tale of siblings, of whom only one is legitimate, and history is written in the tale of the relationship of Israel and Rome: Rome as Israel's brother, counterpart, and nemesis. Rome is what stands in the way of Israel's, and the world's, ultimate salavation, and not a (merely) political Rome but a political and messianic Rome, participating in the sacred (i.e., the familial) history of Israel. At stake is Rome as surrogate for Israel, Rome as obstacle to Israel. Further, "Rome" as family shades into "Rome" as empire and state, comparable to "Israel" as a nation or state—and as the coming empire, too. Therefore, although "Rome" stands for "Esau," the metaphorization of Rome moves into fresh ground, because Rome is differentiated from other nations, and hence the exegetical task of the new politics shifts from the differentiation of entities within Israel to the comparison and contrast of entities outside.

Accordingly, "Rome" is a family just as is "Israel," and, more to the point, "Rome" enters into "Israel's" life in an intelligible way precisely because both are part of that same family. The comparison of "Israel" and "Rome" to states, nations, peoples, and empires rests on, comes to expression in, and is generated by the genealogical metaphor. That singles out Rome alongside Israel: "Rome" is like "Israel" in a way in which no other state or nation is. Rome emerges as both like and also unlike "Israel," in ways in which no other nation is ever represented as "like Israel"; it follows that "Israel" is like "Rome" in ways in which "Israel" is not like any other people or nation.

The counterpart category thus introduces illegitimate power and explains it. Within its own logic, that initiative then requires the differentiation of outsiders, who, being different from the outsider, Rome, by definition are—can be—no longer all the same. Nevertheless, the genealogical account takes no systemic risks[8] in simply turning the outsider into an illegitimate insider. The metaphor that joins past to present, household to household—the whole, then, to "all Israel"—in fact encompasses the other noteworthy social entity and takes it into full account, providing a powerful and successful field theory. That the theory is a distinctively political one hardly requires extended argument: Rome imposes sanctions illegitimately; Israel, legitimately. The one forms the opposite of the other; the politics of the one is the mirror image of the other's.

The systemic focus—the exegetical task imposed by the requirement of differentiation—has shifted, however, so there is a new work of differentiation. Specifically, identifying Rome as different from other outsiders of political consequence required differentiation among the other outsiders, and that led directly to a unified, coherent account of the history of the empires and of Israel's place among them. Once introduced, Rome took a place in the unfolding of the empires—Babylonia, Media (Persia), Greece, then Rome. Israel takes its place in that unfolding pattern, and hence is consubstantial with Babylonia, Media, Greece, and Rome. In that context, "Rome" and "Israel" do form counterparts and opposites. Still more important is that Rome is the penultimate empire on earth; Israel will constitute the ultimate. The illegitimacy of the one politics will be replaced in due course by the legitimacy of power exercised by Israel through its anointed king. Politics now enters history: change, movement, direction, purpose. The initial system bore no explicit teleology; the successor system is all teleology, wholly historical in medium, entirely historical in message. That systemic message pointed to the shifts in world history to elicit a pattern and to place Israel at the apex.

In context, the metaphorical thinking moves beyond the metaphor of genealogy. This required the invention of a new metaphor, and the chosen trope, borrowed from Daniel, bears a not very subtle polemic that compares various nations with various animals. Only Israel is spared an assignment in the political bestiary. The main point, of course, is

Esau. Esau is compared not only to Israel—unambiguous Israel—but also to a pig, the most ambiguous of beasts within the levitical taxonomy. The analogy is apt, for the pig exhibits public traits expected of a suitable beast, in that it shows a cloven hoof, such as the levitical laws of acceptable beasts require, but it does not exhibit the inner traits of a suitable beast, in that it does not chew the cud. Accordingly, the pig confuses and deceives.[9] Here is how the matter is expressed in a passage that rings the changes on all of the relevant themes: legitimate as against illegitimate power, the complex genealogy of Israel and Rome, the victim and the victor now and in the end of history:

Leviticus Rabbah XIII:V.9

A. Moses foresaw what the evil kingdoms would do [to Israel].

B. *"The camel, rock badger, and hare"* (Deut. 14:7). [Compare: *"Nevertheless, among those that chew the cud or part the hoof, you shall not eat these: the camel, because it chews the cud but does not part the hoof, is unclean to you. The rock badger, because it chews the cud but does not part the hoof, is unclean to you. And the hare, because it chews the cud but does not part the hoof, is unclean to you, and the pig, because it parts the hoof and is cloven-footed, but does not chew the cud, is unclean to you"* (Lev. 11:4-7).]

C. The camel (GML) refers to Babylonia, [in line with the following verse of Scripture: *"O daughter of Babylonia, you who are to be devastated!]* Happy will be he who requites (GML) you, with what you have done to us"* (Ps. 147:8).

D. *"The rock badger"* (Deut. 14:7)—this refers to Media.

E. Rabbis and R. Judah b. R. Simon.

F. Rabbis say, "Just as the rock badger exhibits traits of uncleanness and traits of cleanness, so the kingdom of Media produced both a righteous man and a wicked one."

G. Said R. Judah b. R. Simon, "The last Darius was Esther's son. He was clean on his mother's side and unclean on his father's side."

H. *"The hare"* (Deut. 14:7)—this refers to Greece. The mother of King Ptolemy was named "Hare" [in Greek: *lagos*].

I. *"The pig"* (Deut. 14:8)—this refers to Edom [Rome].

J. Moses made mention of the first three in a single verse and the final one in a verse by itself [(Deut. 14:7, 8)]. Why so?

K. R. Yohanan and R. Simeon b. Laqish.

L. R. Yohanan said, "It is because [the pig] is equivalent to the other three."

M. And R. Simeon b. Laqish said, "It is because it outweighs them."

N. R. Yohanan objected to R. Simeon b. Laqish, " '*Prophesy, therefore, son of man, clap your hands [and let the sword come down twice, yea thrice]*' (Ezek. 21:14)."

O. And how does R. Simeon b. Laqish interpret the same passage? He notes that [the threefold sword] is doubled (Ezek. 21:14).

In the apocalypticizing of the animals of Leviticus 11:4-7/Deuteronomy 14:8—the camel, rock badger, hare, and pig—the pig, standing for Rome, emerges as different from the others and more threatening than the rest. Just as the pig pretends to be a clean beast by showing the cloven hoof but in fact is an unclean one, so Rome pretends to be just but in fact governs by thuggery. Edom does not pretend to praise God but only blasphemes. It does not exalt the righteous but kills them. I cannot imagine a more expressive antipolitics than this composition.[10] Of greatest importance is that although all the other beasts bring further ones in their wake, the pig does not: "It does not bring another kingdom after it." It will restore the crown to the one who will truly deserve it, Israel. Esau will be judged by Zion, so says Obadiah 1:21. Beyond Rome, standing in a straight line with the others and providing a caesura in history, lies the true shift in politics, the rule of Israel and the cessation of the dominion of the nations.

Metaphor hardly limited the modes of systemic thought. Israel also found representation as beyond all metaphor. Seeing "Israel" as *sui generis* yielded a sustained interest in the natural laws governing "Israel" in particular, statements of the rules of the group's history viewed as a unique entity within time. This nomological bent produced three results. First, the historical-eschatological formulation of a political teleology moved from an account of illegitimate power to a theory of the inappropriate victim, that is to say, of Israel itself. Sentences out of the historical record formed a cogent statement of the laws of "Israel's" destiny, laws unique to the social entity at hand. Second, the teleology of those laws for *sui generis* Israel focused on salvation at the end of history, that is, an eschatological teleology formed for a social entity embarked on its own lonely journey through time. Third, the conception of "Israel" as *sui generis* reached expression in an implicit statement that Israel is subject to its own laws, distinct from the laws governing all other social entities. These laws may be discerned in the factual, scriptural record of "Israel's" past, and that past by definition belonged to "Israel" alone. It followed, therefore, that by discerning the regularities in "Israel's" history, implicitly understood as unique to "Israel," sages recorded the view that "Israel," like God, was not subject to analogy or comparison. Accordingly, although not labeled a genus unto itself, Israel was treated in that way.

The theory of Israel as *sui generis* produced a political theory in which Israel's sole legitimate ruler is God, and whoever legitimately governs does so as God's surrogate. The theory of legitimate sanctions then is recast into a religious statement of God's place in Israel's existence, but it retains its political valence because the sage, the man most fully "in our image, after our likeness," governs in accord with the law of the Torah.

This static tableau reveals the structure of the politics, but what of its system, its account of how things actually work from day to day? Leviticus Rabbah also presents recurrent lists of events in Israel's (unique) history, meaning Israel's history solely in scriptural times down through the return to Zion. The lists, which concern the exercise of power, whether legitimate or not, again and again ring the changes on the one-time events of the generation of the Flood; Sodom and Gomorrah; the patriarchs and the sojourn in Egypt; the Exodus; the revelation of the Torah at Sinai; the golden calf; the Davidic monarchy and the building of the Temple; Sennacherib, Hezekiah, and the destruction of northern Israel; Nebuchadnezzar and the destruction of the Temple in 586; the life of Israel in Babylonian captivity; Daniel and his associates; and Mordecai and Haman. These individuals and events occur over and over again, serving as paradigms.

In fact, there is a fairly standard repertoire of scriptural heroes or villains, on the one side, and conventional lists of Israel's enemies and their actions and downfall, on the other. The boastful, for instance, include the generation of the flood, Sodom and Gomorrah, Pharaoh, Sisera, Sennacherib, Nebuchadnezzar, and the wicked empire (Rome), which is contrasted to Israel, "despised and humble in this world." The four kingdoms recur again and again, always ending with Rome and the repeated message that after Rome will come Israel. But Israel has to make this happen through its faith and submission to God's will. Cain, the Sodomites, Pharaoh, Sennacherib, Nebuchadnezzar, Haman—all exemplify the illegitimate use of power, which expresses arrogance. So the political virtue is its opposite: to be politically correct is to eschew power; to be politically illegitimate is to exercise power. I cannot think of a finer example of what it means to compose a counterpart category, an antipolitics in place of a politics.

Who rules legitimately? It can only be the sage, who defines the political class and the political institution of Israel, rightly construed. Israel is *sui generis* in that it exhibits the traits of the sages; in the sages' view, these traits have their counterpart not in this world but only in Heaven. In God's image, after God's likeness, "our rabbi" Moses forms the model for sages, and sages, in turn, for "Israel." Conformity to the sages' rule, which is the sole legitimate power within Israel, defines the condition for the Messiah's coming, that is, the establishment of a legitimate politics in place of the illegitimate government. That conviction comes to expression in repeated calls for "repentance," meaning, of course, conformity to the Torah as sages represented it. Here is a rather general statement of matters, speaking not of the sage in the model of Moses but only of conformity to sages' norms:

Y. Taanit 1:1:IX

J. " 'The oracle concerning Dumah. One is calling to me fron Seir, "*Watchman, what of the night ? Watchman, what of the night* " (Isa. 21:11)' "

K. The Israelites said to Isaiah, "O our Rabbi, Isaiah, What will come for us out of this night?"

L. He said to them, "Wait for me, until I can present the question."

M. Once he had asked the question, he came back to them.

N. They said to him, "Watchman, what of the night? What did the Guardian of the ages tell you?"

O. He said to them, "The watchman says: '*Morning comes; and also the night. If you will inquire, inquire; come back again*' (Isa. 21:12)."

P. They said to him, "Also the night?"

Q. He said to them, "It is not what you are thinking. But there will be morning for the righteous, and night for the wicked, morning for Israel, and night for idolaters."

R. They said to him, "When?"

S. He said to them, "Whenever you want, He too wants [it to be]—if you want it, He wants it."

T. They said to him, "What is standing in the way?"

U. He said to them, "Repentance: *'Come back again'* (Isa. 21:12)."

V. R. Aha in the name of R. Tanhum b. R. Hiyya, "If Israel repents for one day, forthwith the son of David will come.

W. "What is the Scriptural basis? *'If today you would hearken to his voice'* (Ps. 95:7)."

The realization of true, legitimate government for Israel depended on adherence to the sage and acceptance of his discipline. Here again is the successor system's antipolitics: Israel, God's nation, conformed to a law different from the nations', worked out a history that was subject to its own rules, and constituted a social and political entity with no counterpart, not merely as to species but especially as to genus. Thus, only sages should rule unique Israel, and when that happens, Israel will assume that power that its submission and humility yield, legitimate power coming from abnegation of power, legitimate sanctions being autonomously self-imposed.

David, the ideal king in the past and model of the coming messiah in the future, provides a more concrete portrait of legitimate power. What mattered is that David adhered to the successor system's model of the sage. If David, king of Israel, was like a latter-day rabbi, then the rabbi would prefigure the son of David who is to come as king of Israel. He was the sage of the Torah, the avatar and model for the sages of this later time. David and Moses are represented as students of Torah, just like the disciples and sages who produced the successor writings. An important presentation shows how David is represented as a rabbi, and how, specifically, what made David exemplary was his devotion to study of the Torah:

Y. Berakhot 1:1.XII

A. *"I will awake the dawn"* (Ps. 5:7, 8)—I will awaken the dawn; the dawn will not awaken me.

P. David's [evil] impulse tried to seduce him [to sin]. And it would say to him, "David. It is the custom of kings that awakens them. And you say, 'I will awake the dawn.' It is the custom of kings that they sleep until the third hour [of the day]. And you say, 'At midnight I rise.' " And [David] used to say [in reply], "[I rise early] *because of thy righteous ordinances* (Ps. 119:62)."

Q. And what would David do? R. Phineas in the name of R. Eleazar b. R. Menahem [said], "He used to take a harp and lyre and set them at his bedside. And he would rise at midnight and play them so that the associates of Torah should hear. And what would the associates of Torah say? 'If David involves himself with Torah, how much more so should we.' We find that all Israel was involved in Torah [study] on account of David."[11]

Because systems set forth their messsages through their selection of opposites, I turn to ask how legitimate power finds its exact match in the illegitimate kind. Modeled after David and educated in the Torah of Moses, the archetypal rabbi, the sages weigh in the balance against pagan kings, in the model of every malefactor in scriptural times. At stake in the outcome is God's rule and presence upon earth: once more, the sole legitimate power. That the stakes in politics have been revised upward—infinitely upward—is shown in the following statement that illegitimate power aims at destroying knowledge of God in the world and that legitimate power aims at nurturing that knowledge and consequent submission to God's will:

Genesis Rabbah XLII:III.2

A. "*And it came to pass in the days of Ahaz*" (Isa. 7:1):

B. "*The Aramaeans on the east and the Philistines on the west devour Israel with open mouth*" (Isa. 9:12):

C. The matter [of Israel's position] may be compared to the case of a king who handed over his son to a tutor, who hated the son. The tutor thought, "If I kill him now, I shall turn out to be liable to the death penalty before the king. So what I'll do is take away his wet nurse, and he will die on his own."

D. So thought Ahaz, "If there are no kids, there will be no he-goats. If there are no he-goats, there will be no flock. If there is no flock, there will be no Shepherd; if there is no Shepherd, there will be no world."

E. So did Ahaz plan, "If there are no children, there will be no adults. If there are no adults, there will be no disciples. If there are no disciples, there will be no sages. If there are no sages, there will be no prophets. If there are no prophets, the Holy One, blessed be He, will not allow his presence to come to rest in the world." [Lev. R.: . . . Torah. If there is no Torah, there will be no synagogues and schools. If there are no synagogues and schools, then the Holy One, blessed be He, will not allow his presence to come to rest in the world.]

F. That is in line with the following verse of Scripture: "*Bind up the testimony, seal the Torah among my disciples*" (Isa. 8:16).

G. R. Huna in the name of R. Eleazar: "Why was he called Ahaz? Because he seized (*ahaz*) synagogues and schools."

The vision is of an "Israel" as a political entity defined by the absence of power and the presence of humility and submission, an entity that takes shape around synagogues and schools, which none could possibly (then or now) have identified with a political structure and system.

That judgment requires qualification, however, for the master in the setting of the school also served as clerk in the administration and court. Moreover, the sage as clerk exercised power not of abnegation or denial but of material sanctions. So the political theory of humility and powerlessness contrasts with the representation of a political reality wherein sages forcefully intervene into the social order. Sages' political authority was practical and involved power; sages formed a political class in the this-worldly sense. The first and most important sort of power a rabbi maintained he could exercise, under some circumstances and in some cases, was the power to sort out and adjudicate rights to property and personal status affecting property. The rabbi is described as able to take chattel or real estate from one party and give it into the rightful ownership of some other.

The second sort of power rabbis are supposed to have wielded was the right to tell people what to do or not to do in matters not involving property rights. Sages also are represented as defining the status of persons so as to affect property and marital rights and standing. Rabbis declare a woman married or free to marry; permitted as the wife of a priest to eat food in the status of leave-offering or prohibited from doing so; entitled the support of a husband's estate or left without that support; and entitled to collect a previously contracted marriage settlement or lacking that right. The rabbis held that they governed the Jewish community as effective political authorities in all these ways, as much as in their control of real estate, commercial, and other material and property transactions among Jews.[12]

The sage, moreover, is represented as mediating between Jews and the outside world. He is represented not as negotiating but only as accommodating and could permit actions normally prohibited in the law. The unstated supposition is that Israel stands in a subordinated relationship, able to resist only with difficulty, and then at a very high cost. The alternative to submission is assumed to be death. The rabbi's authority as representative of the Jewish nation and mediator between that nation and the gentile world in general, and the government in particular, bore heavy symbolic weight. The legitimacy of that mediation derived solely from his mastery of the law. The rabbi as a public official was expected to perform certain supernatural deeds — power in its legitimate form. He stood at the border between heaven and earth, as much as he stood at the frontier between Israel and the nations: wholly liminal and entirely exemplary at the same time.

What is important here is the representation of the rabbi as public authority deemed to exercise supernatural power. His task was to use his supernatural power in pretty much the same context and for the same purpose as he used his political-judicial and legal power and learning, on the one side, and his local influence and moral authority, on the other. What is striking is that sages exercised their responsibility equally through this-worldly and other-worldly means. One example of legitimate power suffices to make the point:

Y. Taanit 3:4.I

A. There was a pestilence in Sepphoris, but it did not come into the neighborhood in which R. Haninah was living. And the Sepphoreans said, "How is it possible that that elder lives among you, he and his entire neighborhood, in peace, while the town goes to ruin?"

B. [Haninah] went in and said before them, "There was only a single Zimri in his generation, but on his account, twenty-four thousand people died. And in our time, how many Zimris are there in our generation? And yet you are raising a clamor!"

C. One time they had to call a fast, but it did not rain. R. Joshua carried out a fast in the South, and it rained. The Sepphoreans said, "R. Joshua b. Levi brings down rain for the people in the South, but R. Haninah holds back rain for us in Sepphoris."

D. They found it necessary to declare a second time of fasting, and sent and summoned R. Joshua b. Levi. [Haninah] said to him,

"Let my lord go forth with us to fast." The two of them went out to fast, but it did not rain.

E. He went in and preached to them as follows: "It was not R. Joshua b. Levi who brought down rain for the people of the South, nor was it R. Haninah who held back rain from the people of Sepphoris. But as to the Southerners, their hearts are open, and when they listen to a teaching of Light [Torah] they submit [to accept it], while as to the Sepphoreans, their hearts are hard, and when they hear a teaching of Light, they do not submit [or accept it]."

F. When he went in, he looked up and saw that the [cloudless] air was pure. He said, "Is this how it still is? [Is there no change in the weather?]" Forthwith, it rained. He took a vow for himself that he would never do the same thing again. He said, "How shall I say to the creditor [God] not to collect what is owing to him?"

True, God could do miracles, but if the people caused their own disasters by not listening to rabbis' Torah teachings, they could hardly expect God always to forgo imposing the sanction for disobedience, which was holding back rain. Accordingly, there were reliable laws by which to deal with the supernatural world, which kept those laws, too. The particular power of the rabbi was in knowing the law. (The storyteller nonetheless took for granted that in the end the clerk could bring rain in a pinch.)

If the sage stood for the legitimate exercise of power, then who represented illegitimate power within Israel? It was not only the patriarch,[13] but—much more to the point—the illegitimate Messiah. And what makes a Messiah a false Messiah is not his claim to save Israel, but his claim to save Israel without the help of God. The meaning of the true Messiah is Israel's total submission to God's yoke and service through the Messiah's gentle rule. Israel does not save itself. The antipolitics under study never permits it to control its own destiny, either on earth or in Heaven. The only choice is whether to cast fate into the hands of cruel, deceitful men or to trust in the living God of mercy and love. This critical position is spelled out in discourse about the Messiah in the Talmud of the Land of Israel.

Bar Kokhba, above all, exemplifies arrogance against God. He lost the war because of that arrogance, and in particular, he ignored the authority of sages:

Y. Taanit 4:5.X

J. Said R. Yohanan, "Upon orders of Caesar Hadrian, in Betar they killed eight hundred thousand."

K. Said R. Yohanan, "There were eighty thousand pairs of trumpeteers surrounding Betar. Each one was in charge of a number of troops. Ben Kozeba was there, and he had two hundred thousand troops who, as a sign of loyalty, had cut off their little fingers.

L. "Sages sent word to him, 'How long are you going to turn Israel into a maimed people?'

M. "He said to them, 'How otherwise is it possible to test them?'

N. "They replied to him, 'Whoever cannot uproot a cedar of Lebanon while riding on his horse will not be inscribed on your military rolls.'

O. "So there were two hundred thousand who qualified in one way, and another two hundred thousand who qualified in another way."

P. When he would go forth to battle, he would say, "Lord of the world! Do not help and do not hinder us! *'Hast thou not rejected us, O God? Thou dost not go forth, O God, with our armies'* (Ps. 60:10)."

Q. Three and a half years did Hadrian besiege Betar.

R. R. Eleazar of Modiin would sit on sackcloth and ashes and pray every day, saying "Lord of the ages! Do not judge in accord with strict judgment this day!"

S. Hadrian wanted to go to him. A Samaritan said to him, "Do not go to him, until I see what he is doing, and so hand over the city [of Betar] to you. [Make peace . . . for you.]"

T. He got into the city through a drain pipe. He went and found R. Eleazar of Modiin standing and praying. He pretended to whisper something into his ear.

U. The townspeople saw [the Samaritan] do this and brought him to Ben Kozeba. They told him, "We saw this man having dealings with your friend."

V. [Bar Kokhba] said to him, "What did you say to him, and what did he say to you?"

W. He said to [the Samaritan], "If I tell you, then the king will kill me, and if I do not tell you, then you will kill me. It is better that the king kill me, and not you.

X. "[Eleazar] said to me, 'I should hand over my city.' [I shall make peace . . .]."

Y. He turned to R. Eleazar of Modiin. He said to him, "What did this Samaritan say to you?"

Z. He replied, "Nothing."

AA. He said to him, "What did you say to him?"

BB. He said to him, "Nothing."

CC. [Ben Kozeba] gave [Eleazar] one good kick and killed him.

DD. Forthwith an echo came forth and proclaimed the following verse:

EE. " 'Woe to my worthless shepherd, who deserts the flock! May the sword smite his arm and his right eye! Let his arm be wholly withered, his right eye utterly blinded!' (Zech. 11:17).

FF. "You have murdered R. Eleazar of Modiin, the right arm of all Israel, and their right eye. Therefore may the right arm of that man wither, may his right eye be utterly blinded!"

GG. Forthwith Betar was taken, and Ben Kozeba was killed.

There are two complementary themes here. First, Bar Kokhba treats Heaven with arrogance, asking God merely to keep out of the way. Second, he treats an especially revered sage with a parallel arrogance. The sage had the power to preserve Israel, but Bar Kokhba destroyed Israel's one protection. The result was inevitable.

Bar Kokhba, an Israelite, stands for illegitimate power; the sage, in the form of Eleazar of Modiin, for legitimate and also true power.[14] The one shows how the reality of power is misunderstood; the other, the transvaluation of values that in politics serves as the counterpart to the same rereading of real value accomplished in the formation of the counterpart category to economics. The upshot is that the successor system has reconsidered not merely the contents of the received structure but the composition of the structure itself. In place of its philosophy it provides a new medium for the formulation of a worldview; in place of a way of life formulated as an economics, a new valuation of value; in place of an account of the social entity framed as a politics, a new conception of legitimate violence. So much for the formation of counterpart categories. My task now is to portray the results of this categorical re-formation in the new structure, seen whole and on its own.

Notes

1. That is, as much as in the contrast of real wealth and true value (land and Torah learning) we identify not a revised economics but a counterpart category to the familiar economics.

2. Israel in the successor system is not only a social entity. It also is represented as empowered to make choices and set norms and impose sanctions; hence, it must be deemed also a political entity.

3. The explanation for the shift deriving from the change in Israel's historical political condition begs the question. When the Mishnah was written, Israel did not govern itself through a king, high priest, and sages' court, and such a system was a complete fabrication. There never was a point in the history of Israel in the Land of Israel in which such a fabrication approximated political facts, so if the initial system presented a political fantasy, we have no reason to explain its revision, or complete rejection in factor of a different system, by reason of a change in the facts of the matter. On the contrary, the sages of the successor documents had no more keen interest in empirical observation and verification than did the ones of the Mishnah and its companions. The systemic theory alone accounts for the character of matters. Hence, the shift here and in respect to modes of thought and problems of thought (chapter 4) and to counterpart economics (chapter 5) are explained in a systemic framework rather than in a material, historical, political one. Part 3 sets forth my account of what I conceive to be the reason why.

4. Here is, by the way, another splendid example of *Listenwissenschaft* as practiced in the Midrash compilations, evidence that the framers of those compilations did not differ in fundamental mode of thought and argument from the authorship of the Mishnah.

5. But, as we shall see, the ordering focused on Israel and anti-Israel (Rome), and the point of ordering was to reckon with the temporal sequence of rule: Rome, then Israel.

6. "Israel" on its own terms therefore yielded not merely allusions or references to a given taxonomic classifier but accounts, including narratives or "histories," of "Israel" viewed as a social entity, a group fully defined concretely and autonomously and not only as an abstraction. The appearance in this stratum of the canon of narratives is not accidental but entirely indicative, and that means we must ask systemic questions of narrative and its uses. I have explored this question in a very different context in *Judaism and Story: The Evidence of the Fathers According to Rabbi Nathan* (Chicago: University of Chicago Press, 1991).

7. The polemical purpose of the claim that the abstraction "Israel" was to be compared to the family of the mythic ancestor lies right at the surface. With another "Israel"—the Christian Church—now claiming to constitute the true one, Jews found it possible to confront that claim and to turn it against the other side. "You claim to form 'Israel after the spirit.' Fine, and *we* are Israel after the flesh—and genealogy forms the link, that alone." (Converts did not present an anomaly, for they were held to be children of

Abraham and Sarah, who had "made souls," that is, converts, in Haran, a point repeated in the documents of the period.) That fleshly continuity formed of all of "us" a single family, rendering spurious the notion that "Israel" could be other than genealogically defined. But that polemic seems to me adventitious and not primary. At the same time, the metaphor provided a quite separate component to the sages' larger system.

8. Within their context, systems never take risks, for always at stake is self-evidence.

9. The polemic against Rome as Esau is simple. Rome claims to be Israel in that it adheres to the Old Testament, that is, the written Torah of Sinai. Specifically, Rome is represented as only Christian Rome can have been represented: it superficially *looks* kosher but it is unkosher. Pagan Rome could not never have looked kosher, but Christian Rome, with its appeal to continuity with ancient Israel, could and did and moreover claimed to do so. It bore some traits that validated the claim but lacked others.

10. That these symbols concede nothing to Christian monotheism and veneration of the Torah of Moses (in its written medium) is obvious, but not the point of analysis here. Rome in the fourth century became Christian. Sages responded by facing that fact quite squarely and saying, "Indeed, it is as you say, a kind of Israel, an heir of Abraham as your texts explicitly claim. But we remain the sole legitimate Israel, the bearer of the birthright—we and not you. So you are our brother: Esau, Ishmael, Edom." And the rest follows.

11. Translated by T. Zahavy, *The Talmud of the Land of Israel* (Chicago: University of Chicago Press, 1990), vol. 1,*Tractate Berakhot.*

12. In these paragraphs I summarize the results of my *Judiasm in Society: The Evidence of the Yerushalmi: Toward the Natural History of a Religion* (Chicago: University of Chicago Press, 1983).

13. The patriarch is discussed in chapter 3.

14. That both are Israelites proves that the differentiating criterion is not gentile versus Israelite but virtue within Israel. Gentile power is a fact of life, not a systemically consequential consideration.

Part Three

Enchanted Judaism:
The New Structure

Prologue III
Comparison and Classification
of Systems

What philosophy kept distinct, religion joined together: that de scription defines the transformation of Judaism from philosophy to religion. The reliable rules of sanctification—to invoke theological categories—are joined with the unpredictable event of salvation, and the routine—to call on the classification of Max Weber—meets the spontaneous. Not to be gainsaid, the social order is made to acknowledge what, if disorderly, nonetheless is immediate and therefore necessary. History was omnipresent but carefully ignored in the philosophical Judaism; in the form of not change but crisis it regains its rightful place at the systemic center of the later Judaism.

The classification of the new system—so I shall now show—is religious and not philosophical. Precisely what I mean must be made clear, for the Mishnaic system also was a religious one. The received system was a religious system of a philosophical character, however, and the successor system was not of a philosophical character. What I mean by a religious system of a philosophical character is readily explained: this-worldly data are classified according to rules that apply consistently throughout, enabling a fair degree of accuracy in predicting what will happen and why. Further, a philosophical system of religion then uses data about the order of nature and society to systematically demonstrate the governance of God in nature and supernature, mundane data pointing toward God above and beyond. The God of the philosophical Judaism sat enthroned at the apex of all things, all being hierarchically classified. Just as philosophy seeks the explanation of things, so a philosophy of religion (in the context at hand) will propose orderly explanations in accord with prevailing and cogent rules. The profoundly philosophical character of the Mishnah has already provided ample evidence of the shape, structure, and character of that philosophical system in the Judaic context. The rule-seeking character of Mishnaic discourse marks it as a philosophical system of religion. As I shall now show, the successor system saw the world differently.

It follows that a philosophical system forms its learning inductively and syllogistically by appeal to the neutral evidence of universally applicable rules derived by observing the order of universally accessible nature and society. A religious system, on the other hand, frames its propositions deductively and exegetically by appeal to the privileged evidence of a corpus of truths deemed revealed by God. The difference pertains not to detail but to the fundamental facts taken to matter. Some of those facts lie at the very surface, in the nature of the writings that express the system.

As I have shown, these writings were not freestanding but contingent in two ways. First, they served as commentaries to prior documents, the Mishnah and Scripture for the Talmud and the Midrash compilations, respectively. Second, and more consequential, the authorships cited Scripture passages or Mishnah sentences as both the centerpiece of proof and program of discourse. The differences that prove indicative are not merely formal, however. More to the point, whereas the Mishnah's steady-state, ahistorical system admits no movement or change, the successor system of the Yerushalmi and Midrash compilations tells tales, speaks of change, and accommodates and responds to historical moments. It formulates a theory of continuity within change, of the moral connections between generations, and of the way in which one's deeds shape one's own destiny and that of future individuals as well. What the framers of the Mishnah wanted more than anything else was to explain the order and structure of being. Their successors rejected their generative concern, instead working out their intense desire to sort out the currents and streams of time and change as these flow toward an unknown ocean.

These large-scale characterizations in well-crafted systems do not provide the only pertinent evidence, however; details, too, deliver the message. The indicators for each type of system, as these are attested in their written testimonies, derive from the character of the rhetorical, logical, and propositional-topical traits of those writings. The shift from the philosophical to the religious modes of thought and media of expression—logical and rhetorical indicators, respectively—comes to realization in the recasting of the generative categories of the system as well. That is the lesson of part 2 of this book. These categories are transformed, and the transformation proved so thoroughgoing as to validate characterizing the result as "counterpart categories." By forming such counterpart categories the system encompassed not only the natural but also the supernatural realms of the social order.

That is how philosophical thinking gave way to religious thinking. The transformation shows the category formation that replaced an economics based on prime value assigned to real wealth with one that encompassed wealth of an intangible, impalpable, and supernatural order, but a valued resource nonetheless. It points toward the replacement of a politics serving to legitimate and hierarchize power and differentiate among sanctions by appeal to fixed principles by one that introduced God's valuation of the victim and the antipolitical conception of the illegitimacy of worldly power. This counterpart politics then formed the opposite of the Mishnah's entire this-worldly political system. In all three ways the upshot is the same: the social system, in the theory of its framers, now extends its boundaries upward to Heaven, drawing into a whole the formerly distinct, if counterpoised, realms of Israel on earth and the Heavenly court above. So if I had to specify the fundamental difference between the philosophical and the religious versions of the social order, it would fall quite specifically *on the broadening of the systemic boundaries to encompass Heaven*. The formation of counterpart categories therefore signals not a re-formation of the received system but the formation of an essentially new one.

Nonetheless, the exegetical focus, the critical issue addressed by the new system and the central point of tension and mode of remission thereof, remains to be identified even after the extension of systemic boundaries has been fixed. As a matter of fact, the counterpart categories themselves do not help identify the generative problematic that defined the new system and integrated its components. The issues I have located as the systemic economics and politics—Torah in place of land, the illegitimacy of power and the priority of its absence—although present and indicative in the documentary expression of the system, assuredly do not occupy a principal position within those documents, for the successor documents' categories are not those of philosophy, on the one side, and a politics disembedded from economics, on the other.

In the nature of systemic analysis, therefore, I have brought the categories of the initial system to the data of the successor system, and the result shows how different the two systems are. Still, concerning the transformed Judaism of the late fourth and fifth centuries, I have yet to get to the main thing. In comparing the given to the new I had no choice but to proceed as I have, but what I have done thus far is ask only *my* questions—that is, the systemic questions of philosophy and political economy or philosophical economics and politics. These questions, however, have been put to a literature that dealt with such questions essentially by dismissing them, for the upshot of the formation of counterpart categories turns out to be the destruction of the received categories, now turned on their heads, emptied of all material and palpable content, and refilled only with intangibles of intellect and virtuous attitude. Knowing how a system has revalued value and reconstructed the sense of legitimate power by deeming legitimate only the victim and never the actor is not to know what the system locates at its center.

To identify the system's systemic foci, *its*—and not my—sources of the exegetical problematic and its definition of its generative issues, I must propose as the answer something other than subjective judgment as to what is dominant and commonplace. I must instead set forth an entirely objective claim as to what is essential, definitive, and integrating (which in this context also happens to be commonplace). By objective I mean simply that my results should emerge for anyone else examining the same evidence in accord with the same principles of description and analysis (interpretation is always subjective). Once we concur that a Judaic system by definition responds to the questions deemed compelling with truths regarded as unavoidable and self-evident, then, if my indicative evidence for the system at hand is correctly identified and accurately described, anyone should reach the conclusions I present here. So the task now is to identify those urgent questions and define the self-evident truths that came about by way of response: the way of life and the worldview formed by the Israel that the successor system defined for itself. The issue is joined when I can identify the point of differentiation of one system and integration of another—surely an objective fact.

I begin in the specification of what is integrating, for historians of religion concur that in general the power of religion lies in its capacity to integrate, to hold together discrete components of the social order and explain how they all fit together. And it seems to me a simple fact that the power of philosophy generally lies in its capacity to differentiate, discriminate, make distinctions, and clarify the complex by showing its distinct parts. Thus, a successor system, connected to but independent of its antecedent, will prove philosophical if it continues the labor of differentiation and religious if it undertakes a work of integration. The Judaism before us addresses the principal and striking distinction between economics and politics that characterized the philosophical system it had inherited, (re)integrating what had been kept apart in the sort of theory of political economy that the Pentateuch and Aristotle had laid out but that the framers of the Mishnah had not composed at all.

Let me spell out what I conceive to be the principal success of integration accomplished by the authorships of the Yerushalmi and related writings within a supernatural framework that must be deemed religious and only religious. As mentioned previously,[1] the one striking contrast between the social system put forth by Aristotle and that set out by the framers of the Mishnah lay in Aristotle's superior systematization of politics within the frame of economics, a facet entirely absent in the Mishnah's social system. Aristotle's systemic message, delivered through his philosophy, economics, and politics, was carried equally by economics and politics in such a way that the two formed a single statement of political economy. To state the matter very simply, the principal economic actor of Aristotle's social system, the householder (in the language of the Jewish sources; the landholder or farmer, for Aristotle and Xenophon), also constituted the principal political figure, the one who exercised legitimate power, and the joining of the landholder and the civic actor in a single person moreover provided Aristotle his account of the formation of society: the *polis,* or lowest whole and indivisible social unit of society.

For the framers of the Mishnah, however, the economic actor, the one who controlled the means of production, was the householder, whereas the householder never played a political role or formed part of the political classes at all. That fact is shown by a simple distinction of usage: the subject of most sentences involving the disposition of scarce resources is the householder, whereas that same social entity ("class") never appears in any of the political tractates and their discourses, which choose for the subjects of their sentences such political figures as the king, high priest, (sages') court, and the like. These usages signal the disembeddedness of economics from politics, a fact further highlighted by the Mishnah's separation between the economic entity (the village or town made up of householders) and the political entities (royal government, temple authority, and sages' court); none of the latter correspond with the village or town, that is, the *polis*, in the Mishnah's philosophical system.

What the philosophical Judaism kept apart, the religious Judaism now joined together, and it is just there, at that critical joining, that I identify the key to the system: its reversal of a received point of differentiation,[2] its introduction of new points of differentiation altogether. The source of generative problems for the Mishnah's politics is simply not the same as the source that served the successor system's politics, and, systemic analysis being what it is, it is the union of what was formerly asunder that identifies in quite objective terms the critical point of tension, the sources of problems, the centerpiece of systemic concern throughout. One fundamental point of reversal, uniting what had been divided, is the joining of economics and politics into a political economy through the conception of *zekhut,* a term I define presently.

There is another, less easily discerned point at which what the one system treated as distinct the next and connected system chose to address as one and whole; to see it, it is necessary to ask a question not raised in the Mishnah concerning the character and source of virtue, specifically, the effect on the individual of knowledge, especially knowledge of the Torah or Torah study. To frame the issue very simply, for the Mishnah, one result of studying the Torah is a change in standing and status. Torah study and its effects form a principal systemic indicator in matters of hierarchical classification, joining the *mamzer* and the disciple of sages in a mixture of opposites, for one self-evident example.

How deep is this change? The Mishnah's hundreds of chapters are silent on this question. Virtue and learning form distinct categories, a point I shall underline in the following chapter, and overall mastery of the Torah does not change a sage's virtue, character, or conscience. Still more strikingly, the Mishnah's authorship is silent also about whether Torah study affects the sage's fate in this world and in the life to come. Specifically, that document makes no claim that studying the Torah either changes the individual or ensures salvation. In the successor system, however, as I shall presently show, the separation of knowledge and the human condition is set aside, and studying the Torah is deemed the source of salvation. The philosophical system, with its interest in *homo hierarchicus,* proved remarkably silent about the effect of the Torah on the inner man.[3] The upshot is that at the critical points of bonding, the received system proved flawed in its separation of learning from virtue and legitimate power from valued resources.

From the foregoing, the following conclusion emerges. The comparison between one system and its connected but distinct successor points to quite objective evidence on the basis of which I may characterize the successor in its own terms, for the categories that present themselves derive from the system subjected to description, not from those of the prior system (let alone from my own theory of the components of a theory of the social order). They emerge at that very point—the juncture of differentiation or its opposite, integration—at which systemic description begins, the exegesis of the system's exegesis. Why virtue joins knowledge and politics links to economics in the religious system but not in the philosophical one is obvious: philosophy differentiates, seeking the rules that join diverse data; religion integrates, proposing to see the whole all together and all at once, thus (for an anthropology, for example) seeing humanity whole, "in our image, after our likeness." Religion by its nature (so it would seem from the case at hand) asks the questions of integration, as should be expected of a theory intended to hold together within a single boundary both earth and Heaven, this world and the other. Thus, my observations about the broadening of the frontiers of the social order signal a deeper characteristic of the analysis at hand.

I followed the route that led me to this mode of analysis because what I take to be of special interest in the work of systemic description is not so much theology, doctrine, or belief as the interplay of religion and society, that is, the relationship between contents and context, conviction and circumstance, each viewed as a distinct and independent variable. Religion is a decisive fact of social reality, not merely a set of beliefs on questions viewed in an abstract and ahistorical setting. My task is now to identify the system that the successor documents' authorships formed, and this I do by proposing to define the questions they pursued and the self-evidently valid answers they set forth in making a single and coherent statement about their own condition.

The final part of the book, then, follows an obvious path. The two chapters of systemic description and analysis represent what I have now identified as the two indicative components of the successor system. First, in chapter 7, I discuss its integration of knowledge and virtue, which is to say, its transformation of the entire realm of intellect from a this-worldly to an other-worldly enterprise, its treatment of knowing as a matter of enchantment.

The second systemic innovation, examined in chapter 8, is the formation of an integrated category of political economy, framed in such a way that at stake in politics and economics alike were value and resource in no way subject to order and rule, but in all ways formed out of the unpredictable resource of *zekhut,* which is sometimes translated as "merit," but which, being a matter of not obligation but supererogatory free will, I think should be portrayed as "the heritage of virtue and its consequent entitlements."[4] Between those two conceptions—the Torah as a medium of transformation and the heritage of virtue and its consequent entitlements, which can be gained for oneself and also received from one's ancestors—the received system's this-worldly boundaries were transcended, and the new system encompassed within its framework a supernatural life on earth. Appealing to these two statements of worldview, way of life, and social entity, I can compose a complete description of the definitive traits and indicative systemic concerns of the successor Judaism.

These are the answers I describe in chapters 7 and 8. In chapter 9 I formulate the urgent and compelling question that the system proposed to settle in a definitive and self-evidently valid way. I do so by appealing for an analogy to a contemporary of the authorships of the successor documents, that is, to another principal system builder and framer of the social order who worked in religious rather than philosophical modes of thought. In the same historical context, addressing comparable issues of gross political change, Augustine set forth his account of the social order, the city of God, with results remarkably congruent to the design of the social order set forth in the successor system of Judaism. As I shall soon show, quite specifically and concretely, I find in the pages of the Yerushalmi, Genesis Rabbah, Leviticus Rabbah, and Pesiqta deRab Kahana—but not in the Mishnah and Tosefta—the design of the city of God that Augustine meant to invent.

Notes

1. I refer to my *Politics of Judaism* (Chicago: University of Chicago Press, 1991), briefly summarized in chapter 3.

2. For, after all, the problematic of the Mishnah's politics is the principle

of differentiation among legitimate political agencies: first, between Heaven's and humanity's; second, among the three political institutions of the Mishnah's "Israel."

3. That the system neglected woman altogether, except as a subordinated outcaste, achieving caste status only through the father at first, and then the husband, served the systemic purpose. By the theory proposed here, however, woman (nearly) as much as man should form a systemic actor, because although for hierarchical purposes woman can be treated as collective and abnormal, for the work of integration, woman, as much as man, will exhibit the besought unities. In stories cited in chapters 7 and 8 I note a number of points at which a woman is a principal figure, either counseling the right response to a dilemma or forming a major actor in a tale. These are only preliminary observations, however, and a study of the comparison between the role and representation of woman in the various documents of the unfolding canon will show whether my guess on the systemic difference, and my implicit explanation of that difference, makes sense when tested against evidence. I begin part of this inquiry in *The Canonical History of Ideas: The Place of the So-called Tannaitic Midrashim. Mekhilta Attributed to R. Ishmael, Sifra, Sifé to Numbers, and Sifé to Deuteronomy* (Atlanta, Ga.: Scholars Press for South Florida Studies in the History of Judaism, 1990).

4. In chapter 8, notes 2 and 4, I expand on why "merit" is a poor translation of the word *zekhut*. Indeed, it would be difficult to imagine a more totaly inept and inaccurate translation of *zekhut* than the word merit. Stated simply, in its earliest contextual definition *zekhut* is contrasted with sin and forms the mirror image of sin. Just as sin cannot be inherited but must be done through one's own intention and action, so, by exact contrast, *zekhut* can be inherited and may be attained not through one's own intention and action but by some other person, whether one's ancestor or an influential person in one's own community. Since "merit" must bear the sense of "just desserts, based on one's own deeds," as in, "he merited an award because of his accomplishments," *zekhut* cannot be accurately represented in English by the word *merit*. But there is more to the inaccuracy of "merit" than merely the unmerited character of the entitlement for which *zekhut* stands. I return to this matter when it forms a critical problem in systemic description and analysis.

7
The New Learning:
The Gnostic Torah

In the successor system, knowledge not only informs, it saves. And knowledge that saves is gnostic. Unlike the initial, philosophical system, the religious successor system alleges that Torah study causes a change in the student's very being. This transformation is not only of knowledge and understanding (let alone mere information), or even of virtue and taxic status, but of what the knower is. The student becomes something different, better and more holy, and whether the complement is "the mysteries" or "the Torah" (as taught by sages) makes no material difference.

As a matter of fact, this conception of the Torah as transformative contains another important trait commonly called gnostic, which is the power to do things that were impossible prior to attaining knowledge in the correct way. The marks of the transformation emerge in the supernatural power acquired through this (new) knowledge, namely, learning in the Torah. That is what I mean by the new learning and what justifies the classification of Torah learning as gnostic. When (mere) knowledge so transforms the knower that he or she is deemed "saved" or otherwise transformed into something utterly different from the prior condition marked by ignorance and unredemption, then that knowledge may be called gnostic, for by *gnostic* people generally mean salvific knowledge, transitive, transformative learning that joins the two quite distinct categories of intellect and personal salvation or regeneration.[1]

That jarring juxtaposition, identifying ignorance (not knowing a given fact) with the personal condition of unregeneracy, knowledge with supernatural standing and, hence, also power—that juxtaposition relates what need not, and commonly is not, correlated: the moral or existential condition of the person and the level of intellectual enlightenment of that same person. Certainly the framers of the Mishnah did not imagine that such a correlation could be made, nor did their heirs for quite some time. In the successor system, however, a principal point of integration of what philosophy had deemed distinct was between knowledge and one's condition or classification as to supernatural things. Specifically, knowledge of the Torah changed a person and made him (never her) simply different from what he had been before he acquired that knowledge: physically weaker, but also strengthened by power that we might call magical but they called supernatural. Before proceeding, let me give a good example of what I mean by knowledge of Torah represented as transformative and salvific.

The following story explicitly states the proposition that obeying the Torah, with obedience founded on one's own knowledge thereof, constitutes a source of salvation. In this story, people expect to be saved because they have observed the rules of the Torah. Those who have not observed accept their punishment. The Torah thus stands here for something more than revelation and life of study, and the sage now appears as a holy man, not merely a learned one, because his knowledge of the Torah has transformed him. Accordingly, this category of stories and sayings about the Torah differs entirely from what had gone before. Y. Taanit 3:8, for instance, provides one among numerous examples in which the symbol of the Torah and knowledge of the Torah bear salvific consequence, a claim the Mishnah never set forth in behalf of knowledge, let alone knowledge of the Torah:[2]

II

A. As to Levi ben Sisi: troops came to his town. He took a scroll of the Torah and went up to the roof and said, "Lord of the ages! If a single word of this scroll of the Torah has been nullified [in our town], let them come up against us, and if not, let them go their way."

B. Forthwith people went looking for the troops but did not find them [because they had gone their way].

C. A disciple of his did the same thing, and his hand withered, but the troops went their way.

D. A disciple of his disciple did the same thing. His hand did not wither, but they also did not go their way.

E. This illustrates the following apothegm: You can't insult an idiot, and dead skin does not feel the scalpel.

What is interesting here is how taxa into which the word Torah previously fell have been absorbed and superseded in a new taxon. The Torah is an object: "He took a scroll . . . ," but it also constitutes God's revelation to Israel: "If a single word . . ." The outcome of the revelation is to form an ongoing way of life that is embodied in the sage himself: "A disciple of his did the same thing . . ." The sage plays an intimate part in the supernatural event: "His hand withered . . ." Here the Torah is a source of salvation, for it stands for, or constitutes, the way in which the people Israel saves itself from marauders. This straightforward sense of salvation would not have surprised the author of Deuteronomy, but in the successor documents there is more to the relationship of the Torah to salvation than mere obedience to its rules.

The successor writings express an approach to the mere learning of the Torah — as distinct from obedience to its rules — that promises not merely intellectual enlightenment but personal renewal, transfiguration, or some other far-reaching change. Given that this view presents a gnostic[3] reading of learning, the successor system presents knowledge of the Torah as not merely informing or presenting right rules of conduct but as transforming, regenerating, and saving.[4] In that context and by these definitions, the theory of the Torah and of Torah study set forth in the successor documents promises a fully realized transformation to those who study and therefore know the Torah. They gain not merely intellectual enlightenment but supernatural power and standing. In this context, that transformation encompasses such salvation as will take place prior to the end of time. The new learning, defined as the consequence of Torah study imputed by the Talmud of the Land of Israel, Genesis Rabbah, Leviticus Rabbah, and Pesiqta deRab Kahana — but not by the Mishnah and its companions, tractate Abot and the Tosefta — changes not merely the mind but the moral and salvific condition of the one who engages in that learning.

This conception would have surprised the philosophers represented by the Mishnah,[5] for the Mishnah promises that study of the Torah transforms people only in terms of status in the hierarchical order of being, not in their very characters and essences.[6] Quite to the contrary, as to the Mishnah's generative concerns on taxonomy, knowledge of the Torah changed nothing; the *mamzer* who mastered the Torah remained in the caste of the *mamzer*, so that if he lost his ass along with others, his would be returned first, but he still could not marry the daughter of a priest or even an Israelite. That means the transformation in no way affected the being of the man, but only his virtue. True, M. Hagigah 2:1 contains statements that have suggested to some[7] that knowledge possessed traits of other than wholly secular character, in that correct knowledge required attention to status (sage) and also the source and character of learning ("understands of his own knowledge," whatever that means):

Mishnah Tractate Hagigah 2:1

A. They do not expound upon the laws of prohibited relationships [Lev. 18] before three persons, the works of creation [Gen. 13] before two, or the Chariot [Ezek. 1] before one,

B. unless he was a sage and understands of his own knowledge.

C. Whoever reflects upon four things would have been better off had he not been born:

D. what is above, what is below, what is before, and what is beyond.

E. And whoever has no concern for the glory of his Maker would have been better off had he not been born.

These sentences have been quite plausibly interpreted to refer to personal and not merely intellectual change effected by knowledge, hence to a gnostic reading of learning, but they do not impute to Torah study as a general classification of intellectual activity the potentiality of (dangerous) change in one's own being. They speak of only specific topics and texts, identifying a very few specific passages and omitting any conception that studying the Torah in general constitutes a transformative and salvific action. Their specificity may justify spelling the adjective Gnostic, but not gnostic.[8] At best, therefore, I find within the compilation of the authorship of the Mishnah the possibility *in nuce* of a gnostic approach to knowledge, but that very representation, unrealized in context, hardly extends to the entirety of learning in the Torah and, indeed, by its formulation precludes such a general approach to the act of intellect performed on the Torah.

The following, somewhat protracted survey of the Mishnah's and tractate Abot's theory concerning the relative effects of knowledge and ignorance of the Torah helps show what is fresh and unprecedented in the representation of the same matter in the successor documents.[9] Tractate Abot, a generation beyond the Mishnah, places heavy emphasis on the importance of correlating actions with knowledge. A variety of sayings insist that if one knows the Torah but does not act in accord with its teachings, one gains nothing. A person's life must change to conform with his knowledge of the Torah. That point of insistence invites as its next small step the doctrine that knowing the Torah changes one in being and essence, not only intellectually, by reason of illumination, but taxically, by reason of transformation. Nonetheless, the gnostic Torah, which would treat knowing the Torah on its own as a medium for one's transformation from merely natural to supernatural character[10] would be some time in coming and would make its appearance only in the successor system. A survey of tractate Abot yields no such conception, but only the point that knowledge must be confirmed in deeds, a conception of moral but not existential weight, as in the following saying:

Tractate Abot 1:17

A. Simeon his son says, "Not the learning is the main thing but the doing. And whoever talks too much causes sin."

True, the statement that if one keeps his eye on three things he will not sin can yield the conception that knowledge bears salvific consequence, but that does not speak of a personal transformation in status and condition. The knowledge that saves people from sin is instrumental, not transformative: "Know what is above you: (1) an eye that sees, and (2) an ear that hears, and (3) all your actions are written down in a book." The same conception, that knowledge is essential to attitudes that bring salvation, is stated in the following:

Tractate Abot 3:1

A. Aqabiah b. Mehallalel says, "Reflect upon three things and you will not fall into the clutches of transgression:

B. "Know (1) from whence you come, (2) whither you are going, and (3) before whom you are going to have to give a full account [of yourself].

C. "From whence do you come? From a putrid drop.

D. "Whither are you going? To a place of dust, worms, and maggots.

E. "And before whom are you going to give a full account of yourself? Before the King of kings of kings, the Holy One, blessed be He."

None of this has strayed far from the notion that knowledge of the Torah promises a good reward here and after death because it keeps man from sin, which is Nehorai's position vis-à-vis studying a trade. Here again, the text treats knowledge as necessary in an instrumental sense; it yields a given goal, but it does not effect a desired transformation. A promise that in context is quite consistent is that he who studies the Torah will encounter God:

Tractate Abot 3:2

c. R. Hananiah b. Teradion says, "[If] two sit together and between them do not pass teachings of Torah, lo, this is a seat of the scornful. . . .

E. "Two who are sitting, and words of Torah do pass between them—the Presence is with them, as it is said, *'Then they that feared the Lord spoke with one another, and the Lord hearkened and heard, and a book of remembrance was written before him, for them that feared the Lord and gave thought to His name'* (Mal. 3:16)."

G. I know that this applies to two.

H. How do I know that even if a single person sits and works on Torah, the Holy One, blessed be He, sets aside a reward for him? As it is said, *'Let him sit alone and keep silent, because he has laid it upon him'* (Lam. 3:28)."

Tractate Abot 3:6

A. R. Halafta of Kefar Hananiah says, "Among ten who sit and work hard on Torah the Presence comes to rest,

B. "as it is said, *'God stands in the congregation of God'* (Ps. 82:1).

c. "And how do we know that the same is so even of five? For it is said, *'And he has founded his group upon the earth'* (Amos 9:6).

D. "And how do we know that this is so even of three? Since it is said, *'And he judges among the judges'* (Ps. 82:1).

E. "And how do we know that this is so even of two? Because

it is said, '*Then they that feared the Lord spoke with one another, and the Lord hearkened and heard*' (Mal. 3:16).

F. "And how do we know that this is so even of one? Since it is said, '*In every place where I record my name I will come to you and I will bless you*' (Exod. 20:24)."

"Knowing God" or bringing God into a study circle both certainly represent desirable goals of illumination. As I shall show, however, these do not encompass the transformative experience that the gnostic theory of the Torah promises the one who knows, because even though God has joined the study circle and brought the divine presence to rest among the disciples, they still do not claim supernatural powers as the consequence; neither the Mishnah, the Tosefta, nor Abot claims that the disciple of the sage does miracles by reason of his learning.[11]

The contrast in the following saying between getting a good name and getting the world to come also is not quite to the point: "[If] one has gotten a good name, he has gotten it for himself. [If] he has gotten teachings of Torah, he has gotten himself life eternal." This speaks of repute, a form of virtue, but not of wonder working. The same point as Simeon's above comes to the fore in the following:

Tractate Abot 3:9

A. R. Haninah b. Dosa says, "For anyone whose fear of sin takes precedence over his wisdom, his wisdom will endure.

B. "And for anyone whose wisdom takes precedence over his fear of sin, his wisdom will not endure."

C. He would say, "Anyone whose deeds are more than his wisdom—his wisdom will endure.

D. "And anyone whose wisdom is more than his deeds—his wisdom will not endure."

Tractate Abot 3:17

I. He would say, "Anyone whose wisdom is greater than his deeds—to what is he to be likened? To a tree with abundant foliage, but few roots.

J. "When the winds come, they will uproot it and blow it down,

K. "as it is said, '*He shall be like a tamarisk in the desert and shall not see when good comes but shall inhabit the parched places in the wilderness*' (Jer. 17:6).

L. "But anyone whose deeds are greater than his wisdom — to what is he to be likened? To a tree with little foliage but abundant roots.

M. "For even if all the winds in the world were to come and blast at it, they will not move it from its place,

N. "as it is said, '*He shall be as a tree planted by the waters, and that spreads out its roots by the river, and shall not fear when heat comes, and his leaf shall be green, and shall not be careful in the year of drought, neither shall cease from yielding fruit*' (Jer. 17:8)."

Tractate Abot 4:5

A. R. Ishamel, his son, says, "He who learns so as to teach — they give him a chance to learn and to teach.

B. "He who learns so as to carry out his teachings — they give him a chance to learn, to teach, to keep, and to do."

Indeed, a variety of sayings explicitly identify not Torah learning but other virtues as primary and furthermore scarcely concede to Torah learning transformative, let alone salvific, power:

Tractate Abot 4:13

C. R. Simeon says, "There are three crowns: the crown of Torah, the crown of priesthood, and the crown of sovereignty.

D. "But the crown of a good name is best of them all."

Tractate Abot 4:17

A. He would say, "Better is a single moment spent in penitence and good deeds in this world than the whole of the world to come.

B. "And better is a single moment of inner peace in the world to come than the whole of a lifetime spent in this world."

These and similar sayings attest to a variety of modes of human regeneration, none of them connected with Torah learning in particular.

In the successor documents, a quite different theory of Torah learning predominates. In these texts, knowledge of the Torah changes the one who knows. He becomes physically weaker[12] but gains supernatural power in compensation. The legitimating power of the Torah and study thereof imputed in the pages of the Talmud of the Land of Israel is explicit: knowledge of the Torah changes a man into a sage and also saves Israel. The Torah then involves not mere knowledge (e.g., correct information and valid generalization) but gnosis: saving knowledge.[13]

To the rabbis, the principal salvific deed was to "study Torah," by which they meant both memorizing Torah sayings by constant repetition, and as the Talmud itself amply testifies (for some sages), conducting profound analytic inquiry into the meaning of those sayings. Such "study of Torah" imparted supernatural power; for example, by repeating words of Torah, the sage could ward off the angel of death and accomplish other kinds of miracles as well. So Torah formulas served as incantations. Mastery of Torah transformed the man who engaged in Torah learning into a supernatural figure, able to do things ordinary folk could not do. In the nature of things, the category of "Torah" was vastly expanded so that the symbol of Torah—a Torah scroll—could be compared to a man of Torah, namely, a rabbi. Given that what made a man into a sage, a disciple of a sage, or a rabbi was studying the Torah through discipleship, what is at stake in the symbolic transfer is quite obvious.

The Torah is then identified with and personified by the sage, who is changed because of what he knows. That is a material and palpable claim, not merely a mode of ascribing great sanctity that lacks any concrete consequence. That claim vastly expanded the definition of the symbol of "Torah," for the allegation that a sage (or disciple of a sage) himself was equivalent to a scroll of the Torah forms a material, legal comparison, not merely a symbolic metaphor.

Y. Moed Qatan 3:7.X

A. He who sees a disciple of a sage who has died is as if he sees a scroll of the Torah that has been burned.

Y. Moed Qatan 3:1.XI

I. R. Jacob bar Abayye in the name of R. Aha: "An elder who forgot his learning because of some accident that happened to him—they treat him with the sanctity owed to an ark [of the Torah]."

In both instances actual behavior was affected. That view is expressed in stories indicating the belief that while a sage is repeating Torah sayings, the angel of death cannot approach him.

Y. Moed Qatan 3:5.XXI

F. [Proving that while one is studying Torah, the angel of death cannot touch a person, the following is told:] A disciple of R. Hisda fell sick. He sent two disciples to him, so that they would repeat Mishnah traditions with him. [The angel of death] turned himself before them into the figure of a snake, and they stopped repeating traditions, and [the sick man] died.

G. A disciple of Bar Pedaiah fell ill. He sent to him two disciples to repeat Mishnah traditions with him. [The angel of death] turned himself before them into a kind of star, and they stopped repeating Mishnah traditions, and he died.

Repeating Mishnah traditions thus warded off death. It is hardly surprising that stories were told about wonders associated with the deaths of various rabbis. These validated the claim of supernatural power imputed to the rabbis. The repertoire of such stories includes two sorts. First, there is a list of supernatural occurrences accompanying sages' deaths, and second, there are claims of specific miracles that were done by Heaven when a great sage died. The former are as in the following:

Y. Abodah Zarah 3:1.II

A. When R. Aha died, a star appeared at noon.

B. When R. Hanah died, the statues bowed down.

C. When R. Yohanan died, the icons bowed down.

D. They said that [this was to indicate] there were no icons like him [so beautiful as Yohanan himself].

E. When R. Hanina of Bet Hauran died, the Sea of Tiberias split open.

F. They said that [this was to commemorate the miracle that took place] when he went up to intercalate the year, and the sea split open before him.

G. When R. Hoshaiah died, the palm of Tiberias fell down.

H. When R. Isaac b. Elisheb died, seventy [infirm] thresholds of houses in Galilee were shaken down.

I. They said that [this was to commemorate the fact that] they [were shaky and] had depended on his merit [for the miracle that permitted them to continue to stand].

J. When R. Samuel bar R. Isaac died, cedars of the Land of Israel were uprooted.

K. They said that [this was to take note of the fact that] he would take a branch [of a cedar] and [dance, so] praising a bride [at her wedding, and thereby giving her happiness].

L. The rabbis would ridicule them [for lowering himself by doing so]. Said to them R. Zeira, "Leave him be. Does the old man not know what he is doing?"

M. When he died, a flame came forth from heaven and intervened between his bier and the congregation. For three hours there were voices and thunderings in the world: "Come and see what a sprig of cedar has done for this old man!"

N. [Further] an echo came forth and said, "Woe that Samuel b. R. R. Isaac has died, the doer of merciful deeds."

O. When R. Yosa bar Halputa died, the gutters ran with blood in Laodicea.

P. They said [that the reason was] that he had given his life for the rite of circumcision.

Q. When R. Abbahu died, the pillars of Caesarea wept.

R. The [gentiles] said [that the reason was] that [the pillars] were celebrating. The Israelites said to them, "And do those who are distant [such as yourselves] know why those who are near [we ourselves] are raising a cry?"

Y. Abodah Zarah 3:1.II

BB. One of the members of the patriarchate died, and the [burial] cave folded over [and received the bier], so endangering the lives [of those who had come to bury him]. R. Yose went up and took leave [of the deceased], saying "Happy is a man who has left this world in peace."

CC. When R. Yosa died, the castle of Tiberias collapsed, and members of the patriarchate were rejoicing. R. Zeira said to them, "There is no similarity [between this case and the miracle described at BB]. The people's lives were endangered, here no one's life was endangered. In that case, no pagan worship was removed, whereas here, an idol was uprooted [so, consequently, the event described in BB was not a miracle, whereas the event described here was a miracle and a sign of divine favor]."

What is important in the foregoing anthology is the linkage between the holy deeds of the sages and the miracles done at their demise. The sages' merit, attained through study of Torah or through acts of saintliness and humility, was demonstrated for all to see. Thus, the sage was not merely a master of Torah, but his mastery of Torah laid the foundations for all the other things he was: he was changed into something other than what he had been before he studied the Torah, and all else follows.

Second, specific miracles, as distinct from natural wonders, were related with regard to the death of the patriarch.

Y. Ketubot 12:3.IV

E. R. Nathan in the name of R. Mana: "There were miracles done that day. It was the eve of the Sabbath, and all the villagers assembled to make a lamentation for him. They put down the bier eighteen times en route to burial to mourn him, and they accompanied him down to Bet Shearim. The daylight was protracted until each one of them had reached his home [in time for the Sabbath] and had time to fill up a jug of water and light the Sabbath lamp. When the sun set, the cock crowed, and the people began to be troubled, saying, 'Perhaps we have violated the Sabbath.'

F. "But an echo came to them 'Whoever did not refrain from participation in the lamentations for Rabbi may be given the good news that he is going to enjoy a portion in the world to come

G. " 'except for the launderer [who used to come to Rabbi day by day, but did not bother to participate in his funeral].' When he heard this, he went up to the roof and threw himself down and died. Then an echo went forth and said, 'Even the laundryman [will enjoy the life of the world to come].' "

Y. Ketubot 12:3.VII

J. When R. Huna, the exilarch, died, they brought his bones up here. They said, "If we are going to bury him properly, let us place him near R. Hiyya, because he comes from there."

K. They said, "Who is worthy of placing him there?"

L. Said to them R. Haggai, "I shall go up and place him there."

M. They said to him, "You are looking for an excuse, for you are an old man, so you want to go up there and die and be buried there next to Hiyya."

N. He said to them, "Tie a rope to my feet, and if I delay there too long you can drag me out."

O. He went in and found three biers.

P. [He heard,] "Judah, my son, is after you, and no one else. Hezekiah, my son, is after you, and no one else. Joseph, son of Israel, and no one else."

Q. He raised his eyes and looked. One said to him, "Lower your face."

R. Said R. Hiyya the Elder, "Judah, my son, make room for R. Huna."

S. He made a place for him, but [Huna] did not accept being buried [next to Hiyya the Elder, out of modesty].

T. [Haggai] said, "Just as [out of modesty] he did not accept being buried next to him, so may his seed never die out."

U. R. Haggai left that place at the age of eighty years, and they doubled the number of his years [so that he lived another eighty years].

That the sage was different from ordinary men seems to me well established, but in context that claim was not surprising; holy men in general were deemed supernatural. What makes this claim distinctive in the later system is not only that it is unprecedented in its canonical context but also that it is a claim of supernatural power gained specifically through the autocephalous act of undertaking to study the Torah.

The Torah was deemed true in this context, and that explained why rabbis were shown more effective than other magicians, specifically in those settings for which all parties conceded that other wonder workers were as able to perform magical deeds as rabbis were. What is important in the following passage is the fact that in a direct contest between a rabbi and another sort of magician (an Israelite heretic) the rabbi was shown to enjoy superior magical power.

Y. Sanhedrin 7:12.III

A. When R. Eleazar, R. Joshua, and R. Aqiba went in to bathe in the baths of Tiberias, a *min* [in context: Israelite heretic] saw them. He said what he said, and the arched chamber in the bath [where idolatrous statues were put up] held them fast, [so that they could not move].

B. Said R. Eleazar to R. Joshua, "Now Joshua b. Hananiah, see what you can do."

C. When that *min* tried to leave, R. Joshua said what he said, and the doorway of the bath seized and held the *min* firm, so that whoever went in had to give him a knock [to push by], and whoever went out had to give him a knock [to push by].

D. He said to them, "Undo whatever you have done [to let me go].

E. They said to him, "Release us, and we shall release you."

F. They released one another.

G. Once they got outside, said R. Joshua to that *min*, "Lo, you have learned [from us whatever you are going to learn]."

H. He said, "Let's go down to the sea."

I. When they got down to the sea, that *min* said whatever it was that he said, and the sea split open.

J. He said to them, "Now is this not what Moses, your rabbi, did at the sea?"

K. They said to him, "Do you not concede to us that Moses, our rabbi, walked through it?"

L. He said to them, "Yes."

M. They said to him, "Then walk through it."

N. He walked through it.

O. R. Joshua instructed the ruler of the sea, who swallowed him up.

IV.4.A

4A. When R. Eliezer, R. Joshua, and Rabban Gamaliel went up to Rome, they came to a certain place and found children making little piles [of dirt]. They said, "Children of the Land of Israel make this sort of thing, and they say, 'This is heave-offering' [priestly ration] and 'That is tithe.' It is likely that there are Jews here."

B. They came into one place and were received there.

C. When they sat down to eat, [they noticed] that each dish that they brought into them would first be brought into a small room and then would be brought to them, and they wondered whether they might be eating sacrifices offered to the dead. [That is, before the food was brought to them, it was brought into a small chamber, in which, they suspected, sacrifices were taken from each dish and offered to an idol.]

D. They said to [the host], "What is your purpose, in the fact that, as to every dish which you bring before us, if you do not bring it first into a small room, you do not bring it in to us?"

E. He said to them, "I have a very old father, and he has made a decree for himself that he will never go out of that small room until he will see the sages of Israel."

F. They said to him, "Go and tell him, 'Come out here to them, for they are here.' "

G. He came out to them.

H. They said to him, "Why do you do this?"

I. He said to them, "Pray for my son, for he has not produced a child."

J. Said R. Eliezer to R. Joshua, "Now, Joshua b. Hananiah, let us see what you will do."

K. He said to them, "Bring me flax seeds," and they brought him flax seeds.

L. He appeared to sow the seed on the table; he appeared to scatter the seed; he appeared to bring the seed up; he appeared to take hold of it, until he drew up a woman, holding on to her tresses.

M. He said to her, "Release whatever [magic] you have done [to this man]."

N. She said to him, "I am not going to release [my spell]."

O. He said to her, "If you do not do it, I shall publicize your [magical secrets]."

P. She said to him, "I cannot do it, for [the magical materials] have been cast into the sea."

Q. R. Joshua made a decree that the sea release [the magical materials] and they came up.

R. They prayed for [the host], and he had the merit of begetting a son, R. Judah b. Bathera.

S. They said, "If we came up here only for the purpose of begetting that righteous man, it would have been enough for us."

T. Said R. Joshua b. Hananiah, "I can take cucumbers and pumpkins and turn them into rams and hosts of rams, and they will produce still more."

These long extracts leave no doubt that the Talmud imputed to Israel's sages precisely the powers generally assigned to magicians. The sage did precisely what the magician did, only he did it better. When the magician then pretended to do what Moses had done, it was his end. The story about Joshua's magic in Rome is similar in its explicit reference to sympathetic magic at K through L. The result was the discovery that the childless man had been subject to a spell.

There can be no doubt that distinctions between magic and supernatural power meant nothing to the Talmud's storytellers. The clerks were not merely holy men, they were a particular kind of holy man. A natural consequence of believing that rabbis had magical powers was to impute to rabbis the ability both to bless those who favored them and to curse those who did not.

Thus far I have shown only that sages studied the Torah, through which study they gained supernatural standing (e.g., when they were buried) and power that they imputed to their knowledge of the Torah. What I have yet to demonstrate is that knowledge of the Torah itself changed the sage so that he not only could manipulate the supernatural power inhering in the Torah but also could himself join in the processes of forming the Torah. I have alleged that the man himself was transformed through Torah study, but what I have already offered in evidence demands an explanation of how that transformation took place, for the allegation that knowledge in particular changes the person can itself refer to a merely instrumental power: if I know thus and so, I can do such and such. At stake in the gnostic Torah was much, much more.

Specifically, one who knows the Torah can join in the making of the Torah, and that claim in the sage's behalf forms solid evidence for the allegation that studying the Torah not only endows the sage with power but actually changes him from what he had been into something else. He had been ordinary; now he is not merely powerful but holy. His holiness is shown by the fact that the Torah may be studied not only in its written and oral forms but also in its quotidian form; the sage himself, his gestures, and his actions form precedents valid within the practice of the Torah itself. If the change in an individual engendered by Torah study allows him to join the process of revealing the Torah, studying the Torah provides a gnostic experience of transformation, regeneration, and salvation. Accordingly, I now must demonstrate that the supernatural status accorded to the person of the sage endowed his deeds with normative, and therefore revelatory, power.

What the sage did had the status of law; the sage was the model of the law, having been changed, transformed, regenerated, saved, and turned into the human embodiment of the Torah by studying the Torah. That gnostic view of Torah study as transformative and salvific—now without explicit appeal to deeds in conformity to the law, though surely that is taken for granted—accounts for the position that the sage was a holy man, for what made the sage distinctive was his combination of this-worldly authority and power and other-worldly influence. In the Yerushalmi's view, the clerk in the court and the holy man on the rooftop praying for rain or calling Heaven to defend the city against marauders were one and the same. The tight union between salvation and law, the magical power of the sage and his law-giving authority, was effected through the integrative act of studying the Torah, and that power of integration accounts for the successor system's insistence that if the sage exercised supernatural power as a kind of living Torah, his very deeds served to reveal law as much as his word expressed revelation.

The sage's capacity to participate in the process of revelation is illustrated in two types of materials. First of all, tales told about rabbis' behavior on specific occasions immediately are translated into rules binding for the entire community. Accordingly, he was a source not merely of good example but of prescriptive law. Here is a humble and mundane case of how that view came to expression.

Y. Abodah Zarah 5:4.III

    x. R. Aha went to Emmaus, and he ate dumplings [prepared by Samaritans].

    y. R. Jerimiah ate leavened bread prepared by them.

    z. R. Hezekiah ate their locusts prepared by them.

    AA. R. Abbahu prohibited Israelite use of wine prepared by them.

As statements of the law on eating what Samaritans cooked, these reports of what rabbis had done enjoyed the same authority as did citations of traditions in the names of the great authorities of old or of the day. What someone did served as a norm if the person was a sage of sufficient standing.

Far more common in the Talmud are instances in which the deed of a rabbi is adduced as an authoritative precedent for the law under discussion. It was everywhere taken for granted that what a rabbi did, he did because of his mastery of the law. Even though a formulation of the law was not in hand, a tale about what a rabbi actually did constituted adequate evidence on how to formulate the law itself, so a law might be framed from the practice of an authority quite independent of the person of the sage. The sage thus functioned as a lawgiver, as Moses did. Among a great many instances of that mode of generating law are the following:

Y. Abodah Zarah 3:11.II

A. Gamaliel Zuga was walking along, leaning on the shoulder of R. Simeon b. Laqish. They came across an image.

B. He said to him, "What is the law as to passing before it?"

C. He said to him, "Pass before it, but close [your] eyes."

D. R. Isaac was walking along, leaning on the shoulder of R. Yohanan. They came across an idol before the council building.

E. He said to him, "What is the law as to passing before it?"

F. He said to him, "Pass before it, but close [your] eyes."

G. R. Jacob bar Idi was walking along, leaning upon R. Joshua b. Levi. They came across a procession in which an idol was carried. He said to him, "Nahum, the most holy man, passed before this idol, and will you not pass by it? Pass before it but close your eyes."

Y. Abodah Zarah 2:2.III

FF. R. Aha had chills and fever. [They brought him] a medicinal drink prepared from the phallus of Dionysian revelers. But he would not drink it. They brought it to R. Jonah, and he did drink it. Said R. Mana, "Now if R. Jonah, the patriarch, had known what it was, he would never have drunk it."

GG. Said R. Huna, "That is to say, 'They do not accept healing from something that derives from an act of fornication.' "

What is important is GG, the restatement of the story in the form of a fixed rule, hence as a law. The example of a rabbi served to teach how one should live a truly holy life. The requirements went far beyond the measure of the law, extending to refraining from deeds of a most commonplace sort. The example of rabbinical virtue, moreover, was adduced explicitly to account for the supernatural or magical power of a rabbi. There was therefore no doubt among the people that the reason rabbis could do the amazing things people said they did was that they embodied the law and exercised its supernatural or magical power. The correlation between learning and teaching, on the one side, and supernatural power or recognition, on the other, is explicit in the following:

Y. Ketubot 12:3.VII

A. R. Yosa fasted eighty fasts in order to see R. Hiyya the Elder [in a dream]. He finally saw him, and his hands trembled and his eyes grew dim.

B. Now if you say that R. Yosa was an unimportant man [and so was unworthy of such a vision, that is not the case]. For a weaver came before R. Yohanan. He said to him, "I saw in my dream that the heaven fell, and one of your disciples was holding it up."

C. He said to him, "Will you know him [when you see him]?"

D. He said to him, "When I see him, I shall know him." Then all of his disciples passed before him, and he recognized R. Yosa.

E. R. Simeon b. Laqish fasted three hundred fasts in order to have a vision of R. Hiyya the Elder, but he did not see him.

F. Finally he began to be distressed about the matter. He said, "Did he labor in learning of Torah more than I?"

G. They said to him, "He brought Torah to the people of Israel to a greater extent than you have, and not only so, but he even went into exile [to teach on a wider front]."

H. He said to them, "And did I not go into exile too?"

I. They said to him, "You went into exile only to learn, but he went into exile to teach others."

This story shows that the storyteller regarded as a fact of life the correlation between mastery of Torah sayings and supernatural power—visions of the deceased, in this case. That is why Simeon b. Laqish complained (at E–F) that he had learned as much Torah as the other and so had every right to be able to conjure the dead. The greater supernatural power of the other then was explained in terms of the latter's superior service to "Torah." The upshot is that the sage was changed by Torah learning and could save Israel through Torah.

More precisely, sages appealed to the character of the saints of Scripture to explain the transformation effected by the study of the

Torah. Seeing Scripture in their own model, they took the position that the supernatural power and salvific promise of the Torah of old continued among themselves in their own day. By studying the Torah, they turned themselves into the model of those sages whose holy deeds the Torah recorded; thus, for example, they called Moses, David, and Isaiah rabbis. In consequence, the promise of salvation contained in every line of Scripture was to be kept in every deed of learning and obedience to the law effected under their auspices. Learning in the Torah was salvific because it turned ordinary men into saints in the model of the saints of the Torah.

That fact helps explain the constant citation of Scripture in the context of sages' rulings and doings. It was not to establish authority alone; rather, it was to identify what was happening just then with what had happened long ago. The purpose was not merely to demonstrate and authenticate the bona fide character of a new figure of salvation but also to show the continuity of the salvific process, a process that relied for its persistence on learning in particular. In the successor system, the act of Torah study had to be endowed with gnostic status, a supernatural power to save, because the act of learning formed the medium for the transmission of not merely lessons but also supernatural power. The Torah presented examples of holiness in addition to rules, and salvation lay in sanctification: "Today, if you repent," that is, conform now as not before; accept transformation, regeneration, salvation.

It followed that the pattern and promise of salvation contained therein lay within the sages' way of life: studying the Torah in discipleship. That is the meaning of the explicit reading of the present into the past—the implicit arrogation of the hope of the past to the salvific heroes of the present, namely, the sages themselves. To state matters simply, if David, king of Israel, prefigured the rabbi, then the rabbi would be the figure of the son of David who was to come as king of Israel. It is not surprising, therefore, that among the many biblical heroes whom the Talmudic rabbis treated as sages, principal and foremost was David himself, now made into a messianic rabbi or a rabbinical Messiah. He was the sage of the Torah, the avatar and model for the sages of their own time. That view was made explicit, both specifically and in general terms. If a rabbi was jealous to have his traditions cited in his own name, it was because that was David's explicit view as well. In more general terms, both David and Moses are represented as students of Torah, just like the disciples and sages of the current time. Recall how David is represented as a devoted student of the Torah. Here is one re-presentation of a bliblical story in the mode of an academic tale:

Y. Sanhedrin 2:6.IV

A. It is written, "And David said longingly, '*Oh, that someone would give me water to drink from the well of Bethlehem* [which is by the gate]' (1 Chron. 11:17)."

B. R. Hiyya bar Ba said, "He required a teaching of law."

C. "*Then the three mighty men broke through [the camp of the Philistines]*" (1 Chron. 11:18).

D. Why three? Because the law is not decisively laid down by fewer than three.

E. "But David would not drink of it; [he poured it out to the Lord, and said, '*Far be it from me before my God that I should do this. Shall I drink the lifeblood of these men? For at risk of their lives they brought it*]' (1 Chron. 11:18-19)."

F. David did not want the law to be laid down in his own name.

G. "He poured it out to the Lord" — establishing [the decision] as [an unattributed] teaching for the generations, [so that the law should be authoritative and so be cited anonymously].

Y. Sheqalim 2:4.V

O. David himself prayed for mercy for himself, as it is said, "*Let me dwell in thy tent forever! Oh, to be safe under the shelter of thy wings, selah*" (Ps. 61:4).

P. And did it enter David's mind that he would live forever?

Q. But this is what David said before the Holy One, blessed be He, "Lord of the world, may I have the merit that my words will be stated in synagogues and schoolhouses."

R. Simeon b. Nazira in the name of R. Isaac said, "Every disciple in whose name people cite a teaching of law in this world — his lips murmur with him in the grave, as it is said, '*Your kisses are like the best wine that goes down smoothly, gliding over lips of those that sleep*' (Song of Sol. 7:9).

S. "Just as in the case of a mass of grapes, once a person puts his finger in it, forthwith even his lips begin to smack, so the lips of the righteous, when someone cites a teaching of law in their names—their lips murmur with them in the grave."

David as a model of the disciple of the sage is represented in the following for the virtue of conscious and zealous Torah study:

Y. Berakhot 1:1.XII (trans. by Tzvee Zahavy)

O. "*I will awake the dawn*" (Ps. 5:7, 8)—I will awaken the dawn; the dawn will not awaken me.

P. David's [evil] impulse tried to seduce him [to sin]. And it would say to him, "David. It is the custom of kings that awakens them. And you say, 'I will awake the dawn.' It is the custom of kings that they sleep until the third hour [of the day]. And you say, 'At midnight I rise.' " And [David] used to say [in reply], "*[I rise early] because of thy righteous ordinances* (Ps. 119:62)."

Q. And what would David do? R. Phineas in the name of R. Eleazar b. R. Menahem [said], "He used to take a harp and lyre and set them at his bedside. And he would rise at midnight and play them so that the associates of Torah should hear. And what would the associates of Torah say? 'If David involves himself with Torah, how much more so should we.' We find that all of Israel was involved in Torah [study] on account of David."

These two extracts show how the Talmud's authorities readily saw their concerns in biblical statements attributed to David. "Water" meant "a teaching of Torah"; "three mighty men" were judges. At issue was whether the decision was to be stated in David's own name and so removed from the authoritative consensus of sages. David exhibits precisely those concerns for the preservation of his views in his name that, in earlier sections, were attributed to rabbis. All this, as previously noted, fully reveals the rabbis' deeper convictions, for David the rabbi also was in everyone's mind David the Messiah.

Enough has been set forth to suggest that I mean to represent the gnostic Torah as the centerpiece of the successor system, but the evidence suggests precisely the opposite, for even the stories contained in the Talmud of the Land of Israel in which the priority and sanctity of the sage's knowledge of the Torah form the focus of discourse prevent me from doing so. Time and again, knowledge of the Torah forms a way station on a path to a more distant, more central goal: attaining *zekhut*, which I translate as "the heritage of virtue and its consequent entitlements." Torah study is one means of attaining access to that heritage, of gaining *zekhut*. There are other, equally suitable means, and the merit gained by Torah study is no different from the merit gained by acts of supererogatory grace. Because it is points of integration, not of differentiation, that indicate the systemic problematic in the successor system, it is a serious matter that such stories as the following assign the contingent status of a dependent variable to Torah study.

Y. Taanit 3:11.IV

C. There was a house that was about to collapse over there [in Babylonia], and Rab set one of his disciples in the house, until they had cleared out everything from the house. When the disciple left the house, the house collapsed.

D. And there are those who say that it was R. Adda bar Ahwah.

E. Sages sent and said to him, "What sort of good deeds are to your credit [that you have that much merit]?"

F. He said to them, "In my whole life no man ever got to the synagogue in the morning before I did. I never left anybody there when I went out. I never walked four cubits without speaking words of Torah. Nor did I ever mention teachings of Torah in an inappropriate setting. I never laid out a bed and slept for a regular period of time. I never took great strides among the associates. I never called my fellow by a nickname. I never rejoiced in the embarrassment of my fellow. I never cursed my fellow when I was lying by myself in bed. I never walked over in the marketplace to someone who owed me money.

G. "In my entire life I never lost my temper in my household."

H. This was meant to carry out that which is stated as follows: "*I will give heed to the way that is blameless. Oh, when wilt thou come to me? I will walk with integrity of heart within my house*" (Ps. 101:2).

What I find striking in this story is that mastery of the Torah is only one means of attaining the *zekhut* that had enabled the sage to keep the house from collapsing, and not the primary means. The question at E provides the key, together with its answer at F, for what the sage did to gain such remarkable *zekhut* was not to master so many tractates of the Mishnah, but rather to perform acts of courtesy, consideration, gentility, and restraint. These produced *zekhut,* all of them acts of self-abnegation or the avoidance of power over others and the submission to the will and the requirements of self-esteem of others. Torah study is simply one item on a list of actions or attitudes that generate *zekhut.*

Politics is replicated in a moral setting: the form of power that the system promises derives from the rejection of power that the world recognizes—legitimate violence replaced by a legitimation of the absence of the power to commit violence or of the failure to commit violence. This sort of power derives from *zekhut* gained in a variety of ways, not through the study of the Torah solely or even primarily. The story at hand speaks of a particular sage who has gained *zekhut* by acting not in the way sages are commonly assumed to behave but in a humble way.

In the context of this story, *zekhut* may prove a virtue dependent on the situation of the Torah and its study, in consequence of which I should have to impute to the gnostic Torah systemic priority, indeed centrality, finding in the new learning the key to the successor system as a whole. But that is in fact not so. At hand is not a religious system in which the transformation of the individual through salvific knowledge provides the compelling answer to the question of personal salvation. A different question stands at center stage, and an altogether different answer defines the dramatic tension of the theatrical globe. At stake is a public and a national question, one concerning Israel's history and destiny, to which the individual and his salvation, although important, are distinctly subordinate. Not Torah study, which may generate *zekhut,* but *zekhut* itself defines what is at issue, the generative problematic of the system, and a grasp of the answer provided by *zekhut* is necessary to reach a definition of the question that precipitated the systemic construction and the formation of all its categories, principal and contingent alike.[14]

The importance of the gnostic Torah in no way diminishes given the subordinate position of the Torah in the successor system, for the upshot remains systemically indicative. In unifying the distinct categories of learning and not deeds or virtue but one's personal condition in the supernatural world and in encompassing data not formerly noted or even assembled at all, the transformation of the category of world-view from an intellectual and even moral indicator to a salvific and a supernatural one shows the successor system's novel power of integration. If Torah study changes an individual not only in his knowledge or even virtue but in his relationship to Heaven, endowing him with supernatural power, then the system as a whole signals a union of Heaven and earth that was formerly unimagined. What a person knows concerns not only earth but Heaven; the power that knowledge brings governs in both realms.

Study of the Torah changed the one who studied because through it he entered into the mind of God, learning how God's mind worked when God formed the Torah, written and oral alike, and (in the explicit view of Genesis Rabbah 1:1) when he consulted the Torah in creating the world. And to the framers of the successor system, it was in the intellect of God that humanity gained access to the only means of uniting intellect with existential condition as to salvation. The Mishnah had set forth the rules that governed the natural world in relationship to Heaven, but knowledge of the Torah now joined the one world, known through nature, with the other world, the world of supernature, where intellect ultimately served merely in the quest for salvation. Through Torah study sages claimed for themselves a place in that very process of thought that had given birth to nature, but it was a super-natural process, and knowledge of that process on its own terms would transform and, in the nature of things, save. That explains the integrative power of imputing supernatural power to learning. To realize that this is what was at stake in the gnostic Torah is to understand the full gravity of the simple statement that the system's orbit encircled not the Torah but *zekhut*.

Notes

1. I bypass the word *Gnostic* with a capital *G*, which bears quite specific meanings in the study of late antiquity. A variety of meanings circulate, attached to various writings. What the common adjective, gnostic, and the denotative adjective, Gnostic, have in common is that the latter falls into the class of the former: saving knowledge.

2. Not even at M. Hag. 2:2!

3. Resorting to the adjective "faustian," although defensible, seems to me less exact.

4. Obviously, this "gnostic" is with a small *g*; I in no way mean to identify the Torah of the successor Judaism with the Gnostic systems—Christian, Judaic, and pagan—of which we have knowledge in the same time and place, as well as earlier and later. My supposition is that, in any religious system, the intellectual component by the nature of the systemic setting is going to bear the same transformative and salvific valence as I show here pertained to

the Torah. There are numerous counterparts in other religions that impute salvific power to knowledge of the correct sort in the proper manner. That seems to me to justify treating "gnostic" as a generic classification for religious knowledge. But is there religious knowledge that is not gnostic, but merely (for one example) validating or qualifying? Indeed, there is a great deal of such knowledge, and the Mishnah's conception of knowing, as set forth in the apologetic of tractate Abot, is exactly of that kind. There, as we shall see, studying the Torah brings God's presence to join those who repeat Torah words, whether one or many. But there is no consequent claim that the Torah words' repetition has changed those who have said them, only that God has joined their study circle. And that claim is of a considerably different kind from the one we shall see in numerous stories of the correlation between knowing the Torah and supernatural power.

5. And hardly them alone. For the prevailing philosophical traditions the consequence of enlightenment in intellect cannot be said to have encompassed personal salvation (let alone national salvation, such as the Yerushalmi covered as well). Virtue depended upon right thinking, e.g., knowing what is the good, the true, and the beautiful, but the consequence of that knowledge did not commonly yield supernatural power in the philosophical system of Greco-Roman antiquity. Along these same lines, knowledge of the Torah served, e.g., the Israelite priesthood, as a medium of validation, in that through knowledge they knew how to do their job, but it was a job that they got by reason of genealogy, not knowledge, as Mishnah tractate Yoma 1:3 has already reminded us. So too, the Israelite scribal profession identified knowledge of the Torah as the foundation of their professional qualification.

6. E.g., Mishnah tractate Horayot 3:3-6, given above.

7. It is conventional to read the following as "Gnostic," for instance, note Gershom G. Scholem, *Jewish Gnosticism, Merkabah Mysticism, and Talmudic Tradition* (New York: Jewish Theological Seminary of America, 1960). Taking the attributions at face value, moreover, various scholars, typified by Scholem, have forthwith assigned to "Judaism," or to "the rabbis" a fully realized Gnostic experience. But if they had not decided in advance that these sayings had to mean what they suppose they mean, the proponents of such views about the condition of "Judaism" in the first century would have had to consider a variety of meanings and alternatives, including the one that we simply do not know what is going on in these statements.

8. And here, in the received scholarly tradition in all languages, Gnostic with a capital G is routinely given. But that seems to me to read into the passage much that is not explicit and need not be present at all; still, I admit, I do not claim to understand the passage at all, nor those in proximity in the Tosefta.

9. Without a full review of the sayings on the relationship of learning to one's personal condition as to salvation, what is fully new in the later documents will not be discerned. The nuances of language here do matter, especially because the received reading of the sayings surveyed in the following paragraphs imposes on them the supernatural valence accorded only in the

later writings to Torah knowledge or Torah study. Here the master of Torah learning is saved only by what he does in consequence of what he knows, or by matching what he knows with what he does. Knowing by itself does not save, though it can effect attitudes that will affect one's actions in one way rather than in some other, and right action will then yield salvation. In addition, Torah study will draw God's presence among those who study, but that does not yield the claim either that the sages are changed or that they thereby gain supernatural power. None of the indicators of the gnostic Torah occur, but only by the following survey will readers appreciate how much has been read into the sayings adduced in behalf of the contrary view.

10. Indeed, the emphasis on the importance of correlating learning and deed and on the priority of deed seems to me to deny that very correlation of learning with transformation. Merely knowing is insufficient, but to a gnostic theory of knowledge, merely knowing itself saves. Thus, I suppose, proponents of the theory of a Gnostic Judaism of the first and second centuries will adduce these statements as evidence of not Gnostic Judaism but a reaction against Gnostic Judaism, but the evidence once more would then be asked to bear too heavy a burden of interpretation.

11. The contrary view, that the one who does miracles is not necessarily a disciple of a sage, though he may be a holy man, is presented at Mishnah tractate Taanit 3:8 with reference to Honi, for one instance. What is important to my argument is simply that no one correlates Torah learning with wonder working. Whether the component of the canon represented by the Mishnah and its associated writings favors wonder working or opposes it, fears it or admires it, is not at stake here. What concerns me is the working of the categories, and the process of category formation adumbrated by the correlation of distinct categories simply has not taken place by the end of the formation of the Mishnah's component of the canon of the dual Torah.

12. As I noted in chapter 2.

13. One important qualification is required. Knowledge is not the only medium of salvation. Salvation, as before, derives from keeping the law of the Torah. Keeping the law in the right way is the way to bring the Messiah, the son of David. This is stated by Levi, as follows: "If Israel would keep a single Sabbath in the proper way, forthwith the son of David would come" (Y. Taanit 1:1.IX.X). The issue of not doing but (mere) knowing, of salvation through study of the Torah, is distinct, however.

14. Until this inquiry I had always taken for granted that the center of the Judaism of the dual Torah was located in the theory of the Torah as the critical symbol of the whole, a position conveyed by the title of my textbook *The Way of Torah: An Introduction to Judaism* in all its various revisions and printings. But as I show in the next chapter, Torah is contingent and instrumental, whereas *zekhut* is uncontingent and the system's sole (so it appears at this moment) independent variable. And yet, it seems clear to me that the symbol of Torah does remain the center and heart of the Judaism that emerged from late antiquity. What this impression suggests to me is that in the third stage in the formation of the Judaism of the dual Torah, attested

by the Bavli and associated Midrash compilations, I should find *zekhut* a more peripheral, contingent variable, replaced by Torah as the independent variable and court of final appeal. Whether that will be the case I cannot now predict.

8

The New Order:
The Political Economy
of Zekhut

Zekhut, scarce or common as the capacity for uncoerced action dictated, puissant or supine as strength to refrain from deeds of worldly power decided, accomplished the systemic integration of the successor documents. That protean conception formed into a cogent political economy for the social order of Israel the economics and the politics that made powerlessness into power and disinheritance into wealth. Acts of will consisting of voluntary submission to the will of Heaven endowed Israel with a lien and entitlement on Heaven. What Israel cannot by will impose, it can by will evoke. What it cannot accomplish through coercion, it can achieve through submission. God will do for Israel what it cannot do for itself when it does for God what God cannot make it do. In a wholly concrete and tangible sense, the command is that Israel love God with all its heart, soul, and might. That systemic statement justifies classifying the successor system as religious in as profound and complete a way as the initial system had been wholly and restrictedly philosophical.

Zekhut stands for the supernatural empowerment that derives from the virtue of one's ancestry or from one's own virtuous deeds of a very particular order. No single word in English bears the same meaning, nor can I identify a synonym for *zekhut* in the canonical writings in the original. The difficulty of translating a word of systemic consequence with a single word in some other language (or in the language of the system's documents themselves) indicates something that is unique, beyond comparison and therefore beyond contrast and comprehension. What is most particular to and distinctive of the systemic structure and its functioning requires definition through circumlocution, such as I gave earlier: "the heritage of virtue and its consequent entitlements."[1]

The word *zekhut* for the successor system forms the systemic counterpart to the mythologoumenon of the resurrection of Jesus Christ, unique son of God, for important Christianities.

It follows that *zekhut*, not Torah, defines the generative myth, the critical symbol of the successor Judaism. The signal that the gnostic Torah formed a mere component in a system that transcended Torah study and defined its structure in some way other than by appeal to the symbol and activity of the Torah comes from a simple fact: ordinary folk, not disciples of sages, have access to *zekhut* entirely outside of Torah study. In stories not about rabbis, a single remarkable deed, exemplary for its deep humanity, sufficed to win for an ordinary person the *zekhut*—"the heritate of virtue and its consequent entitlements"—that elicits the same marks of supernatural favor enjoyed by some rabbis on account of their Torah study.

Accordingly, the systemic centrality of *zekhut*, the critical importance of the heritage of virtue together with its supernatural entitlements, emerges in a striking claim. It is framed in an extreme form, which is another mark of the unique place of *zekhut* within the system. Even though a man was degraded, one action of the right sort sufficed to win for him that heavenly glory to which rabbis aspired in lives of Torah study. The mark of the system's integration around *zekhut* lies in its insistence that all Israelites, not only sages, could gain *zekhut* for themselves (and their descendants). A single remarkable deed, exemplary for its deep humanity, could win for an ordinary person the *zekhut* that elicits supernatural favor enjoyed by some rabbis on account of their Torah study. The rabbinical storyteller whose writing I shall consider assuredly identifies with this lesson, for it is the point of his story and its climax.

In defining what the individual must do to gain *zekhut*, the point of the three following passages is that the protagonists' deeds make them worthy of having their prayers answered, which is a mark of the working of *zekhut*. It is deeds beyond the strict requirements of the Torah, and even the limits of the law altogether, that transform the hero into a holy man, whose holiness served just like that of a sage marked as such by knowledge of the Torah. The following stories should not be understood as expressions merely of the clerks' sentimentality concerning the lower orders, for they deny in favor of a single action of surpassing power the sages' lifelong devotion to what the sages held to be the highest value, knowledge of the Torah:

Y. Taanit 1:4.I

F. A certain man came before one of the relatives of R. Yannai. He said to him, "Rabbi, attain *zekhut* through me [by giving me charity]."

G. He said to him, "And did not your father leave you money?"

H. He said to him, "No."

I. He said to him, "Go and collect what your father left in deposit with others."

J. He said to him, "I have heard concerning property my father deposited with others that it was gained by violence [so I don't want it]."

K. He said to him, "You are worthy of praying and having your prayers answered."

The point of K is an obvious reference to the entitlement to supernatural favor, and it is gained through deeds that the law of the Torah cannot require but must favor: what one does on one's own volition, beyond the measure of the law. Here I see the opposite of sin, for a sin is also what one has done by one's own volition beyond all limits of the law. Thus, an act that generates *zekhut* for the individual is the counterpart and opposite.

L. A certain ass driver appeared before the rabbis [the context requires: in a dream] and prayed, and rain came. The rabbis sent and brought him and said to him, "What is your trade?"

M. He said to them, "I am an ass driver."

N. They said to him, "And how do you conduct your business?"

O. He said to them, "One time I rented my ass to a certain woman, and she was weeping on the way, and I said to her, 'What is with you?' and she said to me, 'The husband of that women [me] is in prison [for debt], and I wanted to see what I can do to free him.' So I sold my ass and I gave her the proceeds, and I said to her, 'Here is your money, free your husband, but do not sin [by becoming a prostitute to raise the necessary funds].' "

P. They said to him, "You are worthy of praying and having your prayers answered."

The ass driver clearly has a powerful lien on Heaven, so that his prayers are answered, even while those of others are not. To get that entitlement he did what no law could demand: he impoverished himself to save the woman from a "fate worse than death."

Q. In a dream of R. Abbahu, Mr. Pentakaka ["Five sins"] appeared, who prayed that rain would come, and it rained. R. Abbahu sent and summoned him. He said to him, "What is your trade?"

R. He said to him, "Five sins does that man [I] do every day, [for I am a pimp:] hiring whores, cleaning up the theater, bringing home their garments for washing, dancing, and performing before them."

S. He said to him, "And what sort of decent thing have you ever done?"

T. He said to him, "One day that man [I] was cleaning the theater, and a woman came and stood behind a pillar and cried. I said to her, 'What is with you?' And she said to me, 'That woman's [my] husband is in prison, and I wanted to see what I can do to free him,' so I sold my bed and cover, and I gave the proceeds to her. I said to her, 'Here is your money, free your husband, but do not sin.' "

U. He said to him, "You are worthy of praying and having your prayers answered."

This passage at Q pushes the point still further, for the named man has done everything sinful that one can do, and, more to the point, he does it every day. Thus, the singularity of the act of *zekhut*, which suffices even if done only one time, encompasses its power to outweigh a life of sin—again, an act of *zekhut* as the mirror image and opposite of sin. Here again, the single act of saving a woman from a "fate worse than death" has sufficed.

V. A pious man from Kefar Imi appeared [in a dream] to the rabbis. He prayed for rain and it rained. The rabbis went up to him. His householders told them that he was sitting on a hill. They went out to him, saying to him, "Greetings," but he did not answer them.

W. He was sitting and eating, and he did not say to them, "You break bread, too."

X. When he went back home, he made a bundle of faggots and put his cloak on top of the bundle [instead of on his shoulder].

Y. When he came home, he said to his household [wife], "These rabbis are here [because] they want me to pray for rain. If I pray and it rains, it is a disgrace for them, and if not, it is a profanation of the Name of Heaven. But come, you and I will go up [to the roof] and pray. If it rains, we shall tell them, 'We are not worthy to pray and have our prayers answered.' "

z. They went up and prayed and it rained.

AA. They came down to them [and asked], "Why have the rabbis troubled themselves to come here today?"

BB. They said to him, "We wanted you to pray so that it would rain."

CC. He said to them, "Now do you really need my prayers? Heaven already has done its miracle."

DD. They said to him, "Why, when you were on the hill, did we say hello to you, and you did not reply?"

EE. He said to them, "I was then doing my job. Should I then interrupt my concentration [on my work]?"

FF. They said to him, "And why, when you sat down to eat, did you not say to us 'You break bread, too'?"

GG. He said to them, "Because I had only my small ration of bread. Why would I have invited you to eat by way of mere flattery [when I knew I could not give you anything at all]?"

HH. They said to him, "And why when you came to go down, did you put your cloak on top of the bundle?"

II. He said to them, "Because the cloak was not mine. It was borrowed for use at prayer. I did not want to tear it."

JJ. They said to him, "And why, when you were on the hill, did your wife wear dirty clothes, but when you came down from the mountain, did she put on clean clothes?"

KK. He said to them, "When I was on the hill, she put on dirty clothes, so that no one would gaze at her. But when I came home from the hill, she put on clean clothes, so that I would not gaze on any other woman."

LL. They said to him, "It is well that you pray and have your prayers answered."

The pious man of V enjoys the recognition of the sages by reason of his lien on Heaven, able as he is to pray and bring rain. He is so endowed with *zekhut* by reason of punctilious acts of a moral order: concentrating on his work, avoiding an act of dissimulation, integrity in the disposition of a borrowed object, his wife's concern both not to attract other men and to make herself attractive to her husband. None of these stories refers explicity to *zekhut;* all of them tell about what it means to enjoy not an entitlement by inheritance but a lien accomplished by one's own supererogatory acts of restraint.

Zekhut integrates what has been differentiated. Holding together learning, virtue, and supernatural standing by explaining how Torah study transforms the learning man, *zekhut* further makes implausible those points of distinction between economics and politics that bore the systemic message of the initial philosophy. Hierarchical classification, with its demonstration of the upward-reaching unity of all being, gives way to a different and more compelling proposition: the unity of all being within the heritage of *zekhut,* to be attained equally and without differentiation in all the principal parts of the social order. The definition of *zekhut* therefore goes to the heart of the integrating and integrated religious system of Judaism.

My claim to describe the transformation of one system into a connected but autonomous successor system, therefore, stands or falls not on the unprecedented character of the concept but on the capacity of the category at hand to hold the whole together. What I shall now show is that *zekhut,* an entirely available idea, had been systemically tangential to the philosophical Judaism and proved itself systemically critical only in the successor structure. That fact will accomplish the twin tasks facing anyone who claims to describe the connections between two historically related systems represented by a single canon. Specifically, showing that *zekhut* was both available and systemically inert will both prove the connectedness of the two systems and also show how the successor system transformed the first. That is to say, the system builders represented by the Talmud of the Land of Israel, Genesis Rabbah, Leviticus Rabbah, and Pesiqta deRab Kahana made their own choices within their inheritance. Their system consequently defined its own categories and accomplished through its own medium the integration of its systemic components, the counterpart categories.[2] Before I explore the place and integrating power of *zekhut* within the systemic structure and system, however, I should reconsider the definition of the word that seems to me so critical to the statement of this Judaism.

As Jastrow summarizes the data,[3] the word *zekhut* bears a variety of meanings, and the pertinence of each possible meaning is to be determined in context:

1. acquittal or a plea in favor of the defendant;
2. doing good or blessing;
3. the protecting influence of good conduct or merit; and
4. advantage, privilege, or benefit.

The first meaning pertains solely in juridical (or metaphorically juridical) contexts; the second represents a very general and imprecise use of the word, for a variety of other words bear the same meaning. Only the third and fourth meanings are relevant, for they are particular to this word, on the one side, and also religious, on the other. That is to say, only through using the word *zekhut* do authors of compositions and authorships of composites express the third sense. Moreover, it will rapidly become clear in context that the fourth sense is not to be distinguished from the third, for reading "protecting influence of good conduct" when the word *zekhut* appears always yields "advantage, privilege, or benefit." It follows that, for the purposes of systemic analysis, those passages in which the word bears the third sense, which yields the fourth, will show how it functions.

My simple definition emphasizes "heritage" because the advantages or privileges conferred by *zekhut* may be inherited and passed on; it stresses "entitlements" because advantages or privileges invariably result from receiving *zekhut* from ancestors or acquiring it on one's own; and I use the word "virtue" to refer to those supererogatory acts that demand a reward because they form matters of choice, the gift of the individual and his or her act of free will, an act that is at the same time (1) uncompelled, for example, by the obligations imposed by the Torah, but also (2) valued by the Torah. As I shall show in chapter 9, the systemic importance of the conception of *zekhut* derives from its capacity to unite the generations in a heritage of entitlements; *zekhut* is fundamentally a historical category and concept in that, like all historical systems of thought, it explains the present in terms of the past and the future in terms of the present.[4]

Because *zekhut* is something one may receive as an inheritance, even out of the distant past, it imposes on the definition of the social entity "Israel" a genealogical meaning. It furthermore imparts a distinctive character to the definitions of way of life. So the task of the political component of a theory of the social order, which is to define the social entity by appeal to empowerment, and of the economic component, which is to identify scarce resources by specification of the rationality of right management, is accomplished in a single word that stands for a conception, a symbol, and a myth. In context, all three components of this religious theory of the social order present specific applications for the general conception of *zekhut*. The first source of *zekhut* derives from the definition of Israel as family; the entitlements of supernatural power deriving from virtue are inherited from Abraham, Isaac, and Jacob. The second source is personal: the power one can gain for one's own heirs and, moreover, by virtuous deeds. *Zekhut* deriving from either source is to be defined in context: what can you do if you have *zekhut* that you cannot do if you do not have *zekhut*, and to whom can you do it? The answers explain the empowerment of *zekhut*.

Now in the nature of things, a theory of legitimate power or violence falls into the category of a politics, and a conception of the scarce resource, defined as supernatural power that is to be rationally managed, falls into the category of an economics. That is why the concept of *zekhut* unifies economics and politics into a political economy: it provides a theory of the whole society in its material and social relationships as expressed both in institutions that are given the permanent right to impose order through real or threatened violence and in the assignment of goods and benefits, as systemically defined, through a shared rationality.

Because I have identified as systemically active not the conception but the word and its usages, I shall focus not on general situations (e.g., the receipt of some sort of benefit by reason of an inheritance) but on specific usages of the word at hand.[5] That focus is required not only by the logic of this study but also by the difficulty of knowing what belongs and what does not belong when *zekhut* bears the confusing translation of "merit" and when "merit" promiscuously refers to pretty much anything acquired *not* by one's own merit or just desserts but rather despite what one has done. Scripture, for example, shows that God loves Israel because he loved the patriarchs (Deut. 4:37); the memory or deeds of the righteous patriarchs and matriarchs appear in a broad range of contexts, for example, "*Remember your servants, Abraham, Isaac, and Jacob*" (Exod. 32:13) for Moses, and "*Remember the good deeds of David, your servant*" (2 Chron. 6:42) for David. At stake throughout is giving people what they do not merit, but in these contexts, "remembering" what X did as an argument in behalf of favor for Y does not invoke the word *zekhut,* nor does the context require use of that word.[6] Accordingly, my problem of definition requires limitation to precise usages of a given word. Were I to work back from situations that seem to exhibit conceptual affinities to the concept represented by the word under consideration (cases, for instance, in which someone appeals to what is owing the fathers in behalf of the children), I would not accomplish the goal at hand, which is to define a word that in this system—specifically, in this system's documents— bears a very particular meaning and, more to the point, carries out a highly critical role.

At M. San. 4:1, 5:4, 5:5, and 6:1 *zekhut* appears in the sense of "acquittal"; at M. Ket. 13:6 the sense is "right," as in "right of ownership"; at M. Git. 8:8 the sense is not "right of ownership" in a narrow sense but "advantage" in a broader one of prerogative: "It is not within the power of the first husband to render void the right of the second." These usages bear no point in common with the sense of the word later on, but the evidence of the Mishnah seems to me to demonstrate that the sense of *zekhut* paramount in the successor documents is not original to them. The following usage at M. Qid. 4:14E-I seems to invite something very like the sense that I have proposed here.

> R. Meir says, "A man should always teach his son a clean and easy trade. And let him pray to him to whom belong riches and possessions. For there is no trade that does not involve poverty or wealth. For poverty does not come from one's trade, nor does wealth come from one's trade. But all is in accord with a man's *zekhut.*"

How best to translate the key word in this passage is not self-evident. The context permits a variety of possibilities. The same usage seems to me to be located at M. Sot. 3:4-5, which clearly indicates a conception of an entitlement deriving from some source other than one's own deed of the moment:

Mishnah Tractate Sotah 3:4-5

4E. There is the possibility that *zekhut* suspends the curse for one year, and there is the possibility that *zekhut* suspends the curse for two years, and there is the possibiity that *zekhut* suspends the curse for three years.

F. On this basis Ben Azzai says, "A man is required to teach Torah to his daughter.

G. "For if she should drink the water, she should know that [if nothing happens to her], *zekhut* is what suspends [the curse from taking effect]."

5A. R. Simeon says, "*Zekhut* does not suspend the effects of the bitter water.

B. "And if you say, '*Zekhut* does suspend the effects of the bitter water,' you will weaken the effect of the water for all the women who have to drink it.

C. "And you give a bad name to all the women who drink it who turned out to be pure.

D. "For peole will say, 'They are unclean, but *zekhut* suspended the effects of the water for them.' "

E. Rabbi says, "*Zekhut* does suspend the effects of the bitter water. But she will not bear children or continue to be pretty. And she will waste away, and in the end she will have the same [unpleasant] death."

Inserting "the heritage of virtue and its consequent entitlements" for *zekhut* at each point yields good sense (thus: "For people will say, 'They are unclean, but *zekhut* suspended the effects of the water for them,' " becomes "For people will say, 'They are unclean, but the heritage of virtue and its consequent entitlements suspended the effects of the water for them' "). That is to say, the woman may escape the penalty to which she is presumably condemnable not because her act or condition (e.g., her innocence) has secured her acquittal or nullified the effects of the ordeal but because she enjoys some advantage extrinsic to her own act or condition. She may be guilty, but she may also possess an inherited benefice, hence, heritage of virtue, and so be entitled to a protection not because of her own action or condition but because of someone else's.

That meaning may be sustained by the passage at hand, even though it is not required by it; still, it seems plausible that *zekhut* in the Mishnah bears not only a juridical but a religious sense. If it does, however, that usage is not systemically critical, or even very important. A search of the pages of the Mishnah for places in which, absent the word *zekhut*, the conception in hand is present yields none—not one. For instance, there simply is no reference to gaining *zekhut* through doing one's duty, for example, in reciting the Shema or studying the Torah, and references to studying the Torah, such as at M. Peah 1:1, do not encompass the conception that in doing so one gains an advantage or entitlement either for one's own descendants or for all Israel. On that basis I am on firm ground in holding the twin positions that (1) the word bore, among its meanings, the one important later on, and also that (2) the word played no systemic role in the philosophical system adumbrated by the Mishnah commensurate with its importance and sense in the religious system of the successor writings.[7]

The evidence of tractate Abot is consistent with that of the Mishnah. The juridical sense of *zekhut* occurs at 1:6, "Judge everybody as though to be acquitted," or more comprehensibly translated, "Give everybody the benefit of the doubt," forming a usage reasonably coherent with those important in Mishnah tractate Sanhedrin. Abot, however, provides clear evidence for the sense of the word that seems to me demanded later on. M. Abot 2:2 has the following:

Tractate Abot 2:2

C. "And all who work with the community—let them work with them for the sake of Heaven.

D. "For the (1) *zekhut* of their fathers strengthens them, and their [fathers'] (2) righteousness stands forever.

E. "And as for you, I credit you with a great reward, as if you had done [all of the work required by the community on your own merit alone]."

Here there is no meaning possible other than that I have given above: "the heritage of virtue and its consequent entitlements." The parallel between *zekhut* of clause (1) and *righteousness* of clause (2) demands that the reference is to an advantage gained by reason of inheritance out of one's father's righteousness. Whatever the conceivable ambiguity of the Mishnah, none is sustained by the context at hand, which is explicit in language and pellucid in message. That the sense is exactly the same as the one I have proposed is shown at the following passages, which seem to me also to exhibit none of the possible ambiguity that characterized the Mishnah's use of *zekhut*.

Tractate Abot 5:18

A. He who causes *zekhut* to the community never causes sin.

B. And he who causes the community to sin—they never give him a sufficient chance to attain penitence.

Here the contrast is between causing *zekhut* and causing sin, so *zekhut* is the opposite of sin. The continuation is equally clear that person who attains *zekhut* endows the community with *zekhut,* and one who sins makes the community sin:

C. Moses attained *zekhut* and bestowed *zekhut* on the community.

D. So the *zekhut* of the community is assigned to his [credit],

E. as it is said, "*He executed the justice of the Lord and his judgments with Israel*" (Deut. 33:21).

F. Jeroboam sinned and caused the community to sin.

G. So the sin of the community is assigned to his [debit],

H. as it is said, "*For the sins of Jeroboam which he committed and wherewith he made Israel to sin*" (1 Kings 15:30).

The appropriateness of interpreting the passage in the way I have proposed is self-evident; all that is required is to substitute for *zekhut* the proposed translation:

C. Moses attained the heritage of virtue and bestowed its consequent entitlements on the community.

D. So the heritage of virtue and its entitlements enjoyed by the community are assigned to his [credit],

The sense then is simple. Moses, through actions of his own (of an unspecified sort), acquired *zekhut,* which is the credit for such actions that accrued to him and bestowed on him certain supernatural entitlements; he passed on as an inheritance that credit, a lien on Heaven for the performance of these same supernatural entitlements: *zekhut,* pure and simple.

To define *zekhut* as the initial system explicated in tractate Abot has used the word requires close attention to the antonymic structure. The juridical opposites are guilty as against innocent; the religious ones, sin as against the opposite of sin. That seems to me to require interpreting *zekhut* as an action, as distinct from a (mere) attitude, that is precisely the opposite of a sinful one; it is, moreover, an action that may be done by an individual or by the community at large, and one that a leader may provoke the community to do (or not do). The contrast of sin to *zekhut* requires further attention. Because any two distinct classes that are to be compared in general must constitute opposites, adequately defining *zekhut* requires showing how *zekhut* is precisely the opposite of sin. For one thing, Scripture explicly states that the burden of sins cannot be passively inherited but, to form a heritage of guilt, must be actively accepted and renewed; the children cannot be made to suffer for the sins of the parents unless they repeat them. Then *zekhut,* being a mirror image, can be passively inherited, not by one's own merit[8] but by one's good fortune alone. But what constitutes these *actions* that form mirror images of sins? Answers to that critical question must emerge from the later systemic documents for they do not occur in those of the initial system.

That simple fact, too, attests to the systemic centrality of *zekhut:* it defines a principal point of exegesis.[9] The critical issue is the question left open by the Mishnah's merely episodic and somewhat opaque reference to the matter and by the incomplete evidence provided by its principal apologetic's representation. Precisely which actions generate *zekhut* and which do not? To find answers to those questions, I have to turn to the successor documents, for not a single passage in the Mishnah or in tractate Abot provides information on what one must do to secure for oneself or one's descendants a lien on Heaven, that is, an entitlement to supernatural favor and even action of a miraculous order.

I turn first to the conception of the *zekhut* that was accumulated by the patriarchs and passed on to Israel, their children. Up to this point, the single distinctive trait of *zekhut* has been its transitive quality: one need not earn or merit the supernatural power and resource represented by the feats possible with *zekhut* but impossible without it. One can inherit that entitlement from others, dead or living. Moses not only attains *zekhut,* he also imparts it to the community of which he is leader, and the same is so for any Israelite. That conception is broadened in the successor documents into the deeply historical notion of *zekhut avot,* empowerment of a supernatural character to which Israel is entitled by reason of what the patriarchs and matriarchs in particular did long ago. That conception forms the foundation for the paramount sense of *zekhut* in the successor system: the Israelite possesses a lien on Heaven by reason of God's love for the patriarchs and matriarchs, his appreciation for certain things they did, and his response to those actions not only in favoring them but also in entitling their descendants to do or benefit from otherwise unattainable miracles. *Zekhut,* as I noted earlier, explains the present—particularly what is odd and unpredictable in the present — by appeal to the past and hence forms a distinctively historical conception.

Within the historically grounded metaphor of Israel as a family expressed by the conception of *zekhut avot,* Israel *was* a family in a concrete and genealogical sense, the children of Abraham, Isaac, and Jacob, or children of Israel. Israel hence fell into the genus *family* as the particular species of family generated by Abraham and Sarah. The distinguishing trait of that species was that it possessed the inheritance, or heritage, of the patriarchs and matriarchs, and that inheritance, consisting of *zekhut,* served the descendants and heirs as protection and support. It follows that the systemic position of the conception of *zekhut* to begin with lies in its power to define the social entity; *zekhut* (in the terms of the initial category formation, the philosophical one) thus forms a fundamentally political conception[10] and only secondarily an economic and philosophical one.

Nonetheless, *zekhut* particularly serves the counterpart category that speaks not of legitimate but of illegitimate violence, not of power but of weakness. In context, time and again, *zekhut* is the power of the weak. People who through their own merit and capacity can accomplish nothing accomplish miracles through what others do for them in leaving a heritage of *zekhut.* And, not to miss the stunning message of the three stories cited above, *zekhut* also is what the weak, excluded, and despised can do that outweighs in power what the great masters of the Torah have accomplished. In the context of a system that represents Torah as supernatural, that claim of priority for *zekhut* represents a considerable transvaluation of power as much as of value. Additionally, *zekhut* also forms the inheritance of the disinherited: what you receive as a heritage when you have nothing in the present and have gotten nothing in the past, a scarce resource that is free and unearned but much valued. So let me dwell on the definitive charcter of the transferability of *zekhut* in its formulation of *zekhut avot,* the *zekhut* handed on by the ancestors, the transitive character of the concept and its standing as a heritage of entitlements.

It is in the successor documents that the concept of *zekhut* is joined with *avot.* The patriarchal or ancestral *zekhut* that has been left as Israel's familial inheritance yields the very specific notion, which defines the systemic politics and especially its theory of the social entity, of Israel not as a (mere) community (e.g., as in tractate Abot's reference to Moses's bestowing *zekhut* on the community) but as a family, with a history that takes the form of a genealogy, precisely as Genesis has represented that history.[11] *Zekhut* is thus joined to the metaphor of the genealogy of patriarchs and matriarchs and serves to form the missing link, explaining how the inheritance and heritage were transmitted from them to their heirs. Consequently, the family called "Israel" could draw on the family estate, consisting of the inherited *zekhut* of matriarchs and patriarchs, in such a way as to benefit today from the heritage of yesterday. This notion involved very concrete problems. If "Israel the family" sinned, it could call on the *zekhut* accumulated by Abraham and Isaac at the binding of Isaac (Gen. 22) to win forgiveness for that sin. True, "fathers will not die on account of the sin of the sons," but the children may benefit from the *zekhut* of the forebears. That concrete expression of the larger metaphor imparted to the metaphor a practical consequence, both moral and theological, that was not at all neglected.

A survey of Genesis Rabbah proves indicative of the character and use of the doctrine of *zekhut* because that systematic reading of the book of Genesis dealt with the founders of the family and made explicit the definition of Israel as family. In this context, *zekhut* draws in its wake the notion of the inheritance of an ongoing (historical) family, that of Abraham and Sarah, which worked itself out in the moments of crisis of that family in its larger affairs. So the Israelites later on enjoy enormous *zekhut* through the deeds of the patriarchs and matriarchs. That conception comes to expression in what follows:

Genesis Rabbah LXXVI:V

2A. "... for with only my staff I crossed this Jordan, and now I have become two companies."

B. R. Judah bar Simon in the name of R. Yohanan: "In the Torah, in the Prophets, and in the Writings we find proof that the Israelites were able to cross the Jordan only on account of the *zekhut* achieved by Jacob:

C. "In the Torah: '... for with only my staff I crossed this Jordan, and now I have become two companies.'

D. "In the prophets: *'Then you shall let your children know, saying, "Israel came over this Jordan on dry land'* " (Josh. 4:22), meaning our father, Israel.

E. "In the Writings: *'What ails you, O you sea, that you flee?*

You Jordan, that you burn backward? At the presence of the God of Jacob' (Ps. 114:5ff.).'"

Here is a perfect illustration of my definition of *zekhut* as an entitlement enjoyed by reason of what an ancestor has done, and that entitlement involves supernatural power. Not only did Jacob leave *zekhut* as an estate to his heirs, the process is reciprocal and ongoing. *Zekhut* deriving from the ancestors helped Jacob himself:

Genesis Rabbah LXXVII:III.3

A. *"When the man saw that he did not prevail against Jacob, [he touched the hollow of his thigh, and Jacob's thigh was put out of joint as he wrestled with him]"* (Gen. 32:25):

B. Said R. Hinena bar Isaac, "[God said to the angel,] 'He is coming against you with five "amulets" hung on his neck, that is, his own *zekhut,* the *zekhut* of his father and of his mother and of his grandfather and of his grandmother.

C. " 'Check yourself out, can you stand up against even his own *zekhut* [let alone the *zekhut* of his parents and grandparents]?'

D. "The matter may be compared to a king who had a savage dog and a tame lion. The king would take his son and sic him against the lion, and if the dog came to have a fight with the son, he would say to the dog, 'The lion cannot have a fight with him, are you going to make out in a fight with him?'

E. "So if the nations come to have a fight with Israel, the Holy One, blessed be He, says to them, 'Your angelic prince could not stand up to Israel, and as to you, how much the more so!' "

The collectivity of *zekhut* as well as its transferability is also illustrated here: what an individual does confers *zekhut* on the social entity. It is, moreover, a matter of the legitimate exercise of supernatural power, and the reciprocity of the process extends in all directions. Accordingly, this is first and foremost a matter of the exercise of legitimate violence, hence a political power. *Zekhut* might project not only backward, deriving from an ancestor and serving a descendant, but forward as well. Thus, Joseph accrued so much *zekhut* that the generations that came before him were credited with his *zekhut*:

Genesis Rabbah LXXXIV:V.2

A. "*These are the generations of the family of Jacob. Joseph [being seventeen years old, was shepherding the flock with his brothers]*" (Gen. 37:2):

B. These generations came along only on account of the *zekhut* of Joseph.

C. Did Jacob go to Laban for any reason other than for Rachel?

D. These generations thus waited until Joseph was born, in line with this verse: "*And when Rachel had borne Joseph, Jacob said to Laban, 'Send me away'* " (Gen. 30:25).

E. Who brought them down to Egypt? It was Joseph.

F. Who supported them in Egypt? It was Joseph.

G. The sea split open only on account of the *zekhut* of Joseph: "*The waters saw you, O God*" (Ps. 77:17). "*You have with your arm redeemed your people, the sons of Jacob and Joseph*" (Ps. 77:16).

H. R. Yudan said, "Also the Jordan was divided only on account of the *zekhut* of Joseph."

The passage at hand asks why only Joseph is mentioned as the family of Jacob. The inner polemic is that the *zekhut* of Jacob and Joseph would more than suffice to overcome Esau. Further, Joseph survived because of the *zekhut* of his ancestors:

Genesis Rabbah LXXXVII:VIII.1

A. "*She caught him by his garment . . . but he left his garment in her hand and fled and got out of the house. [And when she saw that he had left his garment in her hand and had fled out of the house, she called to the men of her household and said to them, 'See he has brought among us a Hebrew to insult us; he came in to me to lie with me, and I cried out with a loud voice, and when he heard that I lifted up my voice and cried, he left his garment with me and fled and got out of the house']*" (Gen. 39:12-15):

B. He escaped through the *zekhut* of the fathers, in line with this verse: "*And he brought him forth outside*" (Gen. 15:5).

C. Simeon of Qitron said, "It was on account of bringing up the bones of Joseph that the sea was split: '*The sea saw it and fled*' (Ps. 114:3), on the *zekhut* of this: '. . . and fled and got out.' "

Zekhut is thus both personal and national. The statement at B refers to Joseph's enjoying the *zekhut* he had inherited; at c, to Israel's enjoying the *zekhut* that it gained through its supererogatory loyalty to that same *zekhut*-rich personality. What shows that the *zekhut* left as a heritage by ancestors is in play? Here is an explicit answer:

Genesis Rabbah LXXIV:XII.1

A. "*If the God of my father, the God of Abraham and the Fear of Isaac, had not been on my side, surely now you would have sent me away empty-handed. God saw my affliction and the labor of my hand and rebuked you last night*" (Gen. 31:41-42):

B. Zebedee b. Levi and R. Joshua b. Levi:

C. Zebedee said, "Every passage in which reference is made to 'if' tells of an appeal to the *zekhut* accrued by the patriarchs."[12]

D. Said to him R. Joshua, "But it is written, '*Except we had lingered*' (Gen. 43:10) [a passage not related to the *zekhut* of the patriarchs]."

E. He said to him, "They themselves would not have come up except for the *zekhut* of the patriarchs, for if it were not for the *zekhut* of the patriarchs, they never would have been able to go up from there in peace."

The issue of the *zekhut* of the patriarchs comes up in the reference to the God of the fathers. The conception of the *zekhut* of the patriarchs is explicit, not general. It specifies what later benefit to the heir, Israel the family, derived from which particular action of a patriarch or matriarch.

Genesis Rabbah XLIII:VIII.2

A. "*And Abram gave him a tenth of everything*" (Gen. 14:20):

B. R. Judah in the name of R. Nehorai: "On the strength of that blessing the three great pegs on which the world depends, Abraham, Isaac, and Jacob, derived sustenance.

C. "Abraham: '*And the Lord blessed Abraham in* all *things*' (Gen. 24:1) on account of the *zekhut* that '*he gave him a tenth of* all *things*' (Gen. 14:20).

D. "Isaac: '*And I have eaten of* all' (Gen. 27:33), on account of the *zekhut* that '*he gave him a tenth of* all *things*' (Gen. 14:20).

E. "Jacob: '*Because God has dealt graciously with me and because I have* all' (Gen. 33:11) on account of the *zekhut* that '*he gave him a tenth of* all *things*' (Gen. 14:20)."

Genesis Rabbah XLIII:VIII.3

A. Whence did Israel gain the *zekhut* of receiving the blessing of the priests?

B. R. Judah said, "It was from Abraham: 'So *shall your seed be*' (Gen. 15:5), while it is written in connection with the priestly blessing: 'So *shall you bless the children of Israel*' (Num. 6:23)."

C. R. Nehemiah said, "It was from Isaac: '*And I and the lad will go so far*' (Gen. 22:5), therefore said the Holy One, blessed be He, 'So *shall you bless the children of Israel*' (Num. 6:23)."

D. And rabbis say, "It was from Jacob: 'So *shall you say to the house of Jacob*' (Exod. 19:3) (in line with the statement, 'So *shall you bless the children of Israel*' [Num. 6:23])."

The first of the two preceding passages links the blessing at hand with the history of Israel. The reference is to the word *all,* which joins the tithe of Abram to the blessing of his descendants. Because the blessing of the priest is at issue, this passage treats the origins of the blessing. The picture is clear. "Israel" constitutes a family as a genealogical and juridical fact; it inherits the estate of the ancestors, and it hands on that estate. It lives by the example of the matriarchs and patriarchs, and its history exemplifies events in their lives. *Zekhut* forms the entitlement that one generation may transmit to the next, in a way in which the heritage of sin is not to be transmitted except by reason of the deeds of the successor generation. The good that one does lives onward, the evil is interred with the bones.

To conclude this brief survey of *zekhut* as the medium of historical existence, that is, the *zekhut* deriving from the patriarchs, or *zekhot avot,* let me present a statement of the legitimate power—sufficient to achieve salvation, which in this context always bears a political dimension—imparted by the *zekhut* of the ancestors. That *zekhut* will enable them to accomplish the political goals of Israel: attaining self-rule and avoiding government by gentiles. This statement appeals to the binding of Isaac as the source of the *zekhut,* deriving from the patriarchs and matriarchs, which will in the end lead to the salvation of Israel. What is important here is that the inherited *zekhut* joins together with the *zekhut* of one's own deeds; one inherits the *zekhut* of the past, and, moreover, if one does what the progenitors did, one not only receives an entitlement out of the past, one secures an entitlement on one's own account. So the difference between *zekhut* and sin lies in the sole issue of transmissibility:

Genesis Rabbah LVI:II.5

A. Said R. Isaac, "And all was on account of the *zekhut* attained by the act of prostration.

B. "Abraham returned in peace from Mount Moriah only on account of the *zekhut* owing to the act of prostration: '...*and we will worship* [through an act of prostration] *and come* [then, on that account] *again to you*' (Gen. 22:5).

C. "The Israelites were redeemed only on account of the *zekhut* owing to the act of prostration: '*And the people believe ... then they bowed their heads and prostrated themselves*' (Exod. 4:31).

D. "The Torah was given only on account of the *zekhut* owing to the act of prostration: '*And worship* [prostrate themselves] *you afar off*' (Exod. 24:1).

E. "Hannah was remembered only on account of the *zekhut* owing to the act of prostration: '*And they worshipped before the Lord*' (1 Sam. 1:19).

F. "The exiles will be brought back only on account of the *zekhut* owing to the act of prostration: '*And it shall come to pass in that day that a great horn shall be blown and they shall come that were lost ... and that were dispersed ... and they shall worship the Lord in the holy mountain at Jerusalem*' (Isa. 27:14).

G. "The Temple was built only on account of the *zekhut* owing to the act of prostration: '*Exalt you the Lord our God and worship at his holy hill*' (Ps. 99:9).

H. "The dead will live only on account of the *zekhut* owing to the act of prostration: '*Come let us worship and bend the knee, let us kneel before the Lord our maker*' (Ps. 95:6)."

The entire history of Israel flows from its acts of worship ("prostration") beginning with that performed by Abraham at the binding of Isaac. Every sort of advantage Israel has ever gained came about through that act of worship done by Abraham and imitated thereafter. Israel constitutes a family and inherits the *zekhut* laid up as a treasure for the descendants by the ancestors. It draws on that *zekhut*, but, by doing the deeds they did, it also enhances its heritage of *zekhut* and leaves to the descendants greater entitlement than they would enjoy by reason of their own actions. Nonetheless, their own actions—here, prostration in worship—generate zekhut as well.

Accordingly, as I claimed at the outset, zekhut may be personal or inherited. The zekhut deriving from the prior generations is collective and affects all Israel, but one's own deeds can generate zekhut for oneself, with the simple result that zekhut is as much personal as it is collective. Specifically, Jacob reflects on the power that Esau's own zekhut had gained for Esau. He had gained that zekhut by living in the Land of Israel and also by paying honor and respect to Isaac. Jacob then feared that, because of the zekhut gained by Esau, he, Jacob, would not be able to overcome him. So zekhut worked on its own; it was a credit gained by proper action, which went to the credit of the person who had done that action. What made the action worthy of evoking Heaven's response with an act of supernatural favor is that it was an action not required but to be rewarded if done, an act of will that could not be coerced but must be honored. In Esau's case, it was the simple fact that he had remained in the Holy Land:

Genesis Rabbah LXXVI:II

2A. *"Then Jacob was greatly afraid and distressed"* (Gen. 32:7): [This is Jacob's soliloquy:] "Because of all those years that Esau was living in the Land of Israel, perhaps he may come against me with the power of the zekhut he has now attained by dwelling in the Land of Israel.

B. "Because of all those years of paying honor to his father, perhaps he may come against me with the power of the zekhut he attained by honoring his father.

C. "So he said: *'Let the days of mourning for my father be at hand, then I will slay my brother Jacob'* (Gen. 27:41).

D. "Now the old man is dead."

The important point, then, is that zekhut is not only inherited as part of a collective estate left by the patriarchs but also accomplished by an individual in his or her own behalf. By extension, the successor system opens a place for recognition of the individual, both male and female, as a matter of fact, within the system of zekhut. As I shall now show, what a man or a woman does may win for that person an entitlement on Heaven for supernatural favor of some sort. Thus, the system has space for a private person, and the individual is linked to the social order through the shared possibilities of generating or inheriting an entitlement on Heaven.[13]

The sorts of deeds that generate *zekhut* are those deeds that produce a common result of gaining for their doer, as much as for his or her heirs, an entitlement for heavenly favor and support when needed. That fact concerning gaining and benefiting from *zekhut* leads to the systemic message for the living generation, its account of what now is to be done, and that message proves acutely contemporary, for its stress is on the power of a single action to create *zekhut* sufficient to outweigh a life of sin. The contrast between sin and *zekhut*, then, gains greater depth still. One sin of sufficient weight condemns, one act of *zekhut* of sufficient weight saves; the entire issue of entitlements out of the past gives way, then, in the face of what is actually at stake.

Recall that Torah study is only one means for an individual to gain access to that heritage, to get *zekhut*. There are other, equally suitable means, and the merit gained by Torah study is no different from the merit gained by acts of a supererogatory character. If one gets *zekhut* for studying the Torah, then presumably there is no holy deed that does not generate its share, but when it comes to specifying the things one does to get *zekhut*, the successor documents speak of what the Torah does not require but yet recommends: not what Jews are commanded to do in detail, but what the right attitude, formed within the Torah, leads them to do on their own volition:

Y. Taanit 3:11.IV

C. There was a house that was about to collapse over there [in Babylonia], and Rab set one of his disciples in the house, until they had cleared out everything from the house. When the disciple left the house, the house collapsed.

D. And there are those who say that it was R. Adda bar Ahwah.

E. Sages sent and said to him, "What sort of good deeds are to your credit [that you have that much merit]?"

F. He said to them, "In my whole life no man ever got to the synagogue in the morning before I did. I never left anybody there when I went out. I never walked four cubits without speaking words of Torah. Nor did I ever mention teachings of Torah in an inappropriate setting. I never laid out a bed and slept for a regular period of time. I never took great strides among the associates. I never called my fellow by a nickname. I never rejoiced in the embarrassment of my fellow. I never cursed my fellow when I was lying by myself in bed. In the marketplace I never walked over to someone who owed me money.

G. "In my entire life I never lost my temper in my household."

H. This was meant to carry out that which is stated as follows: "*I will give heed to the way that is blameless. Oh, when wilt thou come to me? I will walk with integrity of heart within my house*" (Ps. 101:2).

What I find striking in this story is that mastery of the Torah is only one means of attaining the merit that enabled the sage to keep the house from collapsing. What the sage did to gain such remarkable merit was not to master so many tractates of the Mishnah, nor does the storyteller refer to carrying out the commandments of the Torah as specified; rather, he performed acts that expressed courtesy, consideration, and restraint. These acts, which no specification can encompass in detail, produced the right attitude, one of gentility, that led to gaining merit. Acts rewarded with an entitlement to supernatural power are those of self-abnegation or the avoidance of power over others—not taking great strides among the associates, not using a nickname, not rejoicing in the embarrassment of one's fellow, not singling out one's debtor—and the submission to the will and the requirement of self-esteem of others.

Politics is replicated here in a moral setting: the form of power that the system promises derives from the rejection of power that the world recognizes—legitimate violence replaced by a legitimation of the absence of the power to commit violence or of the failure to commit violence. Not exercising power over others—that is, the counterpart politics—moreover produced that scarcest of all resources, supernatural favor, by which the holy man could hold up a tottering building. Here then are politics and economics united in the counterpart category formed of *zekhut*: the absence of power yielding supernatural power, the valuation of the intangible, Torah, yielding supernatural power. It was, then, that entitlement to supernatural favor that formed the systemic center.

What must one do to secure an inheritance of *zekhut* for one's heirs? Here is a concrete example of how acts of worth, or *zekhut*, accrue to the benefit of the heirs of those who do them. What makes it especially indicative is that here gentiles have the power to acquire *zekhut* for their descendants, which is coherent with the system's larger interest in not only Israel (as against the faceless, undifferentiated outsider) but the gentiles as well. Here the successor system shows that it may hold within the orbit of its generative conception even the history of the gentiles:

Genesis Rabbah C:VI.1

A. "*When they came to the threshing floor of Atad, which is beyond the Jordan, they lamented there with a very great and sorrowful lamentation, and he made a mourning for his father seven days*" (Gen. 50:10):

B. Said R. Samuel bar Nahman, "We have reviewed the entire Scripture and found no other place called Atad. And can there be a threshing floor for thorns [the Hebrew word for thorn being *atad*]?

C. "But this refers to the Canaanites. It teaches that they were worthy of being threshed like thorns. And on account of what *zekhut* were they saved? It was on account of the acts of kindness that they performed for our father, Jacob [on the occasion of the mourning for his death]."

D. And what were the acts of kindness that they performed for our father, Jacob?

E. R. Eleazar said, "[When the bier was brought up there,] they unloosened the girdle of their loins."

F. R. Simeon b. Laqish said, "They untied the shoulder knots."

G. R. Judah b. R. Shalom said, "They pointed with their fingers and said, '*This is a grievous mourning to the Egyptians*' (Gen. 50:11)."

H. Rabbis said, "They stood upright."

I. Now is it not an argument *a fortiori*: now if these, who did not do a thing with their hands or feet, but only because they pointed their fingers, were saved from punishment, Israel, which performs an act of kindness [for the dead] whether they are adults or children, whether with their hands or with their feet, how much the more so [will they enjoy the *zekhut* of being saved from punishment]!

J. Said R. Abbahu, "Those seventy days that lapsed between the first letter and the second match the seventy days that the Egyptians paid respect to Jacob. [Seventy days elapsed from Haman's letter of destruction until Mordecai's letter announcing the repeal of the decree (cf. Esther 3:12, 8:9).] The latter letter, which permitted the Jews to take vengeance on their would-be destroyers, should have come earlier, but it was delayed seventy days as a reward for the honor shown by the Egyptians to Jacob."[14]

According to Abbahu, the Egyptians gained *zekhut* by honoring Jacob in his death. This same point then registers for the Canaanites. The connection is somewhat farfetched, that is, through the reference to the threshing floor, but the point is a strong one. And the explanation of history extends not only to Israel's history but also to the Canaanites'.

If the Egyptians and the Canaanites, how much the more so Israelites! What is it that Israelites as a nation do to gain a lien on Heaven for themselves or entitlements of supernatural favor for their descendants? Here is one representative answer to that question:

Genesis Rabbah LXXIV:XII.1

A. "*If the God of my father, the God of Abraham and the Fear of Isaac, had not been on my side, surely now you would have sent me away empty-handed. God saw my affliction and the labor of my hand and rebuked you last night*" (Gen. 41:41-42):

B. Zebedee b. Levi and R. Joshua b. Levi:

C. Zebedee said, "Every passage in which reference is made to 'if' tells of an appeal to the *zekhut* accrued by the patriarchs."[15]

D. Said to him R. Joshua, "But it is written, '*Except we had lingered*' (Gen. 43:10) [a passage not related to the *zekhut* of the patriarchs]."

E. He said to him, "They themselves would not have come up except for the *zekhut* of the patriarchs, for it if it were not for the *zekhut* of the patriarchs, they never would have been able to go up from there in peace."

F. Said R. Tanhuma, "There are those who produce the matter in a different version." [It is as follows:]

G. R. Joshua and Zebedee b. Levi:

H. R. Joshua said, "Every passage in which reference is made to 'if' tells of an appeal to the *zekhut* accrued by the patriarchs except for the present case."

I. He said to him, "This case, too, falls under the category of an appeal to the *zekhut* of the patriarchs."

So much for *zekhut* that is inherited from the patriarchs, a now-familiar notion. But what about the deeds of Israel in the here and now?

> J. R. Yohanan said, "It was on account of the *zekhut* achieved through sanctification of the divine name."
>
> K. R. Levi said, "It was on account of the *zekhut* achieved through faith and the *zekhut* achieved through Torah.

Faith despite the here and now, study of the Torah—these are what Israel does in the here and now with the result that its people gain an entitlement for themselves or their heirs.

> L. "The *zekhut* achieved through faith: '*If I had not believed . . .*' (Ps. 27.13).
>
> M. "The *zekhut* achieved through Torah: '*Unless your Torah had been my delight*' (Ps. 119:92)."
>
> 2A. "*God saw my affliction and the labor of my hand and rebuked you last night*" (Gen. 31:41-42):
>
> B. Said R. Jeremiah b. Eleazar, "More beloved is hard labor than the *zekhut* achieved by the patriarchs, for the *zekhut* achieved by the patriarchs served to afford protection for property only, whereas the *zekhut* achieved by hard labor served to afford protection for lives.
>
> C. "The *zekhut* achieved by the patriarchs served to afford protection for propertly only: '*If the God of my father, the God of Abraham and the Fear of Isaac, had not been on my side, surely now you would have sent me away empty-handed.*'
>
> D. "The *zekhut* achieved by hard labor served to afford protection for lives: '*God saw my affliction and the labor of my hand and rebuked you last night.*' "

Here is as good an account as any of the theology of *zekhut*. The issue of the *zekhut* of the patriarchs comes up in the reference to the God of the fathers. Its conception is explicit, not general, specifying what later benefit to the heir, Israel the family, derived from which particular action of a patriarch or matriarch. Acts of faith and Torah study form only one medium, however; hard labor, that is, devotion to one's calling, defines the source of *zekhut* accessible to those many Israelites unlikely to distinguish themselves either by Torah study and acts of faith, encompassing the sanctification of God's name, or by acts of amazing gentility and restraint.

The system here speaks to everybody — Jew and gentile, past, present, and future; *zekhut* therefore defines the structure of the cosmic social order and explains how it is supposed to function. It is the encompassing quality of *zekhut,* its pertinence to past and future, high and low, rich and poor, gifted and ordinary, that marks as the systemic statement the message of *zekhut,* now fully revealed as the reciprocal response between Heaven and Israel to acts of devotion beyond the requirements of the Torah but defined all the same by the Torah. As Scripture had said, God responds to the faith of the ancient generations by super-natural acts to which, on their own account, the moderns are not entitled, hence a heritage of entitlement. But those acts, now fully defined, can and ought to be done by the living generation as well. As a matter of fact, no one at the time of the system builders was exempt from the systemic message and its demands: even steadfastness in accomplishing the humble work of the everyday and the here and now.

The systemic statement made by the usages of *zekhut* speaks of relationship and function, the interplay of humanity and God. One's store of *zekhut* derives from a relationship, that is, from one's forebears. That is one dimension of the relationships in which one stands. *Zekhut* also forms a measure of one's own relationship with Heaven, as attested by the power of one person but not another to pray and so bring rain. What sort of relationship does *zekhut,* as the opposite of sin, then posit? It is not one of coercion, for Heaven cannot force individuals to do those types of deeds that yield *zekhut;* story after story suggests that the definition of a deed that generates *zekhut* is doing what one ought to do but does not have to do. But then, no one can coerce Heaven either, for example, by carrying out the commandments. These are obligatory, but do not obligate Heaven.

Whence then the lien on Heaven?[16] It is through deeds of a super-erogatory character to which Heaven responds by deeds of a super-erogatory character: God grants supernatural favor only to this one, who through deeds of ingratiation to the other, self-abnegation, or restraint exhibits the attitude that precipitates a counterpart attitude in Heaven, hence generating *zekhut.* The simple fact that rabbis cannot pray and bring rain whereas a simple ass driver can tells the whole story. The relationship measured by *zekhut* — Heaven's response by an act of uncoerced favor to a person's uncoerced gift, for example, acts of gentility, restraint, or self-abnegation — contains an element of un-predictability for which appeal to the *zekhut* inherited from ancestors accounts. So though individuals cannot coerce Heaven, they can through *zekhut* gain acts of favor from Heaven, namely, by doing what Heaven cannot require of them. Heaven then responds to their attitude in carrying out their duties—and more than their duties. An act of pure disinterest (e.g., giving an afflicted woman one's means of livelihood) is the one that gains the actor Heaven's deepest interest.

Zekhut thus forms the political economy within the religious system of the social order put forward by the Talmud of the Land of Israel, Genesis Rabbah, Leviticus Rabbah, and related writings. Herein is the power that brought about the transvaluation of value, the reversal of the meaning of power and its legitimacy. *Zekhut* expresses and accounts for the economic valuation of the scarce resource of what we might call moral authority. It stands for the political valorization of weakness, endowing the weak with a power that is not only their own but their ancestors'. It enables the weak to accomplish goals not through their own power but through their very incapacity to accomplish acts of violence—a transvaluation as radical as that effected in economics. And *zekhut* holds together both the economics and the politics of this Judaism, for it makes the same statement twice.

Zekhut is the power of the powerless, the riches of the disinherited, the valuation and valorization of the will of those who have no right to will. In the context of Christian Palestine, Jews found themselves on the defensive. Their ancestry called into question, their supernatural standing thrown into doubt, their future denied, they called themselves "Israel," and the land, "the Land of Israel," but what power of legitimate violence did they possess to assert their claim to form "Israel"? With the Holy Land passing into the hands of others, what scarce resource did they own and manage that substituted for the measure of value that no longer was subject to their rationality? Asserting a politics in which all violence was illegitimate, an economics in which nothing tangible had value, not even real property in the Holy Land,[17] the system through its counterpart categories made a single, simple, and sufficient statement.

Those whom Judaism knows as "our sages of blessed memory" were not the only system builders, however, and theirs was not the only question about the social order framed in historical and theological terms rather than in analytic and philosophical ones. Their contemporary, the bishop of Hippo whom Christianity knows as Saint Augustine, set forth an account of the social order framed in the same terms and addressed to the same urgent and critical question. It is now in the context of comparison to this account of Augustine's that I interpret the system I have described and analyzed: the Judaism transformed from a philosophy to a religion.

Notes

1. The commonly used single word *merit* does not apply, for it bears the sense of reward for carrying out an obligation, e.g., by doing such and such, he merited so and so. *Zekhut,* by contrast, commonly refers to acts of supererogatory free will, and therefore, though such acts are meritorious in the sense of being virtuous (by definition), they are not acts that one owes but that one gives. And the rewards that accumulate in response to such actions are always miraculous, supernatural, or signs of divine grace, e.g., an unusually long life or the power to prevent a delapidated building from collapsing. I return to this matter below, in note 4, when I take up the amplification of the meaning of *zekhut* in response to concrete usages of the word in the earliest document in which it plays a significant role, tractate Abot, where it appears in a context sufficiently broad to allow for philological exegesis to take place.

2. In my *Judaism: The Evidence of the Mishnah,* pp. 230-86, I ask and answer, in terms of the power of intentionality as the medium of classification, what holds the system together. In the counterpart study of the philosophical system of Judaism attested by the Mishnah (*Judaism as Philosophy: The Method and Message of the Mishnah* [Columbia: University of South Carolina Press, in press]) I have identified the integrating and generative problematic, that of hierarchical classification. These two answers seem to me cogent with one another, even though the one appeals to psychological considerations and the other to philosophical ones.

3. Marcus Jastrow, *A Dictionary of the Targumim, the Talmud Babli and Yerushalmi, and the Midrashic Literature* (New York: Pardes, 1950), 398.

4. That is not the whole story, and one of the subtleties of *zekhut* emerges when we realize that it is a basically antihistorical reading of history, as chapter 9 will show.

5. In this context, the concordance is the key. In others, it is not.

6. God's "remembering" is the principal point in the scriptural situations adduced as evidence for the ancient origins of the concept of *zekhut.* The other part of the same concept, that there are deeds I may do that gain *zekhut* for myself, is excluded, and hence *zekhut* as it is revealed in the systemic sources is not represented in the scriptural ones.

7. A rapid review of the Tosefta's usages of the word *zekhut* suffices, for there are no surprises. Juridical usages are at these passages: T. Git. 1:5 (*zekhut* in the sense of an advantage or a benefit); Sanhedrin 1:8, 3:3, 9:1, 2, 3, 4, 10:11; T. Qid. 1:13. An indeterminate sense of *zekhut* in the sense of "ad-

vantage" or "entitlement," without a clear definition of what one must do or why one gains a benefit, is at T. Pe. 1:2 and T. Yoma 5:12, which is identical to T. Ta. 4:9 (*zekhut* in contrast to disadvantage or liability, conceivably a juridical usage). The sense, "by reason of the claim . . ." or "the entitlement of . . ." seems to me justified in context at T. M.S. 5:27, 29, T. Sot. 11:10, and T. B.B.7:9. Overall, I do not find here anything as decisive as what we see in the tractate Abot, though the case may be made that some of the Tosefta's passages use the word in the same sense as is revealed in that tractate. In the balance, nonetheless, I judge that a full-scale review of Tosefta's usages would not greatly change the results just now given for the Mishnah.

8. Indeed, the conception of merit is so alien to the concept of *zekhut*, which one enjoys whether or not one personally has done something to merit it, that I am puzzled why "merit" ever seemed to anyone to serve as a translation of the word. If I can inherit the entitlements accrued by my ancestors, then these entitlements not only cannot be classed as merit(ed by me), they must be classed as a heritage bestowed by others and not merited by me at all. And, along these same lines, the *zekhut* that I gain for myself may entitle me to certain benefits, but it may also accrue to the advantage of the community in which I live (as is made explicit by Abot for Moses' *zekhut*) and also of my descendants. The transitive character of *zekhut*, the power we have of receiving it from others and handing it on to others, serves as the distinctive trait of this particular entitlement, and it must follow from that definitive characteristic that *zekhut* is the opposite of merit; its character is obscured by the confusion created through that long-standing, conventional, but wrong translation of the word.

9. Here again, the exegesis of exegesis defines the history of religion.

10. That political definition of the systemic role and function of *zekhut* is strengthened by the polemical power of the concept vis-à-vis the Christian critique of Israel after the flesh. The doctrine of the *zekhut* of the ancestors served as a component of the powerful polemic concerning Israel. Specifically, that concrete, historical Israel, meaning for Christian theologians "Israel after the flesh," in the literature before us manifestly and explicitly claimed fleshly origin in Abraham and Sarah. The extended family indeed constituted precisely what the Christian theologians said: an Israel after the flesh, a family linked by genealogy. The heritage then became an inheritance, and what was inherited from the ancestors was a heavenly store, a treasure of *zekhut* that protected the descendants when their own *zekhut* proved insufficient. The conflict is a political one, involving the legitimacy of the power of the now-Christian empire, denied by this "Israel," affirmed by the other one.

11. And it is by no means an accident, therefore, that Genesis was one of the two pentateuchal books selected by the system builders for their Midrash exegesis. The systemic centrality of *zekhut* accounts for their selection. In *Judaism and Scripture*, pp. 94-125, I have accounted for the selection of the book of Leviticus, an explanation that accords in a striking way with the one pertaining to Genesis. That means that any system analysis must explain why

one scriptural book, and not some other, has been chosen for the Midrash compilation(s) that that system sets forth alongside its Mishnah amplification.

12. H. Freedman, *Genesis Rabbah* (London: Soncino, 1948), 684, n. 2. It introduces a plea for or affirmation of protection received for the sake of the patriarchs.

13. The philosophical system, by contrast, had regarded as important principally the issue of classifying persons, e.g., by castes or by other indicators; the Mishnah's paramount system of hierarchical classification had treated the individual in the way it treated all other matters, and so, we now see, does the system of *zekhut:* now to be broadened into the defintion, accomplishing a lien upon Heaven.

14. Freedman, *Genesis Rabbah*, 992, n. 6.

15. Ibid., 684, n. 2. It introduces a plea for or affirmation of protection received for the sake of the patriarchs.

16. The answer to that question forms the bridge to the interpretation, in context, of the system as a whole—the determination of the self-evidently valid answer that the system posits—and therefore the identification of the urgent question that precipitated the formation of the system as a whole. Chapter 9 leads to my proposal for the interpretation of the system as a whole, both on its own and in relationship with the antecedent one.

17. A test of this interpretation is whether in the provenance of Babylonia stories are told about the equivalence of owning land and studying the Torah. That is to say, if studying the Torah is represented as outweighing owning real estate in Babylonia as much as in the Land of Israel, then something is awry with my results in chapter 7 and in this chapter. But if a survey, e.g., of the Talmud of Babylonia, shows that in the context of Babylonia and not the Land of Israel stories of the superiority of Torah study over land ownership do not occur, then that would form a fair confirmation of my point here. This test of falsification will be carried on in the context of the next phase of my ouevre, which will bring me deep into the Babylonian part of the canon of the dual Torah.

9

Enchanted Judaism and The City of God

M ake his wishes yours, so that he will make your wishes his.... Anyone from whom people take pleasure, God takes pleasure" (Abot 2:4). These two statements hold together the two principal elements in the conception of the relationship to God that *zekhut* conveys in a single word. Give up, please others, do not impose your will but give way to the will of the other, and Heaven will respond by giving a lien that is not coerced but evoked. The rationality of discipline within yields the power to form rational relationships with Heaven; that is how the system expands the boundaries of the social order to encompass not only the natural but also the supernatural world.[1]

In the successor system, it is the rationality of that relationship to God that governs the social order, defining the three components thereof — ethics, ethnos, and ethos — for that relationship encompasses the model of not merely ethics but economics, not merely private morality in society but the public policy, the politics that delineates the ethnic community, and not merely the right attitude of the virtuous individual but the social philosophy of an entire nation. The nation in question is the this-worldly social order that joins with Heaven, the society that is a unique and holy family, transformed by *zekhut* inherited and *zekhut* accomplished so as to transcend the world order. That ordering of humanity in society, empowered and enriched in an en-chanted political economy, links the private person to the public polity through the union of a common attitude of renunciation that tells Israelites how to behave at home and in the streets and that instructs Israel how to conduct its affairs among the nations and throughout history.

Treating every deed, every gesture, as capable of bringing about enchantment, the successor system imparted remarkable power to the givens of everyday life, at least in their potential. The conviction that, by dint of special effort, an individual may acquire an entitlement of supernatural power turns commonplace circumstances into an arena encompassing Heaven and earth. God responds to the individual's (and Israel's) virtue, filling the space—so to speak—that the individual leaves about himself and his family by forbearing, withdrawing, and giving up what is his and theirs: their space, his self. God responds to such behavior, personal sacrifice evoking memories of Abraham's readiness to sacrifice Isaac;[2] one individual's devotion to another calls up from Heaven what demanding cannot coerce. What imparts critical mass to the conception of *zekhut,* the gaining of supernatural entitlements through supererogatory surrender, is the recasting, in the mold and model of that virtue of surrender, of the political economy of Israel in the Land of Israel. That accounts for the definition of legitimate power in politics as only weakness and of economics as the rational increase of resources that are scarce but need not be, valued things that are capable of infinite increase.

This recasting not only accounts for the inversion of the received categories and their re-formation into mirror images of what the philosophers had made of them; in my view it also explains why a quite fresh, deeply religious system replaced a compelling and well-composed philosophical one. The Mishnah's God can scarcely compete with the God of the Yerushalmi and the Midrash compilations.[3] The God of the philosophers, the apex of the hierarchy of all being, as the framers of the Mishnah positioned God, made the rules and is shown by them to form the foundation of order. All things reach up to one thing; one thing contains within itself many things: these twin propositions of monotheism, which the philosophical system demonstrates in theory and proposes to realize in the facts of the social order, define a God who in an orderly way governs all the palpable relationships of nature as of supernature but who finds a place and comes to puissant expression in not a single one of them. The God of the philosophers assures, sustains, supports, nourishes, guarantees, and governs, but always according to the rule. That is, after all, what natural philosophy proposes to uncover and discern, and what more elevated task can God perform than the nomothetic one accomplished in the daily creation of the world?

God in the successor system gains what the philosophical God lacks, however, which is personality, active presence, pathos, and empathy. The God of the religious system breaks the rules, according an entitlement to this one, who has done some one remarkable deed, but not to that one, who has done nothing wrong and everything right. So a life in accord with the rules—even a life spent in the study of the Torah—in Heaven's view is outweighed by a single moment, a gesture that violates the norm, extending the outer limits of the rule, for instance, of virtue. And who but a God who, like us, feels as well as thinks and responds to impulse and sentiment can be portrayed in such a way as this?

> "So I sold my ass and I gave her the proceeds, and I said to her, 'Here is your money, free your husband, but do not sin [by becoming a prostitute to raise the necessary funds].' "
> They said to him, "You are worthy of praying and having your prayers answered."[4]

No rule exhaustively describes a world such as this. If the God of the philosophers' Judaism makes the rules, the God of the religious Judaism breaks them. This systemic difference is readily extended outward from the personality of God: the philosophers' God thinks, the God of the religious responds, and we are in God's image, after God's likeness, because we not only penetrate the principles of creation through right thinking but also replicate the heart of the Creator through right attitude. Humanity on earth (and the Israelite family in particular) incarnates God on high, and in consequence, earth and Heaven join.

Perhaps, as I shall argue in a moment, the first system contained within itself the flaw that, like a grain of sand in an oyster, so irritated the innards as to form a pearl. And perhaps even the philosophers, with their exquisitely ordered and balanced social world, could have made a place for God to act; but knowing how they thought, they, like later philosophers, probably would have insisted that miracles also follow rules and demonstrate the presence of rules. In the religious Judaism, however, the world is not what it seems. At stake in what is remarkable is what falls beyond all power of rules either to describe or to prescribe.

What is asked of Israel and of the Israelite individual is godly restraint, supernatural generosity of soul that is "in our image, after our likeness": that is what sets aside all rules. That appeal to transcend the norm defined not personal virtue, however, but the sainthood of all Israel, living together in the here and now, so that within what the Greco-Roman world would have called the *polis* of Israel's society, its political and social order, the bounds of earth extend to Heaven. In terms of another great system composed in the same time and in response to a world-historical catastrophe of the same sort, Israel on earth dwells in the city of God. It follows that God dwells with Israel and in Israel: "today, if you will it."[5]

That insistence on the systemic centrality of the conception of *zekhut,* with all its promise for the reshaping of value, draws attention once more to the power of a single, essentially theological conception to impart shape and structure to the social order. The Judaism of the successor documents, while taking full account of circumstance and historical context, portrayed a social order in which individuals and nation alike controlled their own destinies. The circumstance of genealogy dictated whether the moral entity, be it individual or nation, would enjoy access to entitlements of supernatural favor without regard to merit, but whether favored by a rich heritage of supernatural empowerment, as was the nation, or deprived by reason of one's immediate ancestors of any lien on Heaven, in the end both the nation and the individual had in hand the power to shape the future. How was this to be done? It was not alone by obedience to rules about keeping the Torah, studying the Torah, dressing, eating, making a living, marrying, procreating, raising a family, and burying and being buried.

Life in conformity with the rule, obligatory but merely conventional, did not evoke the special interest of Heaven. Why should it? The rules describe the ordinary, but (in language used only in a later document) "God wants the heart," and that is not an ordinary thing. Nor was the power to bring rain or hold up a tottering house gained through a life of merely ordinary sanctity. Special favor responded to extraordinary actions, in the analogy of special disfavor, that is, misfortune deemed to punish sin. Just as culpable sin, as distinct from mere error, requires an act of will (specifically, arrogance), so an act of extraordinary character requires an act of will. As the mirror image of sin, however, such an act would reveal in a concrete way an attitude of restraint, forbearance, gentility, and self-abnegation. A sinful act, provoking Heaven, was one done deliberately to defy Heaven. An act that would evoke Heaven's favor, imposing on Heaven a lien that Heaven freely gave, was one that, equally deliberately and concretely, displayed humility.

The systemic focus on the power of a single act of remarkable generosity, the surrender to the other of what is most precious to the self, whether an opinion, a possession, or a feeling, in no way would have surprised the framers of the philosophical Judaism. They had laid heavy emphasis on the power of human intentionality to settle questions about the status of interstitial persons, objects, or actions within the larger system of hierarchical classification. So in the philosophical Judaism, attitude and intentionality classified what was of doubtful status, forming the active and motivating component of the structure and transforming the structure, a tableau of fixed and motionless figures, into a system of action and reaction. Thus, the successor system's appeal to the critical power of attitude and intentionality is hardly surprising, for what that system contains is a fundamental point of connection. What was specific before, intentionality, is now broadened and made general through extension to all aspects of one's attitude.

The powerful forces coalescing in intentionality gained very precise definition, and in their transformation from merely concrete cases of the taxonomic power of intentionality that worked one way here and another way there into very broad-ranging but quite specific and prescribed attitudes, the successor system took its leave from the initial one without a real farewell. The point of departure is marked by the religious Judaism's intense interest not in the fixed given of normative intentionality[6] but rather in changing people, both individually and nationally, from what they were to something else, and if the change is in a single direction, it is nonetheless also always personal and individual.

To sum up briefly the conclusions of chapters 7 and 8, the change is signaled by the conception that study of the Torah not only illuminated and educated but so transformed the disciple that he gained in supernatural standing and authority. This gnostic conception of knowledge, however, proved only a component of a larger conception of national transformation and personal regeneration, for Torah study produced *zekhut,* and all things depend on *zekhut,* whether possessed by a person or by the nation as a whole. Mastery of what I classify as "the system's worldview" changed a person by generating *zekhut,* that is, by so affecting the person as to inculcate attitudes that would produce the remarkable actions (often acts of omission, restraint, and forbearance) that generate *zekhut*. The change was the end; Torah study, the medium.

Nonetheless, the system's worldview was not the sole, or even the principal, component that showed how the received system was transformed by the new one. The conception of *zekhut* came to the fore to integrate the system's theory of the way of life of the social order, its economics, with its account of the social entity of the social order, its politics. The remarkable actions—perhaps those of omission more than those of commission—that produced *zekhut* yielded an increase in the scarcest of all resources, supernatural favor, and at the same time endowed a person rich in entitlements to heavenly intervention with a power to evoke that vastly outweighed the this-worldly power to coerce in the pursuit of one's purpose.

This rapid account of the systemic structure and system, its inversion of the received categories and its formation of its own anticategories, draws attention to the specificity of the definition of right attitude and puissant intentionality and the generality of those same matters when represented in the philosophical system of the Mishnah. Nevertheless, the quite concrete definition of the attitudes, correct will, and proper intentionality that lead to acts that generate *zekhut* would not have surprised the framers of documents prior to those that express the transformed Judaism, and that fact indicates yet another fundamental continuity between the two systems.

As a matter of fact, the doctrine defining the appropriate attitude persisted pretty much unchanged from the beginning.[7] The repertoire of approved and disapproved attitude and intentionality remained constant through the five hundred years of development of Judaism's canon following the Mishnah: humility, forbearance, accommodation, and a spirit of conciliation. For one thing, Scripture itself explicitly states that God shares and responds to the attitudes and intentionality of human beings. God cares about what humanity feels—he wants their love, for example—so the conception that actions that express right attitudes of humility will evoke in Heaven a desired response would not have seemed novel to the authors of the Pentateuch or the various prophetic writings, for instance. The biblical record of God's feelings and God's will concerning the feelings of humanity leaves no room for doubt. What is fresh in the system under scrutiny is not the integration of the individual with the nation but the provision, for the individual, of a task and a role analogous to that of the nation.

The Mishnah's system treats matters of attitude and emotion in the taxic context of classifying large-scale and collective classes of things. For instance, although the Mishnah casually refers to emotions, (e.g., tears of joy or sorrow), where feelings matter, it always is in a public and communal context. Where there is an occasion of rejoicing, one form of joy is not to be confused with some other, or one context of sorrow with another. Accordingly, marriages are not to be held on festivals (M. M.Q. 1:7); likewise, mourning is not to take place then (M. M.Q. 1:5, 3:7-9). Where emotions play a role, it is because of the affairs of the community at large, for example, rejoicing on a festival or mourning on a fast day (M. Suk. 5:1-4). Emotions are to be kept in hand, as in the case of the relatives of the executed felon (M. San. 6:6). If I had to specify the Mishnah's single underlying principle affecting all forms of emotion, it would be the profoundly philosophical attitude that attitudes and feelings must be kept under control, never fully expressed without reasoning about the appropriate context. Emotions must always lay down judgments.

In most of those cases in which emotions play a systemic and indicative role, not merely an episodic and random one, the basic principle is the same. Feelings can and should be framed in accord with the appropriate rule. In only one case does emotion play a decisive role in settling an issue, and that has to do with whether a farmer was happy that water came on his produce or grain. That case underlines the conclusion just now drawn. If people feel a given sentiment, it is a matter of judgment and therefore invokes the penalties. So in this system emotions are treated not as spontaneous but as significant aspects of a person's judgment.

The doctrine that very specific attitudes, particular to persons, bear the weight of the systemic structure as a whole, which was made so concrete and specific in the conception of *zekhut* as systemically generative in the successor documents, first appears in tractate Abot, which supplies the phrases I cited at the outset to define the theology that sustains the conception of *zekhut*. Tractate Abot, conventionally attached to the Mishnah and serving as the Mishnah's advocate, forms the bridge from the Mishnah to the Yerushalmi and its associated compilations of scriptural exegeses. That tractate presents the single most comprehensive account of religious affections, for in that document above all, emotion defines a critical aspect of virtue. The issue proves central, not peripheral. The very specific and concrete doctrine emerges fully exposed. A simple catalog of permissible feelings comprises humility, generosity, self-abnegation, love, a spirit of conciliation of the other, and eagerness to please. A list of impermissible emotions is made up of envy, ambition, jealousy, arrogance, stubborness, self-centeredness, a grudging spirit, vengefulness, and the like. Nothing in the wonderful stories about remarkable generosity does more than render concrete the abstract doctrine of the heart's virtue that tractate Abot sets forth.

People should aim at eliciting from others acceptance and goodwill and should avoid confrontation, rejection, and humiliation of the other; they are to do this through conciliating and giving up their own claims and rights. Both catalogs thus form a harmonious and uniform whole, aiming at the cultivation of the humble and malleable person, one who accepts everything and resents nothing. True, these virtues, in this tractate as in the system as a whole, derive from knowledge of what really counts, which is what God wants, but God favors those who please others. The virtues appreciated by human beings prove identical to the ones to which God responds as well. Of them all, the single virtue of the heart that encompasses the rest is restraint, which is the source of self-abnegation and humility and which serves as the antidote for ambition, vengefulness, and above all, for arrogance. It is restraint of our own interest that enables us to deal generously with others, humility about ourselves that generates a liberal spirit toward others. And the correspondence of heavenly and mortal attitudes is to be taken for granted—as is made explicit.

So the emotions prescribed in tractate Abot provide variations of a single feeling, which is the sentiment of the disciplined heart, whatever affective form it may take. And where does the heart learn its lessons, if not in its relationship to God? "Make his wishes yours, so that he will make your wishes his" (Abot 2:4). Applied to relationships between human beings, this inner discipline of the emotional life will yield exactly those virtues of conciliation and self-abnegation, humility and generosity of spirit, that the framers of tractate Abot spell out in one example after another. Imputing to Heaven exactly those responses felt on earth, for example, "Anyone from whom people take pleasure, God takes pleasure" (Abot 3:10), makes the point at the most general level.

The successor system, however, contributes two things: (1) the conception that acts of omission or commission expressing an attitude of forbearance and self-abnegation generate *zekhut* in particular, and (2) the principle that *zekhut* functions in those very specific ways that the system deems critical: as the power to attest to human transformation and regeneration, providing, in place of philosophical politics and philosophical economics, the power inhering in weakness and the wealth inhering in giving up what one has that in the end promise the attainment of one's goals. The path from one system to the other is thus in three stages: (1) the philosophical Judaism, portrayed by the Mishnah, assigns systemic centrality to intentionality and attitude; (2) tractate Abot, in presenting in general terms the rationale of the Mishnah's system, defines precisely the affective attitude and intentionality that are required; and (3) the religious Judaism of the Yerushalmi and associated writings joins together the systemic centrality of attitude and intentionality with the doctrine of virtue laid out in tractate Abot.

In joining these received elements, however, the new system emerges as distinct from the old.[8] To deem both the attitude of not aggression but affirmation and acceptance and the intentionality of self-abnegation and forbearance as defining the means for gaining *zekhut* is contrary and paradoxical: if you want to have, then give up; if you want to impose your judgment, then make the judgment of the other into your own; and if you want to coerce Heaven, then evoke in Heaven attitudes of sympathy that will lead to the actions or events that you want, whether rain, long life, or the salvation of Israel and its hegemony over the nations. To rule, be ruled by Heaven; to show Heaven rules, give up what you want to the other. The result is *zekhut*: the lien on Heaven, freely given by Heaven in response to the individual's free surrender to the will and wish of Heaven. By means of *zekhut*, whether one's own or one's ancestors', the social order finds its shape and system, and the individual his or her place within its structure.

The correspondence of the individual to the nation, both capable of gaining *zekhut* in the same way, linked the deepest personal emotions to the cosmic fate and transcendent faith of that social group of which each individual formed a part. The individual Israelite's innermost feelings, the inner heart of Israel, the microcosm, correspond to the public and historical condition of the nation, the macrocosm. In the innermost chambers of the individual's deepest feelings, the Israelite therefore lives out the public history and destiny of the people Israel.

What precipitated deep thought on fundamental questions of social existence was a simple fact. From the time that Christianity attained the status of a licit religion, the Jews of Palestine witnessed the formation of circumstances that had formerly been simply unimaginable: another Israel, in the same place and time, competed with them in their terms, quoting their Scriptures, explaining who they were in their own categories but in very different terms from the ones that they used. I need not explain the profundities of religious doctrine by reducing them to functions and necessities of public policy, but it is a matter of simple fact that the Jews in the fourth century witnessed a drastic decline in their power to exercise legitimate violence as well as in their command of both the real estate of Palestine, which they knew as the Holy Land, and its wealth. The system's stress on matters of intentionality and attitude, subject to the governance of even the most humble of individuals and the most insignificant of nations, exactly corresponded to the political and social requirements of the Jews' condition in that time. The transformed Judaism made necessity a theological virtue, and, by the way, the normative condition of the social order.

From Constantine's great victory and legitimation of Christianity at the beginning of the fourth century to the Theodosian code that subordinated Jewry and limited its rights at nearly the end, Jews confronted a remarkable shift in the character of the Roman Empire. The state first legalized Christianity, then established it as the most favored religion, and—by the end of that century—finally undertook to extirpate paganism and, by the way, to subordinate Judaism. Therein lies the urgency of the critical question addressed by the system as a whole, if not the self-evident truth of its response. Dealing with world-historical change in the character of the Roman Empire consequent on Constantine's legalization of Christianity and the establishment of Christianity as the state religion by his heirs and successors, the transformed Judaism made its statement in answer to the fundamental question confronting the social order: precisely what are we now to do?

That political question—especially the "do" part—concerning the assessment of the legitimate use of violence in this Judaism called into doubt the legitimacy of any kind of violence at all, the Jews' having none. No less subject to reflection, however, was the "doing" that referred to making a living, the economics of the acquisition and management of scarce resources, and to the making of a life, the philosophy of rational explanation of all things in some one way. At stake, then, were the very shape and structure of the social order, reconsidered at what was, and was certainly perceived as, the critical turning.

This utter reordering of society framed a question that had to be faced and could not be readily answered.[9] It concerned the meaning and end of history, Israel's history, now that the prophetic promises were claimed by the Christian competition to have been kept in the past, leaving nothing in the future for which to hope. When, for a brief moment in 361-63, the emperor Julian disestablished Christianity and restored paganism, proposing also to rebuild the Jews' Temple in Jerusalem, Christianity met the challenge and regained power. The Temple was not rebuilt, and Julian's brief reign brought in its wake a ferocious counterrevolution, with the Christian state now suppressing the institutions of paganism, and Christian men in the streets of the towns and villages taking an active role on their own as well. Julian's successors persecuted pagan philosophy. In 380 the emperor Theodosius (379-95) decreed the end of paganism: "It is our desire that all the various nations which are subject to our clemency and moderation should continue in the profession of that religion which was delivered to the Romans by the divine Apostle Peter." Paganism found itself subjected to penalties. The state church—a principal indicator of the Christian civilization that the West was to know—came into being. In 381 Theodosius forbade sacrifices and closed most temples. In 391-93 a new set of penalties was imposed on paganism. And, while tolerated, Judaism, together with the Jews, suffered drastic change in legal standing as well.

The upshot is simple. In the beginning of the fourth century Rome was pagan; in the end, Christian. In the beginning of the century Jews in the Land of Israel administered their own affairs; in the end their institution of self-administration lost the recognition it had formerly enjoyed. In 300 C.E. the area of Palestine where Jews lived was mainly settled by Jews, hence, palpably and visibly, the Land of Israel, whereas in 400, the country was populated with Christian shrines.[10] In the beginning of the century Judaism enjoyed entirely licit status, and the Jews enjoyed the protection of the state; in the end Judaism suffered abridgment of its former liberties, and the Jews of theirs. In the beginning, the Jews lived in the Land of Israel, and in some numbers. In the end they lived in Palestine.

As a matter of fact, each of the important changes in the documents first redacted at the end of the fourth century dealt with a powerful challenge presented by the triumph of Christianity in Constantine's age.[11] The first change revealed in the unfolding of the sages' canon pertains to the use of Scripture. The change at hand specifically is in making books out of the exegeses of Scripture. That constitutes an innovation because the Mishnah and the exegetical literature that served it did not take shape around the order of biblical passages, even when relevant, let alone the explanation of verses of Scripture. In the third and especially the later fourth centuries, other writings that entered the canon took shape around the explanation of verses of Scripture, not a set of topics. What this meant was that a second mode of organizing ideas, besides the topical mode paramount for the Mishnah, the Tosefta, and the Yerushalmi (and the Bavli later on), now made its way.

The second change concerned extensive consideration of the topic of the Messiah, formerly not accorded a principal place among the parts of the social system.[12] The philosophers of the Mishnah did not make use of the Messiah myth in the construction of a teleology for their system. They found it possible to present a statement of goals for their projected life of Israel that was entirely separate from appeals to history and eschatology. The appearance in the Talmuds of a messianic eschatology fully consonant with the larger characteristic of the rabbinic system—with its stress on the viewpoints and proof texts of Scripture, its interest in what was happening to Israel, and its focus on the national-historical dimension of the life of the group—indicates that the encompassing rabbinic system stands essentially autonomous of the prior, Mishnaic system.

Third, the Mishnah had presented an ahistorical and noneschatological teleology and did not make use of the messiah theme to express its teleology. By contrast, the Talmud not only provides an eschatological and therefore a messiah-centered teleology for its system, but its authorship also formed a theory of history and found it appropriate to compose important narratives, episodic to be sure, concerning events that, in prior systemic writings, were treated as mere taxic indicators. Now, *what* happened counted, not only *that* something happened, and the details of events were to be narrated and preserved. So far as the definition of an event comprises a cultural indicator, the telling of stories about events shows that, for the Talmud of the Land of Israel and related writings, the very formation of culture was transformed.

No wonder, then, that the Mishnah's philosophical (therefore also social-scientific) and ahistorical Judaism, a Judaism of rules, gave way to the religious and historical (therefore also eschatological) Judaism of the Talmud of the Land of Israel, a Judaism of exceptions to the rules. These important shifts show that the later system set forth a Judaism intersecting with the Mishnah's but essentially asymmetrical with it. Given the political changes of the age, with their implications for the meaning and end of history as Israel would experience it, the foci of the connected but autonomous system now directed attention to the media for salvation in the here and now, for Israel and the individual alike, and in time to come for all Israel. A single word captured the whole: *zekhut* yielded a broad variety of answers to one urgent question. It was a question encompassing society and history, the present and the coming age, Israel and the nations, the social order in the here and now and the great society comprised by nature and supernature. In response to the question, the religious system set forth in the late fourth- and fifth-century documents offered the following simple statement: the entire social order forms one reality, in the supernatural world and in nature, in time and in eternity.

The sages who wrote the Talmud of the Land of Israel, Genesis Rabbah, Leviticus Rabbah, and Pesiqta deRab Kahana did not stand alone in their profound reflection on how earth and Heaven intersect and how the here and the now form a moment in history. Another system builder was at work at the same time and under similar circumstances of historical crisis. Given the commonalities of the task facing each party and the dimensions that take the measure of the results, it is not difficult to see how different people of the same time, each speaking to his own world, each delivering his own statement, in the end answer the same question in pretty much the same cosmic dimensions and, it would turn out, with the same enduring results for the formation of Western civilization.[13]

Augustine of Hippo's life, which he lived out in North Africa and Italy between 354 and 430 C.E., coincided with the period in which, to the east, the sages of the Land of Israel produced their Talmud in amplification of the Mishnah as well as their Midrash compilations in extension of Moses's books of Genesis and Leviticus. In terms of comparison and contrast to that Judaism, however, his significance is more than merely temporal coincidence; rather, like the sages of Judaism, he confronted the same this-worldly circumstance, one in which the old order was coming to an end and was acknowledged as such.

The changes were those of power and politics. When the Goths took Rome in 410, refugees of Alaric's conquest fled to North Africa (and to the Land of Israel/Palestine, as events even early in the story of Jerome in Jerusalem show).[14] At the very hour of his death, some decades later, Augustine's own city, Hippo, lay besieged by the Vandals. So it was at what seemed the twilight of the ancient empire of Rome that Augustine composed his account of the theology of the social order known as *The City of God*. Within his remarkable oeuvre, it was that work that renders him of special interest here as both the sages' contemporary and their counterpart as a system builder.

Like the critical issue of political calamity facing sages in the aftermath of the triumph of Christianity and the failure of Julian's brief restoration of both paganism and (as to Jerusalem) Judaism, the question Augustine addressed presented a fundamental challenge to the foundations of the Christian order, coming as it did from Roman pagan aristocrats taking refuge in North Africa.[15] What caused the fall of Rome, if not the breaches in its walls made by Christianity? The first three books of *The City of God* responded in 413, and twenty-two books in all came to a conclusion in 426—a gigantic work.[16] Although *The City of God* (re)presents Christian faith "in the form of biblical history, from Genesis to Revelation,"[17] just as the sages present important components of their system in a historical form of narrative, I see no important doctrinal points in common between the program of Israel's sages in the Land of Israel and that of the great Christian theologian and philosopher. Each party presented in an episodic way what can be represented as an orderly account of the social order,[18] each for the edification of its chosen audience; neither, I think, would have understood a line of the composition of the other, in writing or in concept. Nonetheless, that unbridgeable abyss makes all the more striking the simple fact that the distance between the two was slight, for each party addressed questions entirely familiar, I think, to the other, and the gross and salient traits of both in some striking ways prove symmetrical.[19]

The relationship of the opposing cities of God and the devil, embodied in the pilgrim Church and the empirical state, presents the chief systematic problem of *The City of God*.[20] Augustine covered, in five books, "those who worshipped the gods for felicity on earth;" in five, "those who worshipped them for eternal felicity;" and in twelve, the theme of the origin of "two cities, one of God, the other of the world," "their unfolding course in the part," and "their ultimate destinies."[21] True, sages reconsidered the prior disinterest in history, but they did not then produce a continuous account of everything that had ever happened, as Augustine did. Nor do the two literary monuments, Augustine's and the sages', bear anything in common as to form, style, sources, mode of argument, selection of audience, or literary convention of any kind. Despite all that, what makes the two systems so connected as to warrant comparison is that the authorships of Israel and the Christian author not only responded to the same circumstance but also framed the question deemed posed by that common circumstance in the same terms: a recasting, in historical terms, of the whole of the social order, a rethinking, to use Augustine's image, of God's city.

What, then, was the value of the *polis,* which throughout these pages I have rendered as "the social order," and exactly who lived in the city of the earth? It was "any group of people tainted by the Fall," any that failed to regard "the 'earthly' values they had created as transient and relative."[22] To this Augustine responds, "Away with all this arrogant bluffing: what, after all, are men but men!"[23] The rise of Rome is reduced, in Brown's words, "to a simple common denominator . . . the 'lust for domination.' " The Romans were moved by "an overweening love of praise: 'they were, therefore, "grasping for praise, open-handed with their money; honest in the pursuit of wealth, they wanted to hoard glory." ' "[24] But the true glory resides not in Rome but in the city of God: "the virtues the Romans had ascribed to their heroes would be realized only in the citizens of this other city; and it is only within the walls of the Heavenly Jerusalem that Cicero's noble definition of the essence of the Roman Republic could be achieved."[25] The Judaic sages assuredly concurred on whence comes glory, whence shame: the one from humility, the other, pride.

The system of Augustine addresses the crisis of change with an account of history, and it is, therefore, a deeply historical one in the same sense as is the system of the Judaic sages: "The whole course of human history . . . could be thought of as laden with meanings which might be seized, partially by the believer, in full by the seer."[26] Thus writes Brown: "In his *City of God,* Augustine was one of the first to sense and give monumental expression to a new form of intellectual excitement." God communicates through both words and events. Specifically, history proves the presence of a division between an earthly and a heavenly city.[27] I find this historical interest pertinent to my picture of a Judaism's social order because, in Brown's words, "there is room, in Augustine's view of the past, for the consideration of whole societies"[28] The building block of society is relationship, however, and the whole of human history emerges out of the relationship of Cain and Abel, natural man after the Fall, citizen of this world, against a man who built no city: "by hoping for something else . . . he waited upon the name of the Lord."[29] Brown says:

> Augustine treats the tension between Cain and Abel as universal, because he can explain it in terms applicable to all men. All human society . . . is based on a desire to share some good. Of such goods, the most deeply felt by human beings is the need for "peace": that is, for a resolution of tensions, for an ordered control of unbalanced appetites in themselves, and of discordant wills in society . . . the members of the city of earth, that is, fallen men, tend to regard their achievement of such peace in society as sufficient in itself.[30]

The city of Heaven is "the consecrated commonwealth of Israel"; the city of earth is everybody else.[31] With slight alteration, Brown's summary of Augustine's main point epitomizes the sages' views: "What was at stake, in the *City of God* and in Augustine's sermons, was the capacity of men to 'long' for something different, to examine the nature of their relationship with their immediate environment; above all, to establish their identity by refusing to be engulfed in the unthinking habits of their fellows."[32] How alien could the sages, concerned as they were with the possibilities of extraordinary conduct or attitude, have found Augustine's interest in establishing identity by reflection on what others deemed routine? The obvious answer justifies juxtaposing the two systems as to not only their ineluctable questions but also their self-evidently valid answers.

Two further rhetorical questions seem justified: if Augustine spoke of "resident aliens" when referring to the citizens of God's city,[33] then how difficult could sages have found interpreting the identity of their social entity, their Israel, in the same way: here now, but only because of tomorrow, the pilgrim people, en route to somewhere else. Nor would they have been surprised by the way in which Augustine's city of God was permeated by arguments for hope:[34] " 'Lord, I have loved the beauty of Thy house.' From His gifts, which are scattered to good and bad alike in this, our most grim life, let us, with His help, try to express sufficiently what we have yet to experience."[35] Two systems emerged from the catastrophes of the fifth century, Augustine's[36] for the Christian and the sages' for the Judaic West. Constructed in the same age and in response to problems of the same character and quality, the systems bore nothing in common except the fundamentally same messages about the correspondence of the individual's life to the social order, the centrality of relationship, the rule of God, and the response of God to what transcended all rules.

Both systems, each in its own way, join God to the social order, because it is in relationships that society takes shape and comes to expression, and all relationships, whether between one person and another or between mortals and God, are wholly consubstantial.[37] That is why, for Augustine, the relationship between the individuals Cain and Abel can convey and represent the relationships characteristic of societies or cities, and that is why, for the sages, the relationships between one person and another can affect God's relationship to the village needing rain or the householder needing to shore up his shaky dwelling.

True, these are two utterly unrelated systems of the social order, fabricated by different people, talking about different things to different people, each meant to join the society of humanity (or a sector thereof) with the community of Heaven. But both formed quite systematic and well-crafted responses to one and the same deep (and in my judgment, thoroughly merited) perception of disorder, a world that has wobbled, a universe out of line. Rome fallen and home besieged, for Augustine, corresponded to the end of autonomy and the advent of another (to be sure, *soi-disant*) "Israel," for sages, and both called into question orders of society of very ancient foundation. That in turn produced a profound sense that the rules had been broken, generating that alienation (to frame matters in contemporary psychological terms) that was overcome by Augustine in his way, by sages in theirs.[38]

What, in their own language, was the sages' answer to the question of the times? The shaking of the foundations of the social order shows how Israel is estranged from God. The old rules have been broken, therefore the remarkable and the exceptional succeed. What is unnatural to the human condition of pride is humility and uncertainty, acceptance and conciliation. As individual attitudes and national policies these violate the rule, so let God respond to transcending rules. And when—so the system maintains—God recognizes in Israel's heart, as much as in the nation's deliberation, the proper feelings, God will respond by ending that estrangement that marks the present age. Thus, the single word encompassing the question addressed by the entire social system of the successor-Judaism must be *alienation*. The human and shared sense of crisis—whether Augustine reflecting on the fall of Rome or the sages confronting the end of the old order—finds its response in the doctrine of God's assessment, God's response. God enters the social order imagined by sages because God in the natural order proves insufficient, a presence inadequate to the human situation. God must dwell in the city of humanity, and Israel in the city of God. So what in secular terms is a historical crisis or in psychological terms is one of alienation is in religious terms a caesura in the bounds of eternity. The psychological theology of the system joins the human condition to the fate of the nation and the world—and links the whole to the broken heart of God.

Nonetheless, that theological observation about the incarnate God of Judaism does not point toward the systemic center, which within my definitions of what a system is must be social and explain the order of things here and now. For in the end, a religious theory of the social order describes earth, not Heaven.[39] It simply begs the question to claim that the system in the end attended to the condition of God's heart rather than to humanity's mundane existence, for a religious system is not a theological one, and questions about the way of life, worldview, and social entity, though admittedly bearing the theological implications or even making theological statements, in the end find their answers in the reconstruction of the here and now. So I have not identified the central tension and the generative problematic, nor have I specified the self-evident answer to the question that the system in every sentence and all details meant to settle. It is for identifying that generative problematic of the religious Judaism of the fifth century that the comparison between it and the Christianity of Augustine in his *City of God* proves particularly pertinent.

To state matters very simply, Augustine's personal circumstance and that of the sages corresponded, as did Augustine's central question and the fundamental preoccupation of the sages. Augustine's *City of God* and the Talmud of the Land of Israel took shape in changing times, and both systemic statements accommodate questions of history. Both the answer and the question become visible in light of the fact that both did so in the same way.

Specifically, Augustine, bringing to fruition the tradition of Christian historical thought commencing with Eusebius, provided for Christianity a theory of history that placed into the right perspective the events of the day. The sages did the same, first affirming that events required recognition and then providing a theory of events that acknowledged their meaning, that is, their historicity, but that also subordinated history to considerations of eternity. The generative problematic of the successor system concerned history: the authorships not only attended to the vast changes in the political circumstance of Israel and perceived mutations in the tissue of social relationship, they also clearly showed an interest in revising the plain meaning of ordinary words such as value, power, and learning. And the systemic answer for its part addressed questions of long-term continuity, framed in genealogical terms for the now genealogically defined Israel: the past lives in the future, and the system explains in very precise and specific terms just how that takes place, which is through the medium of inherited entitlement or attained entitlement. The medium was indeed the same. The message carried by *zekhut* counseled performance of actions of renunciation, in the hope that Heaven would respond. Power was weakness, value was knowledge, and knowledge was power: all things formed within the Torah.

If that was the answer to the historical question of change and crisis, then how had the question of history come to be formulated? Briefly put, the question was what events should be deemed to constitute history, what changes matter, and what individuals and nations should do. The answer—the sages' and Augustine's alike—was that only certain happenings are eventful, bear consequence, or require attention, and they are eventful because they form paradigms—Cain and Abel for Augustine, Israel's patriarchs and matriarchs for the sages.[40] Thus, history as made by the barbarians at Rome and Hippo and by the Byzantine Christians at Tiberias and Sepphoris ceased to matter, because what happened at Rome or Tiberias was no happening at all, merely happenstance. The upshot is that history does not follow rules: what will be is not predictable.

Augustine did not claim to know what would happen tomorrow morning, and the sages interpreted events but did not claim to shape them, except through the Torah. The upshot is that what is going on really may be set aside in favor of what is really happening, and the story that is history has already been told in (for Augustine) the Bible and (for the sages) the Torah. But that is no longer history at all, merely a past made into an eternal present. So, to specify what I conceive to be the systemic answer, it is that there are some things that matter, many that do not, and the few that matter echo from eternity to eternity, speaking in that voice, the voice of God, that is the voice of silence, still and small.

Thus, the systemic question, not merely chronic but also urgent, immediate, and critical, concerned vast historical change that comprised chains of events. The answer was that, in an exact sense, "event" has no meaning at all. The modes of organizing existence that governed were other than historical, and history in the ordinary sense did not form one of them. Without the social construction of history, there also is no need for the identification of events, that is, individual and unique happenings that bear consequence, for within the system and structure of the successor-Judaism, history forms no taxon, being replaced by *zekhut*, a historical category that was in the deepest sense antihistorical. So it follows that no happening is unique, and, on its own, no event bears consequence.

Neither Augustine nor the sages produced narrative history; both, rather, wrote reflections *on* history, a very different matter. Neither used narrative history, ordinarily a sustained paraphrastic chronicle, as a medium for organizing and explaining perceived experience. Both referred to events in the past, but these were not strung together in a continuing account. They were cited because they were exemplary, not because they were unique. These events then were identified out of the unlimited agenda of the past as what mattered, and these occasions of consequence, as distinct from undifferentiated and unperceived happenings, were meant to explain the things that mattered in the chaos of the everyday.

In responding as they did to what we conceive to be historical events of unparalleled weight, Augustine and the sages took positions that, from our perspective, prove remarkably contemporary. Present-day viewpoints see all histories as the creation of an eternal present: that is, those moments in which histories are defined and distinguished, in which events are identified and assigned consequence, and in which sequences of events (e.g., "this particular thing happened here *and therefore . . . ,*") are strung together like pearls on a string to form ornaments of intellect. Fully recognizing that history is one of the grand fabrications of the human intellect, facts not discovered but invented, explanations that themselves form cultural indicators of how things are in the here and now, may help in appreciating as far more than merely instrumental and necessary the systemic responses to the urgent questions addressed in common by the sages and by Augustine.

Shall I then classify the successor-Judaism as a historical religion,[41] in that it appeals for its worldview to not myth about gods in heaven but the history of Israel on earth—interpreted, nevertheless, in relationship to the acts of God in Heaven? And shall I characterize that Judaism as a religion that appeals to history, that is, to important happenings defined in the ordinary way, for its source of testing and establishing truth? I think not. That Judaism identifies an event through its own cognitive processes. Just as the canon recapitulates the system, so events—things that happen given consequence—recapitulate the system. Just as the system speaks in detail through the canon, so too the system delivers its message through its repertoire of events granted recognition. But just as the canon is not the system, so the recognition of events does not classify the system as historical.

This brings me directly to the final question of systemic description: what exactly does the successor-Judaism mean by events? To answer that question succinctly is simple. In the canonical literature of the successor-Judaism, events find their place, within the *Listenwissenschaft* that characterizes this literature, along with sorts of things that, for our part, we should not characterize as events at all. Events have no autonomous standing; events are not unique, each unto itself; events have no probative value on their own. Events form cases, along with a variety of other cases, making up lists of things that, in common, point to or prove one thing. Moreover, among the taxonomic structure at hand, events do not make up their own list at all, for what is truly eventful generates *zekhut*. It is the act of *zekhut* that unites past and present, and it is the act that gains *zekhut* that makes history for tomorrow.

Events of other kinds, even those that seem to make an enormous and awful difference in Israel's condition, will appear on the same list as persons, places, and things. And the contrary lists—very often in the form of stories—relate events that in and of themselves change biography (the life and fate of an ass driver) and make history. That means that events other than those that gain *zekhut* not only have no autonomous standing on their own, but also that events constitute no species even within a genus of a historical order. For in our way of thinking, persons, places, and things do not belong in the same list as events; they are not of the same order. Within the logic of our own minds, we cannot classify the city of Paris within the same genus as the event of the declaration of the rights of man, for instance, nor is Sinai or Jerusalem of the same order of things as the Torah or the Temple, respectively. But in the logic of the successor-Judaism, Jerusalem stands for sanctity and for Temple; it is of precisely the same taxic order.

What then—to revert to the worldview adumbrated in the Midrash compilations reviewed in chapter 7—of a list that encompasses events and things within the same taxic composition? Answering that question shows how the sages sort out what matters from what does not: events, by themselves, do not form a taxon, and on their own they bear no means and therefore do not matter. One such list made up of events, persons, and places, is as follows:

1. Israel at the sea;
2. the ministering angels;
3. the tent of meeting;
4. the eternal house (the Temple); and
5. Sinai.

That mixes an event (Israel redeemed at the sea), a category of sensate being (angels), a location (tent of meeting and Temple), and then Sinai, which can stand for a variety of things but in context stands for the Torah. In such a list an event may or may not stand for a value or a proposition, but it does not enjoy autonomous standing; the list is not defined by the eventfulness of events and their meaning, nor is it the compilation of matters of a single genus or even a single species (tent of meeting and eternal house are the same species here). The notion of event as autonomous, even unique, is quite absent in this taxonomy, and once events lose their autonomy a process of selection gets under way that transforms one event into history bearing meaning and sets aside as inconsequential in the exact sense all other events.

Because this point is systemically so fundamental, let me give the case of another such list, which moves from events to other matters altogether, finding the whole subject to the same metaphor, hence homogenized. First come the events that took place at the following places or with the following persons: Egypt, the sea, Marah, Massah and Meribah, Horeb, the wilderness, the spies in the Land, Shittim, or Achan/Joshua and the conquest of the Land. This mixture of places and names clearly intends to focus on particular things that happened, and hence, were the list to conclude at this point, I could define an event for the successor-Judaism as a happening that bore consequence, taught a lesson, or exemplified a truth. In the present case, an event matters because it contains the mixture of rebellion and obedience. There would then be no doubt that "event" formed a genus unto itself and that a proper list could not encompass both events, defined conventionally, and also other matters altogether.

But the literary culture at hand, this textual community, proceeds in the same literary context to the following items: the Ten Commandements, the show fringes and phylacteries, the Shema and the Prayer, and the tabernacle and the cloud of the Presence of God in the world to come. The reason for invoking these candidates for the metaphor at hand seems to me clear from the catalog. These reach their climax in the analogy between the home and the tabernacle, the embrace of God and the Presence of God. So the whole is meant to list those things that draw the Israelite near God and make the Israelite cleave to God. To this massive catalog, events are not only exemplary — which historians can concede without difficulty — but also subordinate.

Events belong on the same list as actions, things, persons, and places because they form an order of being that is not to be differentiated between events (including things that stand for events) and altogether other cultural artifacts. A happening is no different from an object, in which case "event" serves no better, and no worse, than a hero, a gesture or action, a recitation of a given formula, or a particular locale to establish a truth. It is all contingent, subordinate, and instrumental. Nor should this be surprising, for all history is transmitted in writing, and it is the culture that dictates how writing is to take place; that is why history can only paraphrase the affirmations of a system and why events recapitulate in acute and concrete ways the system that classifies one thing that happens as an event but totally ignores another thing. In the present instance, an event is not at all eventful; it is merely a fact that forms part of the evidence for what is, and what is eventful is not an occasion at all, but a condition, an attitude, a perspective, and a viewpoint. Thus, events are subordinated to the formation of attitudes, perspectives, and viewpoints — the formative artifacts of not history in the conventional sense but culture in the framework of

Sahlin's generalization that "history is culturally ordered, differently so in different societies, according to meaningful schemes of things."[42]

Events not only do not form a taxon, they do not present a vast corpus of candidates for inclusion into some other taxon. Among the candidates, events that are selected by the successor documents are few indeed. They commonly encompass Israel at the sea and at Sinai; the destruction of the first Temple; the destruction of the second Temple; and events as defined by the actions of some holy men such as Abraham, Isaac, and Jacob (treated not for what they did but for who they were), Daniel, Mishael, Hananiah and Azariah, and the like. It follows that the restricted repertoire of candidates for taxonomic study encompasses surprisingly few events, remarkably few for a literary culture that is commonly described as quintessentially historical!

Then what taxic indicator dictates which happenings will be deemed events and which not? What are listed throughout are not data of nature or history but of theology: the issue of history is one of relationship, just as with Augustine. Specifically, God's relationship with Israel, expressed in such facts as the three events, the first two in the past, the third in the future (e.g., the three redemptions of Israel or the three patriarchs) and holy persons, actions, events, what have you — these are the facts that are assembled and grouped. This is a kind of recombinant theology given narrative form through tales presented individually but not in a sustained narrative. This recombinant theology through history is accomplished when the framer ("the theologian") selects from a restricted repertoire a few items for combination. There is a kind of subtle restatement, through an infinite range of possibilities, of the combinations and recombinations of a few essentially simple facts (data).

The net effect, then, is to exclude, rather than to include: the world is left outside. The key to systemic interpretation lies in the exegesis of the exegetical process that governs selection: what is included, what is excluded. I find the following statement by Jonathan Z. Smith important in this context: "An almost limitless horizon of possibilities that are at hand . . . is arbitrarily reduced . . . to a set of basic elements. . . . Then a most intense ingenuity is exercised to overcome the reduction . . . to introduce interest and variety. This ingenuity is usually accompanied by a complex set of rules.[43] To know the complex set of rules in play here is to understand the system that makes this document not merely an expression of piety but a statement of a theological structure: orderly, well composed and proportioned, and internally coherent and cogent throughout.

The canonical, therefore anything but random, standing of events forms a brief chapter in the exegesis of a canon. That observation draws us back to Smith, who observes that

> the radical and arbitrary reduction represented by the notion of canon and the ingenuity represented by the rule-governed exegetical enterprise to apply the canon to every dimension of human life is that most characteristic, persistent, and obsessive religious activity. . . . The task of application as well as the judgment of the relative adequacy of particular applications to a community's life situation remains the indigenous theologian's task; but the study of the process, particularly the study of comparative systematics and exegesis, ought to be a major preoccupation of the historian of religions.[44]

Smith speaks of religion as an "enterprise of exegetical totalization," and he further identifies with the word "canon" precisely what I have identified as the substrate and structure of the list. If I had to define an event in this canonical context, I should have to call it merely another theological thing: something to be manipulated and combined in one way or in another, along with other theological things.

In insisting that the successor system remains connected to the initial one, I have until now left open the identification of the joining threads of thought—but now I scarcely need to elaborate. The systems are connected because the successor system sustains the generative mode of thought of the initial one, which was list making, but now the lists derive from data supplied by Scripture (as with the bulk of Augustine's historical events of paradigmatic consequence) rather than by nature. Now as before, list making is accomplished within a restricted repertoire of items that can serve on lists; the list making then presents interesting combinations of an essentially small number of candidates for the exercise. When making lists, one can do pretty much anything with the items that are combined; the taxic indicators are unlimited, but the data studied are severely limited. So the systems connect because the successor system has recapitulated the initial system in mode of thought and medium of expression.

The radical shift in category formation and the utterly fresh systemic composition and construction carry forward received modes of thought.

So far as the two systems may both be called Judaisms, and so far as these Judaisms join so as to form one ongoing Judaism, continuity is in not message but method. The history of religion is the exegesis of exegesis, and, for this case, the transformation of Judaism likewise tells two stories. The one portrays successive and essentially distinct, free-standing systems. The other narrates that enduring process that sustains and unites and nourishes—and, therefore, also defines. But definition in religion yields theology, and that next shift in the transformation of Judaism—the final formation of Judaism—would be long in coming.

Notes

1. I use the word "rationality" in the sense in which it is used in the thought of Max Weber: the systemic sense of what is appropriate and proper. The comparison of the rationalities of the initial and the successor systems is undertaken in the closing paragraphs of this chapter. This is not, of course, an account of the concept of rationality in the thought of Weber. I believe my characterization, for the limited purpose of these remarks, is entirely accurate.

2. Note the fine perception of S. Levy in *Original Virtue and Other Studies*, 2-3: "Some act of obedience, constituting the Ascent of man, is the origin of virtue and the cause of reward for virtue. . . . What is the conspicuous act of obedience which, in Judaism, forms the striking contrast to Adam's act of disobedience, in Christianity? The submission of Isaac in being bound on the altar . . . is regarded in Jewish theology as the historic cause of the imputation of virtue to his descendants." It is not an accident, then, as we shall see, that Augustine selected as his paradigmatic historical exemplum the conflict of Cain and Abel, the city of God being inhabited by Abel and his descendants; he required for his argument a virtue pertinent to all of humanity, not to Israel alone, so it seems to me as an outsider to the subject.

3. My initial comments on that matter are in *The Incarnation of God: The Character of Divinity in Formative Judaism* (Philadelphia: Fortress Press, 1988).

4. The full source is given on p. 255.

5. The full source is given on p. 202-3.

6. That is, an assessment of what people will ordinarily think or propose or wish to have happen. The rule is set by that norm, not by exceptions, and on that basis, in the initial system, we are able to determine what (an ordinary person's) intentionality will dictate in a given interstitial case.

7. I have demonstrated that fact in my *Vanquished Nation, Broken Spirit: The Virtues of the Heart in Formative Judaism* (New York: Cambridge University Press, 1987).

8. This is not to suggest that the substance of the doctrine of virtue was

richly revised in the successor writings. That is not so. The transformation was systemic, not doctrinal. Emotions not taken up earlier in the pages of the Yerushalmi did not come under discussion. Principles introduced earlier enjoyed mere restatement and extensive exemplification. Some principles of proper feelings might even generate secondary developments of one kind or another. But nothing not present at the outset—in tractate Abot—drew sustained attention later on. The system proved essentially complete in the earliest statement of its main points. What then do the authors or compilers of the Yerushalmi contribute? They write that temper marks the ignorant person, restraint and serenity, the learned one, but these are mere details.

9. Nor was it answered by the Mishnah's system, which treated history—composed of events in particular—as mere occasions for taxonomic inquiry: classifying this event in one way, according to one overriding rule, that event in some other, according to another rule, and neither rule bore any relationship to history. The regularization and ordering of disorderly events—counterpart to what we know as social science today—denied to history all status as the source of category formation. I have spelled all this out in my *Messiah in Context: Israel's History and Destiny in Formative Judaism,* vol. 2 of *The Foundations of Judaism: Method, Teleology, Doctrine,* 3 vols. (Philadelphia: Fortress Press, 1983-85).

10. Constantine and his mother had built churches and shrines all over the country, but especially in Jerusalem, so the Land of Israel received yet another name, now becoming the Holy Land for another important group.

11. I have spelled these matters out in *Judaism and Christianity in the Age of Constantine: Issues of the Initial Confrontation* (Chicago: University of Chicago Press, 1987); *Midrash in Context: Exegesis in Formative Judaism,* vol. 1 of *The Foundations of Judaism;* and, in summary, in *Judaism in the Matrix of Christianity* (Philadelphia: Fortress Press, 1986).

12. This is worked out in *Messiah in Context.*

13. One need not exaggerate the influence of either St. Augustine or the sages to claim that the Christianity and the Judaism framed by each, respectively, defined norms and set the course for the two great religions of the West.

14. I refer to J. N. D. Kelly, *Jerome: His Life, Writings, and Controversies* (New York: Harper & Row, 1975).

15. The bibliography for this chapter lists the books I have consulted. In no way claiming to know the scholarship on Augustine, even in the English language, I chose to rely primarily on a single work, consulting others mostly for my own illumination. My chief source was the up-to-date and, I think, universally respected account by Peter Brown, *Augustine of Hippo* (Berkeley: University of California Press, 1987). The pertinent passage is on p. 302. My modest generalizations about the intersection of the two systems on some points important to each rests, for Augustine, entirely on Brown. I found very helpful the outline of the work presented by John Neville Figgis, *The Political Aspects of St. Augustine's 'City of God'* (London: Longmans Green and Co., 1921), 1-31, and the characterization of Augustine's thought by Herbert A.

Deane, *The Political and Social Ideas of St. Augustine* (New York: Columbia University Press, 1963). In Deane's lucid account, anyone in search of specific doctrinal parallels between the sages' system and that of Augustine will find ample evidence that there is none of consequence. As will become clear, what I find heuristically suggestive are structural and functional parallels, not points of doctrinal coincidence of any material importance. My sense is that the success of Brown's book overshadowed the important contribution of Gerald Bonner in *St. Augustine of Hippo: Life and Controversies* (London: SCM Press, 1963), a less dazzling, but more systematic and (it seems to me) useful presentation. A brief and clear account of the two cities is in Eugene Teselle, *Augustine the Theologian* (New York: Herder and Herder, 1970), 268-78, who outlines the variety of approaches taken to the description and interpretation of the work: polemical, apologetic; philosophy or theology of history; analysis of political ideology; source of principles of political and moral theory and of ecclesiastical policy; and the like. The achievement of F. Van der Meer, *Augustine the Bishop: Religion and Society at the Dawn of the Middle Ages*, trans. Brian Battershaw and G. R. Lamp (New York: Harper & Row, 1961), is not to be missed: a fine example of the narrative reading of religion by a historian of religion of one useful kind. Precisely what Augustine means by "the city of God" is worked out by John O'Meara in *The Charter of Christendom: The Significance of the City of God* (New York: Macmillan, 1961), where he says that "the city of God exists already in heaven and, apart from certain pilgrim men who are on their way to it while they are on this earth, in heaven only" (43). When I speak of the sages having extended the boundaries of the social system from earth to Heaven, I mean to suggest something roughly parallel, in that, when women and men on earth conform to the Torah, they find themselves in the image and after the likeness of Heaven. The sense of the concept "history," then, is "the story of two cities," so Hardy, p. 267ff. (cf. Edward R. Hardy, Jr., "The City of God," in Roy W. Battenhouse, *A Companion to the Study of St. Augustine* [New York: Oxford University Press, 1955), 257-86]. I find the story of Israel among the nations as the equivalent unifying and integrating conception of history in the doctrine(s) of history in the Yerushalmi and Leviticus Rabbah; this then means Israel forms the counterpart to the city of God, and I think that is the beginning of all systemic comparison in this context (and, I should suspect, in all others).

16. Brown, *Augustine*, 303.

17. John H. S. Burleigh, *The City of God: A Study of St. Augustine's Philosophy: Croall Lectures, 1944* (London: Nisbet & Co., 1949), 153.

18. But the two parties have in common the simple fact that the representation of their respective systems is the accomplishment of others later on, indeed, in the case of the sages, much later on indeed. Note the judgment of Deane that Augustine "was not a system builder. . . . Virtually everything that Augustine wrote . . . was an occasional piece" (*The Political and Social Ideas of St. Augustine*, viii). The sages' documents, it is quite obvious, do not utilize the categories for the description of the social order that I have imposed: ethos, ethics, ethnos; worldview, way of life, doctrine of the social

entity. But systemic description in its nature imputes and of necessity imposes system, and that is so whether the system is deemed social or theological in its fundamental character. I have no difficulty in defending the proposition that the sages' system was in its very essence a system of society, that is, of the holy people, Israel, and the union of social and theological thought in Augustine is signaled by the very metaphors he selected for his work, in his appeal to "the city."

19. When William Green recommended the choice of Augustine and I accepted it, the recommendation and recognition of its rightness bore a certain rationality, too. Drawing a comparison with Augustine is by no means capricious, based merely on the temporal coincidence of the sages of the Yerushalmi and related writings and Augustine. What I think more compelling is the fact that the sages inherited a Middle Platonic doctrine concerning the unity of all being and reworked it in historical-narrative terms, therefore finding in (among other concepts) the notion of *zekhut* a medium for the unification of the generations, past and present. Augustine, for his part, is everywhere described as a reworking the heritage of Platonism, drawing chiefly from Plotinus, so for instance Burleigh, *The City of God*, 157. As a guess, therefore, I would venture that the principal shift in the large-scale modes of thought from the Mishnah through to the Yerushalmi, along with Genesis Rabbah, Leviticus Rabbah, and Pesiqta deRab Kahana, was the movement away from Aristotelian modes of thought, such as characterized the Mishnah, to those of Middle Platonism. But not being a historian of philosophy in antiquity, I am able only to suggest that hypothesis as a subject for further inquiry. In any event, one did not have to adopt the inheritance of Plato, in the formulation of Middle Platonism, Neoplatonism, or Plotinus, to focus on the social order as the centerpiece of philosophical, systematic thought and system building. Aristotle (much less influential in this period, to be sure) provided an equally accessible model for anyone who might wish to rethink the foundations of the *polis* or of the social being of Israel, the holy people, in the Land of Israel, the Holy Land.

20. So Teselle, *Augustine*, 270.

21. Brown, *Augustine*, 303-4. Cf. Burleigh, *The City of God*, 166ff., on Augustine's attitude toward "the concrete political structures of history."

22. Brown, *Augustine*, 309.

23. Ibid.

24. Ibid., 310.

25. Ibid., 311-12.

26. Ibid., 317.

27. Ibid., 319. See Burleigh, *The City of God*, 185ff., "a philosophy of history." He cites the following: "St. Augustine's *De Civitate Dei* . . . may be regarded as the first attempt to frame a complete philosophy of history. . . . It was . . . a singularly unsuccessful attempt; for it contained neither philosophy nor history, but merely theology and fiction." Whether or not so of Augustine, that statement seems to me an apt description of the form of history as invented in the pages of the Talmud of the Land of Israel. My presentation

of the sages' thought on history is in my *Foundations of Judaism,* vol. 2, *Messiah in Context: Israel's History and Destiny in Formative Judaism.* This matter has not played a principal role in my exposition of the successor system, because it seems to me ancillary and not categorically definitive. Burleigh describes the dominant philosophy of the age, characteristic of Augustine as well, as antihistorical. But Augustine's "Platonic Biblicism in effect brings them [history and philosophy] into the closest relation. Biblical History is Platonic idealism in time." That statement seems to me to run parallel to the characterization of the rabbinic uses of history in the form of persons and events as exemplary and cyclical, rather than unique and linear.

28. Brown, *Augustine,* 320.
29. Ibid., 320.
30. Ibid., 322.
31. Ibid., 322.
32. Ibid., 322.
33. Ibid., 323.
34. Ibid., 328.
35. Ibid., 328.
36. Note Burleigh, *The City of God,* 218: "The Fifth Century... was a period of radical historical change." But just as Augustine expressed no sense of "the end of an era," so in the pages of the documents surveyed here I find no world-historical foreboding, only an optimistic and unshakeable conviction that Israel governed by its own deeds and attitudes its own destiny every day. That seems to me the opposite of a sense that all things are changing beyond repair. I can find no more ample representation of the historical convictions of the sages than Burleigh's representation of Augustine's: "Rome might pass away. The protecting fostering power of her emperors might be withdrawn. But God endured. His purpose of gathering citizens into His Eternal City was not frustrated by transient circumstances. St. Augustine had no anxiety for the Empire or for civilization, even 'Christian' civilization, because he found a better security in God." It is interesting to note that Burleigh gave his lectures in 1944, responding, it seems to me, to the impending dissolution of the British Empire in his rereading of Augustine—and dismissing an interest in the fate of empires as essentially beside the point for Augustine. So I think it was for the sages.

37. Burleigh characterizes matters in this way: "He seems to have been satisfied to show... that the exposition and defence of the Christian faith necessitates a survey of all History, which is in its essence God's providential government of the human race" (*The City of God,* 202).

38. The basic motif of alienation—personal, cosmic, political, theological, as much as affective—characterizes the two systems, because it defines the condition that provokes for each system the generative question and because it is in the mode of reintegration that each system finds its persistent statement. True, alienation defines a purely contemporary category and forms a judgment made by us on the circumstance or attitude of ancients, but the category does serve to specify, for our own understanding, what it at stake.

39. To be sure, earth in the model of Heaven, or, as we might prefer, Heaven in the model of earth.

40. But though I think they are primary, as the formation of Genesis Rabbah at this time indicates, they are not alone; Israel at Sinai, David on the throne, and other historical moments serve as well. It is a mere impression, not a demonstrable fact, that the patriarchs and matriarchs provide the primary paradigm.

41. I leave for Augustine scholarship the counterpart question on him.

42. See his *Islands of History* (Chicago: University of Chicago Press, 1985), 172.

43. "Sacred Persistence: Towards a Redescription of Canon," in William Scott Green, ed., *Approaches to Ancient Judaism* (Atlanta, Ga.: Scholars Press for Brown Judaic Studies, 1978), 1:11-28. Quotation, 15.

44. Ibid., 18.

Appendix to Chapter 1
Modes of Making Connections
and Drawing Conclusions in
Midrash Compilations

The purpose of this and the following appendices is to provide further illustrative sources for points made in the exposition. Readers may find burdensome the task of working through an unfamiliar kind of writing, such as the ancient documents of Judaism may present, so I wished to keep to a minimum the abstracts in the body of the text. What is offered here are some further items that seem to me noteworthy.

To supplement chapter 1, I provide a brief sample of a passage in Genesis Rabbah that shows how the modes of making connections and drawing conclusions of the Midrash compilation before us run parallel to those of the Talmud of the Land of Israel. Here a verse of Scripture is cited and then amplified. The verse that is treated is Genesis 1:3: "*And God said, 'Let there be Light.'* " The discussion is made up of three distinct, well-composed thoughts, which I have numbered with Arabic numerals. To underline how the logic of coherent discourse runs parallel to that of the Mishnah, I give the citations of verses of Scripture in italic type.

Genesis Rabbah III:VIII

1A. Said R. Yannai, "At the beginning of the creation of the world the Holy One, blessed be He, foresaw the deeds of the righteous and the deeds of the wicked.

B. " '*And the earth was unformed and void*' refers to the deeds of the wicked.

C. " '*And God said, "Let there be light"* ' refers to the deeds of the righteous.

D. " '*And God saw the light, that it was good,*' refers to the deeds of the righteous.

E. " '*And God divided between the light and the darkness*' means [he divided] between the deeds of the righteous and the deeds of the wicked.

F. " '*And God called the light day*' refers to the deeds of the righteous.

G. " '*And the darkness he called night*' refers to the deeds of the wicked.

H. " '*And there was evening*' refers to the deeds of the wicked.

I. " '*And there was morning*' refers to the deeds of the righteous.

J. " '*One day,*' for the Holy One, blessed be He, gave them one day, [and what day is that]? It is the day of judgment."

2A. ["*One (unique) day*" (Gen.1:3)] Said R. Tanhum, "It was the day on which unique things were made, heaven, earth, and light."

B. Said R. Yudan, "[It was called 'one day'] because on that day, the Holy One, blessed be He, was truly unique in his world."

C. That view accords with the position of R. Yohanan and not with that of R. Hanina.

D. R. Yohanan said, "On the second day of creation, the angels were created. That is in line with this verse of Scripture: '*Who lays the beams of your upper chambers in the waters,*' and it is further written, '*who makes spirits, your angels*' (Ps. 104:3-4)."

E. R. Hanina said, "The angels were created on the fifth day: '*And let fowl fly above the earth*' (Gen. 1:20), and it is written, '*And with two did the angel fly*' (Isa. 6:2)."

3A. R. Luliani bar Tabari in the name of R. Isaac: "Both R. Hanina and R. Yohanan concur that nothing whatsoever was created on the first day. It was so that you should not say, 'Michael was spreading out [the heaven] at the south of the firmament, and Gabriel at the north, with the Holy One, blessed be He, measuring from the middle.'

B. "Rather: '*I am the Lord who makes all things, who stretched out the heavens alone, who spread forth the earth by myself*' (Isa. 44:24)

C. " ' "*By myself*" for who was with me?' So it is written, meaning, '*Who was my partner in the creation of the world?*' "

What joins 1, 2, and 3 is solely the appeal to the common verse,

Gen. 1:3. No single proposition appeals for demonstration, let alone argument, to the three compositions. Number 1 complements the syllogism that God made the world perfect and without blemish with the necessary corollary. Where there are marks of imperfection, they will be removed at the end of days. God knew what he was doing from the beginning, creating both good and evil, as the story of creation makes clear. When will the perfection of creation come to full realization? On that "one day," the day of judgment.

The basic reading of the creation story repeatedly uncovers this single point. It is a stunning mode of argument, based on a text all parties claim to contain the truth. Genesis 1:3 serves as a proof text in making a point quite distinct from the verse at hand. Number 2 (carrying in its wake number 3) reverts to the exposition of the verse and explains, in particular, the meaning of the word "one," that is, not ordinal but cardinal. The possible meanings of that verse then are related to God's situation in the world at the end of the first day. The negative polemic addresses those who say God was not alone in creating the world. So at each point the exegetes address positions contrary to their own, and the compositors have selected what we must find to be cogent and coherent. The upshot is that the logic of fixed association joins two compositions, 1 and 2-3. We therefore see that the joining logic is the same as the Yerushalmi's in reference to Mishnah commentary.

Appendix to Chapter 2

Expressions of the
Polemic against Wealth

The following shows a case in which wealth is made contingent, so that the outsider's high valuation of money is contrasted with the Israelite's low valuation of money and his high valuation of holiness:

Genesis Rabbah XI:IV

4A. Said R. Tanhuma, "There was a case in Rome that took place on the eve of the great fast [the Day of Atonement]. A certain tailor there went to buy himself a fish, and it happened that the governor's bondman was bidding for it too, and one bid for such and so, and the other bid for such and so, until the price reached twelve denars. And the tailor got it.

B. "At dinner the governor said to his servant, 'Why did you not serve fish?'

C. "He said to him, 'My lord, why should I keep the matter from you? Such and so a certain Jew did to me. Do you want me to bring you a fish that cost twelve denars?'

D. "He said to him, 'Who is he?'

E. "He said to him, 'Such and so, a Jew.'

F. "He sent for him and summoned him, and he came. He said, 'Will a Jewish tailor eat a fish for twelve denars?'

G. "He said to him, 'My Lord, we have a day which effects atonement for us for all of the sins of the year, and should we not treasure it?'

H. "He brought proof for his statement, and the governor let him go free."

What is important to this study is the contrast that is drawn between the incorrect and the correct evaluation of wealth. The gentile does not know what counts, the Israelite does. Then by scarce resources, in the passage at hand and countless counterparts, something other than gold is meant.

The polemic against wealth and comfort and in favor of a different value altogether is exemplified in the notion that the generation of the Flood sinned because it had too much prosperity:

Genesis Rabbah XXXIV:XI.2

A. Said R. Aha, "What is it that made them rebel against me? Was it not because they sowed but did not reap, produced offspring and did not have to bury them?

B. "Henceforward: 'Seedtime and harvest,' meaning that they will give birth and then have to bury their children.

C. " 'Cold and heat,' meaning they have fever and ague.

D. " 'Summer and winter,' meaning: 'I shall give the birds the right to attack their summer crops,' in line with this verse, '*And the ravenous birds shall summer upon them and all the beasts of the earth shall winter upon them*' (Isa. 18:6)."

5A. Said R. Isaac, "What is it that made them rebel against me? Was it not because they sowed but did not reap?"

B. For R. Isaac said, "Once every forty years they would sow a crop, and as they made their trip they would travel from one end of the world to the other in a brief span and cut down the cedars of Lebanon. And the lions and leopards made no more of an impression on them than did a louse on their skin."

C. How so? The climate for them was like the climate from Passover to Pentecost.

D. R. Simeon b. Gamaliel said in the name of R. Meir, and so said R. Dosa, "The latter half of Tishre, Marheshvan, and the first half of Kislev are for sowing, the second half of Kislev and Tebet and the first half of Shebat are winter, the latter half of Shebat and Adar and the first half of Nisan are the cold season, the second half of Nisan and Iyyar and the first half of Sivan are the harvest season, the second half of Sivan and Tammuz and the first half of Ab are summer, and latter half of Ab and Elul and the first half of Tishre are the hot season."

E. R. Judah counts from Marheshvan.

F. R. Simeon counts from Tishri.

Humankind had rebelled under conditions of prosperity, so now they will have to endure "hot and cold," "seedtime and harvesttime," interpreted as misfortunes. Lust for money is condemned in countless ways, for people are not supposed to place their trust in real estate, movables, or other things of material value.

Appendix to Chapter 7

The Expansion of the Symbol of Torah
in the Successor System

Scripture, of course, by this time did not exhaust the content of God's revelation to Moses at Sinai. In the pages of the Yerushalmi the conception comes to expression that the Torah encompassed not only revelation formulated and transmitted in writing, but also revelation formulated and transmitted orally. This oral part of the Torah gained priority simply because knowledge of the oral Torah—at this point, the Mishnah and some unspecified traditions of scribes alongside—characterized sages alone and marked them as distinctive in context. That is why, for all their veneration of Scripture and its (rabbinical) heroes, the Talmud's authorities still regarded knowledge of the Mishnah as more important than knowledge of Scripture, citing biblical proof texts in support of that proposition.

The relative value of learning in various collections of Torah teachings is worked out in the following extended unit of discourse.

Y. Horayot 3:5.III

D. This is what has been said: The Mishnah takes precedence over Scripture.

E. And the following supports this tradition:

F. For R. Simeon b. Yohai taught, "He who takes up studies in Scripture—it is a good quality that is no good quality."

G. Rabbis treat Scripture as equivalent to the Mishnah . . .

W. R. Aha interpreted the following verse: " 'A just balance and scales are the Lord's; all the weights in the bag are his work' (Prov. 16:110).

X. " 'A balance'—this refers to Scripture.

Y. " 'Scales' refers to the Mishnah.

z. " 'Just' refers to the Talmud.

AA. " 'Are the Lord's' refers to the Supplement [Tosefta].

BB. " 'All the weights in the bag are his work'—all of them take their reward from one bag."

CC. R. Abba bar Kahana went to a certain place. He found R. Levi sitting and interpreting the following verse: " '*A man to whom God gives wealth, possession, and honor, so that he lacks nothing of all that he desires, yet God does not give him power to enjoy them, but a stranger enjoys them*' (Qoh. 6:2).

DD. " 'Wealth'—this refers to Scripture.

EE. " 'Possessions'—these are the laws.

FF. " 'Honor'—this is the Supplement."

Christians as much as Jews, ordinary folk as much as sages, knew Scripture. One striking point ought not to be missed in the statement at hand. Given that Torah is the source of supernatural power and salvation, what part of Torah is the source of supernatural power and salvation, what part of Torah is to enjoy precedence? It quite obviously will be the Mishnah and its associated bodies of discussion, that is, the component of Torah in the hands of Israel, and Israel's sages, alone. Assigning to knowledge of Mishnah precedence over knowledge of Scripture therefore serves to declare that those who master Mishnah possess a power to attain salvation greater than those who know (merely) Scripture. I take that to be the deeper sense of D-F.

The contrary view at G and at W-BB should not be missed either. Both parties must be right. No one could really maintain that knowledge of the Scripture was secondary to knowledge of the Mishnah. Nor would any sage concur that knowledge of Scripture alone sufficed. So the sense of the passage allows two correct, if distinct, positions to be juxtaposed. For my purpose the fundamental assertion of the identity of Scripture learning and Mishnah learning with "Torah" is the main thing.

When I speak of the gnostic Torah, marking the new learning that promised not merely illumination of an intellectual order but salvation that was both personal and national, it is to this union of written and oral Torah that I refer: that was the gnostic, the salvific Torah.

Bibliography

This topically organized bibliography provides an account both of works I found useful in writing this book and also of prior writings of my own (signified by citation without reference to an author) in which I have elaborated on points made here or that form the monographic basis for the results given here. My earlier books, of course contain their own bibliographics. In the nature of things, there are topics treated here on which I know of no prior studies pertinent to the question I mean to ask, though, of course, there is a considerable literature on aspects of those same topics in no way relevant to my inquiry.

Specifically, chapters 4, 5, and 7 formulate problems and studies with no antecedents known to me, so the bibliography lists only my work. Further, other chapters, particularly chapters 1, 2, 3, 6, and most of 9, draw my own prior work. Where I have worked on a topic and brought my questions to it, I also read the prior treatments of the same topic and listed those I found useful; these are cataloged in the works of mine and are cited here, in particular with reference to the history of economic and political theory. In the present book I did benefit in a direct way from earlier work on the subjects treated in chapters 8 (a few rather confused studies in *zekhut*) and 9 (for Augustine).

I have not undertaken a topical bibliography of every subject treated here because it did not seem productive to gather lists of books and articles that, although dealing with subjects treated here, neither answered in any material way questions about those subjects important to me nor affected my analysis and treatment of them. A catalog of books and articles on the subjects treated here would therefore mislead and, moreover, suggest that I have found prior scholarship helpful; on the contrary, for the most part it simply proved of no consequence whatever for my inquiry into the description of categories based on a particular slice of the canonical writings, on the one side, and the analysis and interpretation of those category formations in systemic context, on the other. No one has ever done work of that kind, and the treatment of most topics addressed here, so far as there has been any, in the extant scholarly literature is utterly confused and simply misleading, ignoring as it does all the questions of literary setting, systemic context, and historical consideration that seem to me decisive for the description, analysis, and interpretation of category formation and the systems composed of such categories.

General Bibliographies of Ancient Judaism

Extensive bibliographies on the literature and religion of Rabbinic Judaism and on the history of the Jews in the first six centuries C.E. occur in the following, which I edited:

The Study of Ancient Judaism, 2 vols. New York: KTAV, 1981.

Preface and Introduction

This books deals in rather abstract terms with structures of ideas, viewed essentially outside the framework of the society to which those structures were meant to pertain. But in the end, the material consequence of ideas defines the context in which all thought took place. Hence, in due course, I shall have to return to a more narrowly historical reading of matters. I found the following item, on the periodization of late antiquity, suggestive and important in considering the larger context in which the history of Judaism unfolded:

Morony, Michael G. "Teleology and the Significance of Change." In *Tradition and Innovation in Late Antiquity,* edited by F. M. Clover and R. S. Humphreys, 21-27. Madison: University of Wisconsin Press, 1989.

The topical program of the preface and introduction is in five parts, as indicated in the following outline:

1. The Theory of Systemic Analysis

My theory of systemic analysis is in these books:

Ancient Judaism: Disputes and Debates. Chico, Calif.: Scholars Press for Brown Judaic Studies, 1984.
Ancient Judaism: Debates and Disputes, 2d series. Atlanta, Ga.: Scholars Press for South Florida Studies in the History of Judaism, 1990.
Ecology of Religion: From Writing to Religion in the Study of Judaism. Nashville, Tenn.: Abingdon, 1989.
First Principles of Systemic Analysis: The Case of Judaism in the History of Religion. Lanham: University Press of America, 1988.
Formation of the Jewish Intellect: Making Connections and Drawing Conclusions in the Traditional System of Judaism. Atlanta, Ga.: Scholars Press for Brown Judaic Studies, 1988.
From Description to Conviction: Essays on the History and Theology of Judaism. Atalanta, Ga.: Scholars Press for Brown Judaic Studies, 1987.
Making of the Mind of Judaism. Atlanta, Ga.: Scholars Press for Brown Judaic Studies, 1987.

Paradigms in Passage: Patterns of Change in the Contemporary Study of Judaism.
   Lanham: University Press of America, 1988.
*Religious Writings and Religious Systems: Systemic Analysis of Holy Books in
   Christianity, Islam, Buddhism, Greco-Roman Religions, Ancient Israel, and
   Judaism,* 2 vols. Atlanta, Ga.: Scholars Press for Brown Studies in Religion,
   1989. (Edited with Ernest S. Frerichs and A. J. Levine.)
Systemic Analysis of Judaism. Atlanta, Ga: Scholars Press for Brown Judaic
   Studies, 1988.
Why No Gospels in Talmudic Judaism? Atlanta, Ga.: Scholars Press for Brown
   Judaic Studies, 1988.
*Wrong Ways and Right Ways in the Study of Formative Judaism: Critical Method
   and Literature, History, and the History of Religion.* Atlanta, Ga.: Scholars
   Press for Brown Judaic Studies, 1988.

2. Theory of the Three Stages in the Formation of Judaism

In the following work I set forth my basic theory of the three successive stages
in the formation of Judaism, the first represented, in literary form, by the Mishnah
and Tosefta, together with Tractate Abot; the second, by the Talmud of the Land
of Israel and associated Midrash compilations, particularly Genesis Rabbah, Leviticus Rabbah, and Pesiqta deRab Kahana; and the third set forth by the Talmud
of Babylonia and its associated Midrash compilations, particularly Lamentations
Rabbah, Ruth Rabbah, Esther Rabbah I, Song of Songs Rabbah, and also by the
Fathers according to Rabbi Nathan.

Major Trends in Formative Judaism, 3d ser. *The Three Stages in the Formation
   of Judaism.* Chico, Calif.: Scholars Press for Brown Judaic Studies, 1985.

As to the so-called Tannaitic Midrashim, these seem to me to belong in a
mediating position between the first and the second stages. My study of that
problem is in the following:

*The Place of the So-called Tannaitic Midrashim: Methodological Experiments in
   the Intellectual Situation of Documents.* Atlanta, Ga.: Scholars Press for
   Brown Judaic Studies, 1990.

3. The Canonical History of Ideas

I have the sense that my method of the canonical history of ideas is now gaining
broad acceptance in Europe and North America. Israeli historical work in this
area rests on the twin premises that if stories are told, then we know precisely
what happened; if a saying is attributed to an authority, he really said it. Most
Israeli historical work, moreover, takes for granted the premise of Orthodox
Judaism that the entire Torah is without bounds, so the fact that one story appears
in an early document and another in a later makes no difference as to the historicity
of the story or as to the interpretation of that story. But in the rest of the scholarly
world these premises are not broadly shared, and Israeli historical and history of

religions work on the history of Judaism is generally ignored, being judged gullible and credulous.

The premise of this book, that we may identify striking shifts in the history of some, but not all, of the principal components of the system of the Mishnah that occur in the system represented by the Talmud of the Land of Israel and related Midrash compilations, is set forth in great detail in the following books. There I have undertaken the work of analysis—comparison and contrast—now yielding the history of the components of the religious system attested in those documents:

The Christian and Judaic Invention of History. Atlanta, Ga.: Scholars Press for American Academy of Religion, 1989.

Foundations of Judaism: Method, Teleology, Doctrine, 3 vols. Philadelphia: Fortress Press, 1983-85.

From Testament to Torah: An Introduction to Judaism in its Formative Age. Englewood Cliffs, N.J.: Prentice-Hall, 1987.

Incarnation of God: The Character of Divinity in Formative Judaism. Philadelphia: Fortress Press, 1988.

Judaism and Christianity in the Age of Constantine: Issues of the Initial Confrontation. Chicago: University of Chicago Press, 1987.

Judaism and Scripture: The Evidence of Leviticus Rabbah. Chicago: University of Chicago Press, 1986.

Judaism in Society: The Evidence of the Yerushalmi: Toward the Natural History of a Religion. Chicago: University of Chicago Press, 1983.

Judaism in the Matrix of Christianity. Philadelphia: Fortress Press, 1986.

Oral Torah: The Sacred Books of Judaism: An Introduction. San Francisco: Harper & Row, 1985.

Writing with Scripture: The Authority and Uses of the Hebrew Bible in the Torah of Formative Judaism. Philadelphia: Fortress Press, 1989.

4. Philosophical and Theological Discourse

The distinction made in the introduction between philosophy and theology undergoes elaboration in this work:

A Religion of Pots and Pans? Modes of Philosophical and Theological Discourse in Ancient Judaism: Essays and a Program. Atlanta, Ga.: Scholars Press for Brown Judaic Studies, 1988.

5. Components of the Social Order: Philosophy, Politics, Economics

Essays in which I set forth the analysis of the categories of philosophy, politics, and economics in ancient Judaism in general terms are in these books:

The Social Foundations of Judaism: Case-Studies of Religion and Society in Classical and Modern Times. Englewood Cliffs, N.J.: Prentice-Hall, 1989. (Edited with Calvin Goldscheider.)

The Social Study of Judaism: Essays and Reflections, 2 vols. Atlanta, Ga.: Scholars Press for Brown Judaic Studies, 1989.

1. Modes of Thought: From Philosophy to Religion

The bibliography on ancient philosophy such as bears on the philosophical classification and character of the Mishnah—method and message alike—is given in
my *Philosophy of Judaism: First Principles* (Baltimore, Md.: Johns Hopkins University Press, 1991). I have not copied it here.

Judaism as Philosophy: The Method and Message of the Mishnah. Columbia:
    University of South Carolina Press, 1991.
The Philosophical Mishnah, 4 vols. Atlanta, Ga.: Scholars Press for Brown Judaic
    Studies, 1989.

2. Scarce Resources: Philosophical Economics Reproduced

This item contains a considerable bibliography on the history of economic theory,
the economics of Judaism, and the economics of the Mishnah, and also forms
the basis for this chapter:

The Economics of the Mishnah. Chicago: University of Chicago Press, 1989.
    For that book I consulted, among other items, the following:
Bell, John Fred. *A History of Economic Thought,* 13-32. New York: Ronald
    Press, 1967.
Blaug, Mark. *Economic Theory in Retrospect.* Cambridge: Cambridge University
    Press, 1978.
Campbell, William F. "The Free Market for Goods and the Free Market for Ideas
    in the Platonic Dialogues," *History of Political Economy* 17 (1985): 187-97.
Cannan, Edwin. *Origins of Economic Theory,* 3. London: P. S. King & Son, 1929.
Cannan, Edwin. *A Review of Economic Theory,* 1-4. London: P. S. King Son,
    1929.
Cipolla, Carlo M., ed. *The Economic Decline of Empires.* London: Methuen,
    1970.
Davisson, William I., and Hames E. Harper. *European Economic History.* Vol.
    1, *The Ancient World.* New York: Appleton-Century-Crofts, 1972.
Denis, Henri. *Histoire de la pensée économique* [The History of Economic Thought],
    7-57. Paris: Presses Universitaries de France, 1966.
Duncan-Jones, Richard. *The Economy of the Roman Empire* London: Cambridge
    University Press, 1975.
Erb, Otto. *Wirtschaft und Gesellschaft im Denken der hellenischen Antike* [Eco-
    nomics and Society in Ancient Greek Thought]. Berlin, 1939.
Finley, M. I. "Aristotle and Economic Analysis." In *Studies in Ancient Society,*
    ed. M. I. Finley. London: Routledge and Kegan Paul, 1974.
Finley, M. I. *Studies in Land and Credit in Ancient Athens, 500-200 B.C.: The
    Horos-Inscriptions.* New Brunswick, N.J.: Rutgers University Press, 1951.
Frank, Tenney. *Aspects of Social Behavior in Ancient Rome.* New York: Cooper
    Square, 1969.
Gordon, Barry. "Aristotle and Hesiod: The Economic Problem in Greek Thought."
    Review of Social Economy 21 (1963): 147-56.

Gordon, Barry. "Biblical and Early Judeo-Christian Thought: Genesis to Augustine." In *Pre-Classical Economic Thought: From the Greeks to the Scottish Enlightenment*, ed. S. Todd Lowry, 43-67. Boston: Kluwar Academic Publishers, 1987. This essay on rational action in regard to scarcity seems to me little more than a paraphrase of ancient writings, with no important analytical side at all. What we have here is not economics but sayings on themes in some way deemed relevant to economics. I find no attention to how people understood the economy to work or even to the conception, in ancient times, of an economy. All of the issues important to Finley and Schumpeter are neglected. What I find is neither "economic analysis" nor any other kind of analysis. This is the sort of writing that gives economic history a bad name for merely collecting and arranging. But Ohrenstein is worse.

Gordon, Barry. *Economic Analysis before Adam Smith: Hesiod to Lessius*. New York: Barnes and Noble, 1975.

Gray, Alexdander. *The Devlopment of Economic Doctrine: An Introductory Survey*. London: Longmans Green and Co., 1931.

Haney, Lewis H. *History of Economic Thought: A Critical Account of the Origin and Devleopment of the Economic Theories of the Leading Thinkers in the Leading Nations*. New York: Macmillan, 1920.

Humphreys, Sally C. *Anthropology and the Greeks*. London: Routledge and Kegan Paul, 1978.

Humphreys, Sally C. "History, Economics, and Anthropology: The Work of Karl Polanyi." *History & Theory* 8 (1962): 165-212.

Humphreys, Sally C. "Economy and Society in Classical Athens." *Annali della Normale Superiore di Pisa* 39 (1970): 1-26.

Jones, A. H. M. *Ancient Economic History*. London: H. K. Lewis, 1948. This important programmatic statement requires rereading every few years, for it shows how a first-rate mind can set forth a problem and then go about solving it.

Jones, A. H. M. *The Roman Economy: Studies in Ancient Economic and Administrative History*. Edited by P. A. Brunt. Oxford: Basil Blackwell, 1974.

Langholm, Odd. *The Aristotelian Analysis of Usury*. Bergen: Universitetsforlaget, 1984.

Lekachman, Robert. *History of Economic Thought*, 3. New York: Harper, 1959.

Lévy, Jean-Philippe. *L'économie antique*. Paris: Presses Universaires de France, 1964. *The Economic Life of the Ancient World*. Chicago: University of Chicago Press, 1967.

Lowry, S. Todd, ed. *Pre-Classical Economic Thought: From the Greeks to the Scottish Enlightenment*. Boston: Kluwer Academic Publishers, 1987. See especially his "Greek Heritage in Economic Thought," 7-30, and its excellent bibliography.

McKeon, R. *Introduction to Aristotle*. New York: Columbia University Press.

Monroe, A. E. *Early Economic Thought*. Cambridge: 1924.

Ohrenstein, Roman A. "Commentary: Some Socioeconomic Aspects of Judaic Thought." In *Pre-Classical Economic Thought: From the Greeks to the Scottish Enlightenment*, edited by S. Todd Lowry, 68-75. Boston: Kluwer Academic Publishers, 1987. This article is entirely uninformed on its subject, as the bibliography by itself proves. I am puzzled by the inclusion of these ramblings in what otherwise appears to me a very competent collection of essays under Lowry's editorship.

Ohrenstein, Roman A. "Economic Analysis in Talmudic Literature: Some Ancient Studies of Value." *American Journal of Economics and Sociology* 38 (1979).

Ohrenstein, Roman A. "Economic Self-Interest and Social Progress in Talmudic Literature." *American Journal of Economics and Sociology* 29 (1970): 59-70.

Ohrenstein, Roman A. "Economic Thought in Talmudic Literature in the Light of Modern Economics." *American Journal of Economics and Sociology* 27 (1968): 185-96.

Ohrenstein, Roman A. "Some Studies of Value in Talmudic Literature in the Light of Modern Economics." *The Nassau Review* 4 (1981): 48-70.

Oppenheim, A. Leo. *Ancient Mesopotamia: Portrait of a Dead Civilization.* Chicago: University of Chicago Press, 1964. Certainly one of the most intelligent books ever written, and an inspiration for a whole generation.

Polanyi, Karl, Conrad M. Arensberg, and Harry W. Pearson. *Trade and Market in the Early Empires: Economies in History and Theory.* Glencoe, Ill.: Free Press, 1957. In that book I found of special interest the essays by A. L. Oppenheim, "A Birds-Eye View of Mesopotamian Economic History," 27-37; and Karl Polanyi, "Aristotle Discovers the Economy," 64-96.

Polanyi, Karl. *The Livelihood of Man,* edited by Harry W. Pearson. New York: Academic Press, 1977. See, in particular, 145-276.

Popescu, O. "On the Historiography of Economic Thought. A Bibliography," *Journal of World History* 8 (1964): 1ff.

Rostovtzeff, M. I. *Social and Economic History of the Hellenistic World.* Oxford: Oxford University Press, 1941.

Schumpeter, Joseph A. *History of Economic Analysis,* edited by Elizabeth B. Schumpeter. New York: Oxford University Press, 1954.

Silver, Morris. *Economic Structures of the Ancient Near East.* London: Croom Helm, 1985.

Singer, Kurt. "*Oikonomia:* An Inquiry into the Beginnings of Economic Thought and Language." *Kyklos* 11 (1958): 29-54.

Soudek, C. J. "Aristotle's Theory of Exchange." *Proceedings of the American Philosophical Society* 5 (1952): 96ff.

Spendler, Joseph J. "Aristotle on Economic Imputation and Related Matters." *Southern Economics Journal* (1955): 21.

Spiegel, Henry William. *The Growth of Economic Thought.* Durham, N.C.: Duke University Press, 1971.

Toutain, Jules. *The Economic Life of the Ancient World.* New York: Alfred A. Knopf, 1930.

Trever, A. A. *A History of Greek Economic Thought.* Philadelphia: Porcupine Press, 1978.

Weber, Max. *Economy and Society: An Outline of Interpretive Sociology,* edited by Guenther Roth and Claus Wittich. Berkeley: University of California Press, 1978.

Weber, Max. *General Economic History.* Glencoe, Ill.: Free Press, 1950.

Weber, Max. *The Agrarian Sociology of Ancient Civilizations,* trans. by R. I. Frank. London: NLB, 1976. The pages on ancient Israel, 134-46, cover only the pre-exilic period.

3. Legitimate Violence: From Hierarchized Foci to Unitary Focus of Power

The first item contains a considerable bibliography on the history of political theory with special reference to Aristotle's *Politics,* the politics of Judaism, and the politics of the Mishnah, and also forms the basis for this chapter:

The Politics of Judaism: The Initial Structure and System. Chicago: University of Chicago Press, 1991.

For that book I found the following items especially important:

Adkins, A. W. H. *From the Many to the One: A Study of Personality and Views of Human Nature in the Context of Ancient Greek Society, Values, and Beliefs,* 170. Ithaca, N.Y.: Cornell University Press, 1970.

Alexander, Jeffrey C. *Action and Its Environments: Toward a New Synthesis.* New York: Columbia University Press, 1988. I read this book with much admiration.

Alexander, Jeffrey C. *Max Weber.* Berkeley: University of California Press, 1983.

Alexander, Jeffrey C. *Twenty Lectures: Sociological Theory since World War II.* New York: Columbia University Press, 1987.

Barker, Ernest. *Greek Political Theory: Plato and His Predecessors.* New York: Barnes & Noble, 1947.

Barker, Ernest. *The Political Thought of Plato and Aristotle.* New York: Russell & Russell, 1959.

de Ste. Croix, G. E. M. *The Class Struggle in the Ancient Greek World: From the Archaic Age to the Arab Conquests.* London: Gerald Duckworth, 1981.

Finley, M. I. *Politics in the Ancient World.* Cambridge: Cambridge University Press, 1983.

Finley, M. I. "Aristotle and Economic Analysis." In *Studies in Ancient Society,* edited by M. I. Finley. London: Routledge and Kegan Paul, 1974.

Fox-Genovese, Elizabeth. *The Origins of Physiocracy: Economic Revolution and Social Order in Eighteenth-Century France.* Ithaca, N.Y.: Cornell University Press, 1987.

Gerth, H. H., and C. Wright Mills, eds. *From Max Weber: Essays in Sociology,* 333 ff. New York: Oxford University Press, 1958.

Hammond, Mason. *City-State and World State in Greek and Roman Political Theory until Augustus.* Cambridge, Mass.: Harvard University Press, 1951.

Kagan, Donald. *The Great Dialogue: History of Greek Political Thought from Homer to Polybius.* New York: The Free Press, 1965.

Lewis, Bernard. *The Political Language of Islam,* 25 ff. Chicago: University of Chicago Press, 1988.

Minio-Paluello, Lorenzo. S.v. "Aristotelianism." Encyclopaedia Britannica.

Mulgan, R.G. *Aristotle's Political Theory.* Oxford: Clarendon Press, 1977.

Nussbaum, Martha C. "Nature, Function, and Capability: Aristotle on Political Distribution." *Oxford Studies in Ancient Philosophy,* 1988, and *Proceedings of the Eleventh Symposium Aristotelicum,* edited by G. Patzig.

Oates, Whitney J. "The Ideal States of Plato and Aristotle." In *The Greek Political Experience: Studies in Honor of William Kelly Prentice,* 197-213. New York: Russell & Russell, 1969.

Raaflaub, Kurt. "Die Anfänge des politischen Denkens bei gen Griechen," [The Origins of Greek Political Thought]. In *Pipers Handbuch der politischen Ideen,* edited by Iring Fetscher and Herfried Münkler, 189-271. Munich: Piper, 1988.

Rosenthal, Erwin I. J. *Political Thought in Medieval Islam: An Introductory Outline.* Cambridge: Cambridge University Press, 1958.

Stalley, R. F. *An Introduction to Plato's Laws.* Indianapolis: Hackett, 1983.

Weber, Max. "Politics as a Vocation." In *From Max Weber: Essays in Sociology,* ed. Gerth and Mills. New York: Oxford University Press, 1958.

4. Learning and the Category *Torah*

I know of no prior studies pertinent to my treatment of this topic as addressed in this book. My *Torah: From Scroll to Symbol,* cited below, forms the basis for my description of the category and counterpart category.

5. The Transvaluation of Value

I know of no prior studies pertinent to my treatment of this topic as I have framed the problem here.

6. Empowerment and the Category *The People Israel*

This chapter draws on the following, which contains a bibliography on the theory of the social entity set forth in a variety of Judaisms of antiquity:

Judaism and its Social Metaphors: Israel in the History of Jewish Thought. New York: Cambridge University Press, 1988.

7. The New Learning: The Gnostic Torah

I know of no prior studies pertinent to my treatment of this topic of how studying the Torah is supposed to change and save the disciple of the Torah. Studies about "Judaism and Gnosticism" presuppose an array of very dubious categories and facts. Gershom G. Scholem's *Jewish Gnosticism, Merkabah Mysticism, and Talmudic Tradition* (New York: Jewish Theological Seminary of American, 1960), for example, is without any value in contemporary scholarship, other than his occasional exercises of erudition, because of the failure to define what he means by such terms as "Jewish," and "gnosticism." He simply takes for granted what is in fact the problematic of the topic, which, in his day, surely was one of definition.

8. The New Order: The Political Economy of *Zekhut*

In redefining the word *zekhut* and showing it means the very opposite of the word that has been used to translate it, which is "merit," I set aside the received agendum of discussion of this matter. The term has been discussed in the polemical context of contemporary Judaic-Christian dialogue, and Judaism has been accused of "arrogance" or "self-righteousness," and described, in the language of Werblowsky in the work cited below, as being "a mercenary religion." My reading of the sources has given an entirely different sense to the word, and I was able, therefore, to get very little help from the prior literature. The article signed by J. H. Sh. in *Encyclopaedia Jadaica* exemplifies the confusion characteristic of treatments of this subject, for in treating *zekhut* only in the context of *zekhut avot,* translated as "merit of the fathers," the author invokes all cases in which "merit of the fathers" spills over into God's remembering or loving the ancestors and therefore favoring descendants, e.g., "The memory or deeds of the righteous forefathers are often invoked in prayers for the forgiveness or welfare of their decendants, for instance, Moses' supplications after the sin of the golden calf, '*Remember your servants, Abraham, Isaac, and Jacob*' (Ex. 32:13)." What happens here is that the term is treated as general, referring to qualities of a given transaction, thus encompassing within *zukhut avot,* and hence within *zekhut,* a variety of relationships that may or may not pertain. My preference has been to work outward from usages of the word in the writings under discussion and, more to the point, to interpret the usages within the context assigned to those meanings by the system that finds systemically indicative and constructive the word and meanings established in context.

That same indifference to documentary context characterizes Marmorstein and explains the confusion that characterizes his treatment of the subject, which is the definitive one to this time and, alas, also the source of an entire agenda of political issues that in fact do not pertain at all. Marmorstein defines the matter in this way: "Men and women can rise by positive deeds to such a height of moral beauty, virtue, and accomplishment, in spite of their natural shortcomings and innate faults, that they are regarded as meritorious before God" (p. 3). That definition simply misses the point of *zekhut,* which is its supernatural dimension in the natural world: the conception of entitlement through deeds of a very particular character, analogous, on the positive side of the balance, to sin on the negative (a point Marmorstein registers without much appreciation). The sources I have selected as definitive of the concept scarcely intersect with Marmorstein's account of the matter, and none of what they do emphasize is present, so far as I read him, in Marmorstein, who I find to be not so much wrong as simply confused throughout. Still, it was of some value to me to find a prior work that at least treated a subject I found critical and did so in a manner that was more than perfunctory.

Levy's "Original Virtue" refers to "the virtues of the fathers," and he claims to have interpreted that phrase as a contrast to "the Christian theory of Original Sin." His "doctrine of Original Value" posits (1) that there is in man a natural tendency to virtue; (2) the virtues of the fathers are rewarded to the children; and (3) some act of obedience, constituting the ascent of man, is the origin of virtue and the cause of reward for virtue. He finds the doctrine of original virtue in the conception of "the good inclination" (*yeser tob*); he contrasts "the sins of the fathers" with "the virtues of the fathers," that is *avon abot* versus *zekhut avot*. He finds the conspicuous act of obedience in contrast to Adam's sin of disobedience in the binding of Isaac on the altar. This seems to me an imaginative and inviting theological exercise, a *jeu d'esprit* of considerable wit, but the essay has no bearing on the problem of this book.

Herford, R. Travers. *Pharisaism*, 212-15; 276-81. London: Williams & Norgate, 1912. The Pharisees "had no fixed doctrine of merit."

Levy, S. *Original Virtue and Other Short Studies*, 1-42. London: Longmans Green and Co., 1907.

Marmorstein, A. *The Doctrine of Merits in Old Rabbinical Literature: And the Old Rabbinic Doctrine of God*, introduction by R. J. Zwi Werblowsky. New York: KTAV, 1968.

Schechter, Solomon. *Some Aspects of Rabbinic Theology*, 170-98. London: Behrman House, 1900. Speaking of "imputed righteousness and imputed sin," Schechter deals with the *zekhut* of a pious ancestry, a pious contemporary, and pious posterity.

Sh., J. H., S.v. "*Zekhut Avot*." Enclyclopaedia Judaica.

9. Enchanted Judaism and *The City of God*

1. On the Issue of the Correspondence of Divine and Human Emotions

This discussion draws heavily on my study of the doctrine of affections or virtue in its canonical unfolding:

Vanquished Nation, Broken Spirit: The Virtues of the Heart in Formative Judaism. New York: Cambridge University Press, 1987.

2. On Augustine

The bibliography on Augustine is immense, and I am in no way a scholar, even with amateur standing, in that subject. My description of Augustine's system as set forth in *The City of God* is based on the books cited in the chapter. In addition, I read these further works:

Battenhouse, Roy W., ed. *A Companion to the Study of St. Augustine*. New York: Oxford University Press, 1955.

Bonner, Gerald. *St. Augustine of Hippo: Life and Controversies.* London: SCM Press, 1963.

Brookes, Edgar H. *The City of God and the Politics of Crisis.* London: Oxford University Press, 1960.

Brown, Peter. *Augustine of Hippo.* Berkeley: University of California Press, 1967.

Burleigh, John H. S. *The City of God: A Study of St. Augustine's Philosophy: Croall Lectures, 1944.* London: Nisbet, 1949.

Chadwick, Henry. *Augustine.* Oxford: Oxford University Press, 1986.

Deane, Herbert A. *The Political and Social Ideas of St. Augustine.* New York: Columbia University Press, 1963.

Dill, S. *Roman Society in the Last Century of the Western Empire.* London, 1898.

Dods, Marcus, trans. *The City of God,* 2 vols. New York: Hafner, 1948.

Figgis, John Neville. *The Political Aspects of S. Augustine's 'City of God.'* London: Longmans Green and Co., 1926.

Fortin, Ernest L. *Political Idealism and Christianity in the Thought of St. Augustine.* Philadelphia: Villanova University Press, 1972.

Gilson, E. H. *The Christian Philosophy of St. Augustine,* trans. by L. E. M. Lynch. New York, 1960.

Hardy, Edward R., Jr. "The City of God." In *A Companion to the Study of St. Augustine,* ed. Battenhouse, 257-86. New York: Oxford University Press, 1955.

Kirwan, Christopher. *Augustine.* London: Routledge, 1989.

Markus, R. A. *Saeculum: History and Society in the Theology of St. Augustine.* Cambridge: Cambridge University Press, 1970.

Marrou, H. I. *Saint Augustine.* New York: Harper & Row, 1957.

O'Meara, John J. *The Young Augustine: The Growth of St. Augustine's Mind up to his Conversion.* London: Longmans Green and Co, 1954.

O'Meara, John. *The Charter of Christendom: The Significance of the City of God.* New York: Macmillan, 1961.

Rickaby, Joseph. *St. Augustine's "City of God": A View of the Contents.* London, 1925.

Teselle, Eugene. *Augustine the Theologian.* New York: Herder and Herder, 1970.

Van der Meer, F. *Augustine the Bishop: Religion and Society at the Dawn of the Middle Ages,* translated by Brian Battershaw and G. R. Lamp. New York: Harper & Row, 1961.

West, R. *St. Augustine.* London: Peter Davies, 1930.

Other

This book furthermore rests on a variety of my prior studies in which I have set forth the literary and intellectual traits of the canon of Judaism in its formative age.

1. Mishnah and Tosefta

My representation of the Mishnah and Tosefta, encompassing description, analysis, and interpretation, is in the following works:

Ancient Israel after Catastrophe: The Religious World-View of the Mishnah: The Richard Lectures for 1982. Charlottesville: University Press of Virginia, 1983.

First Century Judaism in Crisis: Yohanan ben Zakkai and the Renaissance of Torah. Nashville, Tenn.: Abingdon, 1975.

Form Analysis and Exegesis: A Fresh Approach to the Interpretation of Mishnah. Minneapolis: University of Minnesota Press, 1980.

The Formation of the Jewish Intellect: Making Connections and Drawing Conclusions in the Traditional System of Judaism. Atlanta, Ga.: Scholars Press for Brown Judaic Studies, 1988.

Formative Judaism: Religious, Historical, and Literary Studies, series 1-5. Chico, Calif.: Scholars Press for Brown Judaic Studies, 1982-85.

Formative Judaism: Religious, Historical, and Literary Studies, series 6. Atlanta, Ga.: Scholars Press for Brown Judiac Studies, 1989.

From Mishnah to Scripture: The Problem of the Unattributed Saying. Chico, Calif.: Scholars Press for Brown Judiac Studies, 1984. Reprise and reworking of materials in *A History of the Mishnaic Law of Purities.*

From Politics to Piety: The Emergence of Pharisaic Judaism. Englewood Cliffs, N.J.: Prentice-Hall, 1973.

A History of the Mishnaic Law of Appointed Times, 5 vols. Leiden, Netherlands: Brill, 1981-83.

A History of the Mishnaic Law of Damages, 5 vols. Leiden, Netherlands: Brill, 1983-85.

A History of the Mishnaic Law of Holy Things, 6 vols. Leiden, Netherlands: Brill, 1979.

A History of the Mishnaic Law of Purities, 22 vols. Leiden, Netherlands: Brill, 1974-77.

A History of the Mishnaic Law of Women, 5 vols. Leiden, Netherlands: Brill, 1979-80.

In Search of Talmudic Biography: The Problem of the Attributed Saying. Chico, Calif.: Scholars Press for Brown Judiac Studies, 1984. Reprise and reworking of materials in *Eliezer ben Hyrcanus: The Tradition and the Man.*

Judaism without Christianity: An Introduction to the Religious System of the Mishnah in Historical Context. Hoboken, N.J.: KTAV, 1989. Abbreviated version of *Judaism: The Evidence of the Mishnah.*

Judaism: The Evidence of the Mishnah. Chicago: University of Chicago Press, 1981.

Major Trends in Formative Judaism, series 1-2. Chico, Calif.: Scholars Press for Brown Judaic Studies, 1983-84.

The Memorized Torah: The Mnemonic System of the Mishnah. Chico, Calif.: Scholars Press for Brown Judaic Studies, 1985. Reprise and reworking of materials in *Rabbinic Traditions about the Pharisees before 70,* vols. 1 and 3, and *A History of the Mishnaic Law of Purities,* vol. 21.

Method and Meaning in Ancient Judaism, series 1. Missoula, Mont.: Scholars Press for Brown Judaic Studies, 1979.

Method and Meaning in Ancient Judaism, series 2-3. Chico, Calif.: Scholars Press for Brown Judaic Studies, 1980.

Method and Meaning in Ancient Judaism, series 4. Atlanta, Ga.: Scholars Press for Brown Judaic Studies, 1980.

The Mishnah before 70. Atlanta, Ga.: Scholars Press for Brown Judaic Studies, 1987. Reprise of pertinent results of *A History of the Mishnaic Law of Purities,* vols. 3, 5, 8, 10, 12, 14, 16, 17, and 18.

The Mishnah: A New Translation. New Haven, Conn.: Yale University Press, 1987.

The Mishnah: An Introduction. Northvale, N.J.: Jason Aronson, 1989.

The Modern Study of the Mishnah. Leiden, Netherlands: Brill, 1973.

Oral Tradition in Judaism: The Case of the Mishnah. New York: Garland, 1987. Restatement of results in various works on the Mishnah together with a fresh account of the problem.

The Peripatetic Saying: The Problem of the Thrice-Told Tale in Talmudic Literature. Chico, Calif.: Scholars Press for Brown Judaic Studies, 1985. Reprise and reworking of materials in *Development of a Legend: Rabbinic Traditions about the Pharisees before 70,* vols. 1-3.

Das Pharisäische and talmudische Judentum [Pharisaic and Talmudic Judaism], ed. Hermann Lichtenberger, foreword by Martin Hengel. Tübingen: J. C. B. Mohr (Paul Siebeck), 1984.

The Pharisees: Rabbinic Perspectives. New York: KTAV, 1985. Reprise of *Rabbinic Traditions about the Pharisees before 70,* vols. 1-3.

The Religious Study of Judaism, 4 vols. Lanham, Md.: University Press of America, 1986-1988.

Torah from Our Sages: Pirke Avot: A New American Translation and Explanation. Chappaqua: Rossel, 1983.

The Tosefta, translated from the Hebrew, 6 vols. (vol. 1 ed. Neusner). New York: KTAV, 1977-80.

The Tosefta: Its Structure and Its Sources. Atlanta, Ga.: Scholars Press for Brown Judaic Studies, 1986. Reprise of pertinent results in *Purities* vols. 1-21.

Understanding Seeking Faith: Essays on the Case of Judaism, 3 vols. Atlanta, Ga.: Scholars Press for Brown Judaic Studies, 1986-89.

2. The Tannaitic Midrashim

The mediating documents, called "Tannaitic Midrashim" because the authorities cited bear the technical title Tanna, are to be placed in the third or fourth centuries. I have presented and analyzed them in the following:

Mekhilta Attibuted to R. Ishmael: An Analytical Translation, 2 vols. Atlanta, Ga.: Scholars Press for Brown Judaic Studies, 1988.

Mekhilta Attributed to R. Ishmael: An Introduction to Judaism's First Scriptural Encyclopaedia. Atlanta, Ga.: Scholars Press for Brown Judaic Studies, 1988.

Sifra in Perspective: The Documentary Comparison of the Midrashim of Ancient Judaism. Atlanta, Ga.: Scholars Press for Brown Judaic Studies, 1988.

Sifra: An Analytical Translation, 3 vols. Atlanta, Ga.: Scholars Press for Brown Judaic Studies, 1988.

Sifra: The Judaic Commentary of Leviticus, a New Translation. The Leper: Leviticus 13:1-14:57. Chico, Calif.: Scholars Press for Brown Judaic Studies, 1985. (With a section by Roger Brooks.) Based on *A History of the Mishnaic Law of Purities,* vol. 6.

Sifré to Deuteronomy: An Analytical Translation, 2 vols. Atlanta, Ga.: Scholars Press for Brown Judaic Studies, 1987.

Sifré to Deuteronomy: An Introduction to the Rhetorical, Logical, and Topical Program. Atlanta, Ga.: Scholars Press for Brown Judaic Studies, 1987.

Sifré to Numbers: An American Translation, 3 vols. (vol. 3 by William Scott Green). Atlanta, Ga.: Scholars Press for Brown Judaic Studies, 1986.

Uniting the Dual Torah: Sifra and the Problem of the Mishnah. Cambridge: Cambridge University Press, 1989.

3. The Successor Documents to the Mishnah: The Talmud of the Land of Israel, Genesis Rabbah, Leviticus Rabbah, and Pesiqta deRab Kahana

I give a full account of the Talmud of the Land of Israel, Genesis Rabbah, Leviticus Rabbah, and Pesiqta deRab Kahana in the following:

Genesis Rabbah: The Judaic Commentary on Genesis: A New American Translation, 3 vols. Atlanta, Ga.: Scholars Press for Brown Judaic Studies, 1985.

In the Margins of the Yerushalmi: Notes on the English Translation. Chico, Calif.: Scholars Press for Brown Judaic Studies, 1983.

Judaism and Scripture: The Evidence of Leviticus Rabbah. Chicago: University of Chicago Press, 1984.

Pesiqta deRab Kahana: An Analytical Translation and Explanation, 2 vols. Atlanta, Ga.: Scholars Press for Brown Judaic Studies, 1987.

The Talmud of the Land of Israel: A Preliminary Translation and Explanation, vols. 9-12, 14-15, 17-35. Chicago: University of Chicago Press, 1982-1991.

4. Theory of the Successor Documents' Position in the Formative History of the Canon of Judaism

My theory of the literary history and structure of the compilations cited above is laid out in these books:

Canon and Connection: Intertextuality in Judaism. Lanham, Md.: University Press of America, 1986.

Comparative Midrash: The Plan and Program of Genesis Rabbah and Leviticus Rabbah. Atlanta, Ga.: Scholars Press for Brown Judaic Studies, 1986.

From Tradition to Imitation: The Plan and Program of Pesiqta deRab Kahana and Pesiqta Rabbati. Atlanta, Ga.: Scholars Press for Brown Judaic Studies, 1987. (With a fresh translation of Pesiqta Rabbati *Pisqaot* 1-5, 15.)

Integrity of Leviticus Rabbah: The Problem of the Autonomy of a Rabbinic Document. Chico, Calif.: Scholars Press for Brown Judaic Studies, 1985.

Invitation to Midrash: The Working of Rabbinic Bible Interpretation: A Teaching Book. San Francisco: Harper & Row, 1988.

Making the Classics in Judaism: The Three Stages of Literary Formation. Atlanta, Ga.: Scholars Press for Brown Judaic Studies, 1990.

Midrash as Literature: The Primacy of Documentary Discourse. Lanham, Md.: University Press of America, 1987.

Talmud of the Land of Israel: A Preliminary Translation and Explanation, vol. 35. Chicago: University of Chicago Press, 1983.

5. Presentation of Prior Results

I have presented to a broader audience the principal results of my studies in these books:

Lectures on Judaism in the Academy and in the Humanities. Atlanta, Ga.: Scholars Press for South Florida Studies in the History of Judaism, 1990.

Lectures on Judaism in the History of Religion. Atlanta, Ga.: Scholars Press for South Florida Studies in the History of Judaism, 1990.

Medium and Message in Judaism, series 1. Atlanta, Ga.: Scholars Press for Brown Judaic Studies, 1989.

Subject Index

Scriptural Index

A Note on the Author

JACOB NEUSNER is a distinguished research professor of religious studies at the University of South Florida, teaching at campuses at Tampa, St. Petersburg, Fort Myers, Sarasota, and Lakeland. He served as Martin Buber Visiting Professor at the University of Frankfurt, and in 1992 he will be a fellow of Clare Hall, Cambridge University. He is a member of the Institute for Advanced Study, Princeton. Neusner has written or edited nearly 400 books and holds numerous honorary degrees and medals from American and European universities, including the Universities of Chicago, Rochester, Bologna, Cologne, and Tübingen, as well as Columbia, Brown, and Ohio State universities, the Collège de France, and Regione di Campagna, Italy. He has held Guggenheim Fellowships for two years and American Council of Learned Societies Fellowships for two years. He served by presidential appointment on the councils of the National Endowment for the Humanities and the National Endowment for the Arts, 1978–84 and 1984–90, respectively. He formerly taught at Columbia and Brown universities, the University of Wisconsin–Milwaukee, and Dartmouth College and was visiting professor at the University of Minnesota, Iliff Seminary, and Jewish Theological Seminary of America.

.